A COLORADO WINTER

PHOTOGRAPHY BY

JOHN FIELDER

ESSAYS BY M. JOHN FAYHEE

WESTCLIFFE PUBLISHERS

Englewood, Colorado

ISBN: 1-56579-289-0

Photographs copyright, 1998 John Fielder. All rights reserved.
Text copyright, 1998 M. John Fayhee. All rights reserved.

Designers: Mark Mulvany and Tim George
Production Manager: Harlene Finn
Editor: Kiki Sayre

Published by: Westcliffe Publishers, Inc.
　　　　　　　P.O. Box 1261
　　　　　　　Englewood, Colorado 80150

Printed in Hong Kong by C&C Offset Printing Co., Ltd.

Library of Congress Cataloging-in-Publication Data:
Fielder, John.
　　A Colorado winter / photography by John Fielder;
　text by M. John Fayhee.
　　　　p.　　cm.
　　ISBN 1-56579-289-0 (hardcover)
　　1. Colorado—Pictorial works. 2. Colorado—Description
and travel. 3. Mountain life—Colorado—Pictorial works.
4. Winter—Colorado—Pictorial works. I. Fayhee, M. John, 1955-.
II. Title.
　F777.F49 1998
　508.788—dc21　　　　　　　　　　　　　98-16673
　　　　　　　　　　　　　　　　　　　　　　CIP

*For more information about other John Fielder books and calendars
from Westcliffe Publishers, please call your local bookstore, contact us
at 1-800-523-3692, or write for our free color catalog.*

"Dust of Snow" and "Stopping by Woods on a Snowy Evening" from:
THE POETRY OF ROBERT FROST, edited by Edward Connery
Lathem, Copyright 1951 by Robert Frost, Copyright 1923, © 1969 by
Henry Holt and Company, Inc., © 1997 by Edward Connery Lathem.
Reprinted by permission of Henry Holt and Company, Inc.

First frontispiece: Ponderosa pine, Castle Pines

Second frontispiece: Storm, San Isabel National Forest

ACKNOWLEDGMENTS

I'd like to thank all of my backcountry winter skiing companions over
the past 15 years for the following: carrying the food and wine so that
I could carry more camera gear, having the hut warm and breakfast
and dinner ready when I returned from early morning and late evening
photography, and for the great company. I'd especially like to thank
Brian Litz for inviting me along with him and his more experienced ski
friends 15 years ago, and for all of the support and help he has given
me on the ski trail through the years. I'd like, however, to dedicate this
book to Pete Wingle, a ski pioneer who loved winter even more than
the rest of us; and to the World War II ski troops of Colorado's Tenth
Mountain Division, some of whom I've had the pleasure to know, and
whose example of heroism and love for the world of white has been a
significant source of motivation and inspiration for me.

JOHN FIELDER

Numerous people aided and abetted this effort to bring you a feel for
wintertime in the Colorado high country. Among them are picture-taker
extraordinaire Brad Odekirk; Robert Ray; Craig Minor; Nick Logan of
the Colorado Avalanche Information Center; Marcin Kacperek of the
Colorado Mountain School in Estes Park; Ket McSparin, owner of
Mountain Outfitters in Breckenridge, and the good folks at the Keystone
Science School for teaching me why mosquitos don't die out during
the harsh high country winter.

　　　I would also like to thank my bosses, Bob Brown and Michael
Kirschbaum of Eagle-Summit Publishing, for graciously allowing me
to republish in this book several passages that originally appeared in
Summit Outdoors, a weekly publication which I edit in Summit County,
Colorado. And, not for the first time (far from it), and probably not for
the last (not by a long shot), I would like to raise a toast to my wife,
Gay Gangel-Fayhee, who once more kept the home fires burning while
I was out traipsing through the wonderful Colorado backcountry.

　　　I would also like to thank John Fielder for giving me yet
another opportunity to combine two of the things I love most in life:
journeying through the high country and writing about those journeys.

　　　This book is dedicated to my nephews, Jason Gangel, Kyle
Gangel, Bill Koch, Brian Gangel, and Brett Koch, and my niece, Kelly
Koch, in hopes that one of these days they will come to understand
that a lot of Uncle John's yarns are actually true. If not, then I hope
they at least come to understand that truth is often overrated when it
comes to uncles spinning yarns.

M. JOHN FAYHEE

SUNRISE, RUBY RANGE, GUNNISON NATIONAL FOREST

SCARP RIDGE, GUNNISON NATIONAL FOREST

Winter is like sweet fruit that must be peeled before eaten—once you pare away the temperature problem, it's a remarkably agreeable and sensual time of the year. I've been seriously peeling now for fifteen years, since I first began to ski in Colorado's backcountry. For most of us, winter's inconveniences are easily mitigated by dashing from one heated environment to another. In the comfort of a heated sport-utility vehicle, we laugh at winter on the way from our garage at home to the parking garage at work. When the storm becomes too intense, we just ski to the warming shelter and drink hot chocolate. Even in a frigid state like Colorado, we have no reason to be adept at living in the cold for long durations.

That's too bad, because the world of white can't be appreciated from a living room, or from a car, or even from skis moving at high speeds. Though winter may look beautiful from the comfort of a living room, there is so much more to enjoy than just our visual sense of it. The pungent aroma of that first wet spring snowfall enhances my perception of winter as much as the sight of rime ice crystals clinging to tree branches along river bottoms. The sound of water trickling beneath an ice-covered creek on a clear, crisp day stimulates me as much as the views of the Rocky Mountains covered with such a deep blanket of snow that not a hint of summer is visible. The void, itself, of sound in winter is sensual and pacifying. The touch and taste of mountain winter water is different than that of summer.

Though I've always enjoyed the challenge of being outside and photographing during nature's more capricious moments—in wind, rain, heat, and snow—and actually savoring the rigors of carrying big packs up and down mountains, my first forays into the winter landscape presented special difficulties. Until I began going out in winter during my backcountry ski trips, the distraction of snow, wind, and cold precluded the concentration necessary to enjoy the sensuality of winter. Good photography was impossible. Nevertheless, with a little bit of practice and a lot of common sense, I learned how to make almost any winter weather comfortable. Now winter is a season that I anticipate with excitement.

As much as I initially enjoyed the nostalgia of woolen outer clothing and the comfort of cotton undergarments, after a few wet forays on skis and snowshoes in untracked powder I converted to high-tech fabrics! The most important goal of the winter denizen is to stay dry and warm. Wet clothing can be extremely uncomfortable—even deadly—in very cold weather. Perspiration must make its way quickly away from the body. This only happens if the inner clothing does not absorb moisture, and the outer clothing allows water vapor to pass through the fabric to the

outside. Synthetic fabrics, such as polypropylene and capilene, "wick" moisture away from the skin; and membranes, such as Gore-Tex allow water vapor to pass through where water itself can not. Outer garments with "breathable" fabrics and venting systems, such as pit zips, will keep you dry inside. Staying warm is relatively easy when you are dry.

Good photography requires even greater concentration in winter than in other seasons. Like many nature photographers in the 60s and early 70s, my career began with a fascination for Kodachrome film. Was it Simon and Garfunkel's song, or the rich colors and evocative detail? Nature just seemed to look better than it really was on Kodachrome 25. Slap on a polarizer and, "Wow man, look at those psychedelic colors!"

Almost 30 years later, Kodachrome doesn't do it as well as Fujichrome; I don't often use polarizing filters; and frankly, I now see more than color when I make color photographs of nature. Color became such a crutch for so many years that I missed out on producing images made interesting by photographic ingredients such as form, asymmetrical balance, and soft lighting.

So what's this got to do with winter? Simply that winter demands the perception of things not as colorful as fields of flowers and trees of gold. In fact, winter is the least colorful of all seasons (though you might disagree after perusing this book). In order to fully enjoy its visual sense, you must toss away the color crutch and recognize the element of "form." What is form? It is line, shape, pattern, texture, and volume. Lines that have no end, that essentially meet nowhere, attract the eye. Ski tracks in the snow are lines. Shapes are defined by lines where beginning meets end, but they have no depth. A full moon is a shape. A pattern is created by the repetition of essentially similar shapes. Frost on a cold windowpane makes patterns. Texture occurs when the viewer sees detail inside of a shape or pattern. The image of fresh snow draped on spruce trees has texture. Volume combines shape and texture to imply depth. Light and its direction enhance volume, such as the way shadows make snow puffs on river rocks appear ready for chocolate sauce! In the world of white, I reprogram my brain to not depend upon colors. Nevertheless, when I find them I don't let them go, for they are a commodity less commonly found than during other seasons, and are a suitable decoration of form.

So plan a trip to your favorite outdoor retailer to buy good winter clothing, rent snowshoes or backcountry skis, and get to know the winter environment more intimately. Whether on an extended trip to one of our many mountain "huts," or out for an afternoon on the trail, or just by reading from John Fayhee's journals, I hope that you will enjoy the sweet fruit of a Colorado winter.

ENGLEWOOD, COLORADO

GREAT SAND DUNES NATIONAL MONUMENT, SAN LUIS VALLEY

Five feet from where these words are being written—right there on the other side of my home office wall—a full-blown Colorado high country winter storm is raging. The wind is blowing relentlessly, the snow is piling up at the rate of a foot an hour, and the wind-chill factor is well below zero.

Most people would opt to hunker down on their couch, under an afghan with a large mug of hot tea and a good book while this arcticlike tempest buffeted their home territory. But, for better or worse, not me. I just spent several hours walking my dog through the teeth of the storm. There are few things I hate worse than missing an opportunity to go out into severe winter weather. The couch and the hot cup of tea can wait.

I am, and always will be, a child of winter. I was born with ice water flowing freely in my veins and snowflakes in my hair. Not literally, but literally enough. The act of donning hats, gloves, long underwear, coats, and felt-lined boots before going outside into a frigid white world is as natural and reflexive to me as breathing.

For the past 10 winters, I've dwelled happily and contentedly at an altitude of almost 10,000 feet, and the town in which I live boasts an average annual snowfall of more than 300 inches. Here, winter has little or nothing to do with the calendar that controls—or at least orients—most of our lives. Here, winter essentially starts sometime in mid-October and runs through mid-May. While the good folks of northern Minnesota and central Alaska are reaping summer's first vegetables from their gardens, we still have several feet of snow in our yards. If we celebrated May Day where I live, we would do so on snowshoes. Twice since I've lived here, we've had blizzards in town on Independence Day weekend.

Though I love the other seasons, I love winter most. Perhaps that love stems at least partially from a survival mentality that says, since winter where I live is so strong and so long, I might as well develop a taste for it.

And perhaps that love stems at least partially from the fact that I wholeheartedly enjoy partaking in numerous outdoor activities that are winter-specific and winter-dependent. Snowshoeing, cross-country skiing, and ice skating are tough to do sans snow and ice.

But there is a lot more to my love of winter than survival mentality combined with a taste for playing in the great outdoors. I love winter primarily for aesthetic reasons, of which cold and snow top the list. While many people I know spend hours strolling through art galleries, I go out into the winter landscape looking for natural works of art made by the action of wind on snow. I go for late-night walks just to feel the 20-below-zero air on my skin and in my lungs. It's during winter that I feel the most alive and vibrant.

This book came about because of a conversation John Fielder and I once had on the shores of the Dolores River during a 10-day rafting trip in May. We were sitting on a modest beach at the bottom of a deep canyon during a sultry spring evening, sipping wine and talking about the things we love about Colorado. (The list was long.) John went on for about 20 minutes about a full-moon night he experienced while taking photos in the Collegiate Peaks Wilderness above treeline at 12,000-plus feet. The incomparable beauty he described was profound and very easy for me to visualize. Certainly, what he was describing was not a totally comfortable scene, as it was mid-January. Nonetheless, I understood on all levels where he was coming from. I proceeded to describe a couple of my best winter experiences, and John described a few more of his favorites, then, WHAM, the notion of putting together a winter-based book, consisting of his photographic images and my words, was born.

I think best when I'm on the move, so I opted to center the text of this book around a series of journeys, during which I would have the chance to interface with the intense and often overpowering sensuality of winter not just for a few recreation-based hours, but rather for days, as well as nights.

For this book I went on a four-day yurt trip in the South San Juan Mountains; I enrolled in a five-day mountaineering class in Rocky Mountain National Park; I went on a three-day solo camping trip up a river drainage on the east side of the Tenmile Range very near where I live; and I ascended 13,684-foot Mount Baldy.

Several of my friends said to me before embarking on these trips that, after all was said and done, I might come to learn that I don't like winter as much as I thought. Sure, each of these journeys had its hard parts. There were frozen water bottles and chattering teeth and cold toes and windburn on my face. But each trip was beautiful and wonderful. Some degree of discomfort is a given in a Colorado winter. But that's merely the price of admission into one of the most magical settings on earth.

I know it might seem a little crazy to love winter to the degree that John Fielder and I do. If we are crazy to love winter, at least we're happily crazy. I hope that happy craziness comes through on these pages, as this project was indeed a labor of the utmost love, respect, and maybe even adulation.

Join us on this journey into a Colorado winter.

Just remember to bundle up.

BRECKENRIDGE, COLORADO

MOUNT SNEFFELS, MOUNT SNEFFELS WILDERNESS

Red Hill Pass, Park County

Spruce-fir forest, McClure Pass, Gunnison National Forest

SUNRISE, JACQUE RIDGE, GORE RANGE

DOGSLEDS, BELLYACHE RIDGE, WHITE RIVER NATIONAL FOREST

Rifle Falls, Rifle Falls State Park

LIFE IN SNOW

A few miles below 11,500-foot Hoosier Pass lies the Spruce Creek drainage. By Colorado standards, it's remarkable only insofar as it's not especially remarkable. Within a 15-mile radius, there are dozens of other valleys, gulches, and drainages equally as picturesque: Monte Cristo Gulch, Mayflower Gulch, French Creek, the triple-pronged Swan River complex. Splendid all, equally splendid.

Mind you, this isn't to say that Spruce Creek is anything save astoundingly beauteous. This is a place that would adorn tourist office promotional material in at least 40 states. It's just that, in Colorado, Spruce Creek is, when you get right down to it, merely awesome, and, in the high country, "merely awesome" is a dime a dozen; blasé beauty —like all 50 Miss America contestants on stage at once.

LONG AGO I latched onto Spruce Creek as my destination of choice when I have a few extra hours to venture into the woods. There are only two kinds of places I like: those that I visit only once or twice in a lifetime, and those that I visit so often I come to know individual trees and rocks and rivulets and clusters of columbines as friends. I've visited Spruce Creek so many times that I'm able to enter a Zenlike trance as I make my way along its various trails and dirt roads. I'm now comfortable enough with both the long and short views of Spruce Creek that I can enjoy both without being distracted and mentally waylaid by either. Both the macro and micro panoramas within and surrounding Spruce Creek are so lovely and dramatic that they make my heart flutter just thinking about them, but they no longer startle me with either their intensity or their subtlety.

I'm used to the beauty of Spruce Creek, but I don't take it for granted. I just move comfortably within the mosaic of that beauty— like a native New Yorker moves comfortably among the intensity of the skyscraper-dominated environment. I understand on all levels how blessed I am to dwell a stone's throw from this drainage, and I'm often reminded of that when I come across tourists who are suffering from severe cases of scenery-based giddiness as they snowshoe along the Spruce Creek Trail. When they learn that I live nearby, they stress to me how fortunate they believe I am. I know, I tell them; but it's often good to be reminded of the obvious—to be reminded that, no matter how much of an unfocused rogue and borderline ne'er-do-well I've been throughout most of my life, somehow I managed to pull off dwelling in the heart of the Colorado Rockies. Many of my friends from past lives make more money than I do and they own nicer houses. But those houses are in places like Cleveland and the Dallas metroplex. I'll take a slum in paradise any day over a mansion in or near a city.

COLORADO IS TWO STATES IN ONE: the Colorado of winter is a completely different animal than the Colorado of nonwinter. I've heard the same thing said of geishas, that, once they apply their faces and kimonos, they're no longer the same person: they're transformed, not quite like a butterfly emerging from the cocoon, but close. Colorado, with a veil of snow, is likewise transformed, and that transformation transcends the simple covering-up of the landscape with natural makeup. The Colorado high country in winter aesthetically exceeds the sum of its parts.

My wife, a born-and-bred native of this state, says Colorado is only really Colorado in the winter. In the summer, she says, it's an impostor.

Spruce Creek is one of the few places I visit often in both summer and winter. Generally, I have my winter destinations and I have my summer destinations. Sometimes this is because a pleasant summer trail becomes avalanche central when the snow falls. Sometimes it's because a picture-postcard winter scene, when stripped of its snow, becomes nothing more than endless mounds of repulsive mine tailings. Sometimes access is a question in winter; sometimes it's dirt bikers in summer.

But Spruce Creek beckons me year-round, and its dichotomous nature never fails to intrigue me. It's like having a relationship with one beautiful and fascinating woman half the year, and with a completely different beautiful and fascinating woman the other half. That kind of relationship, of course, would be temporarily disorienting during the first few days of the semi-annual transition, but there's nothing wrong with temporary disorientation: It keeps you mentally alert.

Winter generally comes in a day to the Colorado high country. One day the ground lies covered only by fallen aspen leaves—some still retaining their gold and orange tinge—and dried grasses. But a feel of impending change is in the air. Live in a place long enough, and you get to the point where you can intuit climatic change.

Every year, when I feel that winter is well nigh upon my home turf, I go out to Spruce Creek, which is seven miles from my front door. To get there, I have to drive through the polished heart of Breckenridge. Breckenridge was born and raised by the mining boom of the late 1800s, but it was reborn and raised from the dead by the ski industry. It is, therefore, a town that exists for and because of winter; when there is no snow covering its blemishes, its true nature as a money-making machine disguised as a quaint Victorian town is revealed and exposed. In that shoulder season after the wildflowers have withered and before the snow starts falling, Breckenridge, like all ski towns, looks dry and corrupt.

Though Breckenridge is home to the second-largest downhill ski area in the nation, this time of year it is generally quiet, the tourist-oriented "shoppes" open but empty. It used to be that people closed their art galleries, restaurants, and T-shirt emporiums in the high country during the late fall. No longer. The high country never closes these days; it's always open for business.

As I make my way south on Highway 9, the entire Breckenridge Ski Area opens up to the west. Varicose veins of ski runs—dozens and dozens of them—snake their way down the sides of Peaks 7, 8, 9, and 10 of the Tenmile Range, a range which has felt the touch of man in major-league ways over the years. Just south of the ski area lie the gaping wounds of eight massive clear cuts that, in ultimate irony, bear the names of the once pristine drainages they fouled: South Barton, North Barton, Barton Gulch, et al. Those cuts should bear the names of those who allowed them, of those who perpetrated that evil. They should be considered anti–monuments to man's greed and desire to profit from the destruction of Nature.

Then my eye wanders from the clear cuts to the ski runs, and I wonder how they are conceptually and philosophically different from each other. In each case, where there was once thick pine forest blanketing the Tenmile Range, now there is only exposed ground sticking out like a sore thumb amid the woods. The difference being that the clear cuts will one day sport trees again; the ski runs will remain denuded as long as the ski industry continues to exist.

Highway 9 follows the lovely Blue River—here only knee-deep—up toward Hoosier Pass, the second-highest paved pass in the state that is kept open year-round. The valley gets tighter, and the woods get thicker. Though there are houses here, the feel is the antithesis of Breckenridge. The ski area is no longer visible; it's out of sight and out of mind. After a mile-long drive down a winding, single-lane dirt road, I arrive at the Spruce Creek Trailhead. It feels much more remote than it actually is.

The hiking options here are myriad, but on this, what I guess correctly will be my last nonwinter walk of the season, I take a long (maybe 10 miles total) and tiring loop up Spruce Creek Trail, past the Wheeler Trail intersection, past Continental Falls into the tundra surrounding Mayflower Lakes, before descending down Spruce Creek Road back to the trailhead. I try hard to remember every aspect of the terrain for the sake of comparison purposes once the snow falls. This effort is generally an exercise in joyous futility because, once winter strikes, this will no longer be the same place, and those terrain features will take on a completely new life: their life in snow.

THE FIELDERS EN ROUTE TO PEARL PASS,
ELK MOUNTAINS

TWO DAYS AFTER my last nonwinter visit to Spruce Creek, we were hammered by a storm that people still talk about. It wasn't yet November. I called in sick to work, tossed my snowshoes in my truck, and, once again, drove to Spruce Creek Trailhead. On the way, I noticed how shiny, beautiful, and clean those ski runs suddenly looked. A veneer of snow makes a person forgive a lot of transgressions against the natural world.

The plows had just finished their work at the trailhead, and there was a mound of snow almost head-high at the far end of the parking lot. I had to clamor over it to get to the jeep road upon which I would be snowshoeing. Two feet of pure powder had fallen onto a landscape that, only two days before, had been barren and brown.

The Spruce Creek drainage had been reborn via snowstorm, and so had I. I'd shed my summer skin and was now wearing my winter coat.

I was reminded of a statement I once overheard at a bar in Breckenridge: "At 32 degrees, water turns to magic."

Spruce Creek was now magic. It verily shimmered in the bright morning sun under the cobalt Colorado sky.

To live fully is to have a natural energy source that, more than any other, serves to recharge one's spiritual batteries. For some, it's the searing heat of the desert sun. For others, it's the womblike embrace of the ocean. For still others, it's the company of vast fields of wildflowers. I knew a person who drew power from hot springs, and a lady I once dated down in southern New Mexico would walk for hours in the pouring rain because it made her feel more alive for weeks afterwards.

Snow gives me that energy. When I stand in snow, I feel the dynamism of Nature pulsing up through my boots and into my inner being. Wild animals build up their physical energy through the summer so they can survive the winter. I build up my spiritual energy in the winter so that I may survive the summer.

I spent three hours snowshoeing a loop that usually only takes me one hour. I was in an antihurry. I had to reintroduce myself to the landscape and the trees, which, only 48 hours before, I knew intimately.

Winter had descended on Colorado and I couldn't have been happier. A lot of people react to winter's coming with an "Oh, no" attitude. I react by saying, "It's about time."

BY LATE DECEMBER, I had visited Spruce Creek at least 25 times since that first blizzard. All of these journeys were day trips, either on skis or snowshoes. I would go out for a few hours, then return to the warmth of home and hearth. But for years I had wanted to interact with Spruce Creek in a more intimate fashion, by camping in the middle of winter in the middle of the drainage. I finally decided this was the winter to do it.

It was 10 A.M. the day after Christmas when I hoisted my well-laden external-frame pack on my back and began the two-mile snowshoe to the spot I had mentally chosen as my base of operations for the next three days and two nights. Like most Americans these days, I was stressed by the holidays, which were still going on, and I figured a multi-day backcountry foray would chill me out.

Since I wanted to have my tent up by two o'clock, I only had to move at the contemplative pace of a half-mile per hour. That was just fine, as I wanted to examine the route in a slow-motion fashion.

Just up from the trailhead, Crystal Creek joins Spruce Creek. At the intersection is a small gauging station, which is part of a diversion system that supplies the drinking water to Breckenridge and, thus, to my house. Perhaps this is the root of one of the bonds I feel with Spruce Creek: it quenches my thirst on a daily basis. I bathe in water from this heavenly place.

But it isn't the creek, per se, that supplies my water; rather, it's the snow that falls in this valley that eventually melts and makes its way to my kitchen spigot. I have friends who have wells. They express pleasure at the thought of getting their water from the uncorrupted interior of Mother Earth. Perhaps I was indoctrinated too thoroughly by my Sunday school teachers back at Ware Episcopal Church in Gloucester, Virginia, but I shudder when I think of substances spewed

forth from far beneath the soil upon which I stand. It pleases me to know that my water comes not from the dark and dank depths, but, rather, from snowflakes that have fluttered down one by one from the boundless Colorado sky.

Halfway up the first long hill there is a grove of about 20 side-by-side blue spruces that I consider to be amigos. I stop and talk to these trees every time I'm in the neighborhood (so long as no one is looking). They're perhaps 15 feet tall—mere adolescents in tree time. Every year they grow a few inches, and I mark this growth with the same sense of joy that I mark the growth of my next-door-neighbor's little girl. In the summer, these spruces seem to be trying to spread out, to get some space between themselves. In the winter, though, they appear to be huddling as close together as possible, like emperor penguins in Antarctica. In summer, their branches seem to be pushing their neighbors away; in winter, they seem to be hugging each other.

THE FIELDERS INSIDE LINDLEY HUT, ELK MOUNTAINS

JT Fielder

My wife is surprised that I like these spruces so much, as I'm generally a bigger fan of deciduous trees. I prefer coniferous trees as forests, and I prefer deciduous forests as individual trees. But these particular spruces have greeted me on this trail so many times for so many years now that I make a preferential exception for them.

As I've come to know them better, I've come to more appreciate their winter survival strategies. Unlike their deciduous cousins, these trees do not shed their "leaves" at the first touch of cold weather. They keep their leaves year-round, allowing them to photosynthesize even in the darkest depths of winter. But they risk losing heat through their leaves, which, on most tree species, offer the highest vascular system exposure to the elements, like capillary-rich fingers and toes on humans. So, coniferous trees have evolved to the point that their leaves have taken the form of needles, with less surface area exposure for their vascular system. This system has its down side, in that coniferous trees do not photosynthesize as efficiently as, say, aspens. But it seems to work well enough, as the high country woods are dominated by spruces, firs, and lodgepole pines. This is decidedly coniferous land.

Just past this grove of spruces lies a small grove of juvenile aspens that, likewise, I've come to know well enough over the years that I stop and hobnob with them each time I pass. Aspens at this altitude bear leaves for only a few months a year. It astounds me that they're able to produce enough nutrients to survive the winter, but their internal energy-storage systems are very well honed. Aspens are like bears—getting fat in the summer, then living off that fat through the winter.

These adaptations, of course, are no more impressive than those exhibited by saguaros down in the Sonoran Desert. They are, however, impressive enough, for this is a bonafide hostile place, despite its beauty.

I stop for a snack next to what, this time of year, looks like a large, flat field. In the summer, this is a beaver pond-dominated meadow, lush and boggy. Often in July, August, and September, I come here just to sit and watch the beavers tirelessly going about their environment-altering work. The largest dam in this meadow is almost 100 feet long and 10 feet high. Now, with six feet of snow cover, I can't even make out a bump where the dam lies. Down there, somewhere, a family of *castor canadensis*—a monogamous couple that mates for life and probably two newly born kits, is holed up tight, feasting on stored aspen and willow saplings collected at a frenzied pace during the summer, sleeping 20 hours a day, and waiting for the ice to melt. They've been down there for two months already. They have four months—at least—to go.

Winter determines the fate of beavers in the high country. Beaver ponds must be deep enough that they don't freeze all the way to the bottom. As creeks silt up from runoff, beavers have to build their dams higher and higher. In big runoff years, they often can't keep pace, and they either have to move on or die.

Beavers are also one of the few animal species that alters its own habitat so significantly that it sows the seeds of its own eventual destruction. The more trees it gnaws down, the more silt runs off, and the quicker its pond fills up. I think I like beavers so much because I see in them human desires and frailties. They have a compulsion to build things where there were once no things. And that compulsion ultimately spells doom for these cute little rodents. Beaver populations are never, ever perpetual.

Beavers also significantly affected the history of the Colorado high country. This is one of the few places on earth where indigenous people flat out did not winter-over. With the more temperate Front Range and Western Slope only a few days away by foot, there was no logical reason for the Utes and Kiowas to stay here during winter. When the aspens started turning gold in September, the Native Americans hightailed it posthaste back down to the lowlands, their true home. Like many aficionados of the high country today, the Native Americans had second homes up here.

It was only in the 1840s that the first people—in this case, Jeremiah Johnson-like beaver trappers—decided to stay in the high country between September and early June. It must have been splendid and frightening, those first seasons before the mining boom hit in the

1860s and everything up here changed forever. To be the first people to witness the almost unbelievable buildup of snow in verdant alpine valleys like Spruce Creek; to be the first to experience the full-moon frosty-breathed stillness of a January night at 9,000 feet; to be the first people to hole up in a cabin as the February winds raged for days straight outside while the fireplace crackled inside and the wood pile started dwindling piece by piece; to be the very first to watch the gradual warming of the days through March and April and the concomitant near-mystical transformation of the landscape from white to brown to lush green; to be the very first to observe the rebirth of earth as the flowers once again bloomed and the trees and bushes leafed out overnight, must have been astounding.

Of course, after being snowbound for six or seven months, those early trappers were probably thinking of little else save arranging a quick and intense interface with the closest flatland town, but, hey,

JOHN FIELDER BELOW MOUNT SNEFFELS,
MOUNT SNEFFELS WILDERNESS

Brian Litz

even now people who live up here think about leaving for a couple of weeks after a long, hard winter. But I bet as those trappers were drinking in all that civilization (and there was very little in the way of civilization to be had anywhere in Colorado in the 1840s), their minds often returned to visions of the lovely and tranquil high country winter. From what I have read, many trappers wintered up here year after year, and it's my guess that the seeking out of beaver pelts was only part of that lifestyle choice.

Even though the massive beaver dam is well hidden, thousands of willow stems still poke above the snow. Willows are strange plants indeed. Their branches are the least-orderly of any high country plant; they don't grow as much as they seem to explode willy-nilly and wild in every direction. This is the Phyllis Diller of plants. Moreover, willows are the only plant in the alpine environment that are more colorful in the winter than in the summer. Their stems and branches are a veritable crayon box of vibrancy when contrasted against the snow, with yellows, pinks, browns, and reds dominating.

Once again, I marvel at the survival abilities of alpine plants, which have no ability to self-generate heat. Many high-altitude plants possess the ability to resist freezing through a process called "hardening." Hardening must begin in the early fall, prior to any drastic temperature drops. If there is an early freeze, some plants may die because they haven't yet had a chance to harden.

The hardening process—which has three distinct stages, each with its own chemical reactions and cellular changes—usually takes several weeks to transpire. But, if fall temperatures drop gradually enough, hardened plants will likely survive the winter.

One of the most glorious aspects of winter is the lack of insects. In the summer, this beaver pond-dominated area is thick with mosquitoes and flies, both of which I loathe. More than any other species, plant or animal, I am astounded that insects have the ability to thrive this high up—especially when you consider that insects are essentially liquid-filled boxes. In a perfect world, all bugs would freeze to death by November, and there would be no more bugs. But the world is far from perfect. Some insects actually survive the winter by migrating to warmer climes, like their avian counterparts. Some go into dormancy, like bears, protected by internal antifreeze.

Mosquitoes and flies are unable to make it through the winter, but, sad to say, their eggs are perfectly capable of surviving winter's wrath. Down there beneath all that snow are millions of microscopic eggs waiting to form into larvae that will, one hot July day, emerge from the pond to seek me out, specifically.

BEFORE ONE O'CLOCK, I reach the base of mammoth Continental Falls, which, in late December, falls very little. The entire 100-foot cascade, which roars so loudly in the summer you can hear it a mile away, is frozen solid. It takes 10 minutes to stomp out a tent site. I sit for a half hour in the late afternoon sun as the snow where my tent will be hardens. It is only 19 degrees, but, with the sun bouncing off the snow, it feels warm. I soon get my stove going to melt snow for drinking water.

By the time the tent is up, the sun has passed behind a ridge. The temperature plummets, and I hurriedly change into heavy clothing—expedition-weight polypropylene underwear, heavy-pile pants and jacket, heavy down parka, pile mittens with Gore-Tex overshells, a thick wool balaclava, and felt-lined boots. After a cup of hot tea, I pull my headlamp out of the tent and put my snowshoes back on. It's a new moon, and it's time for an evening walk. As I leave, the serrated ridge to the south explodes with light. For little more than a minute, the uppermost peaks glow bright pink, like the tip of a poker that has been sitting in a fire for an hour. Then, equally as suddenly, the last tendrils of sun from the other side of the Tenmile Range go away, and the surrounding mountaintops turn gray and dull.

Then it is dark, but there is enough in the way of ambient light that I am able to safely keep the lamp off as I make my way toward Continental Falls. It is steep going, and before long my glasses are completely fogged up. The world around me is like an impressionist painting, obvious, but not clear.

My goal is a small, dilapidated, ancient, long-abandoned, mining-era cabin that is close to the falls, about one-third of the way

FIELDER SKI FRIENDS, GOODWIN-GREENE
HUT, ELK MOUNTAINS

up. Just before I get there, I stop and look back toward the Blue River valley, some 2,000 feet below and five miles away. I can't see a single light, save the stars. There's no wind, so the only sound comes from my breathing. It would be absolute sensory deprivation, were it not for the cold stinging my face and lungs.

Inside the cabin, I turn on my headlamp and find a small stub of a candle. Though this cabin has seen better days, people still visit here often. In the summer, dozens of hikers peek in daily before heading up the valley to Mohawk Lakes. In winter, occasional parties bunk down here instead of sleeping in a tent. There's a loft with a skanky foam pad, a few benches scattered around the still-functional remains of a fireplace, and a few shelves with pots, pans, cans of Beenie Weenies and Vienna Sausages, and, most importantly, a journal that has been here for years.

It's a desire to read from the journal at night in the dead of winter that has drawn me here. I love perusing old registers and journals, and I've read this one several times. The entries affect me differently each time, depending on my mood or the weather. I enjoy trying to put myself into the moccasins of people trying to speak to anonymous paper from their heart.

Most of the entries were made by summer visitors, and are light and airy, like summer. "The Johnsons from Houston were here 7-24-94. What A Mess! Nice views though!" And: "I thank the Good Lord for this beauty and this beautiful place called Colorado. A. Krenshaw." And: "Can't believe it—we forgot the beer . . ."

The winter entries are more contemplative and they have deeper meaning when read in similar circumstances to which they were penned. There are long introspective narratives about lost loves, and near-terminal loneliness, and decisions poorly made, and the abiding relationship between man and the backcountry, and the beauty of skiing the headwall area of Spruce Creek Valley. On the one hand, it's easy to feel voyeuristic when reading these kinds of screeds, but, at the same time, they were obviously written to be read.

When I finish, I blow out the candle and just sit for a moment. The wind has picked up, and the cabin creeks. I turn quickly, fumbling with my headlamp, thinking someone is behind me.

It's clearly time to leave. There are more demons lurking about in winter than in summer, and that's a fact.

It feels good to get back outside into the night. The clouds have moved on, and the sky is alive with stars. I'm pretty good at identifying winter constellations, but it's so clear that even stars with apparent magnitudes of less than six are shining like spotlights. The entire Little Dipper sticks out like a neon sign, and it has to be pretty clear for that to happen. Except for Orion, the Big Dipper, and the Pleiades, the sky is a jumble of white-light dots.

It takes 35 minutes to make it back down to my tent. When I get there, it's 17-below. Even though my bottles were filled with boiling water and then placed in insulated sleeves only two hours ago, there are ice crystals forming around the mouth. I crawl into the tent, intent upon cooking some dinner despite my desire to crawl into my bag to sleep. As the stove heats my instant soup and rice, I lie back and stare at the sky, pondering a question made obvious by these circumstances: What makes a man love this harsh season to the degree that he would choose to carry a heavy pack several miles into the backcountry so he can sleep on the snow?

Good question, and I'm not really certain I have a good answer.

FOR MOST OF THE HISTORY of mankind —at least in most places—winter was justifiably seen as a heartless, unforgiving enemy lurking and looming on the chronological horizon, ready to consume and discard as many hapless souls as possible. Autumn celebrations of bountiful harvests were as much about crossing one's fingers in hopes of making it through the upcoming winter as they were about having all the pumpkins and squash you could possibly eat in one sitting.

Springtime celebrations like May Day—which go back thousands of years—were not just joyous embracings of warmth and sunshine; they were, first and foremost, institutionalized ways of saying, "Hallelujah, those heregathered have survived yet another winter, with only minimal cases of frostbite and scurvy!"

It wasn't until relatively recently that people began to look at winter from other perspectives. It has only been within the past two or three generations that even a small percentage of this planet's temperate zone-dwelling human population was first able to view the turning of the leaves with any emotion save survival-based dread. This is not to say that, 100,000 years ago, Neanderthal man didn't occasionally glance out of the cave and appreciate the beauty of the snowfall, as his teeth were chattering and he was wondering how much rancid mammoth meat was left. But, in this part of the world, only within our grandparent's lifetime have "we" been afforded the opportunity to view winter from an aesthetic perspective as much as one based totally upon mortality concerns.

And, only within the past generation has winter come to actually be enjoyed, viewed as a friend returning for yet another long

HEADING UP THE MOUNTAIN,
MAROON BELLS-SNOWMASS WILDERNESS

Brian Litz

and pleasant visit. Civilization run amok has wreaked much havoc upon the world, but it has also afforded people the first chance in history to truly embrace and even love winter. We no longer have to spend as much time worrying about how our rancid mammoth meat supply is holding up—which frees up a lot of time and thought that can best be focused on other survival-based activities, like skiing and snowshoeing.

And we now have 20-below down sleeping bags and expedition-style tents and so forth. So, sure, I love the winter at least partially because I am able to interface with it without starving to death or losing any significant body parts to frostbite—at least if I play my cards right.

I understand, however, that in wintertime in a place as intense as the Colorado Rockies, it's not always possible to play your cards right, and that is certainly part of the thrill of being out here in the snow eating food that is fast turning to ice while my moustache is frozen solid. Even in well-conceived, relatively safe circumstances like those in which I now find myself, winter rules, and winter rules big time. It defines the game and determines the winners and losers.

For the next two days, I wander around the valley and over to the nearby Crystal Lakes drainage. I go up to the headwall between Crystal and Pacific Peaks—two of the state's "high thirteeners." I follow the Wheeler Trail past Francie's Cabin, one of the backcountry facilities owned and operated by Summit Huts Association, over to the eastern flank of Peak 10. From the ridge, I can look down into Breckenridge and see most of the ski area. Down there on the slopes, thousands of people are scurrying around in a holiday season frenzy trying to get as much bang for their vacation buck as possible. They are buying wholeheartedly into the notion that you can spend your way to recreational bliss.

I know from experience that there's as much or more stress on Colorado's ski slopes as there is in rush-hour traffic in any big city. It doesn't make me comfortable to make smug and self-righteous observations like that, but what those people are experiencing down there at the ski area is not a direct interaction with Nature; it is, rather, an interaction with Nature modified, coiffed, groomed, and made as comfortable as possible. It's no more pure Nature than a visit to a zoo or an arboretum.

Those people would return to their lives back down in the flatlands and cities so much better rested and refreshed if they snowshoed into the backcountry, cooked over a stove, and slept on the snow-covered ground.

They would, like me, find renewal or maybe even new life in the snow. At least I think so. At least I hope so.

ELK MOUNTAINS, WHITE RIVER NATIONAL FOREST

MOONRISE, GUNNISON NATIONAL FOREST

ALONG THE EAGLE RIVER, EAGLE COUNTY

Through the hush'd Air the whit'ning Shower descends,

At first thin-wavering; till at last the Flakes

Fall broad, and wide, and fast, dimming the Day

With a continual Flow. The cherish'd Fields

Put on their Winter-Robe of purest White.

—*James Thomson*

Out of the bosom of the Air,

Out of the cloud-folds of her garments shaken,

Over the woodlands brown and bare,

Over the harvest-fields forsaken,

Silent, and soft, and slow

Descends the snow.

—*Henry Wadsworth Longfellow*

SUNSET, HOLY CROSS WILDERNESS

HIGHLINE CANAL, ARAPAHOE COUNTY

CHARLES RIDGE, HOLY CROSS WILDERNESS

Sunset, Sneffels Range, Uncompahgre National Forest

SUNRISE, RICHMOND HILL, WHITE RIVER NATIONAL FOREST

HANGING LAKE, WHITE RIVER NATIONAL FOREST

Rio Grande, San Luis Valley

Aspen trees, White River National Forest

Aspen trees, White River National Forest

SUNRISE, ELK MOUNTAINS, WHITE RIVER NATIONAL FOREST

SUNRISE, ELK MOUNTAINS, WHITE RIVER NATIONAL FOREST

Rime ice, Rambouillet Park, Gunnison National Forest

The thin snow now driving from the north and lodging on my coat consists of those beautiful star crystals, not cottony and chubby spokes, but thick and partly transparent crystals. They are about a tenth of an inch in diameter, perfect little wheels with six spokes without a tire, or rather with six perfect little leaflets, fern-like, with a distinct straight and slender midrib, raying from the center. . . . How full of the creative genius is the air in which they are generated. I should hardly admire more if real stars fell and lodged on my coat.

—*Henry David Thoreau*

Come see the north wind's masonry.

Out of an unseen quarry evermore

Furnished with tile, the fierce artificer

Curves his white bastions with projected roof

Round every windward stake, or tree, or door.

Speeding, the myriad-handed, his wild work

So fanciful, so savage, nought cares he

For number or proportion.

—*Ralph Waldo Emerson*

RIME ICE, ANTHRACITE CREEK, GUNNISON NATIONAL FOREST

PONDEROSA PINES, CASTLE PINES

FOWLER-HILLIARD HUT, TENTH MOUNTAIN DIVISION HUT SYSTEM

RIME ICE, RAMBOUILLET PARK, GUNNISON NATIONAL FOREST

GOTHIC MOUNTAIN, GUNNISON NATIONAL FOREST

STAR PEAK, ELK MOUNTAINS, WHITE RIVER NATIONAL FOREST

SUNRISE, WHITE RIVER NATIONAL FOREST

FRESH SNOW, WHITE RIVER NATIONAL FOREST

GORE RANGE, EAGLES NEST WILDERNESS

WHITE RIVER NATIONAL FOREST

RABBITBRUSH, GREAT SAND DUNES NATIONAL MONUMENT

GOODWIN-GREENE HUT, BRAUN HUT SYSTEM

Toklat Chalet, White River National Forest

Aspen trees, Gunnison National Forest

BECKWITH MOUNTAINS, WEST ELK WILDERNESS

The visibility is nearly zero when we arrive at nine o'clock on a January morning at Trujillo Meadows Trailhead, a stone's throw from 10,200-foot Cumbres Pass in the remote and little-visited South San Juan Mountains of southern Colorado. The man we have hired to drive us from the small village of Chama, New Mexico, to the trailhead is obviously anxious about leaving us vehicle-less in such unforgiving—to say nothing of seemingly uncomfortable—conditions. He drops several hints that maybe we ought to consider going back to Chama with him until the weather passes.

We pass on that notion. We enthusiastically pile out of the car and ready ourselves for our four-day, three-night journey, arranging our mammoth packs, donning our bulky boots and pulling on our Gore-Tex.

I am joined by Robert Ray, a water quality specialist with the Colorado Northwest Council of Governments, and Brad Odekirk, a photographer with the Summit Daily News. We are on skis, and our plan is to visit each of the three backcountry yurts owned and operated by the South San Juan Yurt System. We will pause for only one night at each of the yurts—Trujillo Meadows, Flat Mountain, and Neff Mountain. This is considered by many to be the least trying, least dangerous multi-day winter "hut" trip in the state. We planned just four easy miles the first day, four equally easy miles the second day, six even easier miles the third, and two almost embarrassingly easy miles the fourth. And that is just fine with me. In the Colorado high country, experiential intensity is often worshipped as though it were the one and only recreational god. I prefer to operate under the assumption that one need not risk one's life or exert oneself to near expiration in order to "get something" out of a backcountry experience. There is, in my mind, still a place for mellowness on all levels in the Rockies, and I aim to prove it on this trip.

This marks only my second backcountry foray with Robert and my first with Brad. I am more than a little concerned that they will be bored throughout this modest journey, as they both are expert skiers, but my ill-developed skiing skills prevented us from planning a more ambitious trip—thank goodness! I've had the busiest year of my life and am looking forward to a sinfully laid-back trip that will give me the opportunity to observe the winter landscape instead of just trying to make tracks.

It only takes a few minutes before the vehicle and our driver disappear into the whiteout that we're now immersed in. It's not snowing, but it seems to be. The wind is whipping across the pass so violently that snow from three counties away is passing before us at the speed of sound. The wind-chill factor is hovering close to zero, and the light is so flat that we have little depth perception. This is often a problem with traveling through the heart of winter. Snow in the foreground blends with snow in the background into one monochromatic image, and it's hard to tell how far or how close things are. Sometimes, snow-covered humps two feet high and 200 yards away look like looming mountains, and sometimes you can walk right into a hillside because it has blended in with the white background. I've almost walked off cornices because I couldn't see where the snow ended. You have to look for subtle terrain differences to judge distance, but that's often not possible. Winter is a master of camouflage.

The world is a disorienting mix of white and gray, and instantly we're directionally confused. I've brought a Global Positioning System with the coordinates for Trujillo Meadows Yurt already programmed into it, but it's so cold that the GPS is reluctant to wake up and help us out. So much for relying on technology.

The written directions to the yurt are simple enough: Follow Forest Road 118 for two miles, then hang a left. We were told in Chama this would be easy, as the route surely would have been packed down by snowmobiles. But the wind has erased all vestiges of tracks, and the road is far less than obvious in the flat light. We all look at each other, shrug, and smile. It is, I realize, a strange yet wonderful thing to be happy in conditions this intense. Most people, I believe, would wince at the idea of intentionally putting themselves in such a situation. The three of us, however, share a strong love of winter at altitude. Sure, it would be more pleasant if the sun broke through, but pleasant is not always important. If you don't love a place or kind of place during its most extreme weather, then you truly don't love the place. Anyone can wax poetic about the awesome beauty of the Colorado high country in mid-July when the flowers are swaying in the warm breeze and the birds are singing. That's amateur hour. This is the real thing, Colorado-style.

We begin shuffling our way toward the only landmark we can make out—a pine-covered hillside. As we get closer, the cut of the road into the hill becomes obvious. The yurt system owners have marked the route with wooden diamonds painted blue and attached them to the trunks and branches of trees along the road. Yet, with this visibility, or lack thereof, we understand how easy it would be to ski right by a trail junction, ending up God-knows-where. So, in addition to all the requisite hut supplies, like fuzzy slippers, books, shrimp, cookies, and Scotch, we're all carrying basic bivouac gear—heavy sleeping bags, bivy sacks, sleeping pads, a stove and cook kit—just in case we lose our bearings and have to spend the night yurtless in the woods. We don't necessarily mind the thought of dying out here in the South San Juans, but dying unprepared and in such a way that people make jokes about us is simply not a tolerable thought. We don't want to be eulogized as the nitwits who entered one of the most wild mountain ranges in the state in the dead of winter in the middle of a whiteout sans fundamental survival gear. It's well worth carrying the extra weight if it helps prevent that indignity.

We climb into the thick spruce woods as cloud bank after cloud bank rushes over us. Nowhere do clouds seem to move faster than in the high country. On the vast plains and on the wide ocean there are few points of reference by which to judge the speed of clouds, and, therefore, in all but the most vicious storms, they seem to lollygag along. Here, we're in the midst of the clouds. They are whizzing past treetops almost within our reach. It's dizzying.

As we ascend, we begin seeing patches of blue peeking out from behind the dark, thick clouds. We speculated before leaving the trailhead that the foul weather would soon pass, and it looks like our speculation will prove true. That speculation was based far less on optimism than it was on familiarity with high country weather patterns. All three of us have dwelled in the Colorado mountains for a long time, and we all plan to live in there for the rest of our lives. It's wonderful when you come to know a region well enough that you can sniff the air and predict the short-term weather at least as well as the TV meteorologists. Though none of us mind full-blown winter weather, we're all hoping for clear skies, as we have booked Trujillo Meadows Yurt on a full-moon night—tonight. Last night it was snowing and blowing so hard that we couldn't catch even the faintest glimpse of the moon as we drove from our home in Summit County down to Chama. (We were having enough trouble catching a glimpse of the road as we drove!)

JOHN FIELDER GETTING BACKCOUNTRY AIR, GUNNISON NATIONAL FOREST

Brian Litz

Forest Road 118 ascends maybe 500 feet in two miles—enough of a rise to get the heart pumping, but not so steep as to drain the energy or the spirit. As we climb, we start peeling off layers of clothing. It's a lot easier to overheat in the winter than people imagine, and, when you overheat, you sweat—and sweat eventually chills you. Body temperature management is a vital skill that winter travelers must acquire.

Though we're all struggling with packs laden with four days worth of provisions, we keep a steady pace. Robert, who is the most fit, leads the way, breaking trail through the crusty, windblown snow. Brad stops often to take photos, which is fine with Robert and me, as we're in no hurry. With the changing light, the passing clouds, and the snow-covered landscape, Brad is like a kid in a candy store, gleefully snapping off shots every few seconds. I've long envied photographers their enthusiasm, their intensity, and their ability to see patterns in the natural world that, when you get right down to it, exist only through a camera's view finder. But I've long been happy that I was never photographically inclined. Too much trouble; too much work. Too much frustration when you get home and find that you sort of neglected to load film into your camera.

While Brad snaps away, I notice a set of animal tracks heading off into the woods. They're small, perhaps a half-inch in diameter, and they follow a perfect line. There's no side-to-side deviation whatsoever. With last night's recent snowfall, these tracks must have been made this morning. The snow is so new and fresh that a microbe could walk across its surface and leave physical evidence of its passing.

I'm fascinated by animal tracks in snow. Each set of tracks tells a poignant story of survival, of predators tracking prey, and of prey avoiding predators.

Then I look back and see our tracks in the snow. Ordinarily, I prefer backcountry scenes that are free of evidence of man's passing, even if I'm one of the men in question. The exceptions are ski and snowshoe tracks, both of which I consider beautiful. I can live with ski and snowshoe tracks at least partially because they are so ephemeral. When the next storm blows in, they'll be covered or swept away. Ski and snowshoe tracks, in this regard, are performance art. And the foundation of that performance is built upon joy and rapture. Moving across snow by whatever means one enjoys is perhaps only equaled by moving across water.

Just as animal tracks in the snow are sagas of life and death, snowshoe and ski tracks in the snow each tell a saga of mirth and happiness.

Robert and Brad are both wearing well-used telemark skis and boots. I'm experimenting with alpine touring gear—called randonee gear in Europe. This is the first time I have used this system, and it's not long before I'm laboring. The extremely heavy, calf-high boots are made of rigid plastic; the skis are wide and heavy. I'm using climbing skins on the bottom of my skies for traction. Robert and Brad both have their skins stashed in their packs, and have opted to use wax for traction on this benign ascent. With the skins, I'm getting no glide whatsoever—sort of defeating the purpose of using skis instead of snowshoes, which I generally favor. I'm soon tired.

I decided to try the alpine touring gear for the simplest of reasons: though I'm a pitiful skier under any circumstances, I at least have an idea what it is I'm trying and failing miserably to do on alpine gear. I've taken a few telemark lessons, but the lightbulb has never gone on; I've never figured out what it is I'm trying to do.

The alpine touring rig is set up so that my heels move up and down, just like the kick-and-glide of cross-country skiing. On descents, however, I can clamp the heels down and ski alpine-style.

It was worth a try, if for no other reason than to once again marvel at man's ingenuity when it comes to traveling across snow. Moving through snow without bogging down has occupied a lot of creative energy as our species has evolved. There's evidence that skiing has been around for at least 4,000 years in Scandinavia, and I once read that prehistoric man experimented with snowshoes for more than 5,000 years. Now, of course, there are at least four major food groups of skiing, and several genera of snowshoes—to say nothing of snowboards, crampons, dogsleds, and snowmobiles.

Our written directions instruct us to watch for a 90-degree turn to the left two miles from the trailhead, and, by the time we reach the intersection, the sky is void of cloud cover. We are now basking in sunshine. The wind has died down as well. An hour before, we were in an alpine equivalent of a hurricane; now we're in climatic perfection. The only sound is the rhythmic whoosh-whoosh of our skis.

Quiet has always been one of the reasons I like winter so much. Summer, bless its heart, is a veritable cacophony by comparison, even in the boondocks. Summer is sometimes so raucously loud, what with camp robbers screeching and squirrels jabbering, that you can scarcely think a clear thought without being distracted. Summer is George Thorogood and the Delaware Destroyers live in concert; winter is Bach's "Jesu, Joy of Man's Desiring," played by Leo Kottke on an acoustic guitar.

JOHN FIELDER ON THE TRAIL,
WHITE RIVER NATIONAL FOREST

Brian Litz

Both are good, in their own time and place.

Robert and Brad are cruising right along, but I'm struggling to keep up. Despite the fact that I've backpacked thousands of miles, I've never skied with a full pack on my back before, and I'm having trouble getting my rhythm.

Shortly after noon, we make it to the yurt. It's located in an idyllic setting above a broad valley, which stretches out below us for miles and miles.

THIS IS THE FIRST TIME I've ever been on a multi-day hut trip, though yurts are not technically huts. They have more in common with Plains Indians tipis than they do with the backcountry cabins that form the backbone of Colorado's myriad backcountry hut systems. Yurts are the historic dwellings of the nomads of central and western Mongolia. They are hearty, weather resistant, mobile edifices that lay nary an iota of negative environmental impact on the land.

Trujillo Meadows Yurt is delightfully rustic. Twenty or so feet in diameter, it contains a wood stove, two bunk beds, a dining table with benches, and a small kitchen area that includes a two-burner propane stove and a complete set of dishes and cookware. The primitive outhouse is located a few feet from the yurt. There's a healthy pile of wood outside the front door. Atop the woodstove sits a monster-sized pot used for melting snow for drinking water.

After stoking the fire, Robert, who seems to have the energy level of a wolverine, heads out to fill a plastic trash bag with snow. He brings the bag back to the porch, and we use it to fill the snow-melting pan.

It only takes a few minutes before the yurt is warm, cozy, and homey. We all change clothes, prepare hot beverages, make and eat lunch, and ready ourselves for some serious power relaxation. It doesn't take long before snores are emanating from Trujillo Meadows Yurt.

By late afternoon, another storm front is moving in. It looks like our full-moon viewing will be limited. Still, with the wind whipping and the temperature dropping fast, Robert and Brad decide to head down to a clearing for some extracurricular skiing. I opt to stay behind, as I worked up a serious set of heel blisters on the way up. At least that was my excuse. Actually, I was sort of dreading this part of the trip. Just about every single person I've ever known who takes hut/yurt trips does so primarily so he or she can make tracks in the surrounding backcountry. I knew Robert and Brad were thinking along those lines, if for no other reason than the ski in was so benign, and, though beautiful, unexciting.

When I declined the inevitable offer to go for a few runs before dinner, rather than calling me the kinds of names males tend to call other males in these sorts of circumstances, my companions merely smiled and skied off. Within seconds, they were out of sight—their tracks the only evidence that they had passed.

It was nice to be alone in this secluded place. I wanted to mull over a few things going on in my life and, with a soundtrack consisting of nothing more than a crackling fire and the wind sliding by outside in the heart of the deep Colorado backcountry, I found my thoughts flowing free. There's no mental clutter here; there are no distractions—unless you call tossing another log on the fire a distraction. I don't.

Sitting in front of a fire in the middle nowhere was an instant memory-lane maker, reminding me of the old days, when campfires were as much of the backcountry experience as eating gorp and wearing stinky wool. When the environmentally correct understanding that campfires were bad in numerous ways started taking up residence in the psyches of backpackers, we all lost something very pleasant. I agree with the idea that by and large we shouldn't build campfires, but that will never stop me from missing them. This woodstove-bound conflagration was a close approximation of a campfire, and it didn't take long before I slipped into the old sitting-by-my-lonesome-around-the-campsite mindset. I used to be able to stare into campfire flames, sipping a tasty beverage or 12, for hours on end. No reading or writing in my journal or playing my harmonica. Just sitting there, pondering things great and small. Telling mental stories and jokes to myself. Having interior three-part conversations and arguments about political issues. Reciting poetry and singing songs right there between my ears.

Of course, the kind of thinking one tends to do in front of a fire is usually long on process and short on results. I haven't often made decisions or established plans of action while eyeballing a fire. More often than not, I end up complicating my ruminations with extraneous cranial wanderings and meanderings. But that's OK, too. Thinking is very much like walking or cross-country skiing: the process is a lot more important than the destination. I came to no conclusions while sitting there in front of the fire in that yurt, but I sure did enjoy spending some time pondering the subjects.

Just before dark, Robert and Brad returned. Their smiles were ear-to-ear. They didn't need to describe their experience, as the positive vibrations were pulsing from their entire beings. It's heartening to see such honestly earned joy. Brad and Robert had only taken two short runs in the two hours they'd been gone. To begin each of those runs,

THE FIELDERS POSE AT TAGERT HUT, ELK MOUNTAINS

they had to switchback for 30 minutes up a steep slope through waist-deep snow. Their reward was perhaps 20 seconds of enjoying the clean white buzz of carving turns through powder—no ski lifts necessary, thank you very much.

It's Brad's turn to cook dinner. This man takes culinary matters very seriously. When I first started putting this trip together, I asked Brad and Robert if they wanted instant oatmeal or instant cream-of-wheat for breakfast and whether, like me, they preferred Uncle Ben's instant brown rice over Minute Rice. There was a stunned silence during which they were trying to determine if I was joking. They set me straight, letting me know that one of the main joys of hut-staying stemmed from eating food that has a lot more in common with dinner at your grandmother's house than it does with backpacking fare. Omelettes, pasta with veggies, and huge burritos were more like it, I was told. It didn't dawn on me until we were a mile from the trailhead how silly that concept was. I mean, heavy food in a backpack is still heavy, whether you're heading to a yurt or a campsite.

Brad serves up sauteed shrimp and scallops over pasta.

All thoughts of instant rice and cream-of-wheat vanish from my brain.

Before bed, I step out onto the porch. The sky is completely overcast. There's no moon to be seen. Because of the clouds, though, the temperature is a relatively balmy 15 degrees. I peer through the plastic yurt window to make certain my compadres are absorbed in their reading material and unlikely to follow me outside. Only then do I partake in a quick though personally important ritual that my wife considers the silliest thing she has ever seen.

Ever since my college days down in southwest New Mexico, no matter how cold it is, I go out in the winter night before bed, remove my shirt, and stand there for a few minutes feeling the pins and needles of outrageous cold pricking my exposed skin.

This perhaps points to the essence of my love of winter: in literature, scripture, and myth, the scorching desert is most often portrayed as that place which cleanses our spirit and our soul through simple exposure and osmosis, if nothing else. If not the desert, then, ambiguously, the mountains. In my mind, the setting for Nature-based and Nature-borne spiritual enlightenment lies not in a place as much as it does a time and a set of conditions—winter. When I stand shirtless in the vibrantly, aggressively cold winter night, I feel like Moses must have felt wandering through the Sinai. I feel borderline reborn. If enlightenment ever visits me, and I'm not so sure I want it to, it will come on the wings of winter.

After maybe two minutes that feel like an hour, I put my shirt back on and return to the warmth and conviviality of the yurt.

THE WEATHER IS STILL ROUGH in the morning. After a 12-course breakfast that, unfortunately, I have to both cook and clean up, we begin the ski to Flat Mountain Yurt, some two or three hours away, at the crack of ten. According to the map, we have a three-mile gradual uphill—which will pretty much be the end of our climbing on this trip—followed by a gradual one-mile downhill. When I put my boots on, I can't believe the feeling in my feet. I have huge bruises on both ankles and raw blisters the size of cantaloupes on the inside of both heels. Symmetrical agony. At least I won't be limping, as both feet hurt equally.

While Brad and Robert patiently wait, I eat an entire bottle of Nuprin, cut up and apply 12-acres of Mole Foam, and fit several bandanas in my boots to serve as ankle padding. Nothing helps. I'm hobbled.

Under dark and foreboding skies, we make our way slowly through the deep coniferous woods of the South San Juans. Again, we are following an untracked, marked forest road with Robert in the lead. Robert and Brad spend the morning chatting amicably. I am struggling with the skins again and spend the morning several hundred yards behind my chums, wincing with every kick-and-nonglide. Few times in my life have I fantasized more about arriving at a destination. I plan to set the world record for boot removal.

JOE RYAN, MOUNTAINEER EXTRAORDINAIRE,
IN THE MOUNT SNEFFELS WILDERNESS

We spot the yurt, which is located at the top of a large meadow, at 12:15. There are a half-dozen sets of skis stuck in the snow in front of it. Since check-out time isn't until one P.M. at the South San Juan yurts, we're early. Six guys from Santa Fe have been at Flat Mountain Yurt for the previous two nights, and they aren't ready to leave, though they are in the process of packing up. We stand outside while they prepare to egress the yurt. I'm on the verge of offering to pay them $200,000 to let me go in and take my boots off, but, with six adults already moving around in the diminutive dwelling, I decide to bite my tongue and suck it up.

Soon after they leave, a vicious storm hits. It's snowing so hard we become concerned about finding the trail in the morning. Robert immediately dons his skis and sets out to get oriented before the snow gets too deep. It's wonderful having Robert and Brad along. On most backcountry trips I've taken in my life, I end up having to take care of everything, from itinerary-setting to route-finding to food preparation. Such is not the case with these guys; they almost knock each other over trying to do yurt chores.

One of the best things about winter is that you can take a city dump, or a water treatment plant, or an inner-city cinder-block government office building and, by adding just a few inches of snow, you've got yourself a postcard scene. I've heard it said that even urban New Jersey is pretty with snow. But when you have the Colorado Rockies covered with freshly fallen powder, you have something especially scenic; New Jersey this ain't.

New-fallen snow looks its best when covering nicely spaced woods, like those surrounding Flat Mountain Yurt. In Colorado we spend too much time ogling at long vistas—valleys spread out below or awesome peaks or horizon-to-horizon mountain ranges. Winter asks us to appreciate subtlety; it asks us to concentrate more on those things that are unjustifiably overlooked as we search for the long view of life. It points our attention toward spruces and firs holding on their branches six inches of snow so new it is still falling and settling.

The pitter of snow pattering on the yurt's roof is so light it's barely audible. I begin to mentally toy with the fantasy of getting snowed-in, of having to spend a week just hunkered down in this yurt while our families back home fret and fidget over our safety.

I'm starting to get a little nervous about tomorrow's ski to Neff Mountain Yurt. We have six miles to go. My feet are still killing me, and, since our entire route looks to be downhill, I've decided to forego my skins in favor of the blue wax Robert and Brad have been using. I'm having nightmarish visions of flying through the woods with the greatest of ease and speed—until, that is, I pile headlong into a tree.

THE STORM PASSES before morning. It has deposited about eight inches of prototypical Colorado champagne powder. Even though my blisters are causing severe discomfort, I'm so caught up in the incredible beauty of the scenery that my mind soon wanders away from the pain in my feet.

The trail follows a stream drainage downhill, past a couple of heavenly looking privately owned cabins that seem very much out of place and intrusive here in the otherwise pristine Colorado backcountry.

It's a surreal experience. The new snow is so light that it's like skiing through mist. The snow provides no resistance, no friction at all. For the most part, we can see neither our skis nor our feet. Only occasionally does a ski tip poke through, looking like a mini-dorsal fin breaking the snow.

The blue wax on my skis works perfectly. I've long looked at the art of waxing skis as borderline magic. I know that, even if I were to dedicate the rest of my life to the study of ski waxing, I would never in a million years get it right. The few times I've tried waxing my skis without supervision, I've found myself glued to clumps of heavy snow that couldn't be removed with a blowtorch. But Robert and Brad, not surprisingly, know exactly which wax to apply, and I'm merrily gliding along.

The ski is clear and cobalt blue, and the sun is hot. For the first and only time on this trip, we pull our packs off and snack on the trail. Relaxing in the snow is a bit more awkward than sitting near a trail in the summer, but, if you set your pack on the tails of your skis, you can sit down on it without removing them.

As we eat, we notice several different sets of animal tracks heading into the woods. One set I recognize as belonging to a snow-shoe hare: the larger hind feet are up and outside of the smaller front feet. Another set I believe were left by a coyote, a furtive creature that practices "direct registry"—placing a hind foot in the track made by the front foot—as it stealthily makes its way across the snow, looking, possibly, for the hare. And there is one set that could very well belong to a small cat of some kind. It is hard to tell for certain, as the sun has started melting away some of the tracks' dainty features. Even though the woods seem dead-of-winter devoid of animal life, obviously there is some faunal action transpiring all around us.

It only takes three hours to make it to the Neff Mountain Yurt, which is located at the base of a small, steep, ski-track-covered ridge that has Robert and Brad drooling.

Shortly after making ourselves at home, while my partners are napping, I put my boots back on and head out the door. I simply can't pass up exploring such proximate magnificence a little closer. I make my way toward the ridge behind the yurt, winding through the thick woods and trying to avoid hillsides that look like the snow they hold could slide down and bury my revery. It feels like I'm being drawn to something, but I don't know what. I'm hoping against hope I'm not being drawn toward any hard skiing, because that will be tantamount to being drawn toward my demise.

The views to the north suddenly open up, and my jaw drops. There, seemingly 200 feet away, are the high peaks of the South San

Juan Wilderness. And there is Flat Mountain, which I crossed while hiking the Colorado section of the Continental Divide Trail in 1996. It looks the same as it did that wonderful summer, but it also looks different. A veil of deep snow will do that, like make-up will change the visage of a beautiful women. Same woman, same face, yet different.

I ski a few hundred yards further, to a point where I have to decide whether I want to make tracks down the side of a long hill or head back to the yurt unscathed. Just before I turn back, I turn around, and my day—maybe even my decade—is made. There are several dozen Christmas-tree-sized-and-shaped pine trees covered with hanging icicles—*au natural* yuletide-like decorations. I've never seen icicles adorning trees like this. The unimpeded sunlight twinkles brightly off the trees. I'm dazzled, almost hypnotized. The beauty of the scene is so intense that I can't move. I'm riveted, speechless, and humbled all in one fell swoop.

LOST IN THE STORM! ELK MOUNTAINS

Brian Litz

I know that, later, Robert and Brad will ski off to the top of the ridge behind the yurt, and they will return with tales of the steep and deep. But, at this moment, their tales can't hold a candle to the beauty I'm standing before.

This time, when I return to the yurt, it's me who is smiling.

That night, the moon finally breaks through the clouds. I stand in front of the yurt for a long while taking it all in, loving the life I have found myself living here in the wondrousness that is Colorado in the wintertime.

The next morning, as my associates take a couple of last runs, I wait at the yurt, sitting on the deck in the warm morning sunshine. I realize as I hear Brad and Robert whooping it up on the nearby ridge that I don't want to leave. This yurt lifestyle seems like something I could get used to.

It only takes an hour to ski out. We could have made it faster, but we're not in a hurry. I'm usually torn when leaving the backcountry between a desire to turn and run back into the woods, never more to return to civilization, and a desire to sprint toward the closest town and the closest hamburger joint.

This time, I'm not torn. I want to stay. I want to stay very badly. But I can't stay. But I can sure come back.

ELK SCARS, BELLYACHE RIDGE, WHITE RIVER NATIONAL FOREST

Sunrise, Colorado National Monument

BLACK CANYON OF THE GUNNISON NATIONAL MONUMENT

MOUNT SOPRIS, PITKIN COUNTY

DALLAS DIVIDE, OURAY COUNTY

LODGEPOLE PINES, ARAPAHO NATIONAL FOREST

RED CANYON, COLORADO NATIONAL MONUMENT

PIKES PEAK FROM CASTLE PINES

CHARLES RIDGE, HOLY CROSS WILDERNESS

SUNSET, COLLEGIATE PEAKS WILDERNESS

RUBY RANGE, GUNNISON NATIONAL FOREST

Maroon Bells, Maroon Bells-Snowmass Wilderness

MINING STRUCTURE, RED MOUNTAIN PASS

SAGE, EAGLE COUNTY

SUNRISE, WHITE RIVER NATIONAL FOREST

The snow and he are intimate;

I've often seen them play

When heaven looked upon us all

With such severity,

I felt apology were due

To an insulted sky,

Whose pompous frown was nutriment

To their temerity.

—*Emily Dickinson*

But sweeter yet than dream or song of Summer or Spring

Are Winter's sometime smiles, that seem to well

From infancy ineffable;

Her wandering, languorous gaze

So unfamiliar, so without amaze,

On the elemental, chill adversity,

The uncomprehended rudeness; and her sigh

And solemn, gathering tear,

And look of exile from some great repose, the sphere

Of ether, moved by ether only, or

By something still more tranquil.

—*Coventry Patmore*

ASPEN TREES, UNCOMPAHGRE NATIONAL FOREST

RUBY RANGE, GUNNISON NATIONAL FOREST

WATERFALL, GLENWOOD CANYON

CASTLE CREEK, WHITE RIVER NATIONAL FOREST

ALONG CASTLE CREEK, WHITE RIVER NATIONAL FOREST

Dallas Divide, Ouray County

SKI TRACKS ON RICHMOND HILL, WHITE RIVER NATIONAL FOREST

SUNRISE ON SCARP RIDGE, GUNNISON NATIONAL FOREST

Sunrise on Castle Peak, Maroon Bells-Snowmass Wilderness

SLATE RIVER, GUNNISON NATIONAL FOREST

WHETSTONE MOUNTAIN, GUNNISON COUNTY

GREAT SAND DUNES NATIONAL MONUMENT, SAN LUIS VALLEY

Look up at the miracle of the falling snow,—the air a dizzy maze of whirling, eddying flakes, noiselessly transforming the world, the exquisite crystals dropping in ditch and gutter, and disguising in the same suit of spotless livery all objects upon which they fall. How novel and fine the first drifts! The old, dilapidated fence is suddenly set off with the most fantastic ruffles, scalloped and fluted after an unheard-of fashion! Looking down a long line of decrepit stone-wall, in the trimming of which the wind had fairly run riot, I saw, as for the first time, what a severe yet master artist old Winter is.

—*John Burroughs*

Whose woods these are I think I know.

His house is in the village though;

He will not see me stopping here

To watch his woods fill up with snow.

—*Robert Frost*

CHALK CREEK, SAN ISABEL NATIONAL FOREST

SUNRISE ON CASTLE PEAK, ELK MOUNTAINS

Ski tracks below Castle Peak, Elk Mountains

WIND · SNOW · ICE

The wind had been blowing on the eastern side of Rocky Mountain National Park for two weeks straight, the locals said. Gusts of up to 70 miles per hour were commonplace, they said. "Why on earth would you want to go up into the park now?" they asked.

Their concern was justified, as the landscape around Bear Lake Trailhead on Super Bowl Sunday, when our group of four started snowshoeing toward the base of 12,400-foot Flattop Mountain, was so windblown it looked as though a viscous film covered the land. Visibility was not only low, it was distorted, like we were stuck between dimensions in a *Star Trek* episode. Time and time again we passed groups of snowshoers and backcountry skiers enthusiastically leaving the park, and, almost without exception, we were asked variations on the theme of, "You're not going out camping in these conditions, are you?"

We were.

The Estes Park-based Colorado Mountain School had had this beginner mountaineering class scheduled for five months, and there was no way to know in advance that it would transpire in the middle of the biggest blow of the winter. There was nothing to do, save slog on, hoping against hope that the wind would fade away in the next day or two. Or else go home—and that was not an option. Though we possessed a fair amount of weather-based trepidation, it was overcome by our heartfelt desire to get into the woods.

There were three students: Dan, a 48-year-old concrete-pourer from Joplin, Missouri; Dana, a 28-year-old construction foreman from Omaha; and me. Our instructor was Marcin Kacperek, a 28-year-old Polish immigrant with the lean and chiseled physique and features that one automatically associates with people who spend a lot of time outdoors in the winter.

Our plan was to learn as much as possible about the fine art of ascending snow-covered mountains in the depths of winter, then to actually apply that newly gained knowledge by climbing to the top of Flattop via its north ridge. That part of the course would require a four-day, three-night journey into the backcountry of this, Colorado's largest and best-known national park.

The instruction had actually started the day before on a series of frozen waterfalls just east of Estes Park—though "waterfalls" is not quite an accurate description. Few falls of flowing water freeze thoroughly enough to climb safely; in non-winter seasons, this is a trickle coming from a seep in a tight, sunless canyon. When it slowly froze layer by layer, it took on the visage of a waterfall turned to ice. There was no river to this river of ice; the only thing under it was dirt and rock.

In the pantheon of the winter aesthetic, ice ranks well behind and below snow and cold. Whereas snow can justifiably be viewed as a friend and maybe even a playmate, and whereas cold can at least be justifiably viewed as not the hideous enemy many people believe it to be, ice has few conceptual positives, few apologists, few allies. With the possible exception of icicles, ice is rightfully viewed as winter's evil offspring. It's the side of winter that causes us to slip on sidewalks and to skid out of control on highways. We don't get into iceball fights or make ice angels, and even ice cubes are considered out of place in winter.

It came as something of a surprise to learn that we would begin our mountaineering experience on ice rather than snow. It seemed more a way to fill an extra day with hands-on activity than an exercise with practical value. It also seemed a good way to get scared to death before venturing into Rocky Mountain National Park. Maybe that was part of the goal—to sober us up and clean out our arteries before we entered the backcountry and the "real" phase of this mountaineering class.

Dread overcame me on the way to the ice. I don't have a fear of climbing, per se, nor do I have an especially pronounced fear of heights. My fear of falling, however, is well-developed, as is my fear of acting fearful in front of others. I probably wouldn't mind plummeting to my death if I could do so in such a manner that those theregathered would later laud my bravery and coolness of demeanor as I sped toward terra firma. Alas, such would likely not be the case. I suspect that the main topic of conversation at my wake would be how far away my screams could be heard. And that notion flat-out galls me enough that I generally avoid situations that present even the remotest possibility of being terminated with an adrenaline-based shriek.

In order to enter the side canyon where the ice was, we had to cross the infamous Big Thompson River, the very flow that, in 1976 flooded during an especially intense summer thunderstorm, tore down the canyon, and swept more than 100 people to their deaths.

This river is covered by a thick layer of rough, though slippery, ice. Here, it would be possible to break through, though the water is not deep this time of year. It's only when winter starts melting away that the tiny mountain streams of the Colorado high country turn brown and vicious and deadly.

Ice covering a body of water is one of the physical miracles of winter. That there is enough molecular cohesiveness to support four men atop this layer of solid water directly above its liquid counterpart is well past the point of bewildering; it's mystical. Then again, winter is a mystical season.

Though it is late January and though we are at 7,000 feet, there is little snow on the ground, and we are able to hike toward the ice we plan to climb wearing only thick, plastic mountaineering boots. After 15 minutes of calf-wrecking steepness, we stop to put our crampons on. Ice-climbing requires several pieces of gear that could well pass for medieval weaponry. The ice axes would complement any knight-in-shining-armor's combat ensemble and ice climbing crampons look savage and wicked, like something you'd see put to nefarious use in a particularly hideous martial-arts movie. They attach tightly to the boots, which are designed to receive them, and they boast several dozen razor-sharp teeth contrived to dig deeply into the ice. Combined with the well-executed placement of the ice axes, a crampon-adorned climber can support his or her entire weight on the face of a vertical ribbon of ice.

It's a disconcerting though marvelous notion.

The ice climbing itself went well enough; no death or near-death experiences, though it's certainly intellectually captivating to hear the belayers—those in whose hands your life is literally held—below asking the instructor fundamental questions about the process. Things like: "If he falls, do I pull on this end of the rope, or *this* end?" Makes you concentrate mightily on your technique.

Aside from the aforementioned fear of falling and looking like a wuss while doing so, the biggest problem I have with climbing, whether it be on rock or on ice, is the confusion of gear that the sport requires. I'm not a clear enough thinker to deal in an organized fashion with the piles of ropes, slings, nuts, ice screws, and carabiners that come hand-in-hand with even the most modest climbing endeavors. I've always admired people who can keep track of all this gear—to say nothing of using it correctly. I'll never be such a person, and I'm glad to have finally come to a point in life where I can admit that to myself.

JOHN FIELDER SKIS BACKCOUNTRY POWDER! SAN ISABEL NATIONAL FOREST

Brian Litz

We spent the day going up and down a series of three increasingly steep, high, and scary ice falls. But my recollection of the experience in that little notch of a canyon centers less around the climbing than it does on the feel and look of the ice itself. Being a skater since the age of four, I've always had a positive and intimate relationship with ice, though the physics of solid water continue to astound me. (Australopithecus understood the molecular-level aspects of ice better than my decidedly unscientific mind ever could.) But I'd never before looked at ice as a sensual substance. As I was blemishing the surface of those ice falls with my crampons and ice axes, I felt as though I were violating something sacred, like I was taking a steak knife to the *Mona Lisa*. That the nature of the ice would repair its now-pitted surface in due time mattered not one whit to me. You could argue as you were in the Louvre hacking away that someone could one day paint another *Mona Lisa*.

The ice in that otherwise nondescript little canyon was more lovely than anything any man has ever created in the name of art or science. It was smooth in places, with frozen ripples and arches and stalactite-looking pillars in others. There were near-human forms—faces and legs and breasts and arms. It was like there were people in the ice, trying to form themselves, trying to get out. Nature has once again shown herself to be the ultimate sculptor. I took every opportunity to run my hands across the surface of the ice, like I've always wanted to do with the *Venus de Milo*.

Then there was the matter of contorted perspective. While standing at the bottom of the various falls we climbed that day, it looked as though you could safely walk up to the next level in your socks. Once you were climbing, though, the slope of the ice took on an entirely different physical reality. It was like climbing through a slippery cubist painting, where angles were different depending on how you viewed them. While I was climbing, I was no longer standing perpendicular to the ground, rather, I was standing parallel to the ice. Everything was different from that aspect, the aspect of imminent and quantifiable mortality.

All this ice "art" was created by temperature, friction, and gravity only. Very little wind comes into this canyon, and very little sunlight. The art of this lovely series of ice falls was created by subtlety and the corpulent passage of time.

Outside of this little canyon, things were decidedly different. Nature as artist was in a creative frenzy. Her chisel was the wind, and her subject the snow, and she had perhaps been drinking a bit too much coffee lately.

Within a few hundred yards of the parking lot, the trail passed close by Bear Lake, a place that proves increased remoteness does not necessarily equal increased beauty. Many mountain jocks and jockettes in the American West look upon our national parks and monuments as sacrifice zones established more to keep the teeming masses in a manageable setting than for the preservation of world-class natural resources and scenery. Most of us look at designated wilderness areas, rather than national parks, as the places where the true world-class territory lies.

Rocky Mountain National Park takes that arrogant perspective and tosses it directly into the trash bin, where it belongs. Even a stone's throw from a packed parking lot, there is scenery here to rival any in the nation. The backbone of the ridge that travels north from the Indian Peaks Wilderness to the Mummy Range is home to some of the most intense topography in the state. There are serrated ridges and precipitous headwalls and 2,000-foot sheer cliff faces that draw climbers from all over the world.

And it starts right at Bear Lake, the setting for one of the most transcendent outdoor experiences I've ever had. I was here in the early 1990s with a group of 30 or so kids who were attending an annual "Burn Camp," organized by Children's Hospital of Denver. These heroic young people were so disfigured by their burns that it was painful to look upon their sweet, innocent, confused, resigned, bitter faces.

We passed hundreds of people on the trail to Bear Lake on that long-ago August day, and, almost without exception, those people, no matter their age, no matter their gender or bearing, looked away, too mortified to offer these Burn Camp participants the courtesy of gracious eye contact or a simple greeting. The kids knew they were repulsive to look upon, yet they walked along the trail with their heads up, stoic to a fault. They had little choice.

The farther we traveled into the majestic interior of Rocky Mountain National Park, the more these young people loosened up. Soon, they were just kids playing in the woods. They were skipping stones and climbing on rocks and soaking their ravaged feet in the cooling waters of snow-melt streams. Here, they could forget, even if only for a few hours, the indignities of their injuries in a society that places so much importance on physical appearance. They could simply be the children they were, down deep and deep down.

It was here and then, some 25 years after my outdoor life took root and began to grow, that it sunk in just how healing the powers of Nature are. Certainly, the touch of Nature did not return the skin of those burned children to normal, neither did it take away the memories of inconceivable pain and suffering. Nature, though, did lend a soothing

touch to these young people who were so, so hurt. From that afternoon on, I've never looked at the natural world as a simple escape from those things that pollute the human psyche and the human body. Since then, I've looked at Nature as the ultimate in healthful salvation—that which heals the burns and scars that civilization and the hyper-frenetic modern lifestyle lays on all of us all of the time.

I wonder what it would be like to bring the Burn Camp participants up to Bear Lake in the dead of winter, to start a snowball fight with them, to show them the fine art of making snow angels, to let them feel the spirit and energy of a Colorado winter.

BEAR LAKE WAS FROZEN solid, with a layer of snow covering it at least five feet deep. Though we were only 15 or so miles from the bare ground of Estes Park, now we were nuzzled against the ample bosom of winter.

JOHN FIELDER AND VISITOR, RAMBOUILLET YURT,
GUNNISON NATIONAL FOREST

Brian Litz

Under that ice, fish, plants, and micro-organisms are whiling away the months until spring melt, which, here, will be in mid-May. Maybe. In a season dominated by perplexities, this perhaps tops the list. During the winter, water at the top of a relatively deep body of water, such as Bear Lake (we're not talking about beaver ponds here), is coldest near the top rather than at the bottom, where temperatures hover around 4 degrees Celsius. As the surface of lake water freezes, molecular density would seemingly cause the cold water to sink, freezing the lake solid and killing all life within it. But for reasons that can be described at least as well by theologians as they can by biologists, the less dense, warmer water flows toward the bottom.

It's a miracle.

This vertical temperature gradient allows for very little mixing between the water at the bottom of the lake and that at the top, so the top stays frozen, and the bottom stays liquid. The thick ice cover also prevents mixing, which is generally caused by wind. The unfrozen water down below in the darkest depths gives aquatic plants and animals the opportunity to survive the harsh alpine winters.

Were it not for water's unique ability to remain unfrozen at the bottom of lakes, life in the high country would be much different. The entire food chain would be disrupted, and the fishing would be poor. This isn't the first time it has occurred to me that God must be a fisher-man at heart, because fish in so many ways seem to live the most improbable lives of any alpine animal.

The wind is now scouring Bear Lake's snow-covered surface. It's also scouring our faces. Our eyes are watering, our noses are running, and it's hard to stay focused. Heavy wind makes you look at the world sideways; strong and constant wind doesn't allow for a head-on viewing of your surroundings. Yet we can not let this wind get the upper hand. We have to muster survival-based concentration, despite the wind, as we soon leave the well-packed trail and begin a bushwhack across the eastern flank of Flattop Mountain. We're now in avalanche country, and that reality is exacerbated by the wind.

Slope angle is, of course, of paramount concern when you're thinking in terms of not getting buried by a slide. Any snow-covered slope between 30 and 45 degrees is potentially an avalanche waiting to happen. But there's a lot more to it than slope angle, and wind is a big player.

Avalanches are caused by a strong, heavy layer of snow developing over a weaker layer, and wind loads base layers with additional snow while concurrently weakening the crystalline structure of the base. The heavier the wind, the worse the potential scenario—at least on paper. As Marcin says, if people could accurately predict avalanches, no one would ever die in an avalanche. I once spent several hours talking with Nick Logan of the Colorado Avalanche Information Center, and, of all the things he said, it was his observation that there is no such thing as an avalanche expert that hit home the hardest. Even people who have dedicated their lives and their careers to the study of avalanches admit freely that they are only capable of making educated guesses. And this is not false modesty at work. This is grim reality.

WHITEOUT! WHITE RIVER NATIONAL FOREST

Brian Litz

Some places have tornadoes, some have earthquakes, while still others have hurricanes. We have avalanches, and avalanches evince a deep-rooted fear factor where I live. Everyone who ventures into the Colorado backcountry in the winter has let the potential scenario run through his or her mind: If I'm caught in a slide, could I fight my way out? If not, could I remain calm? Could I die with dignity, or would I panic, whimpering and begging Mother Nature to spare me?

Soon we have to cross an open 35-degree slope. We turn our avalanche beacons on. They look so small and fragile. I don't like the idea of placing my life in the hands of technology, but beacons are the single most important piece of gear you can bring with you into the backcountry in the winter. We cross the slope one at a time. As the only other person in the party who is experienced in backcountry winter travel, Marcin asks me to go last. Last is who gets hit the most often, as each subsequent set of ski or snowshoe tracks can weaken the base. I breathe a sigh of relief when I reach the trees unscathed.

AND STILL THE WIND BLOWS, but it's not too cold—perhaps 20 degrees. As we pass through the spruce forest, I take the time to examine the terrain. Since we are on snowshoes, it's easy to contemplate the surroundings without worrying about suddenly flying down the mountainside, which is exactly what I would be doing if we were on skis.

The rugged brownness of aptly named Lumpy Ridge—one of the climbing meccas of the planet—dominates the eastern horizon, while the towering, massive, and fearsome-looking Mummy Range fills the entire northern horizon.

All around, the snow is being forced by the wind into breathtaking artistic visions. There are ripples in the snow reminiscent of those found in the sand on the Outer Banks of North Carolina as the waves retreat to the ocean depths. But these ripples are hard as rocks.

A series of five side-by-side tree stumps, perhaps three feet high, with improbable dollops of snow perched atop them in a physics-defying fashion line the trail. Though the trunks are only a foot in diameter, the rounded snow crowns are three times that. It's like five mushrooms or ice cream cones standing watch. The attraction of molecules to others of their kind will never cease to amaze me.

Farther along, several miniature cornices curl overhead, where the snow has blown itself over a natural terrain feature in slow-motion, breaking in a wave like fashion.

And there's a chest-high "snowman"— but not of the Frosty variety. This one looks like it was just flown in from Easter Island. It consists of one giant head just sitting in the snow. It has closed slits of eyes and a lopsided nose and uneven ears and a mouth frozen in a gasp. It is all that is left of a bank of snow that has been blown away. Why this small statue remained, I can't say. Perhaps the snowflakes in this one spot contained heavier granules of dust at their core. Perhaps a tree upwind was blocking the most direct gusts. Or perhaps Nature was just being intentionally creative. Why not?

For the billionth time in my life, I'm engrossed and absorbed by the work of the wind and the snow—so much so that I nearly overlook the splendor of the windswept flanks of Flattop Mountain as they emerge from behind trees. But there's nothing wrong with being captivated by beauty in small and often overlooked places.

In 1979, I lived in Chicago for six months. During that time, I was a regular at the Chicago Art Institute, and in a gallery populated by Monets and Picassos, I never once saw a painting or a sculpture that was worthy of being described in the same breath as what I'm seeing all around me as I snowshoe my way through Rocky Mountain National Park on this disorientingly blustery day.

And while I was living in Chicago, I once had the pleasure of hearing Sir Georg Solti direct the Chicago Symphony. Never in a program dominated by the works of Haydn, Mozart, and Brahms did I hear a single note that could compare to the sweet noise of this wind blowing through my hair and my teeth in this awesome setting.

No offense intended to Monet, Picasso, Brahms, Mozart, and Haydn, and I'm sure none taken.

WE FIND AN OASIS IN THE SPRUCES where we can pitch our tent in relative calm. It's a tent designed for three, but, in the spirit of learning how it feels to be on a bonafide mountaineering expedition, where extra ounces are anathematic, Marcin has decided that we will all cram into this one tent. There's no room for our packs, so they must remain outside. We can fit only the barest of essentials into the tent with us.

Though it's only two o'clock, we wedge ourselves between the nylon walls. Dan and Dana are somewhat incredulous that we are essentially bedding down for the night at such an early hour. Marcin and I eyeball each other and smile. In the midst of hyper-busy lives, the opportunity to hang out immersed in down and pile in a tent for 17 hours while the cold wind rages a few feet away is wonderful. I often fantasize about taking my tent out into the dead of winter for no other reason than to catch up on shuteye that is always otherwise sacrificed to less-productive enterprises, like working or performing domestic chores or running the endless torrent of errands that seem to dominate and clutter my life.

JOHN FIELDER MAKES FRESH TRACKS,
WHITE RIVER NATIONAL FOREST

Brian Litz

I volunteer to man the stove on this first night out. I melt snow for hot beverages, then prepare one of my standard-fare backcountry dinners—curried couscous with canned chicken. Marcin devours his portion with the enthusiasm of a man who has endured many worse meals in many less comfortable settings. Dan and Dana pronounce theirs "not bad." But I can tell from the looks on their faces that they're having second thoughts about the whole notion of winter camping. Each of them surreptitiously digs into their snack stashes shortly after dinner.

When I offer to heat water to do the dishes, Marcin stops me, saying that, on mountaineering trips, dishes usually remain uncleaned for the duration of the expedition in order to save stove fuel. With the temperature plummeting, the chances of any microbes taking up residence in the pans or bowls are remote. I'm already wondering what tomorrow's instant maple-flavored oatmeal will taste like when combined with the remains of my curried couscous.

We chat for only a few minutes. Then we fall into the contemplative silence that such a setting demands. The wind isn't howling directly where we are, but it's howling close by. It's out there moving snow, constructing monuments, and honing small works of art that will remain unseen by human eyes and that will pass from existence even as they are still being created.

The wind is also destabilizing the snowpack. Avalanches are loading up on all the proximate slopes, waiting for one unwary step to trigger their almost unbelievable ferocity. I dream of massive slides, of entire mountainsides of benign-looking, powdery snow breaking free and moving faster and faster toward some defenseless settlement way down below in a valley. Trees splinter in its 200-mile-per-hour path. The displacement of air causes a roar that sounds like a sonic boom. Friction causes the snow to superheat. When it settles, it has the consistency of concrete. No one who is covered can get out.

I sleep fitfully.

IN THE MORNING, the wind is blowing harder and more relentlessly than ever. After breakfast, we move gingerly and stiffly from the tent. We spend the day working on technical climbing and expeditionary skills within view of camp. We spend three hours finding buried "victims" with the avalanche beacons, which is a serious challenge in these conditions. With our ice axes, we practice over and over and over the self-arrest procedures that will hopefully save our lives if we slip on the side of Flattop Mountain.

We work on crevasse rescue techniques and talk about how we will rope up and proceed toward the summit at dawn's early light. We can't see the summit, only a ridge finger protruding high above our camp. It's almost completely devoid of snow. It seems we could easily ascend via that route, bypassing any avalanche concerns completely. But that route is rock and boulder-filled, and, thus, dangerous in its own right.

After dinner, we finally talk of the possibility that has been eating at the entire party: the wind might be destroying our chances to summit Flattop. Marcin tells us that we will snowshoe to the base of the climb—two miles away—at first light, to check things out. He stresses to everyone that ego can never be part of a climbing decision. He stresses that Mother Nature deplores human arrogance. He tells us several of the kinds of stories that all serious climbers seem to have in an abundance that often defy their years: he speaks of six or eight dead climbing buddies. Some of their deaths stemmed from acts of God, he said. But others stemmed from acts of machismo.

When I tell Marcin I would rather fail than die, he laughs long and hard.

"Usually," he says, "climbers are full of bravado, and they say just the opposite, that they would rather die than fail. Some are kidding; some are not."

The wind blows stronger than ever as Marcin speaks these words.

Inside the warm but cramped tent, Dan, Marcin, and I talk politics and religion for a couple of hours while Dana lies in his bag groaning. He has contracted what appears to be a moderate case of altitude sickness. We're at 11,000 feet, and neither Dan nor Dana have really had the chance to acclimatize. By morning, Dana feels better, but not much. His skin color has progressed in the past 12 hours from off-green to pasty-white.

As we leave the tent, the wind is blowing the taste right out of our mouths. As we trudge along, we have to lean forward just to keep our momentum. Several gusts almost take us off our feet.

We are carrying light packs, filled with only climbing gear, water, and a few snacks. Dan and Dana are both laboring, the altitude and the difficulty of moving through deep snow taking its toll on their flatland legs and lungs. We're moving slowly enough that, even if Marcin deems the avalanche danger to be acceptable, it's obvious we won't have enough time to get up and down Flattop Mountain today. Yet we still move toward the climbing route. Even if we don't attempt it, we all want to see what it looks like.

A mile from camp, we pass beneath a modest and seemingly harmless-looking hillside. Marcin stops us dead in our tracks. "That's the kind of place where people die," he says, stressing that most avalanche fatalities occur not because entire mountainsides of snow let loose, but, rather, because small slabs break away. "All it takes is a slide 20 meters wide and 10 meters tall, and you can be in serious trouble."

We enthusiastically angle away from the base of this particular slope. Winter is beautiful, but disaster lurks in the snow like land mines waiting to be tripped. That fact can never be overlooked or ignored. Mother Nature is indifferent to us and our passing. Just because she has allowed us access to and safe passage within her inner sanctum doesn't mean she loves or even likes us. She could and would kill us all without remorse in a skinny minute. I don't know whether it's bad karma, coincidence, ignorance, or overt malice on the part of

WINTER RAYS! SAN JUAN NATIONAL FOREST

Brian Litz

Mother Nature that makes dying out in the woods so damned easy. Guess it really doesn't matter. All you can do is keep your eyes peeled, your brain cranked, and hope for the best.

When we finally arrive at the base of our climbing route, my jaw drops. Lying in a near-vertical, snow-filled chute, it's at least 1,000 feet high. Now I can see where the ice-climbing training comes into play.

Dan sighs. There's no way he can make it up there, he says. He admits that he totally underestimated the difficulty of traveling through the Colorado backcountry in the middle of winter. He's a strong man, though, and, when he vows to come back better prepared, I believe him. Ditto for Dana. Besides, Marcin says, the avalanche situation is obviously too dicey to risk an ascent on this day. He receives nary a syllable of argument from the group. As we start back towards camp, Dan suddenly stops and turns to me.

"Well, John, I guess we never asked you what you wanted to do."

I look wistfully toward the distant and lofty summit of Flattop Mountain.

"Guess the smart thing to do is go back," I say, shaking my head slowly, hoping to come across like I really want to give the summit a go, no matter the odds. Truthfully, I am taken aback at the seriousness of the chute we had planned to ascend. Earlier, I mentioned that I generally avoid situations that might cause a face-losing scream to leap from my mouth. You might ask why, then, was I taking a mountaineering class? Well, the answer is simple: I had no idea that we would even consider attempting a route so intense. I'd figured that the route would be so benign as to be border-line embarrassing and that our mellow ascent would be laden with observations from the instructor like: "This is what we would be doing if we were *really* climbing."

It didn't bother me at all that Marcin decided to turn us around.

The plan had been to camp one more night, but, since we were back at the tent by noon, we opted to pack up and pack out then and there. Everyone seemed inclined to sprint back to the trailhead. We were all ready to get out of the wind. Winter had alpha-ed us, and, tail between our legs, we whimpered and submitted.

We were whupped.

Aspen trees below Gothic Mountain, Gunnison National Forest

WILLOWS ALONG ANTHRACITE CREEK, GUNNISON NATIONAL FOREST

ASPEN TREES, GUNNISON NATIONAL FOREST

SUNRISE IN THE RUBY RANGE, GUNNISON NATIONAL FOREST

On North Twin Cone Peak, Pike National Forest

Along the Rio Grande, San Luis Valley

EVENING TWILIGHT, WHITE RIVER NATIONAL FOREST

PARADISE DIVIDE, GUNNISON NATIONAL FOREST

ELK MOUNTAINS, WHITE RIVER NATIONAL FOREST

WINTER WIND, SAN ISABEL NATIONAL FOREST

SCRUB OAK, UNCOMPAHGRE NATIONAL FOREST

SUNRISE, SAN LUIS VALLEY

Sunrise, Sawatch Range, White River National Forest

SUNRISE, RUBY RANGE, GUNNISON NATIONAL FOREST

Fresh snow, Arapaho National Forest

SLATE RIVER, GUNNISON NATIONAL FOREST

SKI MOUNTAINEERING IN MOUNT SNEFFELS WILDERNESS

ELK MOUNTAINS, GUNNISON NATIONAL FOREST

SUNRISE, ELK MOUNTAINS, WHITE RIVER NATIONAL FOREST

EVENING TWILIGHT ON CARBONATE HILL, GUNNISON NATIONAL FOREST

SPRUCE-FIR FOREST, WHITE RIVER NATIONAL FOREST

RIME ICE ALONG THE ROARING FORK RIVER, GARFIELD COUNTY

SUNRISE ON THE SLATE RIVER, GUNNISON NATIONAL FOREST

MARGY'S HUT, TENTH MOUNTAIN DIVISION HUT SYSTEM

ALONG THE GUNNISON RIVER, GUNNISON COUNTY

RIFLE CANYON, RIFLE FALLS STATE PARK

ALONG DIFFICULT CREEK, WHITE RIVER NATIONAL FOREST

All night it fell, and when full inches seven

It lay in the depth of its uncompacted lightness,

The clouds blew off from a high and frosty heaven;

    And all woke earlier for the unaccustomed brightness

Of the winter dawning, the strange unheavenly glare:

The eye marveled—marveled at the dazzling whiteness;

    The ear hearkened to the stillness of the solemn air;

No sound of wheel rumbling nor of foot falling,

And the busy morning cries came thin and spare.

—Robert Bridges

The snow is a great tell-tale,

and blabs as effectually as it obliterates.

I go into the woods, and know all that has happened.

I cross the fields, and if only a mouse

has visited his neighbor, the fact is chronicled.

—*John Burroughs*

Ski mountains and the Maroon Bells, White River National Forest

PARADISE DIVIDE, GUNNISON NATIONAL FOREST

SUNSET OVER THE GORE RANGE, WHITE RIVER NATIONAL FOREST

THE COLOR OF WINTER

inter dawned crimson on the eastern flanks of 13,684-foot Baldy Mountain on this late-February day. One instant, the mountain's massive ridgeline was dull and barely visible. Then, minutes before the orb of the sun rose over the highest peaks on the entire Continental Divide—Grays and Torreys— every molecule of Baldy exploded into heart-palpitating brilliance.

I was standing in the middle of that brilliance, at an altitude of more than 12,000 feet. I was on my way to the summit, having left the trailhead at 4:30 A.M., wanting to witness the dawn from as high up the mountain as possible. I thought the most captivating views would be of the sun illuminating the nearby Mosquito, Tenmile, Williams Fork, and Gore Ranges.

I had no idea I would be part of the light show. Up this high on the windswept ridge, there was little snow, only exposed, lichen-covered rocks and dirt, which, as the sun crept toward the horizon, glowed radioactively. Then I looked over at my jet-black dog. She, too, was glowing brightly, almost like her aura was trying to one-up the sun's corona. Her eyes were so red it looked like she had been possessed by some otherworldly demon. I removed my gloves and lifted my hands up in front of my face, and they were seemingly afire. Moving my hands slowly side to side, they left trails of red light behind them, like wakes.

The Navajo consider dawn to be sacred, and, while I've traditionally been a bigger fan of dusk than dawn (perhaps mainly because I've been awake for a lot more dusks than dawns), this experience on Baldy was near spiritual and borderline mystical. At any moment, I expected to be given a set of commandments, or to be abducted by aliens, or perhaps to spontaneously combust. I tried to avert my eyes from my immediate pigmentation situation in order to view the dawn light as it painted the surrounding peaks of the central Rockies, but I couldn't. It's not every day that I glow; I wanted to witness each and every nanosecond of the spectacle.

Then it ended, and the winter world returned to its normal subdued hues. It was like I'd just been transported from colorful Oz, back to black-and-white Kansas—even though Kansas, in this instance, was the summit ridge of one of the hundred-highest peaks in Colorado. Still, after that light show, everything seemed suddenly ordinary, bland, and drab. I felt drained and energized at the same time. I still can't believe I didn't get abducted by aliens or something.

This was clearly going to be a good day.

THE CLIMB UP from the trailhead, some 2,000 feet below, was arduous, as the crusty-surfaced snow was knee-deep. In the dark hours, there was no pausing to enjoy the sights; there was only the rhythmic placing of one snowshoe after another. Occasionally I stopped to catch my breath, feeling the gloriously crisp and clean air fill my lungs, while my headlamp impotently tried to illuminate the trail.

Slowly, the tree cover began to thin as I made my way towards the tundra. By the time the first tendrils of dawn began to lend light to the scene, I was well above the last trees. Since there was scant snow on this ridge, I ditched my snowshoes next to the trail and proceeded wearing only my leather hiking boots.

It was strange to be walking sans skis or snowshoes at this altitude this time of year. But Baldy boasts a justified reputation for being a seriously windblown mountain. Its summit ridge rarely holds snow for more than a few days, even after the harshest blizzard. The snow that falls here gets blown down the eastern, leeward side of Baldy, where it catches in some of the most fearsome-looking chutes in this part of the state. After my recent experience in Rocky Mountain National Park, I had had my fill of boreal conditions. This dawn, thankfully, broke calm.

For several weeks I had perused topographical maps trying to find a peak that could easily and safely be ascended in a solo fashion even in February. I suspected that whatever I came up with would be my last big trek for this Colorado winter, and I wanted to do it alone.

As my amigos are quick to point out, I probably spend too much time by my lonesome in the backcountry. It's not that I'm misanthropic, like many backcountry devotees I know. Actually, I'm an extremely gregarious social animal, at least in civilized settings. When I'm tromping through the mountains, though, I find that solitude is often the best companion. And company in the woods stymies my ability to daydream freely. I like having time by myself to let my imagination wander down whatever path it desires, and there's no better venue for unencumbered musings than the snow-covered mountains of Colorado.

It took quite some time to come up with an appropriate mountain upon which to try the very first dead-of-winter solo ascent of my life, and, when the lightbulb finally went on over my head, the switch was not flipped by some map or guidebook-inspired stroke of genius—rather it was flipped by simply raising my head one day while standing in my front yard. Baldy Mountain not only dominates the horizon east of my abode, it *is* the horizon. It's a neighbor, and it's a friend. It's a peak that I've seen from all angles in all weather and lighting conditions.

It is also a benign peak—at least on the Blue River side—upon which the trail switchbacks up through the coniferous woods, past several old cabins, and, finally up to a couple of weather-scoured ugly old tin edifices that were built to help the people of Summit County receive the blessings of mass communication from Colorado's Front Range. Because of these buildings, and the electronics they once held, television transmissions were finally in the 1960s able to reach over the Continental Divide and into homes that, previously, were only able to receive TV poorly and intermittently —homes where, before, people passed their evenings playing games, talking, and going to bed early.

For some inexplicable reason, we still call this "progress." These buildings are more than just a conceptual abomination, for they visually pollute a gorgeous ridgeline, and, if you can see Baldy, you most likely can see these buildings, gleaming in the sun from a far distance like something valuable and important.

Shortly past these structures, the trail steeply makes its way up toward the first in a long series of false summits. Within minutes, those odious buildings are a faint memory. It feels wonderful to be this deep in the tundra. I've mentioned how much I buy into the spiritual energy of winter in general, and snow specifically. But winter and snow in and of themselves are only part of my personal backcountry Holy

SAFETY IN NUMBERS! GUNNISON NATIONAL FOREST

Brian Litz

Trinity. They are powerful alone and together, but they are incomplete. The tundra is the glue that binds them together. To me, the tundra is my version of the Vatican; it's the sacred center of my psychic universe. It's a place in which I almost feel compelled to remove my shoes and to proceed upon my knees. Almost. It's a smidge too brisk for that now, but my heart's in the right place.

Ever since I first rubbed elbows with alpine tundra atop Maine's Mount Katahdin when I began hiking the Appalachian Trail in 1979, I've tried to get a handle on my love of this wondrous ecological territory. I've ruminated long and hard about what makes Colorado's massive above-treeline areas my favorite life zones in the world, and, believe me, there are plenty of other life zones that I like a lot. I've mentally toyed with the tundra's most obvious feature: its lack of trees. But I'm a big fan of trees, as long as they stay in their places. I've pondered whether my love of this place is based on the tundra's sometimes unsettling and mind-spinning openness. Certainly, that's part of it. But the Llano Estacado of west Texas is open, and that place gives me a case of the heebie-jeebies just thinking about it.

My best guess is that I like the way I feel in the tundra. I would hope that every person in the world has a place where they feel the most like they hope they really are, deepdown. I'm a person who is not the biggest fan of himself. There's a lot of deep-seated animosity between me and I, but, when I'm in the tundra, I either cut myself enough slack that I at least come to tolerate myself, or this place makes me realize, rightly or wrongly, that I'm not the total schmuck I make myself out to be. For John Fayhee, the tundra is a tranquil place, a calming place, a place where my normal scowl is replaced by an easy smile and a good nature.

Not surprisingly, I spend as much of my life as possible above treeline, but most of that time is in the summer, when the tundra is verdant and lush and populated by marmots, pikas, elk, and the greatest wildflowers on earth. I don't venture up this high much in the winter. The avalanche danger above treeline is usually significantly higher than down in the trees, and the elements are often so harsh as to overcome even the strongest love. Self-flagellation via frostbite is a bit much. I chide myself for not spending more time in the tundra in the winter, though, and, as I make my way up Baldy, I promise to schedule at least one trip a week up into the land beyond trees—which is not really that hard, as I can drive to tundra access points on Hoosier or Loveland Passes. Driving, I know, is not the same as sweating your way into the tundra from the bottom of some deep river valley, but, in the workaday world, sometimes you've got to take what you can get.

This day, the elements are giving me a break. The sky is perfectly clear, and, with the sun moving higher, it's even getting a tad toasty, if you can call 15 degrees toasty. Though there's very little snow hereabouts, there's plenty of ice, and the rocks are slick. I slip and slide several times, banging my right elbow solidly on one boulder and almost landing directly atop my cur. I stop for a swig of hot tea from my thermos and regain what few wits I still have. It's time to start taking this modest trek a little more seriously. Even though a long fall is highly unlikely, there are plenty of opportunities for small falls, and a small fall is sometimes all it takes. My wife is out of town for a couple of days, so, if I incapacitate myself, rescue will likely be a long time in coming. Although, I guess if I have to expire someplace, this place will do nicely.

It takes another hour, and several more stumbles, to reach the summit. The threaded pipe holding the summit register is frozen solid. I don't know why I like trail, trailhead, cabin, and summit registers so much. I've spent many an hour perusing them, empathizing with the emotions and observations expressed on the weather-worn pages. This register already holds my name, as well as that of my wife. We hiked up here with our dear friend Currie Craven the previous summer. Ironically enough, the weather that July day was much less pleasant

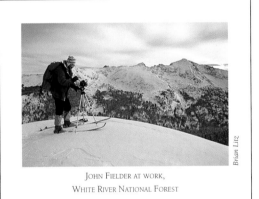

JOHN FIELDER AT WORK,
WHITE RIVER NATIONAL FOREST

Brian Litz

than it is this February day. It was so windy that we lingered up here only a few minutes before rushing down to the protection of the trees. I pull out my lighter and try to thaw the pipe. The only thing I manage to do is burn a hole in my new $80 high-tech gloves. Oh well—that's why they make duct tape.

While eating lunch, I notice a few clouds moving in from the west, just above Breckenridge Ski Area. Though the clouds don't seem foreboding, I decide to get myself down post haste. I have Gore-Tex in my pack, but no bivouac gear, no stove, no cook kit. Surviving a storm at almost 14,000 feet without even rudimentary gear would be trying.

By the time I reach the TV buildings, the wind has picked up to near gale force and an entire bank of malicious-looking gray clouds is about to drop right into my lap.

I should have known, as the weather reports had said it was supposed to remain clear for several more days. One the one hand, it must be a terrible job forecasting winter weather in Colorado. When

you have this degree of altitude and this many mountain ranges, trying to predict which route a storm front will take is a guessing game at best. But, on the other hand, in what other profession can you be totally wrong so often and still keep your high-paid, high-profile job?

In the high country, the veracity of winter weather reports is something of a joke. In the summer, predicting weather here is simple: all you have to say is, "Expect it to be clear tomorrow morning, with thunderstorms moving in by early afternoon and moving out in late afternoon." You could be sitting on a beach in Maui, having never visited Colorado, and correctly predict our summer weather 80 percent of the time.

But winter is another matter, as the storm bearing down upon me fast attests. There was no mention of this storm in yesterday's paper. I want to start running, but the exposed rocks are still icy. When the first snowflakes splat and stick against my glasses, I throw caution to the wind and quicken my pace. This is not dry and light winter snow; this is wet, heavy spring snow, which is strange this time of year, as it's still almost a month till the spring equinox.

THREE DAYS AGO, while out snow-shoeing with my wife up the Spruce Creek Trail, we both stopped in our tracks simultaneously and sniffed the air. There was an unmistakable whiff of spring interfacing with our olfactory systems. Now, I don't know exactly how to describe spring's body odor, except to say it's a combination of mud and budding new life mixed with the smell of last fall's plant decomposition finally being allowed to disperse into the atmosphere. And, if there's such a thing as the smell of relative warmth, there was a trace of that mixed in there as well.

Perhaps spring only has a bouquet in relation to winter, which, because of the frigidity quotient, is pretty much a fragrance-free time of year.

Whatever it was and however it came to pass, my wife and I both caught it—even though it was still the third week of February— much, much too early to be entertaining thoughts of spring in the Colorado high country. Hell, even when it's spring, it's too early to be entertaining thoughts of spring hereabouts. As a matter of fact, one should not act as though spring is officially here until at least summer.

The smell lasted only an instant, but, seconds later, a school of birds flew over. In winter, birds are scarce commodities in the high country. Most species have enough in the way of good sense to wing-it to points south (mainly on the Pacific Coast of Mexico) well before the first snow flies, and those few varieties of birds that choose to remain in the Rockies during the winter keep a relatively low profile, preferring to hunker down until warm weather returns.

My wife and I finished our snowshoe, half expecting to spy a couple of columbines popping up through the snow.

Winter isn't an easy animal to generalize in the high country. Some years, we get hammered by month after month of sub-zero temperatures, while getting little snow. Some years, we get buried by daily blizzards, while the temperatures remain fairly balmy. And some years, we get both buried by snow and hammered by cold.

This Colorado winter, as of February 1, our snowpack was slightly below average, and we've had very few of the arctic cold snaps that generally hit us three or four times a year.

By the time March gets here, though, we're almost assured that the potential for extremely cold temperatures—even up here at 12,000 feet—has passed for yet another season. I've seen some sub-zero temperatures in March, but not many.

It's a different story with snow. The window of snow opportunity throughout the Colorado Rockies is open year-round. Just because we've had a relatively poor snow year till now has no bearing whatsoever on March, April, May, or, for that matter, June. Three years ago, we had such a poor snow year that the word "drought" was being whispered by ski industry mavens all across the state the way "plague" must have been whispered by Europeans in the 1400s. I went so far as to pull my bike out of storage on the last day of March. As I was doing so, a lone cloud moved in. Soon, several more clouds arrived. By nightfall, it was snowing, and it basically didn't stop until the end of May. We got so much snow that spring that it didn't melt out of the high mountains all year.

In these parts, winter doesn't go gently into the good night; it only leaves of its own volition, in its own time. Summer doesn't defeat winter in the Colorado high country; winter decides to simply stop fighting for a season. It's like a big brother getting bored with picking on his little sister.

There may have been a hint of spring in the air as my wife and I were snowshoeing the other day, and there may have been birds tweeting overhead, but all that was simply a tease. Winter will still be with us here in the Colorado high country long after the calendar tells us otherwise.

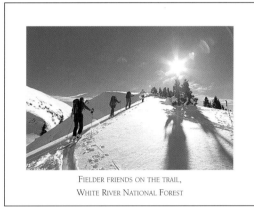

FIELDER FRIENDS ON THE TRAIL,
WHITE RIVER NATIONAL FOREST

By the time I reach my snowshoes, they are half-buried. Another hour, and I might not have been able to locate them, which would have made the descent uncomfortable at best. I strap them on and begin a serious-business beeline toward the trailhead. The flakes are so large and thick that, even though it is noon, I can scarcely see the tips of my snowshoes.

Rather than following the circuitous trail, I opt to dive straight down the side of the mountain. I take several long bounds, my dog leaping happily behind me, until I catch a tip on a submerged downed tree trunk and perform a well-executed somersault, which results in several tons of snow making its way down the back of my shirt. Invigorating. I rise, look around to make certain no one witnessed my spasticity, brush my ego off, and proceed at a more responsible pace.

By the time I near the trees, I'm confident that I'll make it back to my truck all right. So I slow way down, taking time to observe my surroundings. Too many people these days run up and down mountains in Colorado—"bagging" them, rather than savoring them. It's a statewide malady that seems to be reaching epidemic proportions. I refuse to get infected by that silliness, by that unjustified bravado that says, "I came into the mountains, and I conquered." A lot of folks these days are looking at the majestic Rockies as an outdoor workout facility rather than a sacred and special place, and that attitude is all too often translated to an overt lack of respect for these mountains.

It's still snowing hard, but, occasionally, the clouds part, and the sun's rays pour through as intensely as a *USS Enterprise* transporter beam, illuminating an otherwise gray world. The colors of winter are certainly not nearly as varied or intense as their summer counterparts. If winter in Colorado had a representative flag, it would be white, dark green, blue, and some more white. To truly appreciate the chromatic aspect of a Colorado winter, you have to dig for subtlety.

I once stood on the side of Highway 285 in the massive San Luis Valley observing the incomparable Sangre de Cristo Mountains. I was driving home from Mexico just as a storm was moving in from the west. The clouds were serving as a dynamic filter, and the light that was oozing its way through that filter and hitting the heart of the Sangres was changing second-by-second. And it was all blue and gray. That was it—no bright crimson or pink or red sneaking through. Just subdued shades of blue and gray. I counted seven different kinds of blue, and five different kinds of gray, all mixing and striating and swirling. This show took place not only on the the mountains themselves, but in the sky above the mountains and on the ground below. It was a performance-art spectacle that made even the most outlandish rock and roll concert laser light show look elementary and half-hearted by comparison.

Once again, Mother Nature was in her show-off mode.

There was metallic blue against confederate gray against cobalt against charcoal against lilac against electric blue. And this was without clouds to add their magic to the palate. The storm front had yet to cover the mountains. This was just light working on the sky and the earth.

A mile above the Baldy Trailhead, a small creek crosses a lovely little meadow that, in the summer, is home to a splendid wildflower population. With warmer temperatures moving in, the snow covering the creek has receded somewhat, and, in a couple of places, I can actually see water moving through snowbanks that look like miniature white Grand Canyons.

I move closer and observe erosion lines in the snow. It's like a fast-moving working model of how geological time proceeds in the natural world. My dog, upon noticing my close examination of the snow alongside the little creek, decides she ought to investigate. She jumps into the creek, collapsing the snowbanks. A canine asteroid just landed in the middle of my little Grand Canyon. Chaos theory delivered via a mutt.

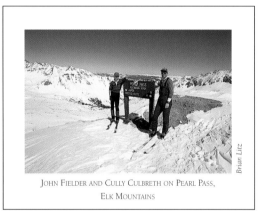

JOHN FIELDER AND CULLY CULBRETH ON PEARL PASS,
ELK MOUNTAINS

The dog clearly thinks it's playtime, so I start packing snowballs and lobbing them across the meadow. One of the main reasons I ever got a dog was to have a good excuse to make and throw snowballs, an activity I take fairly seriously. I consider it a Zenlike pastime.

I've been involved in several fairly heated barroom discussions about snowball technology and dynamics. Some people argue—incorrectly I might add—that the best snowballs are perfectly round. This argument stems from the "baseball school of thought," and I believe it's without merit. Since I grew up playing football, I subscribe to the "oblong snowball theory."

The problem in Colorado is that, with our powdery, dry snow, snowball-making, no matter your shape preferences, is difficult, requiring careful and exacting compression efforts. My dog doesn't seem to mind what form the snowballs take, as long as I keep them flying.

After 15 minutes, we start toward the trailhead, where my truck is parked.

I DRIVE HOME, take a shower, take a nap, and, like on many lazy Saturday afternoons, turn the TV on. I'm fidgety, tapping on the remote-control pad like I'm sending morse code messages that, if translated, would read: I'm becoming an unproductive coach potato, please send help!

It has snowed almost a foot since I returned from Baldy—the biggest storm of the new year. My dog is sitting in front of our picture window, looking wistfully out at the snow, then turning and staring disappointingly at me parked there on the coach with a monster bag of potato chips, sighing, then turning again to look at the new snow some more.

My dog doesn't lightly suffer laziness, even though I could argue to myself, if not her, that we had arisen at four A.M. and climbed and descended one of the highest mountains in Colorado. The hound is right, though—there is no reason to be sitting inside on such a day.

To her surprise, I jump up, put my still-wet pile garments back on, and bound out the door with my fanny pack in hand. We head once more toward Baldy, but via a different route. I decide that, having witnessed dawn on Baldy, it's only appropriate to witness sunset.

The French Gulch winter trailhead parking lot is completely empty. The storm has apparently chased people indoors, so the dog and I have the place to ourselves. We have about 40 minutes before dark. I jump onto my light-touring skis, and we move through the deep, trackless powder toward Sallie Barber Mine, located on a promontory on the side of Baldy, about 35 minutes away.

This is a place I visit only in winter, because under all that snow are some of the most hideous remnants of the mining industry that, from the 1860s to the 1880s, almost destroyed the nature of Summit County. In winter, the endless snow-covered dredge tailings and mine dumps look soft and inviting. In the summer, they are exposed for what they are: nasty-looking piles of rock and dirt that were torn from the bowels of the earth during a frenzied search for gold and silver.

To the northeast, I can see the lights of Keystone Ski Area glimmering. The snowstorm has moved out, and the stars are shining. I'll never cease to be amazed by how quickly and significantly the winter weather changes in Colorado. We can have an entire season's worth of conditions in one afternoon. I've lived in several places where locals smugly say of their weather, "If you don't like it, wait a few minutes."

But people in those places wouldn't know a good case of weather if it bit them on the rump. Here, the weather makes its presence known in ways so intense they can't be reduced to simple, glib phrases. Here in the middle of a Colorado winter, the weather routinely leaves impressions that last years. Whether the weather was so beautiful that the memories give you goosebumps, or whether it was so intensely violent that you shiver recollecting it, there are few climatic scenarios that haven't occurred here. Climatically, everything from good to bad that can happen happens, and happens often.

I've brought with me a backpacking stove, water, a small cook kit, a Crazy Creek chair, a sleeping bag, and a light shovel. I clear away some of the powder, open up my chair, sit down, cover myself with my bag, and start heating up some water for hot chocolate. I plan to enjoy the color of winter as it fades away on this wonderful day into night. It would be much nicer if the lights of Keystone were extinguished, but I'm only partially naive; I understand that the economy of the Colorado high country is booming, much like it was in the 1880s, and certain aesthetic aspects of life here are being compromised for the sake of money the way they've always been compromised. Nothing is left pure on this planet. You can get TV now in the middle of the Amazon Basin, and climbers atop Everest now talk via satellite link-ups to schoolchildren in the Australian Outback.

On top of the Gore Range,
White River National Forest

Life is moving too fast for me. Way too fast. But, are things worse today than they were a century ago, when the earth was being ripped apart at the seams here because people were searching for precious metals? I think not.

For my dog and I, this winter day ends with a perfect earth shadow, pink and purple, just above the lights of Keystone. When the shadow fades, I pack my gear up and head home in the dark. It has started snowing again, and I tilt my head back and let some of the flakes fall into my mouth.

It's been a great winter so far. I've gone outside 78 of the last 81 days. I've slept in a tent 14 nights since December. My nose has been frozen more times than I can count. I've thrown approximately 48,000 snowballs to my dog, and have built three snowmen. I feel healthy and strong and centered, and, without a doubt, it's the Colorado winter that has made me feel this way. I couldn't imagine how I could be happier or more content than I am at this very moment. I hope and pray that circumstances allow me to live out my years here in the high country. I hope that no $100,000-a-year job offer draws me away from this place, or that no family crisis mandates that I move to a place where winter is but a short respite from summer.

As I approach my truck, a poignant realization strikes home: Only a couple of months are left of this Colorado winter.

TRACKS, GUNNISON NATIONAL FOREST

TRACKS, WHITE RIVER NATIONAL FOREST

MOONRISE OVER THE COLLEGIATE PEAKS WILDERNESS

When the nights are calm and the moon full, I go out to gaze upon the wonderful purity of the moonlight and the snow. The air is full of latent fire, and the cold warms me—after a different fashion from that of the kitchen stove. The world lies about me in a "trance of snow." The clouds are pearly and iridescent, and seem the farthest possible remove from the condition of a storm,—the ghosts of clouds, the indwelling beauty freed from all dross. I see the hills, bulging with great drifts, lift themselves up cold and white against the sky, the black lines of fences here and there obliterated by the depth of the snow.

—*John Burroughs*

The moon above the eastern wood

Shone at its full; the hill-range stood

Transfigured in the silver flood,

Its blown snows flashing cold and keen,

Dead white, save where some sharp ravine

Took shadow, or the sombre green

Of hemlocks turned to pitchy black

Against the whiteness at their back.

For such a world and such a night

Most fitting that unwarming light,

Which only seemed where'er it fell

To make the coldness visible.

—John Greenleaf Whittier

MOONSET OVER THE MAROON BELLS-SNOWMASS WILDERNESS

TWILIGHT ON CHAIR MOUNTAIN, GUNNISON COUNTY

SUNSET ON CHAIR MOUNTAIN, GUNNISON COUNTY

ICICLES, BARNARD HUT, WHITE RIVER NATIONAL FOREST

Sandstone outcrops, Roxborough State Park

SUNSET, GUNNISON COUNTY

SUNSET, GUNNISON COUNTY

SUNRISE, ELK MOUNTAINS, WHITE RIVER NATIONAL FOREST

SUNSET, TENMILE RANGE, ARAPAHO NATIONAL FOREST

ELK MOUNTAINS, WHITE RIVER NATIONAL FOREST

ALONG THE SLATE RIVER, GUNNISON NATIONAL FOREST

RUBY RANGE, GUNNISON NATIONAL FOREST

GORE RANGE, WHITE RIVER NATIONAL FOREST

SUNSET, WHITE RIVER NATIONAL FOREST

SUNSET, WHITE RIVER NATIONAL FOREST

SKI TRACKS, ELK MOUNTAINS, WHITE RIVER NATIONAL FOREST

To my precious children, Marissa, Damian, Dominic, and Nino.
I hope this book is a constant reminder of your beautiful Sicilian heritage.

To my beautiful and loving wife, Trina,
who makes me the happiest man I could ever be.

Love, Damian

This book is dedicated to all employees of Carrabba's Italian Grill and Pesce, past and present.
Thanks for the journey—we are looking forward to the future!

Love, Johnny

In memory of Manlio Corrao
We will miss your smiling face and warm Sicilian hospitality.
Only the good die young.

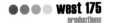

Bright Sky Press

Box 416, Albany, Texas 76430
www.BrightSkyPress.com

Text copyright © 2003 by West 175 Productions, Inc.

10 9 8 7 6 5 4 3 2

Library of Congress Cataloging-in-Publication Data

Carrabba, Johnny, 1958-
  Ciao Sicily / by Johnny Carrabba and Damian Mandola; photographs by Watt M. Casey, Jr.
    p. cm.
Includes index.
    ISBN 1-931721-26-2 (cloth : alk. paper)
1. Cookery, Italian—Sicilian style. I. Mandola, Damian, 1952- II. Title.

TX723.2.S55C37 2003
641.59458—dc21

2003049558

Text: John DeMers
Design: Tina Taylor
Photography: Watt M. Casey Jr., Christine Bruno, Torry Bruno, and PhotoDisc

HoustonPBS

Cucina Sicilia is produced by West 175 Productions, Inc. in association with Houston PBS / KUHT

 west 175 productions

West 175 Productions
2317 24th Avenue East
Seattle, WA 98112
www.cucinasicilia.com

BOLLA

Funding for *Cucina Sicilia* is provided by Bolla Wines

CIAO Sicily

RECIPES FROM THE PBS SERIES

CUCINA SICILIA

DAMIAN MANDOLA & JOHNNY CARRABBA

Foreword by Grace Mandola · Featuring Photography by Watt M. Casey, Jr.

Contents

In front of the Testa's grocery, Sunrise, Louisiana (From left to right) Unidentified man turning the peanut roaster, Damian's great-grandpa, Salvatore Testa; great-grandma, Santa Serio Testa; grandpa, Giuseppe Testa; and an unidentified youth

Foreword
by Grace Mandola

As far as I can tell, being in the food business—
which is basically making people happy with
food—is what our family has always been about.
You might say it's what being Sicilian has always
been about. Even in the worst times, we're always
ready to pitch in with a pot of this or a platter of
that. We believe that eating good things makes
you feel better. And we believe that because we
always make good things with love. If you're not
going to cook with love, then don't even bother
talking to me about food.

Grace Testa Mandola

My mother came to this country from Cefalú, Sicily as a bride
of two weeks, and she couldn't speak a word of English. It wasn't long,
though, before she was reading the newspaper. I'll always remember
her reading the newspaper in her new language, in her new life.
People who couldn't read, all counted on her. What I counted on was
her teaching me about food. When I was a little girl, she taught me
how to do the basic things. Once I was married, I cooked for my

Grace Testa Mandola

family every day, and I'd call Mamma and ask her how to do things. Something she said back then really stuck with me, and it seems to have stuck with my son Damian and my grandson Johnny as well. "Watch me," she said, "and you will learn"—"*Guardami e poi fai.*" Now people all over America get to watch Damian and Johnny. And they're learning a lot of what my mother taught me—from them!

Sometimes I think back on my life—starting in Louisiana and ending up in Texas, being surrounded by Sicilian food every step of the way—and I realize I should have seen this book by Damian and Johnny coming all along. Filling their heads as I did, as our whole family did, with how to make the best Sicilian eggplant, how to roll out the best sweet Sicilian cookies, and which relative made the best Sicilian sausage or meatballs, it only makes sense they'd finally get around to cooking and eating their way back to Sicily. We still have relatives over there, even after all this time in America. They're still family. They're still there to tell us—well no, not just where we came from, but who we really are.

—Grace Mandola

"Every time you go into the kitchen and cook for somebody with love, you're explaining what you believe life is all about. That's the way it still is in Sicily — and in my house — and as Damian and Johnny just can't wait to tell you."

Jenny,
Ciao Ya'll.
Johnny

Introduction

You can't turn back the clock. You can't rewrite history, your own or anybody else's. But you really can go home again.

That's what we found, time and again, as we came face to face with our shared past in the villages and farms and vineyards and markets that our Mandola and Carrabba ancestors left to build lives in the New World. Knowing the opportunity our families found in that strange place called America, (America was named after an Italian boy, so we're not surprised it worked out!), we can't say our time in Sicily made us regret our family's leaving. No, that was the history no one can rewrite, and most of us can understand. What it did teach us was the reality that the grueling trip across a wide ocean, plus several generations of sacrifice and commitment, didn't carry us as far from home as we might have thought. And nowhere did we see this more clearly than in the Sicilian kitchen.

Of course, we had to get into the kitchen first, but that was no problem. Our new Sicilian friends proved as warm and welcoming

as our Sicilian-American families back in Texas. Sure, we Texans know how to bond watching football together or playing golf together, or whatever the day might bring. But we believe one of the best ways to bond, to get to know people for real, and to feel some shared investment in what becomes of us all, is to cook with them. Filming our PBS cooking show, *Cucina Sicilia*, and researching this companion book, we found ourselves not merely allowed, but dragged from this pot to that pot, to taste a friend's grandmother's favorite recipe. Our eyes were shining as much as each cook's were—at all the incredibly rich, deep and even surprising flavors we encountered in Sicily. These are the flavors you'll now encounter in these pages.

What's important to realize is that Sicily is not Italy. Don't worry, we're not trying to launch a rebellion, in Sicily or anyplace else. But we do want you to understand that the broader European traditions that helped form (and in some cases, were formed by) Italian cooking, don't always have a lot to do with how our ancestors cooked and ate in Sicily. In so many ways, Sicily remains what it was for so long, an outpost of ancient Greece. It's not just a bunch of lovely ruins the Greeks left us

in Sicily. It's a lot of lovely recipes that connect us not only to a world better suited to Zorba than Garibaldi but to the most ancient crossroads of Christianity, Judaism and Islam.

And speaking of crossroads, you realize almost daily in Sicily that the winds of culture and cuisine blow up from North Africa just as profoundly than they ever do down from Florence, Genoa or Rome. Just when you think a dish is savory, laden with tomato and garlic and fresh oregano—pow!—your taste buds get slapped with sweet cinnamon or nutmeg. The North African spice trade is alive and well, in the food, memories and longings of every family that ever called Sicily home.

Our homes and families are in Texas now, having become Texans by way of the Gulf Coast. Yet we know now that a piece of our hearts has always resided among the stark, difficult, unrelenting hills and valleys of our ancestors' Sicilia. You *can* go home again. We *have* gone home again. And as in all the best journeys, we've returned to Texas where our story began, and appreciated and knew *this* place for the first time—and our Sicilian heritage even more.

—Damian & Johnny

"Do Sicilians know how to live or what!"

Antipasti
APPETIZERS

Some Americans still get a little confused by the name of this important course in Italian, thinking it automatically refers to pasta in someway—when all it really means is "before the meal." You might think of *antipasti* as *hors d'oeuvres,* except don't show up if you're not hungry or just like wimpy little nibbly things. Sicilians love *antipasti,* and many's the restaurant in Sicily that welcomes its guests with an *antipasti* table almost falling down from the weight of all the chilled and room temperature dishes waiting for you to enjoy. Historically, the notion probably derives from either Greece or Spain, both countries with strong traditions of snacking before dining—especially the *tapas* of Spain. Yet in both cases, the habit may actually hark back to the Arabs, who to this day can practically fill you up with 15 or 20 chopped salads and other items before the real food even starts arriving. We don't know about you, but we think eating is a fine way to work up an appetite!

BRUSCHETTA WITH OLIVE SPREAD
Crostini cu le Olive

Serves 8

1 recipe Bruschetta (see page 180)

1/2 cup Sicilian black olives

1/2 cup Sicilian green olives

1/4 cup sliced carrot

3 teaspoons extra-virgin olive oil

4 cloves roasted garlic, sliced

1 tablespoon chopped fresh oregano leaves

1 tablespoon chopped fresh Italian parsley leaves

1 tablespoon capers in brine, rinsed

Kosher salt and freshly-ground black pepper to taste

TO PREPARE

Put all the ingredients except bruschetta in a food processor and process for 30 seconds until the olives are finely or coarsely chopped as you like. Spread the olive mixture on the bruschetta and arrange on a serving plate.

TO SERVE

Serve at room temperature with your favorite aperitif.

DAMIAN

This is not the most Sicilian dish in the world, but it's a Sicilian variation on something served all over Italy.

JOHNNY

We have a cousin named Mike Benestante who really loves this dish. This is his family's recipe.

DOUBLE CRUST PIZZA WITH ROASTED RED BELL PEPPERS
Sfincione di Pipi Russi

Serves 8

Pizza dough:

2 teaspoons dry yeast

1-1/2 cups water at 100°F

4 cups unbleached all-purpose flour

2 teaspoons kosher salt

2 tablespoons extra-virgin olive oil

Filling:

2 cups whole milk ricotta cheese

3 large eggs

3 tablespoons grated Pecorino Romano cheese

3/4 cup finely-grated Parmesan cheese

3/4 cup coarsely-grated mozzarella cheese

1/2 pound salami, peeled and diced into 1/4-inch cubes

1/2 pound prosciutto, shredded

1/4 cup chopped fresh parsley

1 roasted red pepper, diced (See page 185)

Kosher salt and freshly-ground black pepper to taste

TO PREPARE THE DOUGH

1 Put the dry yeast in a large mixing bowl and stir in the warm water. Let the yeast rest in the water for 10 minutes.

2 Add 1 cup of the flour and mix thoroughly. Add the rest of the flour and salt and knead to a smooth consistency.

3 Brush the dough lightly with olive oil and cover the bowl with a cotton dish towel and set aside to rise for 2 hours or until doubled in size.

4 Place a rack at the lowest setting in the oven and preheat the oven to 350°F.

FOR THE FILLING

1 Put ricotta in a large mixing bowl and stir until smooth.

2 Add the eggs and beat until fluffy.

3 Mix in each additional ingredient until blended into an even mixture. Season to taste with salt and pepper.

4 Put filling mixture in the refrigerator until dough is ready for assembly.

TO ASSEMBLE

1 After the dough is finished rising, punch it down but be careful not to knead it any further so that it will be 'relaxed' to work with. Divide the dough into two balls. Place the first ball on a floured surface and roll out in a circle.

2 Prepare a 9-inch pie pan by rubbing it with olive oil.

3 Lay the first circle of dough on the bottom of the pie pan and trim the edges of the dough to the edge of the pan.

4 Spoon the filling into the pan and smooth it evenly in the shell.

5 Roll out the second ball of dough to about a 10" circle. Lay the circle over the top of the pie and pinch the edges of the dough together.

6 Bake the pie for 45 minutes. The top should be a golden color. Cool the pie on a rack for 10–15 minutes.

TO SERVE

Cut the pie in wedges and serve.

EGGPLANT AND ARTICHOKE PIZZA
Pizza di Milinciani e Cacuocciulu

Serves 8

1 recipe Pizza Dough (see page 178)

8 tablespoons extra-virgin olive oil

1 small eggplant, peeled, diced, salted and drained (see page 184)

2 cups canned crushed tomatoes or 2 large ripe tomatoes, chopped

1 tablespoon roughly-chopped garlic

1-1/2 teaspoons chopped fresh oregano or 3/4 teaspoon dried oregano

Kosher salt to taste

1/4 teaspoon crushed red pepper

1 cup small shards of Pecorino Romano cheese

1 cup quartered artichoke hearts, canned, marinated or packed in water

TO PREPARE

1 Preheat the oven to 400°F.

2 Brush a 16 x 11-inch jellyroll pan with 2 tablespoons of the olive oil.

3 Place the dough in the pan and using your hands, gently press and stretch it out to reach the sides. If the dough springs back and is difficult to stretch, let rest for 5–10 minutes.

4 Brush the dough evenly with 2 tablespoons of the olive oil.

5 Sauté the eggplant in 2 tablespoons of the olive oil in a large sauté pan over medium-high heat until golden brown. Set aside.

6 Combine the tomatoes, garlic, oregano, salt, and red pepper. Set aside.

7 Spread 1/2 cup of the Pecorino Romano cheese over the dough and then top with the eggplant and the artichoke hearts. Gently press the cheese, eggplant and artichokes into the dough. Top with the tomato mixture and the rest of the Pecorino Romano cheese. Drizzle the remaining olive oil over the top.

8 Bake in the oven for approximately 30 minutes, rotating the pizza once so that it browns evenly.

TO SERVE

Cut into wedges and serve hot or at room temperature

JOHNNY

I came up with this dish. It may not be most folks idea of a traditional pizza.

DAMIAN

But the artichoke and eggplant speak volumes about Sicilian cooking. They marry real well in this dish.

CHICKPEA FRITTERS
Panelle

Yields 25 fritters

1 teaspoon extra-virgin olive oil

3-1/2 cups cold water

Sea salt

2 cups chickpea flour
(available in specialty food stores)

1-1/2 cups vegetable oil
or half corn oil and half sunflower oil

1/2 cup extra-virgin olive oil

Thin slices crusty country bread (optional)

TO PREPARE

1 Grease a baking sheet with a teaspoon of olive oil.

2 Heat the water and salt in a deep (5-quart) saucepan. Once the water is boiling sift in the chickpea flour gradually, whisking constantly, to prevent lumps from forming. Once all the flour has been added, whisk vigorously until the batter is very thick and stiff and pulls away from sides. The batter will become hard to whisk when it's done, a process that takes about 5 minutes.

3 With a rubber spatula spread the batter onto the greased baking sheet and place in the refrigerator for 2 hours or overnight, to set up.

4 Heat the oils in a large skillet over medium heat.

5 Remove the batter from the refrigerator and use a sharp knife to cut it into squares of about 3 inches.

6 Line a serving dish with paper towels.

7 When the oil is hot (about 400°F) transfer some of the squares to the hot oil and fry them until lightly golden on both sides. Using a slotted spoon, transfer the cooked fritters to the serving dish lined with paper towels to absorb excess oil. Continue to fry in batches until all the fritters are cooked and drained.

TO SERVE

Remove the paper towels, sprinkle the panelle with salt and serve hot garnished with some fresh flat-leaved parsley

NOTE Sometimes panelle are served like sandwiches between 2 slices of crusty country bread.

JOHNNY

This was the second thing I ever ate in Sicily. The first was cannoli.

DAMIAN

Nothing wrong with starting at dessert and working backwards—specially in Sicily. Sometimes, when you're shopping in the markets there, you can put these between slices of bread and make a sandwich. I always get them at the market—this and a whole lot of other things.

CRISP POLENTA WITH ARUGULA AND RICOTTA SALATA
Polenta cu Rucola e Ricotta Salata

Serves 4–6

1 recipe Polenta (see page 176)

1 tablespoon olive oil

6 cups arugula

2 tablespoons extra-virgin olive oil

1-1/2 teaspoons of balsamic vinegar

1/2 cup ricotta salata

Kosher salt and freshly-ground black pepper to taste

TO PREPARE

1 Cook the polenta according to instructions, pour onto a lightly-oiled cookie sheet to a 1/2-inch thickness and allow to cool for at least 4 hours in a refrigerator.

2 Preheat oven to 450°F.

3 Prepare a baking sheet with a light coat of olive oil.

4 Cut the cooled polenta into 2-inch squares or triangles and using a spatula place the pieces of polenta on the baking sheet. Brush the cut polenta squares with olive oil.

5 Place baking sheet in oven and bake the polenta pieces for 10–12 minutes until they begin to crisp. Flip the pieces over and bake for another 6–8 minutes until very crisp.

6 While polenta is crisping, put arugula in a large salad bowl and drizzle with olive oil. Add vinegar, salt, and pepper, and toss again.

TO SERVE

1 Remove polenta from the oven season with salt and pepper and divide among individual plates.

2 Crumble the ricotta.

3 Portion the tossed greens on top of each piece of polenta and sprinkle the ricotta over the salad and serve.

DAMIAN

The ricotta salata is really interesting, being ricotta cheese that's been drained, pressed and salt-cured. My mother used to put it in her oven with only the pilot light on — for about two weeks.

JOHNNY

This dish is all about the polenta that you cut and bake, then cover it with peppery arugula and that wonderful ricotta salata. It's just great.

PASTA OMELET
Frocia di Pasta

Serves 10–12 (6 as a lunch dish)

8 eggs

1/2 cup shredded fontina cheese

1 cup Pecorino Romano cheese, freshly grated

1/2 cup milk

2 cups cooked pasta, such as spaghetti, drained and rinsed with cool water

1/2 cup pitted Sicilian black olives, coarsely chopped

1/2 cup ham or cooked pancetta, coarsely chopped

Kosher salt to taste

Freshly-ground black pepper to taste

2 tablespoons each chopped fresh parsley, oregano and basil leaves

4 tablespoons extra-virgin olive oil

TO PREPARE:

1 Preheat oven to 350° F.

2 Beat eggs well, in a large bowl. Add the cheeses, milk, pasta, olives, ham or pancetta, seasonings, and herbs and mix well.

3 Heat oil in large heavy nonstick skillet over medium flame. When very hot, pour in the egg mixture. Lower flame (heat) and cook until eggs are set on bottom, about 5 minutes.

4 Finish cooking in the oven for 10–15 minutes, until the mixture is just set. Don't overcook or omelet will be dry and rubbery.

TO SERVE

Loosen the frittata with a spatula and flip over and onto a serving platter. Serve warm or at room temperature.

DAMIAN
No doubt about it, I really love egg dishes. And this frittata is one of the best you'll ever taste, with plenty of cheese and vegetables and olive oil.

JOHNNY
Some of my favorite frittatas are the ones you eat after a late and festive night.

DAMIAN
You know, when you're scrounging around the refrigerator for anything that's real good to eat.

MARINATED ZUCCHINI
Cucuzzini Sott' Olio

Serves 8

12 small tender zucchini

3/4 cup extra-virgin olive oil

2 medium-sized garlic cloves, peeled

1/2 small red onion

10 fresh mint leaves

2 tablespoons red wine vinegar

Kosher salt and freshly-ground
black pepper

Crushed red pepper flakes to taste

TO PREPARE

1   Wash zucchini thoroughly, then cut off both ends. Slice the zucchini into 1/4-inch thick rounds.

2   Line a sheet pan with paper towels.

3   Heat 1/2 cup of the oil in a large skillet over a high heat until very hot. When oil is hot, fry zucchini slices in batches without crowding pan, until golden brown.
Remove zucchini and drain on paper towels.

4   When all zucchini are cooked and drained, transfer them to a serving platter. Sprinkle them with salt and pepper.

5   Finely chop garlic, red onion and mint together on a cutting board. Place in a small mixing bowl. Add remaining 1/4 cup of olive oil and vinegar, salt, pepper, and red pepper. Pour mixture over zucchini and let marinate for 1 hour.

TO SERVE
Pass with slices of crusty Italian bread.

DAMIAN
This is a good old fashioned sott'olio, meaning "under oil." It's very important that you fry the zucchini until it's golden brown.

JOHNNY
And really, you don't want your zucchini slices to be any bigger than a quarter — or maybe one of those new golden dollars. Golden, just like this zucchini!

EGGPLANT TERRINE
Galantina di Milinciani

Serves 8

3 medium eggplants, thinly sliced lengthwise (about 1/8-inch thick)

Kosher salt and freshly-ground pepper to taste

1/4 cup balsamic vinegar

1/2 cup extra-virgin olive oil

1 cup basil leaves, julienned

2 red bell peppers, roasted and then cut into 1/4-inch strips

1/4 cup balsamic vinegar

TO PREPARE

1 First spray a 6-cup rectangular terrine mold with vegetable oil. Line terrine with plastic wrap to allow for easier removal at the end.

2 Next slice the eggplant, brush with olive oil and place on a prepared hot grill. Quickly sear the eggplant on each side. This should take 1–2 minutes per side depending on temperature of your grill. Make sure eggplant is cooked through.

3 Starting at one end of the terrine mold, put the eggplant slices over the sides of the mold, being sure to leave a 2-inch flap of eggplant over the sides of the mold to encase the filling and overlapping the slices by 1 inch to cover any seams or holes. Once the bottom and sides of the mold are covered, add layers of the eggplant lengthwise down the center of the terrine.

4 After 2 layers of eggplant, sprinkle with salt and pepper and a dash of the vinegar.

5 Add a layer of fresh basil and sprinkle with salt and pepper and a dash of the vinegar.

6 Add another layer of eggplant and sprinkle with salt and pepper and a dash of vinegar.

7 Add a layer of the roasted red peppers and sprinkle with salt and pepper and a dash of vinegar.

8 Continue alternating the layers as above, seasoning each layer with salt, pepper, and vinegar. Finish with a final layer of eggplant.

9 Fold over the flaps of eggplant alternating from one side to the other.

10 Next fold over the plastic wrap and top with a piece of cardboard. Place a weight atop the cardboard to press down and firm the contents of the terrine.

11 Place in refrigerator to rest overnight.

TO SERVE

Remove from the refrigerator, remove weights, peel back plastic and invert the mold onto a serving platter. Lift off mold and remove the plastic wrap. Slice the terrine with a sharp knife into 1-inch slices and serve.

GRANDMA'S EGGPLANT
Milinciani della Nonna

Serves 4-6

For the eggplant:

1 medium eggplant

1 teaspoon salt

4 cups Mamma Mandola's Breadcrumbs
(see page 179)

3 eggs, beaten

Vegetable oil

For the stuffing:

1 tablespoon unsalted butter

1/2 medium yellow onion, chopped fine

1/2 cup ricotta cheese

1/4 cup Pecorino Romano cheese, grated

1/3 cup mozzarella, shredded

1/4 cup ricotta salata, grated

1/3 cup pine nuts, toasted

1/4 cup sun-dried tomatoes, coarsely
chopped

2 tablespoons Italian parsley, chopped

Kosher salt and freshly-ground
black pepper to taste

For the assembly:

1 cup Mamma's Marinara Sauce
(see page 176)

1/2 cup Pecorino Romano cheese, grated

6 slices mozzarella cheese

TO PREPARE THE EGGPLANT

1 Slice off and discard ends of eggplant. Cut eggplant cross-wise into 1/4-inch slices. Salt eggplant lightly on both sides and place into colander.

2 Cover eggplant with plate and weight down, a cast iron skillet lid works well to help squeeze bitter fluids from the eggplant. Allow eggplant to drain for 30 minutes.

TO PREPARE THE STUFFING

1 While the eggplant is draining, prepare stuffing. Melt butter in a small skillet over medium-heat. Sauté the onion until translucent and soft. Remove skillet from heat and let cool.

2 In a mixing bowl combine the onion and all the cheeses and mix thoroughly. Add the remaining ingredients and mix well. Taste and correct seasoning. Cover and refrigerate until ready to use.

TO COOK

1 Preheat oven to 350°F.

2 Rinse eggplant and pat dry with a paper towel. Spread bread-crumbs on a large plate. Dip eggplant slices in the egg and let the excess egg run off. Coat the eggplant slices with the breadcrumbs.

3 In a large skillet with enough vegetable oil to come up the sides of the pan about 1/2 inch, fry the eggplant in very hot oil until golden brown. Drain on paper towels.

4 When eggplant is cool enough to handle, lay one slice of eggplant on a work surface.

5 Spoon 2 tablespoons of the stuffing in the middle of the egg-plant and roll up.

6 Place eggplant rolls in a casserole, top lightly with Mamma's Marinara Sauce, sprinkle with Romano cheese and bake in oven 10 minutes.

7 Remove from oven and top with mozzarella and bake 2–3 minutes more until mozzarella melts.

TO SERVE

Serve piping hot from the cooking casserole.

FRIED ARTICHOKES
Cacuocciulu Frittu

Serves 4–6

1/2 ounce brewer's yeast

1/2 cup warm water (100°-110°F)

2 cups all-purpose flour

2 eggs, beaten

1 tablespoon extra-virgin olive oil

1 teaspoon kosher salt

4 medium-sized artichokes

Extra-virgin olive oil for frying

TO PREPARE

1 In a small mixing bowl, dissolve the yeast in the water and let rest 10 minutes.

2 Add the yeast water to the flour in a large mixing bowl.

3 Beat the eggs and blend into the batter along with the olive oil. Season with salt. If the batter is too thick add more warm water to make a semi-thick pancake-like batter. Cover batter with plastic wrap and let rest for one hour.

4 Prepare artichokes (see page 183). Slice artichoke into wedges and place in acidulated water (water with lemon squeezed into it) to keep the artichokes from turning brown.

5 In a large saucepan heat enough oil to deep fry artichokes at 350°F.

6 Drain as many artichoke wedges as you are going to fry. Dip wedges into batter to coat. Fry in hot oil until golden brown, drain on paper towels and sprinkle with salt.

TO SERVE

Transfer to a serving dish and pass with lemon wedges.

NOTE   This batter can also be used for cauliflower, zucchini, or zucchini blossoms. Also, it is important to stir batter each time before use.

JOHNNY

Artichokes are so important to the Sicilian diet because they grow real well there. If you really want to kick this over the top, squeeze a little lemon juice over all.

DAMIAN

Or maybe a lot of lemon juice.

MAMMA'S BAKED EGGPLANT
Milinciani al Furnu

Serves 2–3

3 medium firm eggplant

1 tablespoon salt

Extra-virgin olive oil for frying

3 cups Mamma's Marinara Sauce, cold
(see page 176)

1/2 cup cold water

1 cup Mamma Mandola's Breadcrumbs
(see page 179)

1/2 cup grated Pecorino Romano cheese

20 large basil leaves

TO PREPARE

1 Cut off both ends of eggplant and cut length-wise into 1/2-inch thick slices. Lightly salt both sides of the eggplant and set in a colander to drain the excess water. Lay a plate on top of the eggplant in the colander and then weigh it down—a cast iron pot cover works well—to help squeeze the moisture from the eggplant. Place the colander in the sink or in a pan to catch the juices. Allow eggplant to drain at least 30 minutes—an hour is even better.

2 Preheat oven to 375°F.

3 Rinse eggplant to remove salt and pat dry with paper towels.

4 Heat approximately 1 inch of olive oil in a 12-inch skillet. Fry eggplant until golden on both sides in very hot oil. Drain on paper towels blotting away extra oil.

5 Dilute the marinara sauce with 1/2 cup cold water.

6 Place a small amount of the sauce on the bottom of a 3-quart casserole.

7 Place a layer of fried eggplant slices in the bottom of the casserole. Top with a little more marinara sauce, a dusting of breadcrumbs, some Pecorino Romano cheese and a few torn basil leaves. Repeat until all the eggplant is used, ending with eggplant, marinara, breadcrumbs, cheese, and basil.

8 Place the casserole in the oven for 30–40 minutes or until bubbling hot. Remove from oven and let rest 15–20 minutes.

TO SERVE
Cut into squares and serve.

DAMIAN
In Sicily, you sometimes hear this dish called palmiciane – shutter makers style – because the layering and stacking makes it look a bit like louvered shutters.

JOHNNY
The key is to have your fire hot to cook the eggplant.

DAMIAN
And please, make sure your eggplant is cooked. There's nothing worse than raw eggplant. See Trina shopping for our eggplants in the Capo Market in Palermo.

GRANDPA MANDOLA'S ORANGE SALAD
Nsalata di Aranciu

Serves 6

6 oranges

Several sprigs of fresh mint
or 1/2 cup fresh mint leaves

1/4 cup extra-virgin olive oil

Kosher salt and freshly-ground
black pepper to taste

TO PREPARE

1 Peel the oranges, removing all the white pith beneath the skin as well. Cut the oranges into 1/2-inch rounds, removing any seeds, and place the slices on a platter.

2 Wash mint leaves and cut into ribbons with scissors, or tear each leaf into 2 or 3 pieces. Sprinkle the mint leaves over the orange slices.

3 Add olive oil to small bowl and season with salt and pepper. Mix well. Pour the olive oil mixture over the oranges.

TO SERVE

Allow oranges to marinate for 30 minutes before serving.

JOHNNY

If you want to zip this recipe up, for a different presentation, use those deep red blood oranges everybody in Sicily can't get enough of.

DAMIAN

But whatever color of orange you use, don't use any orange that's not real sweet.

FRITTATA OF POTATO, ZUCCHINI AND SWEET PEPPERS
Frocia di Patate, Cucuzzini e Pipi

Serves 4-6

1/4 cup extra-virgin olive oil

1 medium russet potato, peeled, quartered lengthwise and cross cut into 1/4-inch slices

1/2 medium red or yellow onion, diced medium

1/2 yellow or red bell pepper, cut into 1/2-inch dice

1 medium zucchini, washed, ends trimmed, and sliced into rounds 1-inch thick

3 green onions, sliced

2 cloves garlic, chopped fine

8 eggs

2 tablespoons chopped fresh basil

2 tablespoons chopped fresh parsley

3/4 cup grated Pecorino Romano or Parmigiano cheese

Kosher salt and freshly-ground black pepper

TO PREPARE

1 Preheat oven to 350°F

2 In a large (12-inch) skillet, heat the olive oil over medium-high heat. Add the sliced potatoes and sauté for 5 minutes or until tender. Remove with a slotted spoon to a paper lined plate to drain. Season lightly with salt.

3 In the same skillet add the onion and bell pepper. Cook 3 minutes. There should be enough oil left in the skillet from frying the potatoes. If not, add a tablespoon or so.

4 Add the zucchini and cook until the zucchini is tender. In the last minute add the green onion and garlic. Season lightly with salt and pepper. Remove skillet from heat. Let mixture cool for a few minutes.

5 While mixture is cooling, in a large mixing bowl, beat the 8 eggs and add the remaining ingredients. Add the potatoes and the contents from the skillet to the bowl. Blend with the egg mixture.

6 Pour mixture back into skillet. Place skillet over low heat. Cook until the bottom has set, about 15 minutes. Place skillet in preheated oven or under a broiler until frocia is firm to the touch. Do not overcook or the frocia will be dry.

TO SERVE

Turn frocia over onto a round serving platter. Cut into wedges. Serve warm or at room temperature.

DAMIAN
The next time somebody tells you to eat your vegetable, just kind of smile and say, "Okay, of course."

JOHNNY
That way you can race into the kitchen and whip up this frittata. It's so good, you won't think you're eating your vegetables at all.

PICKLED VEGETABLES
Giardiniera

Yields appox. 3 quarts

1 small head of cauliflower, cored and cut into florets the size of a quarter

3 medium carrots, peeled and sliced into 1/4-inch rings

8–10 cups white wine vinegar

2 bay leaves

3 red bell peppers, cut into strips 1/2-inch wide

3 green bell peppers, cut into strips 1/2-inch wide

30 green olives with pits, left whole

1/2 cup fresh oregano

TO PREPARE

1   Blanch the cauliflower for 5 minutes until just becoming soft; don't overcook. Immediateely, remove the cauliflower from the boiling water and put into ice water to stop the cooking and keep cauliflower crisp.

2   Blanch the carrots for 1–2 minutes and place into ice water as well.

3   Meanwhile place the vinegar and bay leaves into a large saucepan. Bring to a boil, simmer for 1 minute then turn off heat.

4   Remove the cauliflower and carrots from the ice water and pat dry.

5   Place cauliflower, carrots, the rest of the vegetables, and herbs in a large glass or nonreactive bowl and pour the vinegar mixture over the vegetables. Let stand for 2 hours or overnight. You may store these pickled vegetables in a covered container, refrigerated for up to 2 weeks.

TO SERVE

Drain and serve on a vegetable platter or in individual bowls.

JOHNNY

Like a lot of Sicilian dishes, this one was born out of necessity. At harvest time, they'd have more vegetables than they could eat – yet they knew they'd practically starve later on.

DAMIAN

So they learned the art of pickling to keep from starving, until after a while it wasn't about feeding themselves but about loving the taste.

PEPPERS AND ANCHOVIES
Pipi e Anciove

Serves 8

4 medium red bell peppers

4 medium yellow bell peppers

8 whole anchovies packed in salt or 16 fillets in oil or more if you are an anchovy lover

1 cup extra-virgin olive oil

2 teaspoons fresh oregano leaves

3 tablespoons capers in salt or brine, rinsed

4 garlic cloves, lightly crushed

Kosher salt and freshly-ground black pepper

TO PREPARE

1 Place peppers over a hot charcoal grill or directly over a stove burner. Char peppers on all sides until the skin is blistered. Remove the peppers from the grill and place them in a closed paper bag for 15 minutes—the peppers will steam in their own heat and be easier to peel.

2 Peel peppers, removing the charred skin. Don't worry if there are little bits of charred skin left on—it adds to the roasted flavor. Do not rinse under water or you will lose the flavor.

3 Cut the peppers into quarters and trim top and bottom to make even. Remove all the seeds and pulpy core. Place peppers back on the grill to sear them in a cross pattern if you wish.

4 Arrange the peppers in a serving platter, in contrasting colors, overlapping a little. If you are using the whole anchovies, rinse under cold running water and fillet them. If you are using oil packed fillets just rinse under cold running water. Arrange anchovy fillets over the peppers.

5 In a small mixing bowl, combine the olive oil, oregano, capers, and garlic and season to taste with salt and pepper. Pour the olive oil mixture over the peppers. Cover and place the platter in the refrigerator for 4 hours or more. Do not leave the garlic in for more than 24 hours.

TO SERVE

One hour before serving, remove the peppers from the refrigerator and allow to come to room temperature. Serve and enjoy with a crusty Italian bread.

JOHNNY

Tell me, D, is it true you can use just about as many anchovies as you can stand in this recipe.

DAMIAN

Sure, and that's why when I make it they practically have to put anchovies on the endangered list. Actually, Sicily seems to always make more anchovies. The important thing is to balance the saltiness of the anchovies with the sweetness of the roasted peppers.

NONNA TESTA'S
ROASTED MARINATED PEPPERS
Pipi Arroste

Serves 4-6

4 medium red bell peppers, roasted and peeled (see page 185)

1 cup extra-virgin olive oil

1 tablespoon white wine vinegar

2 cloves garlic, crushed

Kosher salt and freshly-ground black pepper to taste

1/2 teaspoon crushed red pepper flakes

TO PREPARE

Cut peppers into 1-inch strips. Place peppers in a jar. Combine all remaining ingredients in a bowl and pour over the peppers. Cover with lid and place in refrigerator for 1 week.

TO SERVE

These peppers are great as part of an antipasto or as a topping for Bruschetta.

DAMIAN

My mom's mom, Nonna Testa, was a really great cook, and my mother learned all the basics from her.

JOHNNY

Try these peppers with that wonderful cheese called caciocavallo and a bit of crunchy bread for an afternoon pick-me-up.

MAMMA'S
GREEN VEGETABLE PIE
Mamma's Torta di Verdure

Serves 8–10

4 pounds Swiss chard

1/2 cup olive oil

1 small yellow onion, finely chopped

3 medium cloves of garlic, finely chopped

1 cup grated Pecorino Romano cheese

1/2 cup Homemade Breadcrumbs
(see page 179)

2 eggs

Kosher salt and freshly-ground pepper
to taste

1/2 cup extra-virgin olive oil

TO PREPARE

1   Bring a large pot of lightly salted water to a boil and place a large bowl of ice water near the sink.

2   Meanwhile, prepare the Swiss chard by trimming a little bit of the stalk and washing in several changes of water. Drain and chop coarsely.

3   Boil the chard until just tender, 5–7 minutes. Strain chard and immediately submerge in the ice water. Strain and squeeze as dry as possible in a cotton dish towel and chop a little more.

4   Preheat oven to 350°F.

5   Place 1/4 cup of the olive oil and the onion in a 12-inch oven-proof skillet over medium heat. When the onion is very soft, add the garlic and cook 1 more minute. Add the cooked chard to the onion and garlic and cook 2–3 more minutes. Season with salt and pepper to taste. Place chard mixture in a bowl, reserving the pan drippings, and let cool about 5 minutes. Don't wash the sauté pan.

6   To the chard mixture add the Pecorino Romano cheese, breadcrumbs and eggs. Taste and re-season with salt and pepper, if necessary.

7   Heat the remaining 1/4 cup of oil in the sauté pan over medium-low heat. Add the chard mixture to the pan and press it with the back of a flat metal spatula. Cook the torta for 5 minutes or so until you think the bottom is set.

8   Place the torta in the oven and cook another 15–20 minutes until it feels firm when touched in the center.

TO SERVE

Remove from the oven, let rest 5 minutes and flip over onto a round serving platter. Cut into pie wedges and serve.

NOTE   This recipe is good prepared with any of your favorite greens, spinach, escarole or even cardoons that are peeled, boiled, and cut into small pieces.

SICILIAN CHICKPEA SPREAD
Purea di Ciciri

Yields 1-1/2 cups

2 cups cooked chickpeas (garbanzo beans) or 1 (15-ounce) can, drained and rinsed

2 cloves garlic

1/2 cup pine nuts

2 tablespoons fresh lemon juice

2 medium fresh basil leaves, chopped

1/4 cup chopped fresh Italian parsley leaves

1/4 cup extra-virgin olive oil

Kosher salt to taste

1/2 teaspoon crushed red pepper flakes

Bruschetta (see page 180)

TO PREPARE

1 Place all the ingredients into a food processor or blender and process for 2–3 minutes until smooth. Taste and season with salt.

2 Pour mixture into a bowl and refrigerate for at least 2 hours.

TO SERVE

Serve as a dip for raw vegetables or with a crusty Italian bread—or spoon atop bruschetta.

JOHNNY

I guess we need to thank the Arabs for this one, D.

DAMIAN

Okay, thanks for this one. Because it's really good and it's really popular all across Sicily — even all across the Mediterranean. If you've ever liked hummus, you're sure to love what Sicilians do with a similar notion.

JOHNNY

We like this dip for spreading on bruschetta — along with Green Olive Spread (see page 17) and Cannellini Bean Spread (see page 19, in our Ciao Y'all book) — we like to give choices!

40 APPETIZERS Antipasti

FRIED STUFFED RICE CROQUETTES
Arancine

Serves 6

For the rice:

6 cups chicken stock

3 tablespoons butter, unsalted

2 cups carnaroli or arborio rice

1 pinch saffron threads

Kosher salt and freshly-ground black pepper to taste

2 eggs yolks, (from extra-large eggs, lightly beaten, whites reserved for the assembly)

1/2 cup grated Romano cheese

For the stuffing:

3 tablespoons extra-virgin olive oil

1 medium yellow onion, finely chopped

2 large garlic cloves, finely chopped

1/2 pound ground beef chuck

1/2 cup dry red wine

1 tablespoon tomato paste

1 cup tomato purée from canned Italian tomatoes, passed through a fine sieve or food mill

1-1/2 teaspoons kosher salt

1/2 teaspoon freshly-ground pepper

1/2 cup fresh peas or frozen baby peas, thawed

8 large fresh basil leaves, finely chopped

For the assembly:

3 cups Homemade Breadcrumbs (see page 179)

1/2 teaspoon kosher salt

4 whites from 4 extra-large eggs, beaten lightly

Extra-virgin olive oil for frying

TO PREPARE THE RICE

1 Bring the stock to a boil in a saucepan and keep it simmering. In a separate 3-quart saucepan, melt the butter over medium heat.

2 Add the rice to the melted butter and stir briskly with a wooden spoon until the rice is completely coated with the butter.

3 Add 1 cup of the stock to the rice and cook over medium heat, stirring with the wooden spoon, until the stock is absorbed, and then add another cup of the stock. Continue adding the stock in this manner, 1 cup at a time and stirring constantly, allowing each cup of stock to be absorbed but not allowing the rice to completely dry out before adding more stock

4 When rice is almost *al dente*, add the saffron, being careful not to add it too soon in the process or it might lose some of its flavor. When the stock is absorbed and the rice is cooked but firm to the bite (you might not use all the stock), remove the pot from the stove. Season with salt and pepper. Pour the rice onto a sheet pan and set aside to cool.

TO PREPARE THE STUFFING

1 Place the olive oil and the onion in a medium saucepan over medium heat and cook until the onion is very soft.

2 Add the garlic and cook 1 minute more. Add the ground meat and brown. Add the wine and cook until the wine has completely evaporated.

3 Add the tomato paste and cook 2–3 minutes and then add the tomato purée. Bring the sauce to a boil, reduce heat and simmer for 10 minutes.

4 Season with the salt and pepper, add the peas and simmer another 20–30 minutes, stirring occasionally.

5 Stir in the basil and remove from heat.

6 Strain the stuffing in a colander over a bowl reserving the juices to add to the rice, and let cool.

FRIED STUFFED RICE CROQUETTES
CONTINUED

TO ASSEMBLE

1 Transfer the cooled rice to a large mixing bowl and add the egg yolks, cheese and reserved stuffing juices, combining well.

2 In a shallow bowl, season the breadcrumbs with the salt.

3 In a separate bowl, lightly beat the egg whites.

4 Take a scant 1/4 cup of rice in your hands and form into a ball. With your finger make a large cavity in the center of rice ball, spoon 2 teaspoons of the meat filling into the cavity, cover with another tablespoon of rice and form the mixture into a ball.

5 Roll the ball first in the egg white and then in the bread-crumbs to coat, knocking off excess breadcrumbs, and transfer to a baking sheet. Repeat with the remaining rice.

6 Fill a heavy pot with oil to about 3 inches deep and heat over a medium-high heat until the thermometer registers 325°F. Fry rice balls in batches, turning frequently, until golden brown, 2–3 minutes. Transfer with a slotted spoon to paper towels to drain.

TO SERVE

Arrange on a serving dish and serve while hot.

JOHNNY

Talk about your classic Sicilian dish. This one is seen all over the island.

DAMIAN

To me, it's all about the open markets. When I go walking through all those great fruits and vegetables and meats and seafoods, well, I get hungry. The name on these fried croquettes means "little oranges," but in the markets I eat them more like hotcakes.

JOHNNY:

Aunt Josie Matranga made the best arancine I've ever tasted.

DAMIAN

You're right about Aunt Josie. And try a hot bite letting the steam come up and the cheese ooze out and — man, are they great!

TUNA MOUSSE
Mousse di Tunnu

Serves 10–12

3 medium-sized potatoes, peeled and quartered

3 cans (6-1/2 ounce) albacore or solid white tuna fish, rinsed and drained

3 salted anchovies, filleted and rinsed, or 6 oil-packed anchovy fillets, drained

3 tablespoons capers, salted or in brine, rinsed

1 teaspoon lemon zest

1/2 teaspoon cayenne

1/2 cup minced Italian parsley

1 tablespoon chopped fresh oregano

1/2 cup roasted red peppers, roughly chopped

1 cup mayonnaise

Kosher salt to taste

TO PREPARE

1 Boil the potatoes in lightly salted water until fork tender, about 25 minutes. Drain and rice the potatoes and set aside.
2 Put the tuna, anchovies, capers, lemon zest, and cayenne in a food processor and pulse until they form fine crumbs.
3 Transfer to a large mixing bowl and add the potatoes, parsley, oregano, peppers, and mayonnaise and mix well. Salt to taste.
4 Transfer mixture to a mold and refrigerate for several hours.

TO SERVE

Unmold onto a platter and garnish with sprigs of parsley and oregano. Serve with a crusty Italian bread.

JOHNNY
This isn't one of those fancy-sounding French mousses — is that the right word, Big D?
DAMIAN
Well, it sure wouldn't be mice!
JOHNNY
Anyway, this is nothing too fancy, just a purée of fish. It has a lot of capers and even anchovies, to make sure nobody forgets it's from Sicily.

"In Sicily they don't have to doctor their food up a lot.

It's all just so fresh and good!"

Primi Piatti
FIRST COURSE DISHES

We hope everybody's keeping count here. First, you have antipasti, cold or room temperature dishes that some of us could make a whole meal off of. Except then we'd be missing *Primi Piatti,* which literally means First Plates but in our case might as well mean First in Line. This course takes in just about anything built around carbohydrates—meaning pasta, of course, but also soups, risotto, gnocchi and a dozen other variations on that wonderful theme. Americans think of pasta and they think of spaghetti and meatballs, and then they picture a large bowl that would feed an army. Pasta servings in Italy tend to be small, usually around 2 ounces per person—though in Sicily, not surprisingly, people tend to eat a little more. The idea is not to be your entrée, but to satisfy your taste buds, thus getting you ready for an even heartier main course, which we'll be telling you about next. Logically, though, you can't have *Secondi* until you've had *Primi,* and that's what this chapter is all about. Of course, at our houses it is allowed to have 'seconds' on 'firsts,' as much as that sounds like the Abbott and Costello routine. With a name like Costello, we're sure at least Lou would have understood.

FUSILLI WITH ZUCCHINI, SAUSAGE AND GOAT CHEESE
Fusilli cu Cucuzzini, Salsiccie e Caprino

Serves 6–8

2 tablespoons extra-virgin olive oil

12 ounces Italian fennel sausage, sliced into 1/2-inch-thick rounds

1 small red onion, chopped

1 teaspoon crushed hot red pepper, or to taste

6 garlic cloves, minced

1 pound Fusilli (corkscrew pasta)

4 large ripe Roma tomatoes, (about 1 pound), seeded and diced

3 small zucchini, (about 1/2 pound), trimmed and sliced very thinly

6 ounces fresh goat cheese, cut into 1/2-inch chunks, at room temperature

1 teaspoon fresh oregano

1/2 cup finely-chopped, fresh Italian parsley

1 cup freshly-grated Parmigiano Reggiano cheese

Salt and freshly-ground black pepper

TO PREPARE

1 In a large sauté pan, heat the olive oil over medium heat. Add the sausage and cook, stirring, until the sausage starts to brown, about 3 minutes. Add the onion and the red pepper and continue to cook until the sausage is cooked through and the onion is soft, another 3–5 minutes. Add the garlic and cook 1 minute more.

2 In a large pot of boiling salted water, cook the pasta until *al dente,* drain well, saving 1 cup of the pasta cooking water.

3 Return the sausage pan back to a medium heat. Add the drained pasta, the tomatoes, zucchini, goat cheese, and the herbs and toss well. Add enough of the pasta water to moisten and make a nice sauce. The goat cheese should totally melt, become creamy and coat the pasta.

4 Add half of the grated Parmigiano Reggiano cheese and toss again. Season to taste with salt and pepper.

TO SERVE

Transfer pasta to a warm serving bowl or pasta platter. Serve, passing the remaining grated Parmigiano Reggiano cheese.

DAMIAN
A great, quick supper.

RIGATONI WITH CACIOCAVALLO AND EGGPLANT
Rigatoni allo Corrao

Serves 4–6

2 (about 1-1/2 pounds) medium firm eggplant, ends trimmed and sliced from stem to end, 1-inch thick

Kosher salt

3/4 cup extra-virgin olive oil

1 medium red onion, peeled, finely chopped

4 large cloves garlic, peeled and lightly crushed

6 anchovy fillets, preferably salt-packed and rinsed or packed in oil, drained, finely chopped

1-1/2 pounds canned whole peeled Italian tomatoes, de-seeded and crushed fine by hand

2 teaspoons sugar

Kosher salt and freshly-ground black pepper to taste

1/2 teaspoon crushed red pepper flakes

2 tablespoons capers, preferably salt-packed from Pantelleria, rinsed of salt or capers in brine, rinsed

4 large fresh basil leaves, each torn into 2-3 pieces

8-10 fresh mint leaves, torn in half

1 pound rigatoni

1/2 cup caciocavallo cheese, cut in shards or roughly chopped (can substitute imported Provolone)

Grated caciocavallo or Romano

TO PREPARE

1   Salt eggplant slices lightly on both sides with kosher salt. Place slices in a colander. Put a plate on top of the eggplant. Place a heavy weight on the plate. Let eggplant sit for 30 minutes. Rinse eggplant with cold water. Pat dry with paper towels. Cut eggplant slices into 1-inch cubes.

2   Heat 1/2 cup of the olive oil in a large skillet over high heat, until very hot. Add the eggplant and cook until golden brown and cooked through. Drain eggplant on a paper towel lined pan. Set aside.

3   Place a large pot with 6 quarts of water on the stove to boil. In a large skillet, heat remaining 1/4 cup of olive oil over medium heat. Add the onion, stirring frequently until the onion is very soft and starting to caramelize.

4   Add the garlic and sauté for 5 minutes, then remove the garlic and add the chopped anchovy. Cook another minute to let anchovy dissolve. Add the tomatoes and sugar. Raise the heat and bring sauce to a boil.

5   Reduce heat, add salt and pepper to taste, and the red pepper, and let sauce simmer 10 minutes, stirring frequently.

6   Stir in the capers, eggplant, and herbs. Add 2 tablespoons of kosher salt to the now boiling water. Drop the pasta in the pot.

TO SERVE

When the pasta is *al dente*, drain and add to the skillet with the sauce, over a low heat. Toss, add the shards of caciocavallo (or Provolone). Toss 1–2 minutes or until the cheese is soft and gooey. Transfer pasta to a warm serving platter. Sprinkle over with grated caciocavallo or Romano. Serve, passing extra grated cheese.

DAMIAN
This dish is named after the beautiful Sicilian family that makes the ceramics we use at the restaurants. They invited my wife Trina and me over to their house for this special dish during our honeymoon.

JOHNNY
The eggplant and rigatoni are perfect. But the cheese that melts with them really completes the dish.

PASTA WITH ONIONS
Pasta cu Cipuddi

Serves 4–6

1/2 cup extra-virgin olive oil

8 cups (about 2-1/2 pounds)
sliced yellow onions, 1/4-inch thick

1 teaspoon sugar

10 large cloves garlic, coarsely chopped

Kosher salt and freshly-ground black pepper

4 cups light chicken stock

1/4 cup fresh mint leaves

6 quarts of water

1 pound fedelini or vermicelli

Freshly-grated Pecorino Romano cheese

TO PREPARE

1 In a 3-quart pot, heat the olive oil over medium-low heat. Add the onions, stir and cover, and cooking slowly for 10 minutes or until onions are tender and translucent. Remove the lid and add the sugar, garlic, 1/2 teaspoon of the salt, and 1/2 teaspoon of the pepper.

2 Continue cooking, stirring often, until the onions and garlic are dark golden brown and caramelized, about 30 minutes more. Add the stock and raise the heat to bring the sauce to a boil.

3 When the sauce comes to a boil, reduce the heat to a vigorous simmer and cook for another 30 minutes. Adjust the salt and pepper for taste and add the mint. Turn heat on the sauce very low while you prepare the pasta.

4 In a large saucepan, bring 6 quarts of water to a boil and add 2-3 tablespoons of salt. Add the pasta to the boiling water and cook until *al dente*.

TO SERVE

Drain pasta and place on a large heated serving platter. Ladle half of onion sauce over pasta and toss. Serve pasta and pass extra sauce around. Sprinkle with a lot of grated Pecorino Romano cheese.

NOTE This is a dish my mamma would serve on Fridays when we couldn't eat meat. It's kind of like pasta with onion soup. If you like onions, especially caramelized onions, you'll love this dish. Once it's on my plate, I like a lot of freshly-cracked black pepper and cheese tossed in.

JOHNNY
One of my best memories is we made this dish at the restaurant one night. Damian said to cook about a pound of pasta, and we figured: Great! — pasta with onions for all of us. But then Damian sat down with this whole platter in front of him — and he ate it all.

DAMIAN
What can I say? My mother really loved this simple pasta dish. And she taught me to love it with plenty of cheese.

SICILIAN SEAFOOD SOUP
Zuppa di Pisci

Serves 12–16

1 cup dried chickpeas, soaked overnight in water, drained and rinsed

6 cups water

1 bay leaf

6 cloves garlic, peeled and sliced

1 teaspoon hot red pepper flakes

3 tablespoons olive oil

2 medium onions, coarsely chopped

2 tablespoons fresh oregano leaves

3 ribs celery, chopped

1 bulb fennel, chopped

2 carrots, diced

1 16-ounce can tomatoes, chopped with juice

2 tablespoons tomato paste

2 cups water

2 cups fish stock or chicken stock

2 zucchini

1 small head cauliflower, broken into small floret pieces

3 pounds fresh fish, shrimp, or shellfish –or a combination (bones and shells removed)

1 cup basil leaves

Bruschetta (see page 180)

TO PREPARE

1   Place the chickpeas in a soup pot with 6 cups of water, the bay leaf, 2 garlic cloves and the red pepper flakes. Bring to a boil then turn the heat down, cover, and cook until chickpeas are just tender. Remove from heat and set aside.

2   Meanwhile, heat the olive oil in a Dutch oven set on medium-high heat. Add the onions and cook until onions become transparent. Add the oregano, garlic, celery, fennel, and carrots and cook another 3 or 4 minutes.

3   Add the tomatoes and the tomato paste and cook an additional 5 minutes. Reduce the heat to low, add the chickpeas and their cooking liquid, and simmer for 1 hour.

4   Increase heat to medium, add the zucchini and cauliflower and cook 15 minutes, stirring occasionally. Add the seafood and basil and continue cooking for 5 minutes, or until seafood is cooked through. Add salt and pepper to taste.

TO SERVE

Remove bay leaf from soup. In each individual soup bowl, place a slice of bruschetta. Ladle the soup into the bowls over the bruschetta. Pass crusty Italian bread or crostini.

JOHNNY
This is the Sicilian version of boulillabaise.

BUCATINI WITH CAULIFLOWER PALERMO STYLE
Pasta chi Vroccoli Arriminata

Serves 4–6

2 pounds cauliflower

2 tablespoons kosher salt

2/3 cup extra-virgin olive oil

1 medium yellow onion, chopped fine

Kosher salt and freshly-ground
black pepper to taste

5 whole salt-packed anchovies filleted or
10 oil-packed fillets, rinsed in cold water
and chopped fine.

1/4 cup pine nuts

1/4 cup dried currants or raisins,
soaked in warm water for 20 minutes

1/2 teaspoon saffron threads

1 pound bucatini pasta

Muddica (see page 180)

TO PREPARE

1 Wash the cauliflower and divide into florets. In a large stock pot, bring 6 quarts of water to a boil and add the 2 tablespoons salt.

2 Add the cauliflower and cook just until tender. Remove the cauliflower with a slotted spoon and transfer to a bowl, reserving the water in the stock pot set on a simmer. In a large (12-inch) skillet, sauté the onion in the olive oil over medium heat until soft, seasoning with salt and pepper.

3 Add the anchovies, pine nuts, currants, saffron and 1/4 cup of the reserved cauliflower water to the skillet, stirring occasionally, and simmer for 2 minutes.

4 Add the cauliflower to the skillet and simmer, stirring occasionally, over low heat for 5 minutes. Adjust seasoning. Bring the cauliflower water back to a boil and add the pasta. When the pasta is *al dente,* drain it, reserving about a cup of the liquid.

TO SERVE

Add the pasta to the skillet and toss well. If dry, add a little of the pasta liquid. Transfer the pasta to a warm serving platter and sprinkle with 1/4 cup of Muddica. Serve, passing more Muddica.

DAMIAN
The word arriminata means "mixed up," and that's about what you can get in Sicily when you think about this main ingredient. They say broccoli when they mean cauliflower.

JOHNNY
Except sometimes, when they really mean broccoli or vroccoli. Whatever it is, when you cook it this way, it's delicious.

DAMIAN
You never see this except in the springtime, when the cauliflower is really young and tender.

JOHNNY
They don't have to doctor their food up a lot. It's all just so fresh and good.

BAKED PASTA
Maccheroni al Furnu

Serves 8–10

For the ragu:

1/2 cup extra-virgin olive oil

1 pound boneless pork butt, cut into 1-inch cubes

1 pound boneless veal round, cut into 1-inch cubes

2 medium yellow onions, chopped medium

4 large garlic cloves, finely chopped

1/2 cup red wine

6 tablespoons tomato paste

4 cups canned Italian tomatoes, passed through a food mill fitted with its smallest holes

5 cups water

Kosher salt and freshly-ground black pepper to taste

Red pepper flakes to taste

1 pound Italian sausage

For the filling:

6 tablespoons of extra-virgin olive oil

4 cloves garlic

2 medium zucchini, washed, ends trimmed, sliced into 1/4-inch rounds

Kosher salt and freshly-ground black pepper to taste

1/4 cup finely-chopped Italian parsley

1 pound fresh mushrooms, shiitake, cremini, or white domestic or mix of these, wiped clean, sliced 1/4-inch (shiitake stems discarded)

1 pound fresh or frozen peas

For assembly:

4 tablespoons kosher salt

2 pounds of pasta tubes, such as anelletti, ditali or ditalini

2 tablespoons butter

1/2 cup Homemade Breadcrumbs (see page 179)

2 ounces grated Pecorino Romano cheese

3/4 pound fresh mozzarella, shredded

2 hardboiled eggs, peeled and sliced 1/4-inch thick

2 ounces sliced salami, 1/16-inch thick, coarsely chopped

2 tablespoons softened butter for dotting

Extra Romano cheese, grated

TO PREPARE THE RAGU

1 In a large pot, heat oil over medium heat. Season the pork and veal with salt and pepper and, when the oil is very hot, add to the pot and brown meat well on all sides. Add the onions to the meat and cook, stirring often, until onions are soft and start to brown. Add the garlic and cook 1 minute more.

2 Deglaze the pan with the red wine, scraping up all of the browned bits on the bottom of the pan. Add the tomato paste and cook 2–3 minutes stirring continuously. Add the puréed tomatoes and the water, bring the contents to a boil and then reduce to a simmer.

3 Season ragu with salt, black pepper, and red pepper and simmer sauce partially covered for 1 hour.

4 Remove the sausage from its casing and break into 1-inch pieces. Add the sausage to the simmering ragu and cook 30 more minutes. Turn off heat and set ragu aside.

TO PREPARE THE FILLING

1 When the ragu is in the last 30 minutes of simmering, place 3 tablespoons of the olive oil and 2 cloves of the garlic, crushed lightly, over medium heat in a large skillet.

2 When the oil is very hot and the garlic starts to brown, remove and discard garlic and add the zucchini. Season with salt and pepper and sauté, stirring occasionally, until the zucchini is browned and cooked through. Add half of the parsley.

3 Transfer the cooked zucchini to a plate or pan and set aside.

4 Add the remaining oil and the other 2 cloves of garlic lightly crushed, over medium heat. When the oil is very hot and the garlic starts to brown, remove and discard garlic and add the mushrooms, season with salt and pepper and sauté, stirring occasionally, until the mushrooms are browned and cooked through. Add the remaining parsley.

5 Transfer the cooked mushrooms to a plate or pan. If using fresh peas, boil in lightly salted water until tender. Drain and submerge in ice water immediately, drain and set aside. If using frozen peas, thaw and set aside.

TO ASSEMBLE

1 Preheat oven to 350°F.

2 Bring 10 quarts of water to boil in a large pot and add the salt. Cook the pasta in the water until 2 minutes from *al dente.* Meanwhile, butter a large deep casserole and coat with 1–2 tablespoons of the breadcrumbs.

3 When the pasta is done, drain and toss it in a bowl with 1/2 of the ragu. Transfer 1/4 of the pasta to the bottom of the casserole. Top with a little of the extra ragu.

4 Distribute the zucchini over the pasta and cover with 1/3 of the grated Romano and 1/3 of the mozzarella. Top with another 1/4 of the pasta, a little sauce, the peas, the sliced hard-boiled eggs, the salami, and another 1/3 of the Romano and the mozzarella.

5 Top with another 1/4 of the pasta, a little sauce, the mushrooms, and remaining grated Romano and mozzarella.

6 Cover with the last 1/4 of the pasta, a little sauce, top with bread crumbs and dot with butter. Bake for 30 minutes at 350°F. Remove from the oven and let rest 15–20 minutes. Serve, passing extra Romano cheese.

EGGPLANT RAVIOLI
Ravioli di Milinciani

Serves 8

For the stuffing:

1/2 cup extra-virgin olive oil

2 pounds eggplant, peeled and cut into 1-inch cubes

1 small yellow onion, finely chopped

4 cloves garlic, minced

1/2 cup grated Pecorino Romano cheese

1/2 cup ricotta, drained overnight in a sieve

1 large egg, lightly beaten

1 teaspoon fresh thyme leaves

Kosher salt and freshly-ground black pepper

1 recipe Basic Egg Pasta (see page 177)

For the sauce:

2 tablespoons extra-virgin olive oil

1 small red onion, peeled and finely diced

2 cloves garlic, minced

3 pounds Roma tomatoes, peeled, seeded and chopped

2 cups chicken stock

1/4 pound unsalted butter, cut in cubes

Small handful basil leaves, torn into 3-4 pieces

Kosher salt and freshly-ground black pepper to taste

1/4 cup grated Pecorino Romano cheese

TO PREPARE THE STUFFING

1 In a large skillet, heat the oil over high heat. When the oil is very hot, add the eggplant and sauté, browning well until the eggplant is tender, approximately 5–8 minutes. Remove the eggplant from the skillet with a slotted spoon and drain on baking sheet or tray lined with paper towels.

2 Remove all but 2 tablespoons of oil from the pan. Reduce the heat and add the onion to the skillet, cooking until the onion is soft and translucent. Add the garlic and cook 1 more minute.

3 Put the onion and garlic in a mixing bowl along with the eggplant. Mash the eggplant mixture well with a fork and allow to cool. When the eggplant mixture is cool, add the Pecorino Romano and ricotta cheeses, the egg, and the fresh thyme and season to taste with salt and pepper.

4 Mix well, cover and chill in the refrigerator at least 2 hours (or overnight) until stuffing becomes firm.

TO PREPARE THE RAVIOLI

1 Cut the pasta dough in half. Wrap one half in plastic wrap while you work with the other half. Roll dough through a pasta machine on its thinnest setting. Lay out on a wooden work surface.

2 Trim the ends so they are straight. Starting about 1 inch from one end and 1 inch in from the sides, place 1/2-tablespoon mounds of stuffing across the sheet, leaving about 1-inch between them. Stop about half way down the sheet.

3 Fold the pasta half with no stuffing over the stuffed side. Press to seal around each mound. With a fluted pastry cutter cut out the ravioli. Press the edges of each piece of ravioli to make sure they are sealed. Place ravioli on cotton dishtowels until ready to cook.

TO PREPARE THE SAUCE

1 Place the olive oil and the onion in a saucepan over medium-low heat and sauté for about 5 minutes. Add the garlic, sauté for another 2 minutes, then add the tomatoes and the chicken stock. Cook for 30 minutes.

EGGPLANT RAVIOLI
CONTINUED

2 Using a whisk add the butter to the tomatoes, one cube at a time, allowing each cube to fully incorporate before adding another cube. Stir in the basil and season with salt and pepper to taste.

TO ASSEMBLE
1 Boil ravioli in 6 quarts of slowly boiling water seasoned with 2 tablespoons of kosher salt. Meanwhile re-warm sauce in a 12-inch skillet, over a low flame. When ravioli are ready, use a large skimmer to retrieve them from the water.
2 Transfer ravioli to the skillet with the sauce. Toss ravioli in the sauce. Add 1/4 cup of grated Pecorino Romano cheese. Toss again.

TO SERVE
Transfer to a warm serving platter. Serve with extra Pecorino Romano cheese.

JOHNNY
The best ravioli maker I know is my uncle, Damian Mandola. His "little pillows" just melt in your mouth.

DAMIAN
I'm a delicate sort of guy.

JOHNNY
For a big guy, he has real soft hands.

PASTA WITH SARDINES AND FENNEL
Pasta Malanisa

Serves 4–6

1/2 cup extra-virgin olive oil

1 medium yellow onion, finely chopped

1 bunch green onions, finely chopped

1 cup chopped fennel fronds

2 tablespoons chopped fresh dill leaves

6 anchovy fillets, packed in oil, or 3 whole anchovies in salt, rinsed, drained and filleted

2 (4-1/2 ounce) cans sardines in oil, drained and de-boned; or 4 fresh sardines, cleaned, boned, and cut into 1-inch pieces

1/2 cup golden raisins

1/4 cup pine nuts

2/3 cup dry white wine

16-ounce can Italian tomatoes, puréed

Kosher salt and freshly-ground black pepper to taste

1 pound bucatini

Muddica (see page 180)

TO PREPARE

1 Place olive oil, onions, fennel and dill in a large sauté pan. Cook over medium heat until onions start to caramelize. Add anchovies, and sardines and cook for 2–3 minutes. Add the raisins and pine nuts. Cook for 5 minutes.

2 Increase heat, then add wine and reduce for another 5 minutes. Add tomatoes and bring sauce to a boil again. Turn heat to low. Season to taste with salt and pepper. Simmer and cook for 1/2 hour.

3 In a large pot, bring 6 quarts water to a boil. Add 3 tablespoons salt. Add bucatini and cook until *al dente*.

TO SERVE

Drain pasta and add to skillet with sauce and toss well. Transfer pasta to a warm serving platter. Ladle the remaining sauce left in pan over the top. Shower liberally with Muddica. Serve with more Muddica on the side.

JOHNNY
You know who makes the best Malanisa, right, Yo!

DAMIAN
What can I say, he's right.

JOHNNY
It's all about the fresh sardines they have in Sicily. They always eat it on St. Joseph's Day, so that makes it a Lent thing. Some people add a lot of sugar — but that makes it too sweet, if you ask me. Kind of like Damian.

PASTA WITH PESTO FROM TRAPANI
Spaghettini cu Pesto alla Trapanese

Serves 4–6

1 cup basil leaves

6 large cloves garlic, peeled

1 cup blanched almonds, roughly chopped

6 very ripe, Roma tomatoes, peeled, seeded and chopped medium

1/2 cup extra-virgin olive oil

Kosher salt and freshly-ground black pepper

1 pound imported Italian dried linguini, or spaghetti

TO PREPARE

1 In a food processor, blend together the basil and the garlic, then add the almonds and blend to a rough chop. Add the tomatoes and olive oil and purée. Season with salt and pepper to taste, then blend again.

2 Bring 6 quarts of water to a boil. Add 3 tablespoons kosher salt. Add the pasta and cook until *al dente*. Drain the pasta, saving some of the water to thin the pesto sauce. Mix enough of the water with the pesto sauce to get the desired consistency.

TO SERVE

Spread about 1/2 cup of the pesto sauce on the bottom of a warm serving platter, and transfer the pasta on top, then pour the remaining pesto on the pasta and toss. Serve immediately.

NOTE   The pesto sauce can be prepared several hours before serving and kept covered, in the refrigerator. Take the sauce out of the refrigerator and let warm to room temperature for at least an hour before using.

DAMIAN
You can make the pesto now in a food processor, but the name tells of half of what the old-timers used — a mortar and pestle. Around the town of Trapani, they were probably inspired by the Genovese.

JOHNNY
By the family?

DAMIAN
No, by the people of Genoa, who kicked off this whole pesto thing in the first place.

JOHNNY
It's really a great dish.

PASTA WITH SICILIAN SQUASH AND FAVA BEANS
Pasta cu Cucuzza e Fave

Serves 6-8

1/2 cup extra-virgin olive oil, plus extra to garnish

1 medium yellow onion, chopped fine

3 large cloves garlic, minced

2 pounds cucuzza, peeled, seeded cut into 3/4-inch cubes

2 cups tenerumi (the last tender 12 inches of cucuzza vines, washed and rough chopped), optional

2 cups canned Italian tomatoes, seeded and crushed by hand

6 large, fresh basil leaves, torn into 2 or 3 pieces

1 cup water

Kosher salt and freshly-ground black pepper

Crushed red pepper flakes to taste

1-1/2 cups shelled fresh fava beans, blanched and peeled

1/2 pound thin spaghetti or fedilini broken into 1-inch pieces

Grated Pecorino Romano cheese

TO PREPARE

1 In a large pot, sauté the onion in the olive oil over medium heat until just golden. Add the garlic. Cook another minute. Add the cucuzza (and the tenerumi, if desired), the tomatoes, basil and the water and stir to blend. (The cucuzza will produce a lot of its own water.)

2 Season lightly with salt, black pepper and red pepper. Reduce the heat, and cook, partially covered, for 10 minutes. Add the fava beans, partially cover again. Continue to cook until the squash and the fava are tender, 20–30 minutes.

3 Bring 4 quarts of water to a boil in a 6 or 8 quart pot. Season with 2 tablespoons of kosher salt and drop the pasta into the pot. When the pasta is about 2 minutes from being *al dente,* remove pot from stove. Drain pasta, reserving 2 cups or so of the water. Transfer the drained pasta to the pot with the cucuzza.

TO SERVE

Add enough pasta water to make the dish as soupy as you like. Season to taste. Transfer pasta to a serving bowl. Drizzle with olive oil and sprinkle with grated cheese and red pepper flakes.

NOTE If you can't find cucuzza, you can substitute zucchini that has been scrubbed, ends trimmed, and cubed. You can substitute fresh, or frozen baby lima beans for the fave.

DAMIAN

It's hard to get two things more Sicilian than fava beans and cucuzza. Fave, of course, are known as lucky beans in Sicily. And even today you find Sicilian-Americans walking around with a bean in their pocket for good luck. It's not superstitious or anything, huh?

JOHNNY

Just a little, maybe. But there's nothing superstitious about the oversized squash called cucuzza. We're lucky to have cousins that grow cucuzza for us. And that's what I really call good luck.

SPAGHETTI WITH SEAFOOD
Spaghetti ai Frutti di Mare

Serves 6

1/2 cup extra-virgin olive oil

1 medium red onion, finely chopped

4 cloves garlic, peeled and mashed

Juice of 1 lemon

1 cup dry white wine

2 pounds fresh tomatoes, blanched, peeled, and seeded, each cut into 8 wedges

Kosher salt and freshly-ground black pepper to taste

Crushed red pepper to taste

1 tablespoon chopped fresh oregano

3 tablespoons salt

1 pound spaghetti

1 pound halibut fillets, or any other firm white-fleshed fish, cut into 1-1/2-inch squares

2 pounds clams, washed well

1 pound mussels, washed well

1 pound medium shrimp, peeled and deveined

TO PREPARE

1 Fill pasta pot with 6 quarts of water and put over high heat and bring to boil. Heat the oil in a 12-inch skillet over medium heat, add onions and cook for 5 minutes, or until soft.

2 Add the garlic to the onions and cook for 1 minute. Add in lemon juice and wine, cooking until liquid evaporates, about 3 minutes. Add the tomatoes and stir, then add salt, black pepper, red pepper, and oregano and cook for 5 minutes.

3 Add 3 tablespoons of salt to the boiling water, stir and add spaghetti and cook until *al dente*. Meanwhile, add the seafood to the sauce, cover and cook until fish is done and the shellfish have opened. Discard any clams or mussels that do not open.

TO SERVE

Drain pasta and transfer to the skillet and toss well. Transfer to a large serving platter. Spoon seafood sauce over the pasta.

DAMIAN

Every coastal town in Sicily has its own version of this spaghetti. This recipe comes from my grandma's town of Cefalú. I ate it there one night in a little restaurant, sitting right on the water, with seafood so fresh it had slept in the bay the night before.

JOHNNY

I guess, in this case, it really did sleep with the fishes!

SPAGHETTI WITH TUNA
Spaghetti al Tunnu

Serves 4–6

1 whole anchovy packed in salt
or 2 filets packed in oil

1/4 cup extra-virgin olive oil

1 medium yellow onion, finely chopped

2 large garlic cloves, finely chopped

2 cups Italian canned whole tomatoes
with juice, passed through a food mill

Kosher salt and freshly-ground black pepper

Crushed red pepper flakes to taste

1 (6-1/2 ounce) can good-quality albacore
tuna packed in oil, drained

1 teaspoon fresh oregano leaves

16 Sicilian black olives, pitted, split in half
lengthwise

2 tablespoons capers in salt or brine, rinsed

3 tablespoons kosher salt

1 pound spaghetti

Garnish:

2 tablespoons extra-virgin olive oil

1/4 cup chopped Italian parsley

Muddica (see page 180)

TO PREPARE

1 Rinse the anchovy packed in salt under cool running water and fillet. If using oil packed fillets rinse under cool running water. Chop anchovy fillets.

2 Put the olive oil in a large skillet and place over medium heat. Add anchovy and dissolve in the oil. Add the onion and cook for about 3–5 minutes or until very soft. Add garlic and cook 1 minute more.

3 Add the tomatoes and cook 5 minutes, stirring frequently. Season with salt, pepper and red pepper. Add the tuna, oregano, olives, and capers reduce heat and simmer 2–3 more minutes. Adjust seasoning.

4 Bring 6 quarts of water to a boil and season with 3 tablespoons of kosher salt. Cook spaghetti until *al dente*. Drain and toss pasta with sauce over a low flame in the skillet.

TO SERVE

Add olive oil and parsley, toss again. Serve on a warm pasta platter. Shower liberally with Muddica. Pass more Muddica.

DAMIAN

Here's a recipe I learned from a young Sardinian chefs Velio Deplane, who has a little trattoria in Houston.

JOHNNY

The thing is, don't try to make it with fresh tuna. This is one of those recipes that call for canned tuna and really is meant to be that way.

SPAGHETTI WITH DRIED TUNA ROE
Spaghetti cu la Bottarga

Serves 4

1 pound spaghetti

4 ounces tuna bottarga (dried and salted tuna eggs)

3/4 cup extra-virgin olive oil

1 small hot fresh red pepper, halved lengthwise, seeds removed

3 cloves garlic

2 tablespoons finely-chopped Italian parsley

Kosher salt to taste

TO PREPARE

1 Grate half of the tuna bottarga. Put aside in a bowl. With a mandolin or a truffle slicer, very thinly slice the other 2 ounces. Set aside.

2 Lightly crush the garlic. Place olive oil in a large skillet along with the garlic and red pepper. Place the skillet over a medium-low flame. Bring oil up to heat slowly letting the oil infuse with the garlic and hot pepper.

3 When the garlic starts to color, remove the pan from heat. Let the oil cool slightly. When the oil has cooled, remove the garlic and pepper. Reserve the skillet for later use. Pour the garlic and pepper infused oil into a blender.

4 Add the grated bottarga to the blender jar with the oil. Purée a few seconds. Return the blended mixture to the skillet. Taste and correct seasonings (careful, bottarga is salty.)

5 Bring 6 quarts of water to a boil and season with 3 tablespoons of kosher salt. Cook spaghetti until *al dente*. Drain pasta, reserving 1/4 cup of the boiling water.

6 Place pasta in the skillet with the sauce, over a low flame. Add a little pasta water if needed to moisten the pasta. Toss well.

TO SERVE

Transfer to a warm serving platter, sprinkle with the shaved bottarga and parsley and serve.

JOHNNY

In Sicily, bottarga is tuna roe but not just tuna roe. It's got to be dried a special way.

DAMIAN

They take the whole roe sac, salt it and flatten it between boards. Then they dry it in the sun for weeks. It has a very earthy seafood taste, kind of funky but real good.

JOHNNY

This is not a dish for the faint of heart.

PASTA WITH EGGPLANT
Pasta alla Norma

Serves 4–6

For the eggplant:

3 medium eggplants

1 tablespoon salt

Extra-virgin olive oil for frying

For the sauce:

1/4 cup extra-virgin olive oil

3 large cloves garlic, finely chopped

2 pounds very ripe Roma tomatoes or 4 cups canned Italian tomatoes, coarsely chopped

Kosher salt and freshly-ground black pepper to taste

Crushed red pepper to taste

12 large fresh basil leaves

For the pasta:

6 quarts of water

1 tablespoon kosher salt

1 pound spaghetti or rigatoni

For serving:

1 cup grated ricotta salata

1 cup grated Pecorino Romano cheese

TO PREPARE THE EGGPLANT

Trim the ends of the eggplant and cut in 1/2-inch slices. Lightly salt the slices and place in a colander in the sink or over a tray. Place a plate on top and something heavy (a cast iron pot lid works well) on top of the plate to squeeze the juices from the eggplant and let sit for 30 minutes to 1 hour.

TO PREPARE THE SAUCE

1 Heat the olive oil and garlic in a large saucepan over medium-high heat. When the garlic starts to take on color, add the tomatoes with a pinch of salt and simmer, stirring occasionally, for about 30 minutes.

2 Pass the tomatoes through a food mill, fitted with the disk with the smallest holes, and then return the tomatoes to the pan over medium low heat.

3 Season the tomato purée with salt, black pepper, and red pepper, if desired, and simmer until sauce is a nice thick consistency, 10–15 minutes, and then remove from stove.

4 Tear each basil leaf into a few pieces and sprinkle over the sauce.

5 Cover the saucepan with a lid and let it sit to allow the basil to steep and perfume the sauce.

6 In a large skillet pour enough olive oil to come up about 2 inches. Place the skillet over medium-high heat until the oil is very hot.

7 Rinse the eggplant slices and dry with paper towels and then fry in batches in the hot olive oil until golden brown. Remove the eggplant from the oil with a slotted spoon and drain on a tray lined with paper towels.

TO PREPARE THE PASTA

1 In a large pot bring 6 quarts of water to a boil and season with kosher salt. Boil the pasta until *al dente*, drain and return pasta to the boiling pot.

TO SERVE

Add enough sauce to the pasta to coat and transfer to a warm serving platter. Top with a little more sauce, arrange the eggplant over the top and sprinkle with ricotta salata. Serve, passing ricotta salata and Pecorino Romano cheese.

LENTIL AND CAULIFLOWER SOUP
Zuppa di Lenticchie e Cavolfiore

Serves 8

1 pound dry lentils

1/2 cup extra-virgin olive oil

1 large yellow onion, finely chopped

2 large celery ribs, finely chopped

4 ounces pancetta, sliced 1/4-inch thick, unrolled and cut into 1/2-inch strips

8 cloves garlic, finely chopped

1 pound canned Italian tomatoes, seeded and crushed fine by hand

1/2 teaspoon dried oregano

4 bay leaves

1/4 cup chopped fresh parsley

10 cups boiling water

1/2 teaspoon crushed red pepper

Kosher salt and freshly-ground black pepper

1/2 head cauliflower, broken into small florets

1/2 pound dried fettuccine, broken into 1-inch pieces.

Extra-virgin olive oil to taste

Grated Pecorino Romano or Parmigiano cheese to taste

TO PREPARE

1 Pick through lentils and make sure there are no stones or foreign matter. Rinse lentils thoroughly and set aside.

2 In a 5-quart stockpot, sauté onion, celery, and pancetta in the olive oil until soft, about 10 minutes. Add garlic and cook 1 minute or more. Add tomatoes and cook 2–3 minutes more. Add lentils, oregano, bay leaves, parsley, water, red pepper, salt, and pepper to the stockpot and bring to a boil. Reduce heat and simmer uncovered 15 minutes (skimming any foam that rises to the top).

3 Add the cauliflower and continue to cook for 15–30 minutes more or until lentils are very tender. Taste and correct for seasoning. Remove the bay leaves.

4 In a separate pot, bring 4 quarts of water to a boil. Add 1 tablespoon of kosher salt to the boiling water and add pasta. Cook pasta until *al dente*. Drain pasta and reserve 2 cups of pasta water.

5 Add pasta to the stock pot with lentils and cauliflower with enough reserved water to achieve a soup consistency. Continue cooking until pasta is done.

TO SERVE

Ladle soup into individual bowls and top with a little extra virgin olive oil and fresh grated Pecorino Romano or Parmigiano cheese.

JOHNNY

My grandmothers always made this rustic soup when the first cold front blew through here each year. And after the summers we have here in Houston, that was usually cause for some celebration.

DAMIAN

Mostly, though, we were happy to finally get our mouths on this soup. Be sure to drizzle a little olive oil over your soup and sprinkle with cheese.

SAINT JOSEPH'S DAY SOUP
Maccu di San Giuseppe

Serves 6–8

1/2 pound dried fava beans, shelled

1/2 cup dried chestnuts

1/2 cup dried beans (kidney, cranberry or barlotti)

1/2 cup dried chickpeas

1/2 cup dried split peas

1/2 cup dried lentils

1 medium yellow onion, sliced medium

2 celery ribs, chopped medium

1 large head escarole, chopped medium

2 sun-dried tomatoes, cut into small pieces

1 teaspoon fennel seeds, toasted and lightly crushed (see page 187)

2 tablespoons finely-chopped fresh fennel fronds

1 tablespoon dill weed, finely chopped

Kosher salt and freshly-ground black pepper to taste

1/4 cup extra-virgin olive oil

TO PREPARE

1 Soak the fava beans, chestnuts, dried beans, and chickpeas, overnight in a pot of cold water. Drain and place in a large stock-pot or terra cotta soup pot with 10 cups of water.

2 Bring to a boil, reduce heat and simmer for about 1 hour. Add the split peas, lentils, onion, celery, escarole, tomatoes, fennel seeds, fennel, and dill weed. Season with salt and pepper. Simmer another 1-1/2–2 hours or until beans are tender. Add more water if needed to thin to a soup consistency.

TO SERVE

Turn off heat, taste and re-season, if needed. Add olive oil.

NOTE This soup can be served as is or with croutons made of rustic country bread fried in extra-virgin olive oil. It can also be served with small pasta. Also, if the fava beans are not already shelled, soak them separately and shell. After they have soaked all night, you can slip off their skins and proceed with the recipe.

DAMIAN

In Sicily, and even among Sicilian-Americans, St. Joseph's Day is a day of prayer, of thanks, and a whole lot of symbolism. Look at those St. Joseph altars, for instance, where just about everything stands for something having to do with life or faith of family.

JOHNNY

And since it's during Lent in a Catholic country, there'd better not be any meat anywhere near a St. Joseph's altar.

DAMIAN

Sure, but we don't miss it much, with this very earthy multi-bean soup. We get our protein and our religion in the same bite.

"Sweet and sour flavors are really big all over Sicily, and they especially love to do fish this way."

CIAO SICILY

Secondi: Pisci
SEAFOOD ENTRÉES

Being on an island is certainly no guarantee you'll have wonderful seafood from local waters every day of the week, but in Sicily it certainly is. The Mediterranean is not only one of the world's most ancient fishing grounds but one of the richest, too. Millions of fish flipper and flutter past Sicily each 24 hours, and every culture that has run the place over the centuries has noted how easy it is to make wonderful meals with Sicilian seafood. Huge swordfish are a specialty, sometimes carried off the boats just long enough to be cut into steaks and slapped on a hot wood grill for brushing with the slightest touch of olive oil, garlic and lemon juice. And what works for Sicilian swordfish works for the island's fresh tuna, sardines and anchovies as well—keep it simple, *stupido*! When we created our newest restaurant in Houston, one that blends the seafood traditions of the Mediterranean with the equally rich ones of our Gulf Coast, we thought of all the seafood we've inhaled in Sicily. For all those reasons and more, we called our new place *Pesce*.

TUNA WITH BEANS
Tunnu cu Fasoli

Serves 4

For the tuna:

4 (6-ounce) tuna steaks

4 tablespoons extra-virgin olive oil
(plus more to cook fish)

1/4 cup black pepper, coarsely ground

4 slices of bacon or pancetta

1/4 cup minced yellow onions

2 cloves garlic, minced

2 (15-ounce) cans cannellini beans, drained

6 Roma tomatoes, seeded and diced

2 cups baby arugula, leaves with large
stems removed

For the dressing:

1/4 cup balsamic vinegar

3/4 cup extra-virgin olive oil

1/4 cup sliced fresh chives

Kosher salt and freshly-ground
black pepper to taste

TO PREPARE THE TUNA

1 Rub the tuna steaks with I tablespoon of olive oil and coat on all sides with crushed black pepper. Set aside.

2 Fully cook the bacon in a large sauté pan over medium-high heat, remove to a paper towel, drain, and crumble. Add onion to the bacon fat and cook until translucent. Add garlic to the onions and cook another 2–3 minutes at low heat.

3 Add the beans, tomatoes, arugula, and the cooked bacon to the mixture and heat thoroughly. Season with salt and pepper.

4 To make the dressing, place all of the dressing ingredients in a blender and pulse briefly.

5 Heat 3 tablespoons of olive oil in a large sauté pan set on medium-high heat until sizzling.

6 Put the tuna steaks in the pan and cook for 2–5 minutes on each side, to reach desired doneness.

TO SERVE

Place each tuna steak on a bed of the beans and drizzle lightly with balsamic dressing.

NOTE   If desired, spinach can be substituted for the arugula.

DAMIAN

I don't know, maybe this started out as a Tuscan dish, but it sure went south in a hurry.

JOHNNY

Meaning it went to Sicily, which is a great idea, if you ask us. After all, the Sicilians love tuna and beans too.

DAMIAN

And let's face it, tuna and beans are a great combination. I like to make this dish in the cooler months.

FISH WITH SWEET AND SOUR ONIONS
Pisci cu Cipuddi in Agra Duci

Serves 4

1-1/2 pounds pearl onions

1/4 cup extra-virgin olive oil

2 tablespoons sugar

1/3 cup high-quality white wine vinegar

4 tablespoons extra-virgin olive oil

1/3 cup oil-packed sun-dried tomatoes, cut into thick slices

1/4 cup currants, plumped in hot water, drained with liquid saved

3 tablespoons chopped fresh mint plus additional sprigs for garnish

4 fillets of cod, snapper, flounder, halibut, or sea bass

Kosher salt and freshly-ground black pepper to taste

TO PREPARE
1 Preheat the oven to 450°F.

2 Drop the onions in boiling water for 2–3 minutes then drain, remove the outer skins and set aside. Heat the oil in a large sauté pan and add the onion. Stir in the sugar, allowing it to dissolve and then start to caramelize with the onion.

3 Add the vinegar and stir well. Cover and simmer gently over low heat for about 30 minutes or until onions are fork tender and the flavors in the sauce have combined. If the sauce becomes too thick, add some hot water, as needed.

4 Add the sun-dried tomatoes, currants, and mint to the onions and cook for a few minutes.

5 Taste and adjust for seasoning, adding salt and pepper as desired. Taste and adjust for the sweet-and-sour ratio, heightening sweetness by adding some of the currant soaking liquid.

6 Season the fillets with salt and pepper and place in an oiled baking dish. Cover with the onions. Bake for 8–10 minutes, or until the fish is done. Serve hot.

TO SERVE
Season with a little more freshly-ground black pepper and garnish with sprigs of fresh mint.

JOHNNY
Everybody always thinks of Chinese food when they hear the words "sweet and sour." But they'd better not say anything about that to the Sicilians. Right, D?

DAMIAN
Better not. Sweet and sour flavors are really big all over Sicily, and they especially love to do fish this way. Still, there are connections here to other parts of Italy. Way up north in Venice, people are always munching on a dish they call "in saor," which with its vinegar and olive oil is pretty much the same thing.

JOHNNY
And the onions, man, they add this really nice sweetness.

BAKED SWORDFISH
Pisci Spada al Furnu

Serves 4

4 (6-ounce) swordfish steaks, about 1-inch thick

3/4 cup extra-virgin olive oil

Kosher salt and freshly-ground pepper

6 leaves fresh basil, chopped

4 garlic cloves, thinly sliced

1 cup dry white wine

Juice of 1 lemon

TO PREPARE

1 Preheat oven to 350°F.

2 Rub both sides of each steak with olive oil. Place the steaks in a 9 x 13-inch baking dish. Sprinkle lightly with salt and pepper, basil, and sliced garlic. Pour the wine and remaining olive oil over the fish. Bake the fish in the oven, uncovered, for 15–18 minutes.

TO SERVE

Transfer the fish to a serving dish and sprinkle with lemon juice. Serve with risotto and freshly steamed asparagus.

JOHNNY

These two recipes for swordfish are as simple as it gets— in Sicily that means as good as it can get!

BROILED SWORDFISH WITH OLIVE OIL AND LEMON
Pisci Spada cu Olio e Limone

Serves 4

1/2 cup extra-virgin olive oil

1 large clove garlic, chopped

3 tablespoons fresh parsley, chopped

Juice of one lemon

1/2 cup white wine

Kosher salt and freshly-ground black pepper

4 swordfish steaks

TO PREPARE

1 Combine the olive oil, garlic, and parsley, and beating with a wire whisk, add lemon juice and white wine.

2 Season with salt and pepper to taste. Set aside for 1 hour to allow flavors to combine.

3 Broil swordfish 5 minutes on each side. Pour marinade onto of fish and broil another 1–2 minutes. Serve immediately.

DAMIAN

The sauce we use here is like classic salmorighiu, except that you usually put it on the fish after cooking. Here we change things up a bit broiling the fish with the sauce.

STUFFED SARDINES
Sarde Chini al Arrustutu

Serves 6

For the stuffing:

1 cup of Homemade Breadcrumbs,
(see page179)

1 (3-ounce) can oil-packed tuna, drained

1/2 fennel bulb, white part, cleaned and
finely chopped

1/4 cup finely-chopped fennel fronds

1/4 cup Italian parsley, finely chopped

Kosher salt and freshly-ground
black pepper to taste

1/4 cup extra-virgin olive oil

18 thoroughly cleaned sardine fillets,
(9 sardines)

All-purpose flour

For the sauce and serving:

1/2 cup extra-virgin olive oil

1 teaspoon dried oregano, or 2 teaspoons
fresh oregano

2 tablespoons dry white wine

Kosher salt and freshly-ground
black pepper to taste

Juice of 1 lemon

1 tablespoon chopped fresh Italian parsley

TO PREPARE THE STUFFING

1 Put breadcrumbs, tuna, fennel, parsley, salt, and pepper into a food processor and pulse for 10 seconds. Add 2 tablespoons of the olive oil (more if necessary) through the feed tube of the processor to moisten the breadcrumbs.

2 On a flat work surface, line up half of the sardine fillets skin side down, season lightly with salt and pepper. Spoon equal amounts of the breadcrumbs across each sardine. Cover with the remaining fillets, boned side down. Press each sardine sandwich gently together and dredge in flour.

3 Heat the remaining olive oil in a large, deep, frying pan until hot but not smoking. Cook the sardines in batches until golden brown on each side, carefully turning with tongs or 2 spoons. Drain the sardines on paper towels.

TO PREPARE THE SAUCE

Heat the olive oil with oregano and wine in a small pan over medium-high heat until it just boils. Season with salt and pepper to taste. Pour the lemon juice into the sauce and add the parsley.

TO SERVE

Arrange the sardines in a serving platter and sprinkle with lemon juice. Pour the sauce over the top and serve.

JOHNNY
Just when we keep saying Sicilians like to keep their fish simple, we stumble on these wonderful stuffed sardines.

DAMIAN
Man, don't the Sicilians love sardines – you know, the fresh ones, not the ones we get here in little flat cans. And yes, the stuffing can be a bit of a chore, but it's the one thing Sicilian cooks will put themselves out to do with fish, recipe after recipe.

JOHNNY
Of course, anything that sits still long enough might end up stuffed in Sicily. They love what stuffing brings to a dish.

BAKED STRIPED BASS
Branzino al Furnu

Serves 4-6

4 whole striped bass, 2–2-1/2 pounds each, scaled, cleaned and rinsed in salt water

Kosher salt and freshly-ground black pepper

4 cloves garlic, sliced

4 rosemary branches, cut to 4-inch lengths

12 sprigs Italian parsley

8–12 basil leaves, whole

8 lemon slices, 1/4-inch thick

1 cup chicken stock

1/2 cup dry white wine

Juice of 1 lemon

TO PREPARE

1 Preheat oven to 500°F.

2 Season the fish inside and out with salt and pepper. Stuff each fish with I sliced garlic clove, one rosemary branch, 3 sprigs parsley, 2 basil leaves, and two lemon slices. Oil a II x 13-inch baking pan. Place the fish in the pan.

3 Pour the chicken stock and wine over the fish. Bake, uncovered, for 15–20 minutes, turning once. Transfer the fish to a serving plate and keep warm.

4 Pour cooking juices in to a saucepan. Bring to a boil. Reduce this sauce by half and season with salt and pepper.

TO SERVE

Pour sauce over fish and drizzle with extra-virgin olive oil and juice from I lemon, Serve extra sauce on the side.

NOTE If striped bass is unavailable, substitute whole rockfish or red snapper.

DAMIAN
Seems like everybody is suddenly serving branzino, even though a few years ago almost no Americans had ever heard of it. It's a terrific saltwater bass they really love in Sicily. The meat is white, with just the right amount of oil for flavor.

JOHNNY
It's a wonderful tasting fish. And again, the idea is that, as much as possible, you keep things simple and let the fish speak for itself.

STUFFED CALAMARI
Calamari Chini

Serves 4

12 medium-sized squid

1/4 cup extra-virgin olive oil

1 small yellow onion, finely chopped

1 clove garlic, peeled and minced

1 cup Homemade Breadcrumbs
(see page 179)

3 anchovy fillets, salt or oil packed,
rinsed and chopped

1/4 cup capers, salt or brine packed,
rinsed and drained

1/4 cup pine nuts, chopped medium

1/4 cup raisins, plumped in water for
30 minutes, chopped

3/4 cup Italian parsley, chopped

2 eggs

2 (15-1/2-ounce) cans imported Italian
tomatoes, crushed

Kosher salt and freshly-ground
black pepper to taste

TO PREPARE

1 Clean the squid by removing the head, the fins and all contents of the body sac, being sure to leave the body tubes intact. Remove the tentacles from the head, by cutting just below the eyes. Chop tentacles fine and set aside for the stuffing. Wash the tubes. Peel off skin.

2 Heat 2 tablespoons of olive oil in a frying pan and brown the chopped squid tentacles. Add onion and cook for 5 minutes. Add garlic and cook for another minute.

3 In a bowl, mix the breadcrumbs, anchovies, capers, pine nuts, raisins, 1/2 cup parsley, and the eggs. Add the browned chopped squid, onion, and garlic. Mix well. Season with salt and pepper to taste. Stuff the calamari tubes with the breadcrumb mixture and seal with toothpicks. Place the remaining 2 tablespoons of olive oil in frying pan over medium heat. Add the stuffed squid, and brown on all sides.

4 Add the chopped tomatoes. Season with salt and pepper to taste. Bring to a boil, partially cover and simmer for about 20 minutes.

TO SERVE

Transfer to a serving bowl and garnish with the remaining parsley.

DAMIAN

There are about as many recipes for stuffing calamari in Sicily as there are swordfish in the Straits of Messina. It's way better to use fresh calamari for this. But if you're in a bind and can't find any, frozen will be good too.

JOHNNY

We need to make sure everybody knows this is the whole squid you're stuffing here, not those little rings you get fried in just about every restaurant these days. And the stuffing of anchovies, capers, raisins and pinenuts is terrific.

DAMIAN

With calamari, you either cook them a real short time or a real long time. Anything in between will make them like rubber bands. But when you cook them right, like we do here, there's nothing more delicious.

ORANGE SCALLOPS
Cunchigghie alle Aranchiu e Finocchio

Serves 4

16 sea scallops

1/2 cup all-purpose flour

Kosher salt and freshly-ground black pepper

1/4 cup extra-virgin olive oil

2 shallots, minced

1/2 fennel bulb, thinly sliced, save fronds for garnish

1 clove garlic, thinly sliced

1/4 cup Sambuca liqueur

1 tablespoon orange zest

1/3 cup fresh orange juice

1/2 cup white wine

1 tablespoon unsalted butter, chopped into pieces

2 tablespoons chopped fresh chives

TO PREPARE

1 Clean and rinse the scallops and set aside. Combine the flour with the salt and pepper.

2 In a large skillet, heat oil over medium-high heat. Dredge the scallops in the flour mixture, shaking off any excess. Cook the scallops until they are golden on both sides, being careful not to overcook—it makes them tough. Remove scallops and set aside.

3 Add the shallots and fennel to the sauté pan and cook over medium heat for about 2 minutes.

4 Add garlic and cook 1 minute more. Remove the pan from the heat and add the Sambuca. Return the pan to the heat and add the orange zest, the orange juice, and the wine and simmer until slightly thickened, 3–5 minutes.

5 Whisk in the butter and the chives and add back the scallops long enough to heat through. Turn onto a platter and serve immediately.

DAMIAN

Time after time, dishes are lifted to heaven by just adding the wonderful citrus grown all over the island. Sometimes it's lemon, sometimes it's one or more types of orange, sometimes it's some other citrus. But there's always this incredible sweetness, balanced by the fruit's own natural acidity.

JOHNNY

And while you're busy oohing and ahhing over all those wonderful orange flavors, be careful not to overcook the scallops. There aren't too many things more delicious or more delicate in the whole ocean.

MARINATED MUSSELS
Cozzule alla Marinata

Serves 6-8

3 pounds mussels

1 cup dry white wine

2 tablespoons finely-chopped red onion

1 bay leaf

1 tablespoon finely-chopped fresh fennel fronds

1/4 teaspoon coarsely-ground or crushed black pepper

For the dressing:

2 tablespoons wine vinegar

1/2 cup extra-virgin olive oil

2 tablespoons roasted, peeled, chopped sweet red pepper

2 tablespoons fennel bulb, chopped fine

1 tablespoon capers, in salt or brine, rinsed

1/2 small red onion, finely chopped

1 teaspoon fresh fennel fronds, finely chopped

1/2 cup chopped Italian parsley

Salt and freshly-ground black pepper to taste

TO PREPARE THE MUSSELS

1   Scrub mussels under cold water and remove "beards." Place mussels in a large stockpot along with wine, onion, bay leaf, fennel, and pepper. Cover and steam mussels for about 5 minutes or until they open. Be sure to discard any mussels that do not open.

2   Transfer mussels to a bowl, reserving the steaming liquid. Strain steaming liquid and put it back in the stockpot. Bring the liquid to a boil and reduce it to 1/2 cup. Remove stockpot from heat and allow liquid to cool. Shuck the mussels, reserving the shells, and put mussels in reduced cooled liquid.

3   Place vinegar in a mixing bowl and slowly whisk in olive oil and remaining dressing ingredients. Strain the reduced mussel liquid into the dressing and blend well. Place mussels back in half shell, spoon marinade over the mussels, and marinate for a few hours in the refrigerator. Place mussels on a serving platter.

DAMIAN

We used to serve this dish a lot at my restaurant Damian's, and people would just love it.

JOHNNY

And these mussels are real convenient if you're throwing a party at home, because you can just poach them in advance and keep them a few hours in the refrigerator while they marinate.

DAMIAN

What Johnny really means is: While they keep getting more and more wonderful.

GRILLED TUNA WITH SAUCE OF GREEN HERBS
Tunnu Arrustutu cu Erbe Virdi

Serves 4

For the tuna:

2 anchovy fillets, salt- or oil-packed, rinsed

2 tablespoons extra-virgin olive oil

2 pounds tuna steaks, 3/4- to 1-inch thick

For the sauce:

1/2 cup extra-virgin olive oil

5–6 garlic cloves, minced

2 bay leaves

1 tablespoon lemon zest

5–6 tablespoons finely-chopped fresh herbs, any combination of Italian parsley, rosemary, oregano, thyme, and mint

1 tablespoon capers, salt- or brine-packed, and rinsed

Juice of one lemon

Kosher salt and freshly-ground black pepper to taste

TO PREPARE

1 Mash the anchovies in the olive oil until smooth. Spoon the anchovy oil over the tuna steaks. Let marinate for at least an hour or overnight in the refrigerator.

2 To make the sauce, warm the olive oil, garlic, and bay leaves in a small saucepan over low heat for 2–3 minutes. Remove the sauce pan from the heat, add the remaining ingredients, and mix well. Adjust salt and pepper to taste. Set aside.

3 Over a preheated grill, grill the tuna steaks to desired doneness.

TO SERVE

Serve tuna with the green herb sauce.

NOTE   This sauce is good with most any grilled seafood, shellfish, poultry, or meat.

DAMIAN

Italians from all over the country love green herb sauces, especially on fish. But this one gets a kick in the pants from the anchovies, the capers and that wonderful splash of Sicilian lemon.

JOHNNY

It's a bit like the pesto you find up north in Genoa – you know, the place Columbus came from.

DAMIAN

Be great if while he was off discovering Americans, the Sicilians were discovering a better recipe for pesto. Besides, enough of us would figure out where America was later.

SWORDFISH STEWED WITH TOMATO, POTATOES, OLIVES AND CAPERS
Pisci Spada alla Messinese

Serves 6–8

1/4 cup extra-virgin olive oil

1 red onion, skin removed and cut into 1-inch dice

2 Yukon gold potatoes, diced into 1/2-inch cubes

2 cloves garlic, finely chopped

1 tablespoon fresh sage, chopped

1 tablespoon capers, rinsed of salt or brine, coarsely chopped

1/4 cup green olives, preferably Sicilian, pitted and coarsely chopped

2 cups canned tomatoes, preferably Italian, crushed

2 cups dry white wine

Juice of 1/2 lemon

1 cup water, if needed

Kosher salt and freshly-ground pepper to taste

1-1/2 pounds swordfish, cut into 1-inch cubes

TO PREPARE

1   In a large skillet, heat the olive oil. Add the onion and cook for 2 minutes, stirring so it doesn't burn. Add the potatoes and stir and cook for 2 more minutes.

2   Add the garlic, sage, capers, olives, and tomatoes and stir thoroughly. Add the wine and the lemon juice and season with the salt and pepper.

3   Cover the skillet and reduce heat. Simmer for 15–20 minutes or until the potatoes are tender, adding more water if the liquid has reduced too much (it should be a little saucy). Season the swordfish with salt and pepper and add to skillet, cooking for 8–10 minutes, just until the swordfish is done.

TO SERVE

Transfer the swordfish to a serving platter. Garnish with parsley and serve.

JOHNNY

Seems to me we don't eat enough fish stews in America. I mean, they're some of the best things you can get anywhere along the Mediterranean.

DAMIAN

And this particular fish stew is nothing generic. It's a classic from Messina, the closest point to the mainland, looking at Italy right across those famous straits. Generally in Sicily, the more you add to a stew like this – more potatoes, more tomatoes – the better it gets. In the end, you can just about taste the sunshine.

JOHNNY

And the more hungry mouths you can feed too. Especially served over pasta or rice.

STUFFED ROLLED SWORDFISH
Involtini di Pisci Spada

Serves 4-6

For the stuffing:

1/4 cup extra-virgin olive oil

1 small yellow onion, finely chopped

2 large cloves garlic, finely chopped

3/4 cup Homemade Breadcrumbs, (see page 179)

1/4 cup Italian parsley, finely chopped

3 tablespoons grated caciocavallo or Pecorino Romano cheese

1/4 cup golden raisins or dried currants, soaked in warm water 30 minutes, drained

1/4 cup toasted pine nuts

Kosher salt and freshly-ground black pepper to taste

For the swordfish:

12 slices swordfish, 1/4-inch thick, about 3 x 4 inches

Extra-virgin olive oil

1 cup Homemade Breadcrumbs, (see page 179)

1 large red onion, peeled and quartered

12 fresh bay leaves

TO PREPARE THE STUFFING

1 Place the oil and onion in a medium skillet. Place skillet over medium-low heat.

2 Cook onion until very soft, about 5 minutes. Add garlic and cook 1 minute more.

3 In a mixing bowl, combine the breadcrumbs, the onion-garlic mixture, the parsley, and cheese. Chop the raisins or currants and pine nuts coarsely. Add them to the bowl. Toss, seasoning with salt and pepper. If the stuffing seems a little dry, add a little more olive oil.

TO COOK

1 Soak wooden skewers in water for 1 hour.

2 Light your grill, or preheat your broiler, or preheat your oven to 400°F. Season swordfish lightly with salt. With the widest side facing you, place about 1 tablespoon of stuffing on each slice and roll up.

3 Place a little olive oil on a plate. Put the breadcrumbs on another plate. Roll the swordfish in the oil, then in the breadcrumbs to coat lightly. Peel apart the layers of the onion. Place a slice of onion on a wooden skewer, then a swordfish roll and then a bay leaf. Repeat until you have 4 rolls on each skewer.

4 Drizzle rolls with olive oil. Place on grill turning for 10–15 minutes. Or, broil turning for 10–15 minutes. Or, bake in oven for 15–20 minutes.

TO SERVE

Remove from skewers. Serve with lemon wedges and, if you like, a drizzle of extra-virgin olive oil.

JOHNNY
I think this is one of the best dishes we ever cooked on the show.

DAMIAN
I remember I first tried it in a little village near Palermo called Ferrocavallo. It was a revelation, because Italians don't usually mix cheese with seafood. But down south in Sicily, this is a classic local dish.

CIAO SICILY

SHRIMP IN TOMATO, CAPER AND PINE NUT SAUCE
Gamberetti al Sarsa di Chiappari e Pignoli

Serves 6

2 pounds medium-sized shrimp, peeled and de-veined

1/2 cup extra-virgin olive oil

1 medium red onion, finely chopped

1 small fennel bulb, thinly sliced

2 medium cloves garlic, minced

1 pound very ripe tomatoes or 2 cups drained canned tomatoes, preferably imported Italian

Kosher salt and freshly-ground black pepper to taste

4 tablespoons pine nuts

6 tablespoons capers, salt- or brine-packed, rinsed

8 bay leaves

1 lemon, cut in half

1/4 cup chopped fresh basil leaves

1/4 cup chopped fresh parsley leaves

TO PREPARE

1 Place a Dutch oven on stove with the oil over medium heat. When warm, add the onion and fennel. Sauté for 15 minutes, stirring occasionally with a wooden spoon.
2 Add garlic and stir 1 minute more. Add tomatoes to pan. Cook for 15 minutes, stirring occasionally with a wooden spoon. Season with salt and pepper to taste. Add pine nuts and capers to skillet. Cook for 10 minutes more.
3 Arrange all the shrimp over the sauce. Distribute bay leaves over shrimp, squeeze lemon over shrimp and cook, covered, for 3–5 minutes, depending on size of shrimp. Discard the bay leaves.

TO SERVE

Transfer to a terra cotta serving dish. Serve sprinkled with basil and parsley leaves.

JOHNNY
Everybody's always grilling shrimp these days, D. So why are we here doing just about the exact opposite?
DAMIAN
Simple. Because I like shrimp better cooked this way. Fennel and seafood always work so well together. And I like shrimp best when they're sautéed and then stewed a little bit in this wonderful sauce.
JOHNNY
It's sure not your every day tomato sauce, with all the fennel and capers and pine nuts.

"Every Sicilian family has their own versions of dishes, and they'll be quick to tell you your version is wrong."

CIAO SICILY

Secondi: Carni
MEAT ENTRÉES

Though an island rich in seafood, Sicily features meat in its cuisine in ways both satisfying and symbolic. Surely no one enjoying roast spring lamb as part of an Easter celebration in any Sicilian city, town or village can doubt meat's importance in this culture. The dishes that follow are usually called *Secondi* (Seconds) because, of course, they tend to follow *Primi* (Firsts), but they're also referred to sometimes as *Forti*. This word, meaning "strong" or, in this case, "substantial," says a mouthful about the Sicilian approach. *Secondi* tend to be hearty roasts, braises and stews, not silly little slices of meat that look forlorn in the center of some huge white platter in someplace like California. This is what Sicilian Mammas use to feed their families, good times and bad, from everyday meals to seasonal celebrations. There's a lot of lamb served in Sicily, cooked just about any way you can imagine. There's chicken, as just about everywhere. And there's pork, a wonderful meat all by itself, yet one that finds life's true meaning ground up and turned into sausage. It's not for nothing all the Carrabbas and Mandolas in Texas and Louisiana have at least one relative they can count on for richly seasoned sausage.

GRILLED BUTTERFLIED LEG OF LAMB
Agneddu cu Pipi

Serves 6

1 boned and butterflied leg of lamb, about 3 pounds

2 teaspoons chopped fresh oregano

4 sprigs of fresh rosemary, leaves stripped and chopped

2 teaspoons chopped fresh lemon thyme or thyme

3 cloves garlic, finely chopped

Kosher salt and freshly-ground black pepper to taste

1 cup extra-virgin olive oil

Juice of 2 lemons

6 red sweet peppers, grilled or roasted

TO PREPARE

1 Use a container that is just large enough to hold the lamb. Combine the herbs, garlic, salt, and pepper and rub into meat thoroughly. Pour olive oil over the meat. Turn and coat lamb with olive oil and more freshly-ground black pepper. Squeeze lemon juice over lamb. Cover container and refrigerate for 2–4 hours.

2 Remove the lamb from the refrigerator, and let rest at room temperature for 30 minutes if time permits.

3 Preheat the grill and arrange a rack at least 6 inches away from the coals or gas flame.

4 Cook the meat on the grill until it reaches desired doneness. Remove lamb from grill and allow to rest on a heated platter for a few minutes. Slice into serving pieces.

TO PREPARE PEPPERS

Grill peppers over hot coals, turning frequently until skins blacken on all sides. Remove from grill, put in paper bag, closed tightly, for 5–10 minutes. Remove from bag, and gently scrape away the charred skins, slit peppers and remove seeds, cut peppers into lengthwise strips, and arrange with lamb on the serving platter.

TO SERVE

Arrange lamb on serving platter with grilled sweet red peppers—a delicious combination and a beautiful, colorful dish.

JOHNNY
This is one of those classic Sicilian dishes.

DAMIAN
All the great herbs and the marinating can make any lamb taste like young spring lamb.

JOHNNY
Sicilians like their lamb pretty cooked through, with the wonderful flavors coming from the herbs.

DAMIAN
I like to put some herb stems especially rosemary right onto my hot coals for some mysterious toasted herb flavor.

LAMB STEW
Agneddu Agglassatu

Serves 4–6

2 cinnamon sticks

5 thyme sprigs

Small bunch parsley

4 strips bacon, chopped into small pieces

3 pounds lamb shoulder, cut into
1-inch cubes

Kosher salt and freshly-ground black pepper

1 cup flour

6 cloves garlic, minced

2 cups full-bodied red wine

1 (35-ounce) can imported Italian tomatoes with juice, crushed

1 cup pitted green olives, preferably Sicilian

2 bay leaves

5-1/2 cups chicken stock

TO PREPARE

1 Preheat oven to 300°F.

2 Tie cinnamon sticks, thyme, and the parsley in a bundle with kitchen string. In a large pot over medium-high heat, cook the bacon. Remove bacon, leaving the bacon fat in the pot.

3 Season the lamb with salt and pepper, dredge in flour and then brown in the bacon fat. Add garlic, cooking for about 2 minutes, then pour in the wine and reduce liquid by half. Add the tomatoes, green olives, bay leaves, salt, and pepper along with the bundle of seasonings and the bacon. Cook for 5 minutes.

4 Add the chicken stock to the stew, bring to a boil, reduce heat to simmer, re-season with salt and pepper, then partially cover and cook in oven for 2–2-1/2 hours.

TO SERVE

Remove the bay leaves and seasoning bundle from the stew. Taste and adjust seasoning. Serve in large soup bowls with crusty Italian bread and a crisp green salad.

DAMIAN

My mother always made wonderful lamb stews. Growing up, I'd bring friends over who'd never tasted lamb, and they would love it. This is based on my mother's recipe. There's nothing better than lamb stew to make a man feel Sicilian.

JOHNNY

Well, I feel Sicilian already, but everybody needs a booster shot every now and then.

LAMB CHOPS ARNO
Costolette di Agneddu

Serves 4

8 center cut lamb chops

Kosher salt and freshly-ground black pepper to taste

1/4 cup extra-virgin olive oil

1 teaspoon minced garlic

1 teaspoon chopped fresh rosemary

1 teaspoon anchovy paste

1 cup red wine

1 tablespoon good-quality balsamic vinegar

2 tablespoons butter

TO PREPARE

1 Preheat oven to 200°F.

2 Season lamb chops with salt and pepper. Heat oil in a large skillet and brown lamb chops rapidly on both sides over medium-high heat (approximately 4 minutes per side for medium rare).

3 Remove chops to warm plate and put into oven while you complete the sauce. You may have to cook chops in batches. Add garlic, rosemary, and anchovy paste to the skillet and cook, stirring, for 1 minute.

4 Add red wine and vinegar to the skillet and deglaze the pan, scraping up all the pan drippings, reducing the sauce to a slightly syrupy consistency. Lower heat. Add cold butter and stir until melted, and adjust for salt and pepper.

5 Remove chops from oven and return to pan for 2 minutes, turning them in the sauce.

TO SERVE

Remove chops to serving platter and top with sauce.

DAMIAN
There used to be this restaurant in Houston in the 70s, called Arno's — yes, the same name as the river that runs through Florence up in Tuscany. Janice Arno Beeson always had these lamb chops on her menu. I fell in love with — and barrowed the recipe.

JOHNNY
Yeah, Arno's was a really great restaurant.

PORK CHOPS
WITH CAPER SAUCE
Cutuletta di Maiali cu Sarsa di Chiappare

Serves 4

4 lean center-cut pork chops,
1-1/4 inches thick

Kosher salt and freshly-ground
pepper to taste

1 tablespoon extra-virgin olive oil

1/2 cup finely-chopped yellow onions

2 teaspoons finely-chopped garlic

2 teaspoons red wine vinegar

1 cup chicken broth

4 tablespoons capers, drained and rinsed

1 tablespoon Dijon mustard

1 tablespoon tomato paste

1 tablespoon finely-chopped fresh rosemary

1 tablespoon butter

4 tablespoons finely-chopped fresh parsley

TO PREPARE

1   Sprinkle the chops with salt and pepper. In a skillet large enough to hold the chops in one layer, heat the olive oil over medium-high flame.

2   Add the chops and cook until lightly browned, approximately 7 minutes, then turn and cook the other side. Remove chops, set aside, and keep warm. Pour off the excess fat from the skillet.

3   Add the onions and garlic to the skillet and cook until wilted. Add the vinegar and reduce by half. Add the chicken broth, capers, mustard, tomato paste, and rosemary. Cook and reduce by half.

4   Remove the sauce from the heat and add any juices that may have accumulated around the pork chops. Swirl the butter with the sauce and adjust salt and pepper according to taste.

TO SERVE

Spoon the sauce over the meat and sprinkle with parsley.

DAMIAN
I love pork or veal with caper sauces.

JOHNNY
And if you're on a budget, pork is cheaper.

DAMIAN
Try to find capers that are packed in salt.
They have a much better flavor.

PORK LOIN ROASTED with GARLIC, ROSEMARY and FENNEL
Arrustu di Maiali

Serves 8–10

12 large cloves garlic

3 tablespoons rosemary leaves

2 teaspoons fennel seed, toasted and lightly crushed

1-1/2 tablespoons kosher salt

1-1/2 tablespoons freshly-ground black pepper

2 pounds russet potatoes, peeled and cut into 1-inch cubes

3 tablespoons extra-virgin olive oil

4 pounds center cut pork loin, boned with a little fat left on the loin, reserve the rib rack

TO PREPARE:

1 Preheat oven to 375°F.

2 Chop the garlic, rosemary, and fennel together on a cutting board, remove to a bowl and combine with the salt and ground pepper.

3 In a separate bowl, toss the potatoes with the 2 tablespoons of the olive oil and 2 tablespoons of the herb mixture.

4 Place the loin on a cutting board and butterfly open. Rub 1 tablespoon of the herb mixture over the inside surface. Fold the loin over the herb mixture length wise and tie every 2 inches with butcher string. Make a few punctures in the outside of the loin with a small knife, about 1/2-inch deep, and stuff the holes with a little of the herb mixture.

5 Rub the remaining herb mixture over the outside of the loin and the rib rack. Place the loin in a roasting pan and cover the loin with the rib rack. Roast approximately 30 minutes.

6 Remove the loin from the oven and set the rib rack to the side of the loin, curved side up.

7 Add the potatoes to the pan, return to the oven and continue roasting for 30 minutes, then increase heat to 450°F and roast for another 10–20 minutes or until the internal temperature is 145°F.

8 Remove from the oven and let rest 10 minutes before slicing. Remove the strings and slice loin and cut the rack into ribs.

TO SERVE

Arrange individual plates with 3 slices of loin, 2 ribs and some potatoes. Pour the roasting juices over the loin and serve.

DAMIAN
Here's a dish that's similar to one beloved up in Tuscany, except down in Sicily they have all that wonderful fennel. Be careful you don't overcook this one, since pork is a very lean meat.

JOHNNY
Yeah, you might want to use a meat thermometer to be sure. That way you can take the pork's temperature.

GRILLED PORK TENDERLOIN
Controfiletto di Maiale Ripieno

Serves 4

4 pieces pork tenderloin, each about 4 inches long

3 ounces prosciutto, finely diced

3 ounces provolone cheese, finely chopped

1 tablespoon chopped fresh parsley

2 tablespoon extra-virgin olive oil

1-1/2 tablespoons chopped garlic

1-1/2 teaspoons chopped fresh sage leaves

1 tablespoon crushed red pepper flakes

Kosher salt and freshly-ground black pepper to taste

TO PREPARE

1 Remove all of the membrane that covers the pork and make a lengthwise slit in the middle of each piece with a long, thin-bladed knife.

2 In a small bowl, mix the prosciutto, provolone, and parsley. Stuff the slit of the tenderloin pieces with this mixture, pressing well with your fingers. Hold closed with a toothpick, or truss with kitchen string.

3 Brush the tenderloin pieces with 1 tablespoon of oil and roll them in a mixture of the chopped garlic, sage, and pepper flakes until well coated. Wrap with plastic wrap and refrigerate for a few hours to allow flavors to penetrate the meat.

4 Preheat the grill and arrange a rack at least 3 inches away from the coals or gas flame. Remove the pork from the refrigerator, brush with the remaining oil and sprinkle with salt and pepper.

5 Cook the meat on the grill until it reaches desired doneness. Let rest on a heated platter for a few minutes before serving.

DAMIAN
I love pork any way I can get it.

JOHNNY
And believe me, this is one great way to get it.

DAMIAN
And when I change things up a little and cook it with Mamma's Sunday Gravy, I wish every day could be Sunday.

ROAST PORK SHANKS
Stinco di Maiali al Furnu

Serves 4

For the marinade:

4 pork shanks, cut into 2-inch bone lengths, from the meaty part of the shank, trimmed of as much fat as possible (you may have your butcher do this)

1 teaspoon kosher salt

1/2 teaspoon freshly-ground pepper

2 cups dry red wine

6 juniper berries, crushed

1 orange peel, cut into long pieces

1 tablespoon chopped fresh rosemary

1 tablespoon chopped fresh sage

For the roasting:

3/4 cup extra-virgin olive oil

2 large red onions, thinly sliced

2 cups canned imported Italian tomatoes;

2 pounds potatoes, peeled and cut into 1-inch cubes

For the herbed breadcrumbs:

1 cup Homemade Breadcrumbs (see page 179)

1/4 cup extra-virgin olive oil

1 tablespoon orange zest

1 clove garlic

4 whole fresh sage leaves

1/4 cup fresh parsley leaves

Kosher salt and freshly-ground black pepper

TO PREPARE THE MARINADE

Place the shanks in large non-reactive dish and season with salt and pepper. Add wine, juniper berries, orange peel, and the herbs and combine well, turning the shanks in the marinade so they are completely covered. Cover and refrigerate overnight or for at least 4 hours, turning occasionally.

TO COOK

1 Preheat oven 350°F.

2 Put 1/4 cup olive oil in a frying pan and bring to medium heat. Add onions and let cook about 10 minutes until caramelized, turning with a wooden spoon as they cook. Meanwhile, drain the shanks, reserving the marinade, and pat dry with a paper towel.

3 Heat 1/2 cup of the olive oil in a large Dutch oven over medium-high heat, add the shanks and brown thoroughly. Add the caramelized onions, tomatoes, potatoes, and reserved marinade, bring to a boil. Season to taste with salt and pepper.

4 Put the lid on the pan and roast in the oven for 2 hours, occasionally turning and basting shanks with sauce. Remove the lid and roast uncovered for another 30 minutes.

5 During the last 30 minutes of roasting, prepare the topping.

6 Put breadcrumbs into a mixing bowl, and add the olive oil and orange zest and combine. Chop garlic, sage, and parsley together, add to breadcrumbs. Adjust salt and pepper to taste.

TO SERVE

Remove the Dutch oven from the oven and place the shanks and vegetables on a large platter with all the sauce. Sprinkle with the herbed breadcrumbs and serve.

DAMIAN

Stinco is Italian for shank. It's not an attractive name in English, I guess, but it sure does taste good.

JOHNNY

I really love the herbed breadcrumbs on top. They give the dish a nice crunch and a real good flavor — plus it's just something Sicilians love to do.

ROLLED STUFFED FLANK STEAK
Farsumagru

Serves 8–10

4 pounds beef flank steak

Kosher salt and freshly-ground black pepper to taste

1/2 pound prosciutto, thinly sliced

1/4 pound provolone, thinly sliced

1/2 pound ground beef

1/2 pound Italian sausage, removed from casings

1 egg, beaten

1/2 cup grated Pecorino Romano cheese

1/2 cup fresh or frozen peas

1/4 cup finely-chopped Italian parsley

2 cloves garlic, finely diced

1 small onion, finely diced

1/4 cup plus 2 tablespoons extra-virgin olive oil

8 eggs, hardboiled

1/4 cup flour

1 cup dry red wine

5 tablespoons tomato paste

1-1/2 cups chicken or beef stock.

TO PREPARE

1 Preheat the over to 350°F.

2 Place the flank steak between two pieces of plastic wrap and gently pound the meat, being careful to keep the rectangular shape and to avoid tearing the meat. Spread the meat on a flat working surface, grain running left to right. Season lightly with salt and pepper

3 Put the slices of prosciutto and provolone on top of the meat, overlapping the slices down the length of the meat and leaving a 1-inch border.

4 In a large mixing bowl combine the ground beef, sausage, egg, grated Pecorino Romano cheese, peas, parsley, garlic, onion, salt, pepper, and 2 tablespoons of the olive oil and combine well. Spread the mixture over the prosciutto and provolone.

5 Remove the shells from the hardboiled eggs. Trim the tips of the eggs to reveal the yolks and lay the eggs lengthwise on top of the prosciutto, provolone and spread mixture, near the end closest to you.

6 Roll meat carefully, tucking in the edges burrito style. Tie together with kitchen string. Heat the remaining olive oil in a large sauté pan until very hot. Dust the meat roll with flour and add to the sauté pan, searing on all sides about 2 minutes a side. Remove the meat from the sauté pan and set aside.

7 Add the wine to the pan and cook for 10 minutes or so, scraping the brown bits from the pan and allowing the wine to reduce. Combine the tomato paste and the stock and add to the wine reduction, cooking for 2–3 minutes.

8 Put the meat in a roasting pan and add enough sauce to reach about halfway up the side of the meat roll. Save the remaining sauce for possible later use. Cover the pan with foil and place in the oven and cook for 1–1-1/2 hours or until done, turning and basting the meat with the sauce every 30 minutes. Add additional sauce if needed.

9 Remove from the oven, cool to room temperature, cover and refrigerate overnight.

TO SERVE

1 Preheat oven to 350°F.

2 Cut the twine and slice the meat, 1/2-inch thick and arrange in a casserole. Remove any congealed fat from the sauce and spoon over steak slices. Warm in oven covered for 30 minutes and serve.

SICILIAN POT ROAST
Arrustu di Carni

Serves 4–6

2-1/2–3 pounds boneless beef chuck roast

Kosher salt and freshly-ground black pepper to taste

Flour for dredging

3 tablespoons extra-virgin olive oil

2 tablespoons melted butter

3 pounds onions, peeled and sliced

3 bay leaves

6 cloves garlic, sliced

1 teaspoon crushed red pepper flakes

2 teaspoons chopped fresh thyme

2-1/2 cups dry white wine

1 cup dry Marsala wine

4 cups chicken stock

TO PREPARE

1 Season the roast with salt and pepper, then coat with flour, shaking off excess. Put 2 tablespoons of olive oil in a Dutch oven on medium heat and brown the roast on all sides.

2 Transfer the roast after browning to a large bowl and set aside. In the Dutch oven, combine the remaining olive oil and the butter. Sauté the onions, bay leaves, garlic, red pepper flakes, thyme, and 1 teaspoon of salt. Cook, stirring occasionally, for about 5 minutes, or until the onions are soft .

3 Add the white wine and Marsala, increase heat to high and bring to a boil, stirring continually, for 6–8 minutes and reduce by half. Add the browned roast along with any juices that have accumulated in the bowl.

4 Add enough chicken stock to reach about halfway up the side of roast and bring to a boil. Reduce heat to low, cover and simmer for 2 hours, turning meat every 30 minutes. Remove the meat to a carving board to rest and increase the heat under the Dutch oven to high.

5 Bring the sauce to a boil, stirring frequently, and cook until reduced by half, about 30 minutes, and sauce is quite thick and light brown in color. Adjust seasoning.

TO SERVE

Cut the meat in thin slices and arrange on a large platter with sauce on the side.

DAMIAN
We love doing pot roasts. In this case, the Marsala from Sicily gives a certain nuttiness and sweetness.

JOHNNY
And be sure to cook this meat until it just falls apart with your fork. The flavor is amazing.

CITRUS CHICKEN
Gaddina all'Agrumi

Serves 4–6

1 whole chicken, cut into 8 pieces

Kosher salt and freshly-ground black pepper to taste

1 tablespoon chopped fresh rosemary

2 cloves garlic, thinly sliced

2 tablespoons olive oil

2 bay leaves

5 oranges

1 lemon

TO PREPARE

1 Season the chicken with salt, pepper, and rosemary.

2 Zest 2 oranges and the lemon. Juice the oranges and lemon and remove seeds. Set zest and juice aside until needed.

3 In a large skillet over medium heat, add the chicken, skin-side down, making sure not to overcrowd.

4 When the skin-side is browned, approximately 5–6 minutes, turn and cook the other side, for 3–4 minutes. Add the garlic and bay leaves, and cook for 1 minute. Add the orange and lemon zest and juice. Cover and continue to cook another 15 minutes or until chicken is cooked through.

TO SERVE

Discard the bay leaves and use a slotted spoon to transfer the chick to a warm platter. Pour the sauce over the chicken and serve.

DAMIAN

Ah, that Sicilian love of citrus again. It's a real simple dish, with wonderful flavors.

JOHNNY

I don't think anybody's going to complain about how simple it is. Not after they taste it, for sure.

COUSCOUS WITH CHICKEN AND SEAFOOD
Couscous alla Trapanese

Serves 6

For the couscous:

6 cups chicken stock

2 bay leaves

Pinch of saffron

1/2 teaspoon kosher salt

1/2 teaspoon freshly-ground black pepper

4 cups instant couscous

1/4 cup chopped fresh parsley

For the stew:

1 red onion, chopped

1/4 cup extra-virgin olive oil

6 cloves garlic, minced

4 tablespoons tomato paste

3 cups chicken stock

1-1/2 pounds tomatoes, blanched, peeled, seeded, and coarsely chopped

12 leaves fresh basil, torn

1/2 cup parsley, coarsely chopped

Kosher salt and freshly-ground pepper to taste

1 3-pound chicken, cut into 14 pieces (see page 113)

1-1/2 pounds halibut, cut into 6 pieces

2 pounds calamari, cleaned and cut into 1/2-inch rings

1 pound large shrimp, cleaned with the tails left on

TO PREPARE THE COUSCOUS

1 In a large saucepan over medium-high heat, bring the chicken stock to a simmer. Add the bay leaves, saffron, salt, and pepper and cook for 5 minutes.

2 Spread the couscous over the bottom of a 9 x 13-inch baking dish. Pour the stock over couscous and gently stir with a fork. Cover with plastic wrap and let couscous sit for 10–15 minutes.

TO PREPARE THE STEW

1 In a large saucepan over medium heat, sauté the onion in the olive oil until soft, approximately 5 minutes. Add garlic and cook another 2–3 minutes. Add the tomato paste and cook an additional 3 minutes.

2 Add the chicken stock, tomatoes, basil, and parsley. Bring to a simmer and season with the salt and pepper. Cook until reduced by half, about 30 minutes. Season the chicken, add to the stock and cook for 20 minutes.

3 Add the halibut and calamari to the stock and cook for another 10 minutes, or until the seafood is cooked. Add the shrimp and cook for another 5 minutes.

TO SERVE

Fluff the couscous with a fork and spread on a serving platter. Pour the stew with the chicken and seafood over the bed of couscous. Garnish with chopped parsley.

CHICKEN BREAST STUFFED
WITH ITALIAN SAUSAGE
Involtini di Gaddina

Serves 4

For the chicken breast:

2 bunches fresh baby spinach, stems removed, washed in 2 or 3 changes of cold water

1 small yellow onion, finely chopped

2 cloves garlic, finely chopped

1/4 cup extra-virgin olive oil

3/4 pound Italian sausage, removed from casing

1/2 cup grated Parmigiano Reggiano cheese

1 egg

Kosher salt and freshly-ground black pepper to taste

8 chicken breast halves, with skin, bones and cartilage removed

For cooking:

1/2 cup flour

2 tablespoons unsalted butter

1/4 cup olive oil

1/2 cup dry Marsala wine

1/4 cup chicken stock

1 stick (4 ounces) cold butter, cut into 8 pieces

Kosher salt and freshly-ground black pepper to taste

TO PREPARE THE CHICKEN

1 Place washed spinach, with leaves still wet, in a large pot over medium heat. Cover pot and steam spinach. When wilted, drain the spinach, and run under cold water to cool completely. Squeeze out as much liquid as possible. Chop fine.

2 Sauté the onion and garlic in the olive oil in a medium-sized pan over medium heat. When the onions are translucent, add the sausage and stir well to break up the sausage meat. Cook until the meat loses its pink color.

3 Add the chopped spinach to the sausage and cook, stirring for 2 more minutes. Season to taste with salt and pepper. Remove mixture from heat, transfer to a mixing bowl and let cool.

4 Stir in the grated cheese and the egg and mix well. Taste and adjust seasoning if necessary.

5 Butterfly each chicken breast half by cutting almost in half horizontally. Lightly pound each breast between sheets of plastic wrap to a level degree of flatness. Lightly season the chicken with salt and pepper.

6 Place approximately 2 tablespoons of the filling near the widest side of each breast half and roll tightly to enclose the filling, tucking in the edges burrito-style as you go. Place the chicken on a sheet pan, cover and refrigerate for 2–3 hours or overnight to help the *involtini* to hold their shape while cooking.

TO COOK

1 Heat the butter and the olive oil in large skillet over medium heat. Lightly season the chicken with salt and pepper and dredge the rolls in flour, shaking off any excess. Sauté the chicken for 8–10 minutes until it is lightly browned on all sides.

2 Tilt the skillet and drain out all but 2 tablespoons of the fat. Add the Marsala and the chicken stock to the skillet and cook, stirring and scraping the pan to deglaze. Let liquid reduce until all but about 1/4 cup remains. Reduce heat to low.

3 Add cold butter 2 pieces at a time and shake and swirl pan, adding 2 more pieces of butter as the previously added butter melts and the sauce becomes creamy. Do not raise heat and boil sauce or the sauce will "break." When all of the butter has been incorporated and the sauce is creamy, taste and adjust seasoning.

TO SERVE

Place the chicken on a serving platter. Pour sauce over the chicken and serve.

DAMIAN
This has got to be one of our Top 10 favorite dishes at Carrabba's. We only have it as a special maybe once a month, and people go crazy for it.

JOHNNY
And like every good Sicilian son, I'm here to tell you my daddy makes the best Italian sausage.

CHICKEN HUNTER'S WIFE STYLE
Gaddina alla Cacciatura

Serves 4

3-pound frying chicken

1/4 cup extra-virgin olive oil

Kosher salt and freshly ground black pepper to taste

1/2 cup flour

1 small red onion, sliced 1/4-inch thick

1 leek, cleaned, with white and some green, sliced 1/4-inch thick

1 small carrot, peeled and cut into 1/4-inch pieces

1 small red or yellow bell pepper, seeded and cut into 3/4-inch pieces

2 cloves garlic, finely chopped

1/2 pound mixed mushrooms, stemmed shiitake, cremini, chanterelle, or domestic, sliced 1/4-inch thick

1/2 cup dry white wine

1/4 cup chicken stock

1 cup canned Italian plum tomatoes with juice, crushed fine by hand

3 whole medium tomatoes, peeled and seeded

1/4 cup fresh or frozen peas

1 teaspoon chopped fresh thyme leaves

2 tablespoons chopped fresh Italian parsley leaves

TO PREPARE THE FRYER

1 Wash chicken inside and out and dry thoroughly. Turn breast side down. Cut down both sides of backbone and remove for stock.

2 Cut chicken in half by cutting down the center of the breast. Remove breasts from the thighs and legs. Cut off the wings from the breasts, leaving some of the breast meat with the wings. Cut off wing tips. Reserve tips for stock.

3 Cut breasts in half crosswise. Separate legs from the thighs. Cut the thighs in half across the thighbone. Cut off the leg ends where they start to widen, saving the thin ends for stock. Cut the meaty part of the leg in half across the leg bone. You should now have 14 pieces. Your chicken is now ready to cook.

TO COOK

1 Heat oil in a 12-inch skillet over medium-high heat until very hot. Season chicken with salt and pepper. Dredge lightly in flour. Shake off excess flour. Add to hot oil skin side down. Leave chicken undisturbed for 4–5 minutes or until well browned. Turn and brown chicken very well on the other side. Remove the chicken to a platter.

2 Add the onion, leek, carrot, and bell pepper to the sauté pan. Season with salt and pepper and cook for 5 minutes. Add the garlic and cook 1 minute. Add the mushrooms and cook 3 more minutes, stirring frequently.

3 Return the chicken to the pan along with any juices that may have accumulated on the plate. Add the wine and reduce for 2 minutes. Add the stock, tomatoes, and the peas.

4 Reduce the heat to a simmer and cook, turning every few minutes, until the chicken is cooked through, about 15 minutes. Stir in the thyme and parsley. Adjust seasoning. Transfer to a warm platter and serve.

RABBIT IN SWEET AND TART SAUCE
Cunigghiu all' Agru-Duci

Serves 4

3-pound rabbit, cut into pieces
1/2 cup capers in brine or salt, rinsed
1 cup pitted prunes
1 cup green olives, preferably Sicilian
3/4 cup extra-virgin olive oil
1 cup red wine vinegar
2 cups dry white wine
4 cloves garlic, minced
3 bay leaves
3 tablespoons minced fresh oregano
2-1/2 teaspoons kosher salt
1 teaspoon black pepper
1/4 cup brown sugar
1 cup almond flour

TO PREPARE

1   In a deep dish, add capers, prunes, green olives, olive oil, vinegar, wine, garlic, bay leaves, oregano, salt, and pepper. Marinate rabbit overnight in dish. Save marinade.

2   Preheat oven to 325°F.

3   Pat rabbit dry. In a medium skillet, brown rabbit pieces in a little olive oil and transfer to an ovenproof casserole dish. Pour marinade over rabbit. Sprinkle brown sugar and almond flour over rabbit. Cover casserole dish. Bake 2–3 hours, until rabbit is tender and falls off the bone. Serve in casserole dish.

DAMIAN

The Sicilian sweet and sour thing works well for lighter meats like rabbit, pork and veal. If rabbit isn't part of your repertoire, you should try it. It's delicious.

JOHNNY

And cooking the rabbit with the bone-in, gives a better flavor.

ROASTED RABBIT WITH OLIVE OIL~HERB SAUCE
Arrustu di Cunigghiu all' Salmorighiu

Serves 4–6

4 cloves garlic, minced

1/4 cup fresh oregano, coarsely chopped with the stems removed

1 teaspoon kosher salt

1 teaspoon freshly-ground black pepper

1 rabbit (about 3 pounds), cut into 8 pieces

1/2 cup extra-virgin olive oil

1/2 cup Italian parsley, coarsely chopped with the stems removed

1/4 cup lemon juice

Zest from 1 lemon

1 teaspoon crushed red pepper flakes

Salt and pepper to taste

3–4 slices bacon or pancetta

TO PREPARE

1   Combine half the garlic, 1 tablespoon of the oregano, salt, and pepper. Rub the rabbit with the mixture and let marinate in the refrigerator for 2 hours or overnight. Remove the rabbit from the refrigerator and let it come to room temperature before cooking.

2   Preheat oven to 450°F.

3   Heat the oil in a small saucepan over medium heat. Add the remaining garlic and cook, until just softened and fragrant. Remove from heat and let cool.

4   Add the chopped parsley, remaining oregano, lemon juice, lemon zest, and pepper flakes to the olive oil and garlic and mix well. Place the rabbit in a baking dish and drizzle a little less than half of the lemon juice mixture over the rabbit until well coated. Lay bacon strips over rabbit.

5   Cook in the oven for about 20 minutes, until the rabbit begins to brown. Spread the rest of the lemon juice mixture over the rabbit and continue roasting until cooked through, approximately 20–30 minutes.

TO SERVE

Serve on a platter with pan juices spooned over the top.

DAMIAN

In this case, you use the salmorighiu to cook the rabbit in. It gives such a nice piquancy to the light and tender white meat.

JOHNNY

And to make it really pop right out at you, add some chopped olives and some more fresh herbs right at the end.

VEAL RIB ROAST
Arrustu di Viteddu

Serves 4–6

3–4-pound bone-in veal rib roast

Kosher salt and freshly-ground
black pepper to taste

2 tablespoons extra-virgin olive oil

3 Italian sausages, cut into thirds

1 medium red onion, coarsely chopped

2 medium carrots, peeled and coarsely
chopped

2 stalks celery, sliced into 1-inch chunks

2 tablespoons chopped fresh Italian parsley

2 tablespoons chopped fresh sage

1/2 cup dry white wine

TO PREPARE:

1 Preheat the oven to 350°F.

2 Season the veal with the salt and pepper. Heat the olive oil over medium heat in a roasting pan.

3 Add the veal to the pan and brown on all sides, approximately 3 minutes per side. Remove the veal from the pan and set aside.

4 Add the sausage to the roasting pan and brown. Add onion, carrots, and celery to the pan, along with half the parsley and the sage, and cook for several minutes.

5 Add the wine to the vegetables and deglaze the pan, scraping the brown bits from the bottom. Remove the pan from heat.

6 Put the rib roast back into the roasting pan and place in the preheated oven. Cook for 1 hour, turning the roast every 15 minutes. Remove the roast from the oven and place on serving platter, letting it rest for 10 minutes before carving, preserving the juices in the roasting pan.

7 Heat the roasting pan with the juices, add the rest of the herbs and pour over the sliced meat.

DAMIAN
I love this dish!
JOHNNY
I do too. You get that nice flavor from the sauce and the herbs. It's one of our favorite dishes to cook at home.
DAMIAN
And of course the sausage gives the lean veal a real nice punch.

VEAL STEW WITH FENNEL AND ORANGE

Spezzateddu di Viteddu cu Finocchiu e Aranciu

Serves 4

2 pounds veal shoulder, cut into 1-inch cubes

Kosher salt and freshly-ground black pepper to taste

1/4 cup extra-virgin olive oil

4 ounces pancetta, cubed

1 medium red onion, finely chopped

2 fennel bulbs, quartered and then halved

2 cloves garlic, lightly crushed

2 tablespoons tomato paste

4 large tomatoes, peeled, seeded, and coarsely chopped

4 ounces whole green olives, preferably Sicilian, slightly crushed

1/2 cup dry white wine

1-1/2 cups chicken stock

1 orange, juice and zest

2 tablespoons chopped fresh oregano

3 tablespoons chopped fresh Italian parsley

TO PREPARE

1 Preheat oven to 350°F.

2 Season the veal with the salt and pepper. Heat the olive oil in an ovenproof casserole over medium-high heat. Add the seasoned veal and brown on all sides. Remove veal from pan and set aside. Add the pancetta, onion, and fennel the casserole and cook until lightly browned.

3 Add garlic, cook for 1–2 minutes. Add the tomato paste and cook for 2 minutes.

4 Return veal to the casserole along with the tomatoes, olives, wine, chicken stock, orange juice, half of the oregano and parsley.

5 Bring to a boil, season with salt and pepper, cover and place in the oven and cook for 1–1-1/2 hours or until meat is tender. Add the rest of the herbs and the orange zest. Adjust seasoning. Serve immediately.

DAMIAN

Now this is a very Sicilian dish. The fennel and orange go together so well, especially with the delicate veal.

JOHNNY

Sicilians being the kings of citrus, they think of using it with just about everything.

VEAL SHANKS WITH ARTICHOKE SAUCE
Ossobuco cu Cacuocciulu

Serves 4

For the sauce:

6 artichokes, cleaned, trimmed and quartered

1 lemon

4 veal shanks, about 3 pounds

Kosher salt and freshly-ground black pepper

1/2 cup flour

1/4 cup extra-virgin olive oil

2 carrots, peeled and finely diced

1 small yellow onion, finely diced

2 celery stalks, finely diced

2 bay leaves

1 tablespoon chopped fresh thyme

4 cloves garlic, minced

2 tablespoons tomato paste

1 pound fresh tomatoes, peeled and seeded

2 cups dry white wine

3 cups chicken stock

For the gremolata:

1 tablespoon capers, rinsed and chopped

1 tablespoon pine nuts, toasted

1 cup chopped fresh parsley leaves

Zest of 2 lemons

1 teaspoon kosher salt and freshly-ground black pepper to taste

5 Sicilian black olives, pitted and minced

2 cloves garlic, minced

TO PREPARE

1 Preheat oven to 300°F.

2 Soak the artichokes in a bowl of cold water with the juice of 1 lemon. Season the shanks with salt and pepper. Dust with flour and brown in olive oil in a pot just large enough to hold the shanks. Remove and set aside.

3 Reduce heat to medium, add carrots, onion, celery, drained artichokes, bay leaves, thyme, and garlic. Cook until golden and slightly soft. Add tomato paste and stir to coat. Add tomatoes and cook 2 minutes more.

4 Add wine and reduce by about half. Return veal shanks to the pot, add enough chicken stock just to cover and return to a boil. Cover with a heavy lid and place in the oven for 2-1/2 hours, basting about every 30 minutes. Remove lid and cook uncovered for 30 minutes more.

TO SERVE

Prepare *gremolata* by combing all ingredients in a medium bowl. Adjust seasoning. Serve veal shanks with *gremolata*.

DAMIAN

I'm sure Sicilians started loving these tough cuts of meat because they were cheaper than the tender cuts. But I love them because they have more flavor. I remember my grandmother eating veal shanks when I was a little boy. And believe me, she didn't leave much on or in the bone.

JOHNNY

And artichokes are so good in these long, slow-braised dishes. You cook the shank until the meat cooks right off the bone.

DAMIAN

It's classic Sicilian cooking, the perfect thing for a cold winter night. The uncooked gremolata condiment contributes an interesting crisp texture to the earthy, slow-cooked ossobuco.

ELEPHANT EAR VEAL CHOPS
Orecchi di Elefante alla Savit

Serves 4

For the salad:

1 small red onion

1/2 pound fresh ripe tomatoes, seeded and diced

1/4 pound baby arugula

6 radishes

3 tablespoons, extra-virgin olive oil

1 tablespoon lemon juice, freshly squeezed

Kosher salt and freshly-ground black pepper to taste

Parmigiano Reggiano cheese to taste

For the veal chops:

4 (12-ounce) veal rib chops

4 eggs, lightly beaten

1/4 teaspoon of kosher salt

2 cups Homemade Breadcrumbs (see page 179)

3 cloves garlic, finely chopped

1/2 cup finely-chopped fresh Italian parsley

Kosher salt and freshly-ground black pepper to taste

Extra-virgin olive oil for frying

TO PREPARE THE SALAD

1 Peel and thinly slice the red onion and soak in a bowl of cold water for 30 minutes.

2 Place the diced tomatoes in a mixing bowl. Wash arugula, removing any large stems, spin dry and add to the bowl with the tomatoes. Wash the radishes, trim ends, slice into thin rounds and add to the tomatoes and arugula. Set bowl in the refrigerator.

TO PREPARE THE VEAL

1 Preheat oven to 350°F.

2 Remove the meat and fat from along the rib leading up to the main eye of the rib (a process called *Frenching*). Place the chops flat between two pieces of plastic wrap and pound until only 1/4-inch thick.

3 In a large bowl, season the eggs with salt, add the chops and let them to soak for about 30 minutes. In a separate bowl, combine the breadcrumbs with the garlic, parsley, salt, and pepper.

4 Heat enough olive oil to cover the bottom of a large 12–14 inch nonstick skillet over medium-high heat. While the oil is heating, remove 2 chops from the eggs and coat well on both sides with the breadcrumb mixture.

5 Fry the chops in the olive oil, turning only once, until lightly golden on each side, about 2–3 minutes per side. Transfer the chops to a small sheet pan and dab with paper towels to remove excess oil.

6 Discard the skillet oil, wipe clean and repeat with the other two chops. Place the sheet pan with the four chops in the oven for 5–6 minutes to finish cooking around the bone.

7 Drain onions and lightly squeeze dry, and add to the arugula salad. Add olive oil, salt, and pepper and toss. Add lemon juice and toss again.

TO SERVE

Remove chops from the oven. Divide chops on 4 plates. Re-toss the salad, mound on top of each chop and serve.

NOTE   Shaved Parmigiano Reggiano cheese makes a nice addition to the salad.

"Nothing wrong with starting at dessert and working backwards. Especially in Sicily."

CIAO ✱ SICILY

Dolci DESSERTS

Call them Saracens, call them Moors or call them Arabs—but don't call them late for dessert. To this day, the Arab influence on Sicily is perhaps clearest in the sweet tooth—we mean, the *very* sweet tooth—possessed by anyone who ever learned to eat there. In fact, a century after the last great immigrations, Americans of Sicilian descent continue to think it's entirely fine to enjoy a dessert sweetened with fresh and dried fruit, nuts, honey, and plenty of sugar. In this, they share taste buds not only with the sweet-crazed modern Arab world but with other cultures influenced by the Ottoman Empire. Think of Greeks downing baklava, for instance. Italian restaurants in America were for years best known at dessert time for two Sicilian favorites, *cannoli* and *cassata*. But ask any Sicilian mamma: the island has a lot more desserts than those.

ORANGES WITH WINE SAUCE
Arancie al Vino

Serves 12

8 navel oranges

1 tangerine and/or 1 lemon, sliced and unpeeled

3 cups full-bodied red wine

1/2 cup hot water

1 cup granulated sugar

2 tablespoons whole cloves

4 sticks cinnamon

1/2 cup slivered or crushed almonds optional

TO PREPARE

1 Peel two oranges with a vegetable peeler removing just the peel and leaving the white membrane attached. Slice this thin peel into narrow julienne strips. Set aside.

2 Peel all the oranges with a sharp knife removing all the white membrane. Cut into 1/4-inch slices and set aside in a glass bowl.

3 In an enamel, Pyrex or other non-reactive saucepan, combine the wine, water, and sugar. Add all but 1/4 cup of the julienned peel, tangerine or lemon slices, cloves, and cinnamon. Bring to a boil, immediately lower the heat, and simmer until reduced by half and sauce has become syrupy, about 35–45 minutes. Strain out the spices and fruit peel—though you may wish to reserve the cinnamon sticks for garnish.

TO SERVE

Pour the warm, or chilled, wine sauce over individual portions of the sliced oranges. Garnish with a cinnamon stick, a sprinkle of almonds, a few curls of julienned orange peel (optional)—and another glass of your favorite red wine.

NOTE The sauce may be prepared ahead and stored for up to three weeks refrigerated. In cool weather we serve the sauce warm, if convenient. In summer we serve this sauce chilled with other fresh fruits, berries, figs, peaches, or pears.

BAKED CASATTA
Cassata alla Siciliana al Furnu

Serves 10–12

For the crust:

5 ounces unbleached all-purpose flour

1 pinch of salt

1 ounce shelled walnuts

1/2 cup granulated sugar

8 tablespoons unsalted butter

1 extra-large egg

1 tablespoon heavy cream

4 tablespoons cold water or dry white wine

For the filling:

4 egg yolks

8 tablespoons granulated sugar

1 tablespoon corn starch

3 large pieces orange rind

1 cup milk

4 tablespoons candied orange rind, cut into very small pieces

4 tablespoons candied citron, cut into small pieces

1 teaspoon jasmine extract or 2 drops if imported from Italy

30 ounces ricotta, well drained

1 ounce grated bittersweet chocolate

TO PREPARE THE CRUST

1 Place flour in a mound on a board. Make a well in it. Put the pinch of salt in well.

2 Using a food processor or blender, finely grind the walnuts with the sugar. Pour walnut mixture and the butter in well of the flour mixture. Use a dough scraper to chop the butter, incorporating it into the flour compound.

3 Make another well and pour the egg and heavy cream into it. Add the water and quickly mix the liquids together.

4 Start incorporating the flour mixture using your hands to form a ball of dough. Wrap dough in plastic wrap. Refrigerate for 1 hour before using it.

TO PREPARE THE FILLING

1 Make a custard cream. Beat together the egg yolks, sugar, corn starch, orange rind, and the milk, in a double boiler over boiling water until the custard thickens.

2 Transfer prepared custard to glass bowl. Cover the bowl with plastic for 10 minutes. Refrigerate until needed. At that time, remove orange rind from custard cream.

3 Add candied orange rind, citron, jasmine extract, ricotta, and chocolate. Mix again. Refrigerate while you finish the pastry.

TO ASSEMBLE AND SERVE

1 Preheat oven to 375°F.

2 Lightly butter a 12-inch cake pan with a removable bottom. With a rolling pin, stretch pastry between 2 pieces of plastic wrap, into a disc about 18 inches in diameter.

3 Peel off the top plastic wrap from the pastry. Flip pastry into buttered pan. Press sides of pastry into the bottom and against sides of pan. Remove second piece of plastic wrap. Pour in prepared filling.

4 Use pastry wheel to cut off excess pastry around sides of pan. With excess pieces of pastry, prepare several strips about 1-1/2 inches wide to make criss-cross top crust and brush the strips with melted butter.

5 Bake for 1-1/2 hours. Remove from oven and let cake rest in pan for at least 1/2 hour before lifting out of cake pan. Serve at room temperature.

PISTACHIO CAKE
Torta ai Pistacchi

Serves 6–10

For the cake:

8 ounces pistachios

3/4 cup granulated sugar

2 tablespoons water

1 teaspoon vanilla

2 tablespoons unsalted butter, at room temperature

2 whole eggs

4 large eggs, separated

1 large orange

1 cup all-purpose flour

1/2 teaspoon salt

2 teaspoons baking powder

For the glaze:

8 ounces powdered sugar

3–4 tablespoons orange juice

A large pinch of saffron threads

TO PREPARE THE CAKE

1 Preheat oven 350°F.

2 Shell and blanch nuts for 1 minute in salted boiling water. Dry them on a cookie sheet in preheated oven for 10 minutes. Leave the oven on.

3 In a food processor, place the pistachios and 1/4 cup sugar. Process until smooth. Add the water and vanilla and process until mixture becomes a paste.

4 In an electric mixer, cream butter, and the remaining 1/2 cup sugar. Add the 2 whole eggs, one at a time, mixing well. Add the 4 egg yolks, one at a time, mixing well with each addition. Add ground pistachio mixture, the juice and zest of 1 orange.

5 Combine flour, baking powder and salt and add to the batter. Stir until completely blended.

6 Beat egg whites in a separate bowl until soft peaks form. Fold into the batter.

7 Pour into a loaf pan that has been lined with parchment paper. Bake for 50 minutes. Remove from oven. Transfer to a cooling rack. Cool for 15 minutes.

8 Turn pan over and take cake out of pan. Peel off parchment paper and turn back over and place on a large plate.

9 Peel and slice oranges into 1/4-inch thick slices. Remove seeds and set aside in a glass bowl.

TO PREPARE THE GLAZE

Sift powdered sugar into a small saucepan. Add 3 tablespoons of reserved orange juice and saffron. Mix well. Set pan over very low heat. Stir constantly, until sugar and saffron are completely melted and texture is smooth.

TO SERVE

Pour the glaze over the cake. Let cake cool for at least 15 minutes, slice and serve warm with orange slices and pistachios.

DAMIAN

This Sicilian tradition was one of the best cakes we ever made on the show. And I've made it at home many times.

JOHNNY

I love this one at home with a great big cold glass of milk.

CIAO SICILY

BLOOD ORANGE CAKE
Torta di Taroco

Serves 6–8

For the cake:

1 cup unsalted butter

2 tablespoons almond paste

2 cups granulated sugar

1 teaspoon orange zest

4 eggs

3 cups all-purpose flour, sifted

1 tablespoon baking powder

1 teaspoon baking soda

1/2 teaspoon salt

1/2 cup milk

1/2 cup fresh orange juice (preferably from blood oranges)

1/4 cup lemon juice

1 teaspoon vanilla

For the filling:

1/2 cup granulated sugar

6 egg yolks

2 tablespoons flour

2 cups milk

1 cinnamon stick

Orange peel

1 stick cold butter, cut into small cubes

1 cup heavy cream

For the glaze:

3 cups blood orange juice

1 cup powdered sugar

TO PREPARE THE CAKE

1 Preheat the oven to 350°F.

2 Butter and flour two 9-inch round cake pans and set aside. In a large mixing bowl, combine the butter, almond paste, and sugar. Beat at medium speed with hand mixer until smooth.

3 Add the orange zest and beat in the eggs one at a time. In a separate bowl, combine the flour with the baking powder, baking soda, and salt. Fold half the dry ingredients into the batter.

4 Add the milk, orange juice, lemon juice, vanilla, and the rest of the dry ingredients.

5 Mix until evenly blended and transfer to the baking pans. Bake for about 35 minutes, or until golden brown and done in the center.

TO PREPARE THE FILLING

1 In a medium saucepan, mix together the sugar and the egg yolks. Blend in the flour, mixing well, and set aside.

2 In a separate pan, heat the milk, cinnamon, and orange peel until almost boiling. Remove the milk from heat and temper the eggs by mixing approximately 1/2 cup of the heated milk into the egg mixture.

3 Add the tempered egg mixture to the milk and heat, stirring constantly, until almost boiling. Remove from heat.

4 Remove the cinnamon stick and orange peel, whisk in the butter and let cool. Add the heavy cream to the mixture and whisk until thoroughly mixed.

TO PREPARE THE GLAZE

Boil the orange juice until reduced in volume by half. Whisk in the powdered sugar until smooth.

TO ASSEMBLE

When cake is cool, use a serrated knife to level the top of each layer. Put 1 layer on a plate and top with the filling. Add the top layer and drizzle with the glaze and a dusting of powdered sugar.

TO SERVE

Serve cake with additional orange slices.

NOTE   Sicily is famous for many things, including miniature donkeys, lemons that look like huge limes, and the spectacular blood orange, *taroco*. Blood oranges look like tangerines on the outside, but on the inside they are bright and deep red, redder than pink grapefruit. You can make this cake with regular oranges, but if blood oranges are available, they make a spectacular dessert.

JOHNNY

The first time I had Sicilian blood orange juice,
I thought Damian had ordered me some tomato juice.
I got mad at him, because I wanted orange juice.

DAMIAN

I said, "Take a sip."

JOHNNY

So I did. I swear, it was like drinking flowers.

WALNUT AND FIG TORTE
Torta di Nuci e Fichi

Serves 8

1-1/4 cups granulated sugar

3/4 cup shelled walnuts

1/2 teaspoon ground cloves

1/2 teaspoon of ground cinnamon

1/2 cup Homemade Breadcrumbs
(see page 179)

Grated peel of 1 lemon

2 extra-large eggs

4 extra-large eggs, separated

4 tablespoons (2 ounces) sweet butter
at room temperature

1 cup dried figs, stemmed and coarsley
chopped

To bake:

2 tablespoons (1 ounce) sweet butter

1/3 cup Homemade Breadcrumbs
(see page 179)

1 tablespoon granulated sugar

For the garnish:

1/4 cup chopped walnuts

1 heaping teaspoon powdered sugar

TO PREPARE

1 Preheat oven to 325°F.

2 Finely grind 1/4 cup of sugar and the walnuts in a food processor. Add the clove, cinnamon, breadcrumbs, and grated lemon peel and continue to process until combined. Transfer to an electric mixer bowl.

3 Butter the bottom and sides of a 10-inch round springform cake pan. Line the bottom with buttered parchment paper. Line the sides of the cake pan with 1 tablespoon of the breadcrumbs.

4 Transfer the breadcrumb mixture to the electric mixer bowl and add remaining 1 cup of sugar, the 2 whole eggs, and the 4 egg yolks, mixing until well combined. Add the figs to the batter and mix at low speed.

5 In a seperate bowl whisk the 4 egg whites until they form soft peaks. Add 1 large spoonful of the beaten egg whites to the batter and fold in by hand with a spatula. Gently fold in the rest of the egg whites.

6 Transfer the batter to the prepared pan and bake for 20 minutes. Sprinkle a tablespoon of granulated sugar over the top and bake for 20 minutes more. Transfer to rack and cool for 30 minutes.

TO SERVE

Unmold torte into a round serving platter and let cool. Sprinkle chopped walnuts and powdered sugar over the cake. Cut cake into wedges and serve.

DAMIAN

Figs are very important in Sicily. In Texas, both of my grandmas had fig trees, and they do so well down here, too.

JOHNNY

This was one of your Grandma Testa's favorite cakes.

CHOCOLATE HAZELNUT CAKE
Torta Savoia

Serves 12

For the syrup:
1/2 cup granulated sugar
1/2 cup water
6 tablespoons dark rum

For the filling:
1 13 ounce jar Nutella
1-1/2 cups heavy cream
1 teaspoon vanilla

For the cake:
6 eggs, separated
3/4 cup granulated sugar
1 tablespoon hot water
1 teaspoon vanilla
Zest of 1 lemon
1/2 teaspoon baking powder
1/4 teaspoon salt
1-1/4 cups cake flour

For the glaze:
2 tablespoons butter
12 ounces semisweet chocolate chips
1 cup heavy whipping cream

TO PREPARE THE SYRUP

Combine the sugar and water in a small saucepan, bring to a boil and boil until the sugar is dissolved and the mixture is reduced by 1/4. Cool, and stir in the rum. Set aside.

TO PREPARE THE FILLING

Put Nutella in a saucepan over low heat. Stir in the heavy cream. Add vanilla. Cook until mixture is smooth, and then set aside.

TO PREPARE THE CAKE

1 Preheat oven to 350°F.

2 Butter and flour a 9-inch cake pan. In a large nonreactive bowl, with an electric mixer, whip the egg yolks with 1/2 cup of the sugar. Add the water, vanilla, and lemon zest and beat until light yellow. Add the baking powder and salt and mix thoroughly. Sift in the flour and stir.

3 In a separate bowl, with clean beaters, whip the egg whites until soft peaks form. Whip in the remaining 1/4 cup of sugar until stiff peaks form.

4 Take one large spoonful of the egg whites and fold it into the egg yolk mixture thoroughly. Then add the rest of the egg whites, folding gently.

5 Spread the batter evenly in the prepared 9-inch cake pan and bake for 35 minutes. Set upside down on a cooling rack and cool completely before removing from pan. When cake is cooled cut cake into three 1/2-inch layers.

TO ASSEMBLE

1 Put one layer on the cake plate. Spread a thin layer of syrup evenly over the cake. Then spread half of the filling mixture over the cake. Let cool for 10 minutes.

2 Add the second layer and repeat the process. Now add the third layer of cake to the top and spread with the final amount of syrup. Cover with plastic and put in the refrigerator for 2–4 hours.

TO PREPARE THE GLAZE

Put the butter and chocolate in a double boiler. Melt the butter and chocolate together until you have a smooth mixture. Slowly stir in the cream keeping the mixture smooth.

TO SERVE

Take the cake from the refrigerator and remove the plastic. Using a spatula smooth the glaze evenly around the sides of the cake and then spread over the top of the cake. Let the glaze set before serving. Serve with a few roasted hazelnuts on top and pass a bowl of whipped cream—or a pitcher of heavy cream—mmm so good.

DAMIAN
Chocolate and hazelnut go together like love and marriage. Or even better, like cake and ice cream.

JOHNNY
I just love this torta.

DAMIAN
I had it in this little pastry shop in Noto, with a great cup of espresso.

CIAO SICILY

CARAMELIZED
CUSTARD APPLES
Mele al Caramello

Serves 6

For the custard cream:

4 extra-large egg yolks

4 tablespoons granulated sugar

1 tablespoon cornstarch

1 1/2 cups whole milk or heavy cream

For the apples:

3 large apples, ripe but not over ripe, preferably Rome apples or red or yellow Delicious

6 tablespoons golden raisins

12 amaretto cookies

1 cup granulated sugar

3 tablespoons of water

Juice of 1/2 lemon, plus 1 whole lemon

2 teaspoons orange extract

TO PREPARE THE CUSTARD CREAM

1   Bring some water to a boil in bottom of a double boiler.

2   Put egg yolks into a glass bowl. Add sugar and corn starch. Stir with a wooden spoon, until sugar is completely incorporated and the egg yolks turn a lighter color.

3   Add the milk or heavy cream. Stir very well. Transfer contents to top part of double boiler and insert it over boiling water. Stir constantly with a wooden spoon.

4   Just before it boils, the custard should be thick enough to coat the wooden spoon. **Absolutely** do not allow to boil.

5   Immediately remove the top part of the double boiler from the heat. Stir the contents for 1 minute longer. Transfer the sauce to a crockery or glass bowl to cool completely, about 1 hour.

TO PREPARE THE APPLES

1   Preheat oven to 350°F.

2   Rough chop raisins. Put raisins and cookies in food processor and process until a smooth mixture forms. Carefully wash apples. Dry with paper towels.

3   Cut apples in half. Remove core from each half. Fill the hole with raisin filling.

4   Place a casserole pan large enough to hold all six apple halves in a single layer over low heat on top of stove.

5   When casserole pan is warm, sprinkle 1/2 cup of sugar evenly over bottom, add water and stir the sugar mixture until it begins to boil and remove from heat.

6   Place apples, cut part facing down, in casserole. Sprinkle with remaining sugar and the lemon juice. Cut off ends of whole lemon. Divide it into 8 slices. Be sure all seeds have been removed. Arrange all lemon slices in the pan, in between the apples.

7   Sprinkle orange extract over contents of pan. Remove pan from stovetop and place in preheated oven. Bake for 15–20 minutes. Carefully watch that the sugar does not become too dark.

TO SERVE

Put a large spoonful of custard cream on a dessert plate. Place an apple half with some caramelized sugar in the middle of the cream.

VISCOTTI
Twice Baked Cookies

Yields 48 viscotti

2 cups flour

2/3 cup granulated sugar

1/2 teaspoon salt

1/2 teaspoon baking powder

1/2 teaspoon baking soda

1 teaspoon ground cinnamon

1/2 teaspoon ground cloves

3 eggs

1 teaspoon vanilla

1 cup almonds (or shelled pistachios, pecans, walnuts or hazelnuts)

2 extra egg yolks, slightly beaten

TO PREPARE

1 Preheat oven to 350°F.

2 Mix dry ingredients including spices together in a large mixing bowl. In a separate bowl, beat eggs with vanilla. Make a well in the center of dry ingredients. Pour egg mixture into the well.

3 With a rubber spatula or your clean hand, mix the dry ingredients into the eggs, bringing dry ingredients into the center well, little by little, until thoroughly incorporated and evenly mixed, resulting in a soft dough.

4 Scoop dough out onto a floured flat surface. Flour your hands and pat out into a square. Spread the almonds evenly over the surface of the dough and press them down gently into the dough.

5 Fold the dough in half and press out into a square again and

refold. Repeat the folding several times until the almonds are well distributed throughout. Dust the surface with a little more flour to prevent sticking as you refold and flatten the dough.

6 Dust a large cookie sheet with flour. Divide the dough into 2 equal lumps and roll each lump into a 12-inch log and carefully transfer to the cookie sheet.

7 With a pastry brush, paint the top of each dough log with the beaten egg yolk, being careful not to let the egg yolk drip onto the cookie sheet. Bake for 25–30 minutes until the logs are a light golden brown and feel firm to the touch.

8 Reduce oven temperature to 300°F.

9 Remove from the oven and, as soon as you can handle without burning your hands, slice on a diagonal, 1/2-inch slices. Reform the log-loaves on the cookie sheet, with slices standing on the bottom edges, but leave 1/2-inch spaces between the slices.

10 Carefully return the viscotti to the oven, being careful to keep the slices upright. Bake for 15–20 minutes until the slices are very dry.

TO SERVE

Remove from the oven and eat a few while hot with a little butter (the children's favorite), allow the rest to cool before storing in a tightly covered cookie jar or tin.

DAMIAN
Every region and every town and every grandma has a viscotti recipe. I have a couple hundred recipes all by myself. But this one with Sicilian almonds is one of the best.

JOHNNY
These are great dunked in a cappuccino.

VARIATION

For chocolate viscotti, add to the basic viscotti dough 4 tablespoons dry, unsweetened cocoa and dip one end of each twice baked viscotti in the following chocolate glaze.

6   ounces semi-sweet chocolate squares
1   tablespoon vanilla
2   tablespoons amaretto

Melt ingredients together carefully over boiling water until chocolate is melted. Whisk together gently until well combined and smooth. Cool completely on wax paper before storing in cookie jar or tin.

CHOCOLATE ALMOND TARTLETS
Dolcetti al Liquore

Yields 1 dozen tartlets

1/3 cup golden raisins

1-1/2 cups rum

2 cups blanched almonds

2 cups granulated sugar

1 teaspoon vanilla

1 teaspoon almond extract

1/2 cup semisweet chocolate

1 teaspoon vegetable oil

1/2 cup chopped pecans or walnuts
for dusting

TO PREPARE

1   Plump raisins in 1 cup hot water for 1 hour. Drain well. And then soak them in rum for at least 12 hours.

2   Put almonds, sugar, vanilla and almond extract in a food processor and process until a paste forms.

3   On marble slab, or other cold surface, roll out almond paste 1/4-inch thick. Dust surface and rolling pin with cornstarch to prevent sticking.

4   Use round cookie cutter, cut out 24 2-inch circles. Place 12 circles in small fluted molds or muffin tins.

5   Fill each tartlet with 1 teaspoon of the raisins, and top with a little rum. Cover tartlets with remaining circles. Press edges together with fingers.

6   Cut away excess almond paste and chill for an hour. Remove tartlets from molds.

TO SERVE

Melt chocolate in a double boiler or microwave. Stir in oil.
Dip top half of each tartlet into the chocolate and dust with chopped nuts. Set on rack to harden. Serve or store in airtight container.

DAMIAN

These are just molded almond paste, stuffed with raisins and dipped in chocolate. They're really sweet and nice.

JOHNNY

They're terrific for any party.

CREAM FILLED DOUGHNUTS
Krapfen

Yields 24 doughnuts

1/2 cup butter

2 cups water

1/3 cup granulated sugar

1 teaspoon salt

1 package active dry yeast

6 cups all-purpose flour

4 egg yolks

1 quart vegetable oil

1 recipe Vanilla Cream Filling (see page 182)

Powdered sugar

TO PREPARE

1 Put butter in a small saucepan and melt over medium heat. Stir in the water, sugar, and salt and bring to 100°F. Remove from heat. Add the yeast and allow to sit for five minutes. Yeast should begin to foam.

2 Put flour in a large mixing bowl and make a well in the center.

3 Pour the yeast mixture into the well and add the egg yolks. Work mixture with a wooden spoon until all flour is blended.

4 Spoon mixture onto a lightly-floured surface and knead for 8 minutes until smooth.

5 Put the dough in a lightly-oiled bowl, cover with a towel and let rise for 1-1/2 hours

6 Put dough on floured surface and roll out to 1/2-inch thickness. Using a floured glass or cookie cutter, cut rounds and place on a lined baking sheet. Cover with a towel and let rise for 30 minutes until doubled in size.

7 In a large frying pan, bring vegetable oil to 350°F. Fry the rounds in the hot oil, turning until nicely browned. Remove rounds and place on a paper lined baking sheet to cool.

TO SERVE

Split the cooled doughnut with a sharp knife about halfway around and fill with pastry cream. Dust with powdered sugar and serve.

DAMIAN

No, it's not your imagination. The name for these doughnuts really is German, but it just made it to Sicily somehow. It's similar to the bombolini you find up in Tuscany.

JOHNNY

I love the pastry cream these things are filled with. If you love any kind of doughnuts, you'll love these.

PISTACHIO~RICOTTA SWEET FRITTERS
Frittelle di Ricotta e Pistachio

Serves 8–10

15 ounces whole-milk ricotta, very well drained

1/3 cup granulated sugar

1/2 cup unbleached all-purpose flour

1/2 cup pistachio nuts, ground

2 extra-large eggs and 1 egg yolk

Grated peel of 1 lemon

For cooking and serving:

About 1 cup unbleached all-purpose flour

3 extra-large eggs

1 cup Homemade Breadcrumbs (see page 179)

3 cups vegetable oil (1/2 cup sunflower oil, 1/2 cup corn oil)

Granulated sugar

TO PREPARE

1 Place ricotta in a medium-sized crockery or glass bowl. Add sugar and flour. Mix very well. Add ground pistachio nuts. Add to bowl along with eggs, egg yolk, and grated lemon peel.

2 Mix very well with wooden spoon to form a very smooth, thick batter. Using tablespoonfuls of mixture, form into individual balls. Lightly flour.

3 Lightly beat eggs in glass bowl. Spread breadcrumbs on sheet pan. Heat oil in skillet over medium heat to 375°F.

4 Dip each ball in the beaten egg. Coat with breadcrumbs. Fry until golden all over, about 1 minute. Transfer balls to a serving platter lined with paper towels to drain excess oil.

TO SERVE

When all fritters are on serving platter, remove paper towels and sprinkle with some granulated sugar. Serve hot—with more pistachios.

NOTE Texture of fritters should be very crusty on outside and extremely creamy on inside.

DAMIAN

Johnny and I had a lot of fun making this recipe on the show. I guess I just love any kind of fried pastry. On the show we made a mistake. We dipped the first fritters in salt by mistake—surprised the tasters! We made a quick correction.

JOHNNY

These are so light and delicious.

DAMIAN

They are like eating clouds.

LEMON COOKIES
Taralli

Yields 3 dozen cookies

For the cookie dough:
3-1/2 cups all-purpose flour
1/2 teaspoon salt
1-1/2 teaspoons baking powder
1 teaspoon baking soda
1 cup granulated sugar
Grated zest of 1 lemon
8 tablespoons unsalted butter, softened
1 cup milk
2 large eggs
1 teaspoon vanilla extract
Juice of 1/2 lemon

For the glaze:
2 cups sifted powdered sugar
Grated zest of 1/2 lemon
Juice of 1/2 lemon
2 to 3 tablespoons milk

TO PREPARE
1 Preheat oven 350°F.
2 Lightly flour 2 or 3 baking sheets lined with parchment paper. For the cookies, combine flour, salt, baking powder, baking soda, sugar, and lemon zest in mixing bowl. Make a well.
3 Add butter, milk, eggs, vanilla, and lemon juice. Mix dough with your hands until mixture stretches out into a ribbon when you lift it out of the bowl with your hand. Dough will be very sticky.
4 Pick up 1 tablespoon of dough. Roll it into 1/2-inch a rope. Roll out another tablespoon of dough into a rope and twist the two pieces together. Form the rope into a circle and pinch the ends together.
5 Place rings 1 inch apart on baking sheets. Continue with remaining dough. Bake for 15–20 minutes, or until very lightly browned and puffed. Cool thoroughly on the pan.
6 Make the glaze by combining the confectioners' sugar, lemon zest, and lemon juice. Add just enough milk to make medium-thick icing. With pastry brush, dust excess flour from bottom of cookies. Brush the top of each cookie with glaze.

TO SERVE
Place on racks or clean pans until glaze is dry. Store cookies in a tightly sealed container.

JOHNNY
Sicilians do anything and everything with citrus.
DAMIAN
In this wonderful simple recipe, lemon zest and lemon juice are both used in the cookie dough, and they give a nice citrus zing to the glaze as well.

VIRGINS' BREASTS
Minni di Vergine

Yields 3 dozen cookies

For the pastry:
2-2/3 cups unbleached all-purpose flour
2/3 cup granulated sugar
1/2 cup cold butter
1 egg
1/4 cup milk

For the pastry cream:
6 eggs, separated
3/4 cup granulated sugar
1/2 cup cornstarch
4 cups milk
Rind of 1 lemon, grated
1 teaspoon vanilla extract
1/4 teaspoon of ground cinnamon

TO PREPARE THE PASTRY

Use an electric mixer, food processor, or pastry cutter. Combine the flour, sugar, butter, and egg. Add milk as needed to make soft dough (you may not need to use all of the milk). Chill dough for 30 minutes.

TO PREPARE THE PASTRY CREAM

1 In the top of a double boiler, with a wire whisk, beat together egg yolks and sugar. Stir in cornstarch and the milk. Add lemon rind, vanilla extract, and cinnamon. Heat mixture over very hot water. Stir continuously, until very thick.
2 Set pastry cream aside to cool.

TO ASSEMBLE

1 Preheat oven 375°F.
2 On a floured surface, roll out half of the dough. Drop heaping tablespoonfuls of pastry cream in rows on the dough. Space drops of cream about 1/2 inch apart.
3 Roll out remaining half of dough and lay it carefully on top of layer dotted with filling. Press down between the lumps to seal the filling in. Cut the cookies in rounds, each containing filling.
4 Transfer the cookies to a baking sheet. Bake for 45 minutes.

TO SERVE

Sprinkle with confectioner's sugar just after they come out of the oven.

DAMIAN

I was in Erice with my wife Trina, taken there by our Marsala producers, Orazio Lombardo and his wife Federica. We stopped in the little pastry shop of Maria Grammatico — when these little pastries were just coming out of the oven.

JOHNNY

You told me about those. You thought you'd died and gone to Sicily.

FRIED PASTRY SHELLS
WITH TWO FILLINGS
Cannoli

Yields 12–18 cannoli

For the pastry shells:

2 cups all-purpose flour

1 tablespoon granulated sugar

1 teaspoon cinnamon

1 tablespoon lard or vegetable shortening

1 egg

1/2 teaspoon vanilla

1/2 cup Marsala wine

1 quart vegetable oil for frying

For the pistachio filling:

3/4 cup shelled pistachios

3/4 cup granulated sugar

5 egg yolks

1-3/4 cups milk

Zest of one lemon

1/4 cup water

3 tablespoons cornstarch

1 teaspoon vanilla

For the chocolate filling:

8 ounces semisweet chocolate pieces

1-1/2 cups milk

5 egg yolks

1/2 cup granulated sugar

1 teaspoon vanilla

1 teaspoon almond extract

3 tablespoons cornstarch

1/2 cup water

TO PREPARE THE PASTRY TUBES

1   Sift the flour, sugar, and cinnamon into a bowl. Cut in the lard and mix into the flour mixture. Add the egg and vanilla. Add enough wine to make a firm dough. Knead the dough until elastic. Wrap in plastic and let rest for 30 minutes

2   In a 3-quart pan or Dutch oven, preheat the oil to 350°F. Roll the dough paper-thin on a cutting board and cut into equal 4-inch squares.

3   Place a metal tube diagonally on each square and bring the two corners over to meet in the middle. Press gently to seal.

4   Gently drop them a few at a time into the hot oil and cook until they are a deep golden brown. Remove them from the oil with tongs and immediately slide the shells off the metal tubes. Cool the shells on a rack lined with paper towel.

TO PREPARE THE PISTACHIO FILLING

1   Fill a small saucepan with 2 cups of water and bring to a boil. Put the pistachios in the water for 30 seconds and drain water. Spread the pistachios on a sheet of paper towel, dry and peel off skins.

2   Put the pistachios in a food processor with 1/2 cup of sugar and process until you have a powder.

3   In a large mixing bowl, whisk together the egg yolks and 1/4 cup of sugar. Add the ground pistachio mixture and blend well. Put the milk and lemon zest in a saucepan and stir over medium heat until almost boiling.

4   Add 1/2 cup of the hot milk into the bowl with the egg-pistachio mixture and mix well. Add the remaining hot milk and mix well. Return batter to saucepan over medium heat.

5   Put the water in a small bowl and mix in the cornstarch until smooth. Add the cornstarch liquid to the batter and stir until thickened. Add the vanilla and stir until completely blended.

6   Pour the filling into a glass bowl, cover with plastic wrap placed directly on the surface of the filling, and put in the refrigerator to chill.

TO PREPARE THE CHOCOLATE FILLING

1 In the top of a double boiler, put the chocolate pieces and the milk. Bring the water in the double boiler to a boil and stir the milk and chocolate until you have a smooth mixture.

2 In a small mixing bowl, combine the egg yolks, sugar, vanilla, and almond extract and whisk until fluffy. Add 1/4 cup hot chocolate milk stirring constantly. Then add this slurry to the remaining hot milk in the double boiler.

3 In a small bowl, mix the cornstarch and water until completely blended. Add the cornstarch to the mixture in the double boiler and over medium heat, stir until it thickens. Pour filling into a glass bowl and cover the top with plastic to prevent a skin from forming. Put the filling in the refrigerator to chill.

TO ASSEMBLE

When the fillings have chilled through, using a pastry bag with no tube on the end, fill cannoli with either filling or some of each. Sprinkle with powdered sugar and place finish with a candied cherry or other candied fruit on each end.

DAMIAN

Along with cassata, this is the classic Sicilian dessert. There's all kinds of variations in every village on the island, but they're all about wonderful pastry stuffed with ricotta and candied fruit.

JOHNNY

I remember having this chocolate version at a pastry shop is Bisaquino. I was a little reluctant to take something away from tradition, but I loved it anyway.

LEMON AND CHOCOLATE BISCUIT BALLS
Tatú

Yields 24 cookies

For the cookie dough:
4-1/2 cups all-purpose flour
1 tablespoon baking powder
1-1/4 cup granulated sugar
1 teaspoon pure vanilla extract
2/3 cup melted butter
2 cups milk

For lemon glaze:
1 cup water
1-1/4 cups powdered sugar
1/4 cup lemon juice
Zest of 1 lemon
1 tablespoon heavy cream

For chocolate glaze:
8 ounces semisweet chocolate pieces
1/4 cup of melted butter
1-1/4 cups powdered sugar
1 tablespoon heavy cream

TO PREPARE THE COOKIES

1 Preheat oven to 350°F.

2 In a large bowl, combine the flour, baking powder, and 1-1/4 cup of the sugar. Add vanilla and the melted butter. Slowly stir in milk, mixture will be firm.

3 Form dough into balls the size of walnuts. Arrange balls on the baking sheet lined with parchment paper a few inches apart. Bake for about 10 minutes. Remove and cool on rack. Arrange and bake the next batch.

TO PREPARE THE GLAZES

1 For lemon glaze, put water, sugar, lemon juice, and lemon zest in a bowl. Whisk until sugar has melted and add a touch of cream. Dip each cookie into lemon glaze to cover half of the cookie. Let set on a cooling rack.

2 For chocolate glaze, put chocolate pieces, butter, sugar, and cream into a small saucepan. Cook on low heat while stirring continually until melted. When the glaze is completely smooth, set aside to cool for five minutes.

TO SERVE

Dip the other half of the cookies in the chocolate glaze. Let dry on cooling rack. Serve with tea or sweet wine.

DAMIAN
These are some really famous Sicilian cookies. And like all Sicilian cookies, they tend to be on the dry and crispy or crunchy side.

JOHNNY
What I like, though, D, is the zest of lemon. You put some citrus in and it really starts tasting Sicilian to me.

SICILIAN FIG COOKIES
Cucidate

Yields 200 cookies

For the stuffing:
4 pounds dried figs (stems removed)
1 pound pitted dates
1 pound white raisins
zest of 2 lemons
zest of 2 oranges
2 tablespoons ground cinnamon
3 tablespoons allspice
2 tablespoons nutmeg
2 tablespoons ground cloves
1 pound pecans
1 pound almonds (blanched and toasted)
1 pound walnuts
2 cups red wine
2 cups simple syrup (plus more if needed)

For the simple syrup (1):
2 cups sugar
2 cups water

For the dough:
4 pounds flour
1 pound vegetable shortening
3 cups white wine
2 cups simple syrup

For the simple syrup (2):
2 cups sugar
1 cup water

For the glaze:
1 cup powdered sugar
1/2 teaspoon vanilla
2 tablespoons fresh orange juice
Multicolored nonpareils, for garnish, optional

TO PREPARE FILLING

1 Dissolve sugar in the water over medium heat.

2 Chop the nuts and place in a mixing bowl large enough to hold all the ingredients.

3 In a food processor grind the figs, dates, raisins, lemon and orange zests. Place ground fig mixture into the mixing bowl with the nuts.

4 To the bowl add the spices, wine and simple syrup (1) and mix thoroughly. Cover with plastic wrap. Leave stuffing room temperature until ready to use.

TO PREPARE DOUGH

1 Dissolve sugar in the water over medium heat.

2 Place flour and shortening in a large bowl and mix until shortening is well blended and crumbly. Add wine and simple syrup (2) and mix until dough comes together adding water if necessary.

FINAL ASSEMBLY

1 Cut off a piece of dough and roll it out into a long strip, about the same thickness as pie dough. Trim the dough strip to be about 3-inches wide.

2 Place a mound of fig filling down the center of the dough strip about the size of a cigar and fold the dough over the filling overlapping the dough. Roll the filled cookie "rope" over pressing and forming a round shape with the seam on the bottom. Gently tap the top to flatten slightly. Cut the strip into cookies on a bias about 2-1/2-inches long. With the tip of a very sharp knife, make tiny slits on the side of the fig cookies while flicking the wrist, and add a few decorative carvings on top.

3 Bake on ungreased cookie sheets for about 25 minutes at 350°F or until lightly browned. Cool, add glaze if desired and store in an airtight container.

4 If glaze is desired, while first batch of cookies bake, whisk together powdered sugar, vanilla, and enough orange juice to make a pourable icing.

5 Brush glaze on warm cookies and decorate with nonpareils (if using), then cool completely, and store in an airtight container.

DIAMIAN

In our part of Sicily, our family called these cucidati. In other parts of Sicily, people called them buccidati. I love this recipe. When our whole family gets together right after Thanksgiving each year, we make these fig cookies.

JOHNNY

And we make a lot of them.

GRANDMA MANDOLA'S CHOCOLATE PUDDING
Ciucculatta Manciari

Serves 4–6

1/2 cup cornstarch

1/4 cup plus 2 tablespoons cocoa powder

3/4 cup plus 2 tablespoons granulated sugar

1 quart milk

Ground cinnamon

Semi-sweet chocolate bar

Fresh mint sprigs (optional)

TO PREPARE

1 In the top of a double boiler mix cornstarch, cocoa and sugar. With a whisk gradually stir in milk. Place top of double boiler over simmering water. Stir mixture constantly with a wooden spoon until pudding is thick.

2 Pour pudding into a shallow platter and let cool 5 minutes. Shave the chocolate bar with a vegetable peeler. Sprinkle pudding with cinnamon and shaved chocolate.

TO SERVE

Chill pudding at least 2 hours before serving. Spoon into individual dessert dishes and garnish with sprigs of fresh mint.

DAMIAN

This pudding is traditionally made as vanilla pudding – "Bianca Mangiare" in Italian – or "Blanc Manger" in French. My grandma made this chocolate version. And when she made it, the aroma filled the whole house.

JOHNNY

And you knew you were in for a real treat.

WATERMELON PUDDING
Gelo di Melone

Serves 6

1 5-pound ripe red watermelon

3/4 cup granulated sugar

4 packets of gelatin

1/4 teaspoon rose water or 2 tablespoons jasmine water

1/3 cup semisweet chocolate chips

1/3 cup squash or citron preserves, diced

3 tablespoons unsalted pistachios, chopped

Jasmine flowers

TO PREPARE

1 Set out six 6-ounce custard cups, or six small dessert bowls or prepare a mold by rubbing it with vegetable oil and lining with plastic.

2 Halve or quarter the watermelon. Remove the flesh and cut into chunks, removing and discarding the seeds. Purée fruit and press through a fine mesh sieve lined with double thick cheesecloth. Discard pulp. Measure out 4 cups juice.

3 In a large saucepan, whisk juice and sugar until smooth and no lumps remain.

4 Over medium heat, bring mixture to a boil and cook. Add 4 packets of gelatin and whisk constantly until thick and glossy (about 2 minutes). Remove from heat.

5 Add rosewater or jasmine water. Cool until lukewarm. Stir in chocolate bits. Spoon the pudding into cups, bowls or a mold. Refrigerate until well chilled.

TO SERVE

Unmold the pudding. Garnish with squash or citron preserves, pistachios, and jasmine flowers.

DAMIAN
I tried this one in a little mountain town near Cefalú on a hot summer day on our honeymoon. There were these famous candymakers who had all these puddings and ices.

JOHNNY
You loved it, D. You said this was like eating watermelon without the watermelon.

PEACH GRANITA
Granita di Pesche

Serves 6

2 cups granulated sugar
4 cups water
4 fresh peaches
Juice of 2 lemons

TO PREPARE

1 Combine sugar and water in saucepan. Cook over medium heat until sugar dissolves.

2 Boil for 5 minutes to make light syrup. Pour mixture into a wide bowl. Let cool.

3 Peel, pit, and slice peaches, then toss in a bowl with the lemon juice. Purée peaches in a food processor until smooth. Stir the purée into the saucepan with the syrup.

4 Transfer to metal ice trays or shallow metal pan. Place the pan in the freezer, stirring every hour with a fork. The granita is done when it takes on a slush-like consistency.

TO SERVE

Scoop into serving glasses and serve immediately.

NOTE   You can make this granita with about 1 pound of any fruit. The more perfumed the fruit, the better the granita will be. Use more sugar if the fruit is not very sweet.

DAMIAN
My grandma, Rose Testa, used to make a lemon granita like this in the summer, and it was so refreshing.

JOHNNY
If you've got good, sweet peaches, like the ones we get in Texas from Fredericksburg, this is a great way to cool off.

BRIOCHE ROLLS FOR GELATO OR ICE CREAM
Brioscia

Yields 24

For the rolls:
3 packages active dry yeast
1/2 teaspoon sugar
3/4 cup lukewarm or warm milk
3 cups unbleached all-purpose flour
2 tablespoons granulated sugar
1/2 teaspoon salt
5 extra-large eggs
1-1/2 cups unsalted butter, softened

To bake the rolls:
Greased cookie sheet
2 extra-large eggs

TO PREPARE

1 Dissolve yeast in warm milk with 1/2 teaspoon sugar and let stand for 10 minutes. Place flour, and the 2 tablespoons sugar, salt and 5 eggs in a bowl and mix thoroughly. Add the dissolved yeast and mix well. Add the butter, 2 tablespoons at a time, and mix well until a smooth dough is formed.

2 Take dough out of bowl and work gently on a lightly-floured board. Let rest in a covered greased bowl until doubled in size, about 30 minutes. Then put in refrigerator for 2 hours and chill.

3 Remove dough from refrigerator, and knead lightly on a lightly-floured board, and roll out dough. Take small pieces of the dough and roll them into ball shapes, golfball-sized. Lay out on a cookie sheet, cover and let rise for 2 hours.

4 Preheat oven at 350°F.

5 Lightly beat additional eggs with 1 tablespoon of water and quickly brush top of each roll. Bake about 20 minutes.

TO SERVE

Remove rolls from oven. Split each roll and put two small scoops of your favorite ice cream in roll and serve.

DAMIAN:
In Sicily, and on the mainland of Italy, you almost never see people eating gelato from a cone, the way we usually do over here. They eat it more like a sandwich.

JOHNNY:
There's an art to eating those things.

DAMIAN:
There's an art to making them too. And they even eat ice cream sandwiches for breakfast. Do those Sicilians know how to live or what!

MOCHA ICE
Granitta di Mocha

Yields about 1 quart

2 cups water
2 cups granulated sugar
1/4 cup powdered cocoa
2 cups freshly-brewed espresso
4 ice cube trays

TO PREPARE

1   In a medium saucepan stir water, sugar, and chocolate powder together and bring to a boil. Remove from the heat and add the espresso.

2   Pour into ice cube trays or shallow metal pan and put in freezer. When ice crystals begin to form stir with a fork and return to freezer. Repeat every 20 minutes until granita is completely frozen and slushy.

TO SERVE

Serve the granita in individual dessert cups.

JOHNNY
Up until recently, Americans didn't know or care too much about iced coffee, even when it's real hot in the summertime.

DAMIAN
But if you love coffee and if you love chocolate, you'll just go crazy over this. The Sicilians serve it with a dollop of whipped cream.

DATE CANDY
Confetta di Dattula

Yields about 2 dozen pieces

2-1/2 cups granulated sugar
1/2 cup milk
2 tablespoons butter
2 cups pecans
1 pound dates, chopped

TO PREPARE

Cook sugar and milk until it forms a ball. Add butter, pecans, and dates. Beat 5 minutes and let cool. Beat until creamy and pour onto damp cloth and roll. When firm, cut into slices.

THE SICILIAN

PANTRY

Nobody knows what's in the pot,
but the spoon that stirs it."

—GRACE MANDOLA

The Sicilian Pantry

LIKE ANYBODY ELSE ON EARTH, *Sicilians love to cook and eat food the reflects who they are and what they've got. If you line up all the conquerors who've spent time on the island and turn them loose in one big historic kitchen with what they could grow, hunt or fish for, you'd end up with something like authentic Sicilian cuisine. Here are some of the most important ingredients that make up the Sicilian culinary personality.*

Almonds and Dried Apricots

Artichoke

Italian Breads

ALMONDS:

Often mentioned in many of the world's most ancient and cherished books, including the Bible, almonds are a part of the Greco-Roman tradition of the Mediterranean that came to be shared with the Arab world right across Homer's "wine-dark sea." The Greeks were the first to cultivate almonds in Sicily, and Sicilians love to get their hands on them toasted or raw, whole or sliced in savory or sweet applications.

ANCHOVIES:

You'd better like anchovies if you're going to like many Sicilian dishes — but don't give up if all you know are those tiny, salty, sometimes too-fishy things found in a can. Anchovies are, naturally, best when eaten fresh, and they can grow considerably larger than people who've only opened cans have ever seen them. Sicily is an island, after all, surrounded by some of the Mediterranean's most profitable fishing grounds. The presence of anchovies, sometimes as movie star, sometimes as mere extras, is a reminder of this culture's links to the sea. For preserved anchovies we like the ones packed in salt rather than in oil. Salted or oil-preserved anchovies are used more as a seasoning ingredient for a dish.

ANISEED:

The herb anise, native to the Mediterranean, is prized for its licorice-like flavor. The seed also produces anise oil. Anise has been considered a digestive aid for thousands of years. The seed and oil are used in baking.

APRICOTS:

Sicily, then as now, is less a Garden of Eden than first-time visitors might think. A lot of terrain here is dry and Spartan, and apparently it was even more so before conquerors imported various plants and trees. Apricots were introduced by the Arabs, who used them, fresh and dried in sweets, of course, but also in interesting ways in fish and meat dishes.

The Sicilian Pantry

ARTICHOKES:

For Sicilian-Americans, the artichoke is one of the top 5 foods when you think of home. From the Gulf Coast to New York's Little Italy to Boston's North End, artichokes are prime ingredients for frying, stuffing, or baking in a thousand variations in Grandmother's casserole. They've been grown in Sicily since 1290, most famously in the kitchen gardens of Palermo.

BASIL:

Sicilians love fresh herbs, and basil, "The King of Fresh Herbs" sits right at the top of their list with oregano. It grows year-round in Sicily, so the very thought of using dried basil would strike most Sicilians as sacrilege. Fresh basil is available year 'round in most American supermarkets. Still, if in the winter months you can't find fresh basil, you can substitute dried—using a good deal less, of course, because the flavor is more concentrated. The Sicilian trinity of tomatoes, eggplant, and zucchini seldom venture out of the kitchen without at least a sprinkling of fresh basil.

BAY LEAVES:

The tough yet flavorful leaves of the bay tree are an important part of Sicilian cooking, not the least because most Sicilians can simply step outside and pick what they need. Two or three leaves are perfect in almost any soup or stew, or perhaps even spread around some roasted or grilled meat. Because of their chewiness, be sure to remove bay leaves before you serve the dish.

BOTTARGA:

Make no mistake about it: Sicilians love the taste of fish at its most assertive. Along with anchovies and sardines, these tuna eggs (called bottarga) are used all over the island. The eggs are formed into flat sheet cakes and cut into 1-inch thick blocks, which can be shaved over pasta.

BREADCRUMBS:

Sicilians use breadcrumbs to form a nice crust on top of baked starches and vegetables, sprinkled over certain pasta or soup dishes, and just plain adding interesting texture to almost anything. Yet the seasoned variation actually finds its way into stuffings for meat, seafood and vegetables. Simple rule: when making Italian breadcrumbs, rustic Italian bread works best.

Basil

The Sicilian Pantry

Cinnamon Sticks

Eggplant

Fava Beans

Fennel

CACIOCAVALLO:

This is a popular cow's milk cheese aged 3 months or longer and therefore perfect for grating. According to Sicilian tradition, the cheese is shaped into balls and tied together two-by-two with raffia. Once it's aged, it can be, and is grated for use in place of the Parmesan enjoyed on the Italian mainland.

CANDIED FRUIT:

It's not just for Christmas fruitcake anymore. Sicilians love to use candied fruit in a variety of ways, an obsession they picked up from the Arabs. The citrus fruits grown all over the island tend to turn up most often—the candied lemon and orange peel. It's hard for us to picture a Sicilian kitchen without a collection of home-candied fruit at the cook's disposal.

CAPERS:

These tiny, pungent orbs—the flower buds of a spiny shrub—have been popular in Sicily since Greek times. Sicilians will insist the best capers come from Pantelleria, and are larger and bigger in flavor than the ones from French Provence. In Sicily, capers are usually preserved with salt rather than brine. Their strong, peppery flavor is one of the most distinctive aspects of Sicilian cooking.

CHICKPEAS:

Chickpeas, called *ciciri* in Sicily and garbanzos in the Hispanic world, are one of the more notable signatures of the Arab World—a product of the same Moorish Spain that gives us the graceful Islamic swirls of Cordoba and the lush, fountain-filed gardens of Granada. Dried chickpeas need to be soaked for 6–8 hours or overnight and cooked over low heat for a long time, 2–3 hours until tender.

CINNAMON:

Here's an addition to the "Italian" pantry that you won't find much if you travel even a few miles north into Italy. Cinnamon, the aromatic, inner bark of trees of the *Cinnamonium* genus, rolled into sticks or ground into powder, was a favorite spice of the ancient Arabs. It traveled to north Africa with the caravans from the east, and made the crossing to Sicily with the conquering Arabs, often referred to as Saracens. As elsewhere, cinnamon is perfect for pastries and desserts, but don't be shocked to taste it with seafoods, meats, and vegetables.

The Sicilian Pantry

CURRANTS:

Sicilians are all about "currant events." There are two distinctly different fruits called currants. The first a tiny dark raisin, is a seedless, dried, small grape, *passoli*. The other is a tiny berry related to the gooseberry. In Sicilian cooking we are talking about the raisin. If you can't find the tiny raisins just use regular raisins as we did here in these recipes, and as I saw in Sicily most of the time. The intensified sweetness from drying is not only a taste to be cherished all by itself, but one to bring extreme exoticism to numerous Sicilian stuffings when paired with pine nuts. This duo is usually called *passoli e pignoli*.

EGGPLANT:

In the 10th century, the eggplant and its appreciation spread to two destinations that now practically wouldn't know how to cook without it. It spread to Greece, becoming part of several dishes (like *moussaka*) that are as "Greek" as you can get. And it spread to Sicily, those coming to dominate the recipes written or remembered by Sicilians coming to America. Sicilians prefer an eggplant variety known as Tunisian. It's large, egg-shaped, and a nice, pale purple. The old cooks say these are very sweet, and therefore don't have to be salted and leached of bitterness before cooking.

FAVA BEANS:

On any list of things not to joke with Sicilians about, you should include these "lucky beans." A pagan superstition that (like so many things in Sicily) resisted centuries of attack by Catholic doctrine, fava beans are considered a Sicilian's "ace in the whole," whether the wish is for love, money, health or a favored spot in the hereafter. Since Greek times, fave have been eaten raw, especially with pecorino cheese, as well as cooked in a wonderful peasant soup called *Maccu*.

FENNEL:

Wild Sicilian fennel has been important to the island's cuisine since antiquity, producing a people who love the bulb's mild licorice flavor. Fennel is found in numerous Sicilian braises and pasta sauces and, most simply, sliced and served uncooked in a salad with citrus fruits and olives. If you love what Americans call Italian sausage (especially the kind our family still makes in Texas according to some very old Sicilian recipes), then you almost certainly love the taste of fennel seed. Because Sicilian wild mountain fennel is not available in the United States we like to add some dill weed when using fennel fronds to season a dish. This gives the dish a somewhat wild fennel taste profile.

The Sicilian Pantry

Figs

Garlic Cloves

Mint

Black Olives

FIGS:

Fresh figs are grown all over Sicily, often just outside many a kitchen window. When figs are in season, the race is on to use them as many ways as possible. Thus, Sicilian cuisine is full of savory and sweet dishes using fresh figs. And, perhaps most strategically, there's a long tradition of making fig preserves—the ultimate way to extend the life of any perishable product. Dried figs are also used extensively, as in our *Cucidati*.

FLOUR:

Sicily was the ancient granary for Rome. All recipes in this book are based on all-purpose unbleached, un-bromated flour. The other famous flour in Sicilian cooking is hard wheat Semolina. Semolina is used for the famous and delicious *Pane Siciliani*.

GARLIC:

Surely this is one of the cornerstones of Sicilian flavor. It's hard to imagine virtually any Sicilian savory dish without the sweet, pungent aroma and taste of garlic. A mere whiff of garlic sizzling in just a bit in olive oil is enough to throw nearly any Sicilian-American back to childhood as his mother cooked Sunday dinner for the family. But beware, garlic is to be used judiciously.

LEMONS:

Sicily is quite the eye-opener for people to think lemon is just for iced tea. Since lemons and other citrus have grown in abundance on the island since they arrived with the Arabs in the 10th century, a battery of uses has evolved —fish to poultry to lamb, from salad to sherbet to pastries—and candied peel.

MARSALA:

This distinctive sweetish wine has an aroma and taste hard to confuse with any other, even with other sweet wines from elsewhere. Veal Marsala is, of course, the famous namesake. But the wine also adds a particular sweetness to the dough used for *Cannoli* and airiness to the classic *Zabaglione*. Finer Marsala, Superiore or Vergine are excellent sipping wines similar to sherries.

MINT:

Always used fresh, mint adds a refreshing taste to drinks, salads, meat, sauces, and desserts.

NUTMEG:

Another Sicilian weapon borrowed from the Arabs, this spice if often found in savory dishes along with the unexpected sprinkle of cinnamon— thus linking Sicilian cuisine more with Morocco than the Italian mainland. It's used to flavor pasta, fish sauces, some vegetables, and of course many desserts.

The Sicilian Pantry

OLIVES:

The green olives are usually cured in brine while Sicilian black olives are oil cured. If you can find Sicilian olives please use them. If not, a good Italian, Spanish or Greek olives can work.

OLIVE OIL:

Sicily is profoundly part of the Mediterranean world, within the Olive Belt that takes in Spain, Provence (south of France's Cream and Butter Zone), Italy, Greece, the Eastern Mediterranean around Lebanon, and all of North Africa back to the tip of Spain. To achieve the best flavors in your Sicilian cooking, use only cold-pressed extra virgin olive oil, (preferably Sicilian), which happily is found is most supermarkets these days.

ORANGES:

Arabs introduced the very first oranges to Europe by way of Sicily, a bitter orange that soon was grown by the emirs around Palermo. This citrus fruit proved perfect, along with limes and shaddock, for making candies, preserves and essences. Today, the sweet oranges of Sicily are known as Portugals. But an even more striking variant is the blood orange called *taroco* (named for its deep red color inside), ideal for a Sicilian orange salad.

OREGANO:

Oregano is an essential herb for cooking across the island, contributing a strong, spicy flavor to sauces for grilled fish or roasted meats, as well as for now—worldwide pizza, pasta, and chicken dishes.

PARSLEY:

Sicilians and Italians alike use the fresh flat-leaf parsley, *pitrusini*. It has a stronger more pronounced flavor than the curly variety. It is indispensable in the Sicilian-Italian cucina.

PECORINO:

Fresh Pecorino, *primo sale*, is a sheep's milk cheese with a taste similar to feta, though a good bit less salty. Aged pecorino is also common, usually grated over pasta or served with raw fava beans.

PINE NUTS:

Known as pignoli, these are an essential ingredient in many sweet and savory dishes, as well as in fillings for just about anything. They come from the cone of the stone pine and are native to the Mediterranean.

Marsala

The Sicilian Pantry

Pistachios

Pomegranate

Tomatoes

Canned Tuna

PISTACHIOS:

These exotically colored, distinctive green nuts are reflective of today's Italian flag and are another important contribution of the Arabs. Sicilians believe the very best is the *Pistachio di Sicilia* (naturally), which comes from Bronte in the province of Catania.

POMEGRANATES:

Brought to Spain and Sicily by the Arabs, the brilliant blooms and fruits of this shrub add color and beauty to their lush gardens. After making peace with enjoying them despite the over-abundance of seeds, Sicilians enjoy pomegranates as a fruit, as a garnish on dishes from savory to sweet, and as a juice.

RICE:

Sicilians prefer to cook either *Arborio* (famous in risottos from Italy to the north) or *Vialone* rice. In addition to serving as starch in many a meal, rice takes on magic as the beloved Sicilian street food *arancini* (little oranges), fried balls of cooked rice stuffed with meat, green peas and cheese.

RICOTTA:

Best known to Americans as the cheese used in lasagna. The best ricotta is made with sheep's milk. Ricotta is a byproduct, using the whey that's left after turning out mozzarella and provolone, reheated (re-cotta, cooked) and skimmed. In addition to savory service in *lasagna* and *manicotti*, look for ricotta when it's time to make Sicilian desserts like *cannoli*.

ROSEMARY:

The minty-pine-scented, evergreen herb is grown all over Sicily. The flat, needle shaped leaves are wonderful flavoring for pork, poultry, and lamb.

SARDINES:

Another of those fish, along with anchovies, that most Americans know from small, lesser examples in a can full of oil. Fresh sardines are very popular in Sicily used in stews and sauces. The most famous Sicilian sardine dish is *Sarde a Becafico*. Sardines are also the named star of the Sicilian national dish *Pasta cu li Sarde*.

SQUASH:

Sicily is a great garden in many ways, with marrow or summer squash playing a role in the local diet since the Middle Ages. Called *zucca* in

The Sicilian Pantry

Italian, the many squash types are a favorite vegetable. A larger and longer variety called *cucuzza* is such a part of the Sicilian personality that Sicilian-Americans quickly started growing them in their new homeland.

TOMATOES:

If Italian-Americans are known for their love of red sauce, or even "red gravy," it's because such large proportions of them hailed from Sicily. Tomatoes, brought to Europe by Columbus, are a near-mandatory addition to pasta, pizza, and a thousand other sauces, lovingly tended by a mamma who always knew how long to cook the sauce. Pulling into Corleone one Sunday afternoon in late summer looking for some Carrabba family members, we were struck by how eerily quiet the town was. Later we came to find out that the Carrabbas and most of the town were in the countryside, picking tomatoes and canning their tomatoes for the winter.

TUNA (CANNED):

Good albacore tuna packed in olive oil is always great to have on hand for a quick pasta sauce or antipasto. Always drain the oil from the can and use your best extra-virgin oil. The oil tuna is packed in will not be of the best quality.

VINEGAR:

Always have good red and white wine vinegar on hand for salads, sweet and sour sauce and for preserving vegetables.

VINO COTTO:

This is a syrup made from non-fermented grapes. No doubt stemming from the great Arab love for sweet tastes, this liquid is used to bring exactly that to innumerable Sicilian dishes.

WATERMELON:

The Arabs introduced watermelon to Sicily, possibly as early as the 10th century. In addition to the sweet, refreshing pulp, the seeds were roasted and then pounded into a paste — or sometimes crushed into cakes. There are two kinds of watermelon in Sicily: one round with a light green skin, the other larger and darker green. Watermelon juice is a quick, cold drink in Sicily, and also the flavoring in a popular pudding, *Gelo di Melone*, page 154.

Rosemary

BASICS & TECH

NIQUES

"My mother came to this country from Cefalú, Sicily.... When I was a little girl, she taught me how to cook the basic things...."

—Grace Mandola, *from the Foreword*

Basics & Techniques

BASIC MEAT BROTH
Makes 6 about quarts

2 gallons cold water

3 pounds beef meat with bones, beef shanks preferred

1 3-pound whole chicken

2 onions, peeled and coarsely chopped

3 carrots, peeled and coarsely chopped

3 celery stalks, coarsely chopped

2 medium tomatoes coarsely chopped

2 bay leaves

8 peppercorns

4 thyme sprigs

1 bunch parsley

TO PREPARE

1 Place beef and chicken in a stockpot. Cover with cold water and slowly bring to a simmer. Try to keep from boiling the water or the resulting broth will not be clear. It should take 1 to 2 hours to come to a simmer. Skim off any scum or foam that comes to the top. Skimming throughout the cooking process is very important if you want a good-tasting, clear broth.

2 With a piece of cheesecloth, make a sachet with the bay leaves, peppercorns, thyme, and parsley. Tie this sachet and place it in the stockpot along with the vegetables. Bring broth back to a simmer. Skim, skim, skim!

3 Cook for 4 more hours, skimming all the while.

4 When done pour broth through a fine mesh sieve lined with several layers of dampened cheesecloth. Discard the boiled meat, bones, and vegetables. Cool broth rapidly in an ice bath until you don't see any steam. Refrigerate. The next day remove all solidified fat from the broth. You should have about 6 quarts of broth. For a stronger broth, reduce the broth as you like.

USES

Use this broth on it,s own or as a base for any soup to add depth and flavor It will keep well in the refrigerator for up to 4 days, or in re-sealable plastic bags in the freezer for up to 2 months.

Basics & Techniques

BEEF STOCK
Makes 4 quarts

1 tablespoon olive oil

3 pounds beef bones

2 onions, peeled and cut into large dice

3 carrots, peeled cut into large dice

3 celery stalks, cut into large dice

2 tablespoons tomato paste

2 bay leaves

8 peppercorns

4 thyme sprigs

1 bunch parsley stems

2 cups red wine

TO PREPARE

1 Preheat the oven to 400° F.

2 Brush a cookie sheet or sheet pan with the olive oil and spread the bones on the sheet pan. Place in the oven and roast until browned, approximately 1 hour.

3 In a large bowl, mix the vegetables with the tomato paste to evenly coat. Set aside.

4 Remove the bones from the oven and transfer to a 6-quart stockpot leaving the olive oil on the sheet pan.

5 Pour off the excess oil from the sheet pan. Place the coated vegetables on the same cookie sheet and roast for approximately 30–45 minutes, or until lightly browned. Remove the vegetables from the oven and transfer to the stockpot.

6 With a piece of cheesecloth, make a sachet with the bay leaves, peppercorns, thyme, and parsley stems. Tie this sachet and place it in the stockpot.

7 Pour 1/2 cup of the red wine on the baking sheet and scrape up any bits of vegetables or bones left on the pan. Pour this into the stockpot along with the remaining wine.

8 Place the stockpot on the stove and fill it with cold water to cover the bones. Bring to a boil and then turn down to simmer. Cook for 8–12 hours, skimming off any scum that floats to the top within the first 2 hours of cooking.

9 You can cook this overnight and strain it the next day through a wire mesh sieve. Discard the bones. Return the stock to the stove and reduce the volume by half.

USES
Use this stock as a base for any soup you want to add some depth and flavor to. It will keep well in the refrigerator for up to 4 days, or in re-sealable plastic bags in the freezer for up to 2 months.

Basics & Techniques

CHICKEN STOCK
Makes about 4 quarts

4 pounds chicken bones, or chicken necks or backs

2 cups white wine

1 medium onion, peeled and cut into large dice

2 large carrots, peeled and cut into large dice

3 ribs celery, cut into large dice

1 fennel bulb and 3–4 stalks

Water to cover

2 bay leaves

8 peppercorns

1 bunch of parsley stems

5 thyme sprigs

TO PREPARE

1 Preheat the oven to 400° F.

2 Place the chicken bones on a baking sheet and roast in the oven for 35–45 minutes, or until dark brown. Remove the bones from the oven and place in a 6-quart stockpot.

3 Add approximately 1 cup of the wine to the sheet pan and place on the stove top. With a wooden spoon, loosen the bits and pieces stuck to the pan and pour into the stockpot.

4 Roast the vegetables for about 30 minutes on the same pan until they are nicely browned. Transfer the vegetables to the stockpot and add the remaining wine to the sheet pan and loosen the vegetable bits with a wooden spoon. Add them to the stockpot as well.

5 Next fill the pot to cover the bones and vegetables with cold water. With a piece of cheesecloth, make a sachet with the bay leaves, peppercorns, parsley stems, and thyme. Tie this sachet and place it in the stock-pot.

6 Bring to a boil, then turn down to a simmer and cook for 2–3 hours.

7 Strain the stock through a wire mesh sieve and discard the bones. If you would like a richer stock, reduce the volume by half.

USES

This stock is great as a base for any soup or sauce. For the classic light chicken stock, omit roasting the vegetables and simply put all the ingredients into a stockpot. Cook for 2–3 hours and strain. Either version of this recipe will keep well in the refrigerator for up to four days, or in re-sealable plastic bags in the freezer for up to 2 months.

Basics & Techniques

FISH STOCK
Makes about 1 gallon

3 pounds fish bones, preferably white fish such as
halibut, snapper, sole or grouper. You can use the heads
for more flavor, but make sure the gills are removed.

1 gallon cold water

2 cups white wine

3 ribs celery, coarsely chopped

1 bunch leeks, cleaned and coarsely chopped, white part only

1 small onion, peeled and coarsely chopped

2 bay leaves

8 peppercorns

1 cup parsley stems

1/4 cup thyme stems or tarragon stems, (a small handful)

TO PREPARE

1 In a large stockpot, place the bones, water, wine, and vegetables.

2 With a piece of cheesecloth, make a sachet with the bay leaves, peppercorns, parsley stems, thyme, or tarragon stems. Tie this sachet and place it in the stockpot.

3 Put on stove and bring to a boil.

4 Once the liquid is boiling, turn the heat down to simmer. With a large spoon or ladle, skim off the scum that floats to the top.

5 Cook for 30 minutes and then turn off the stove. Let this mixture sit for 15 minutes, pressing down the vegetables and bones to extract all the flavor.

6 Strain the mixture through a large piece of cheesecloth into a large bowl and place the bowl in an ice bath. (To make an ice bath, put a couple of trays of ice cubes in a large pot of water and place the bowl into the water.)

7 Stir to cool evenly. Refrigerate or freeze the stock until ready to use.

USES

You can use this stock for any fish soup recipe such as gumbo, *cioppino* or even chowder. If you refrigerate the mixture, it will keep for 4–6 days. If frozen, it will keep for up to 2 months.

Basics & Techniques

MAMMA'S MARINARA
Yield approximately 3 cups

3 cups extra-virgin olive oil

1 small yellow onion, finely choppd

3 medium cloves garlic, finely choppd

1 35-ounce can Italian tomatoes with juice passed
   through a food mill fitted with the smallest holes

Kosher salt and freshly-ground black pepper to taste

10 large basil leaves torn in several pieces

TO PREPARE

1 In a stainless steel saucepan place the olive oil,
onion, and garlic, over medium heat and cook, stirring occasionally, for 8–10 minutes, or until onions
are soft and translucent.

2 Add tomato purée, bring sauce to a boil, reduce
to a simmer, season with salt and pepper and cook
for 30 minutes, stirring frequently to keep sauce
from burning.

3 When the sauce is thickened, adjust seasoning.
Turn off the stove, add the basil leaves to the top of
the sauce and cover tightly. Let sauce sit for a few
minutes and then remove the lid and stir in the basil
that was sitting on top of the sauce. Cool sauce if
not using immediately and store in the refrigerator
in a plastic container with a tight fitting lid.

POLENTA
Serves 12

1 pound cornmeal

2 quarts cold water

3 tablespoons salt

2 cups grated Parmigiano or Pecorino Romano

TO PREPARE

1 Bring 2 quarts of water with 3 tablespoons salt to
boil.

2 Lower heat to medium. Drizzle polenta in a little
at a time, always stirring in the same direction. When
all the polenta has been stirred in, the polenta will
start to thicken.

3 Stir vigorously and constantly over low flame, in
the same direction for about 7 minutes.

4 Remove from heat. Add 2 cups grated cheese
and blend thoroughly.

5 Polenta may now be served immediately—just like
grits or mashed potatoes.

ALTERNATE METHOD

6 Lightly coat work surface or sheet pan with olive
oil. Pour polenta onto surface. Spread polenta evenly
until 2-inch thick and let cool completely. Cut
polenta into rectangular shapes about 2 x 3-inches
or desired size.

6 The polenta rectangles may now be toasted or
quickly sautéed.

Basics & Techniques

BASIC EGG PASTA
Yields 1 pound

4 cups all-purpose unbleached flour

4 extra-large eggs

1 teaspoon olive oil

Pinch salt

TO PREPARE

1 Place the flour in a mound on your work surface. Make a well in the center of the flour. Add the eggs, oil, and salt to the center of the well. With a fork, start beating eggs in the center of the well as you incorporate the flour a little at a time.

2 Little by little, incorporate more flour from the bottom of the well, until the dough can be handled. When the dough is firm enough to handle, move it to the side. Scrape up the remaining flour.

3 Sift the flour, discarding the unwanted particles and set aside. Return to the pasta dough and start kneading, incorporating the sifted flour until you have a very firm smooth dough. This process should take about 5 minutes. Flatten the ball of dough. Run the dough through the widest setting of the pasta machine.

4 Flour the dough only on the bottom. Fold dough into thirds. Press to seal the folds together with your fingers. Run the dough through the widest setting again making sure the dough is turned so the open side goes in first, letting the air escape. Repeat this process 8–10 more times or until the dough is very smooth and elastic.

5 Lightly flour the dough on both sides. Turn the setting on the pasta machine to make the rollers closer together. Pass the pasta through the rollers. Repeat this process until you reach the desired thickness.

6 If you are making long cuts, let the pasta dry a few minutes before running the sheets through cutter. If you are making stuffed pasta, like ravioli or tortelli you will need to work quickly and stuff the pasta promptly to achieve a good seal.

Basics & Techniques

PIZZA DOUGH
Makes one 10–12-inch round pizza or
One 15-1/2 x 10-1/2-inch rectangular pizza

1/2 teaspoon dry yeast
3/4 cups water at 100° F
1 tablespoon olive oil
1 teaspoon salt
2 cups all-purpose flour

TO PREPARE

1 In a large mixing bowl, dissolve the yeast into 1/4 of the water. Let it sit for 10 minutes to dissolve. Stir in the oil and salt.

2 Add 1/2 cup of flour to start and mix thoroughly. Now start adding more water and flour, alternating and mixing well after each addition. Once you've added all the water and flour, a sticky dough should be forming.

3 Turn the dough out onto a lightly-floured surface and knead for 10 minutes. It should still be slightly sticky.

4 Place the ball of dough into a large bowl, lightly coated with olive oil. Cover with plastic wrap and let it rise for 1–1-1/2 hours, or until doubled in size. (You can easily double this recipe—just increase the rising time to two hours.)

5 Punch the dough down and be careful not to knead it any further as you want the dough to be "relaxed" and easy to work with. If you have doubled the recipe by increasing the rising time, divide the dough into 2 balls after you have punched it down, and freeze one of the balls.

6 If you're using a pizza stone to shape the dough, sprinkle a generous amount of flour over the surface of a pizza paddle, or alternatively you can get a 1/2-inch flexible piece of board from the hardware store and cut into about a 14 x 14-inch square.

7 Lightly flour a wooden work surface and place dough on work surface. Flour your hands, start from the center of the dough, and begin to shape, using a patting and stretching combination, until you achieve a 10–12-inch round (depending on how thin or thick you want it). It does not have to be perfectly round!

8 If you are using a pizza pan, brush the bottom with a little olive oil first and then start from the center of the dough, using a patting and stretching combination until you reach the edges. You may need to gently pull and stretch some parts to reach the edges.

NOTES

To freeze the dough, wrap the ball of dough in plastic wrap and place in a freezer bag, or wrap with aluminum foil. It can be frozen for up to six months. To thaw, place in the refrigerator overnight and then remove from the plastic bag or foil, and bring to room temperature in an oiled bowl covered with plastic wrap. When it is at the point of beginning to rise again, it is ready for making pizza according to the recipe.

Basics & Techniques

HOMEMADE BREADCRUMBS
Makes 4–5 cups, depending on size of loaf

1 loaf stale rustic Italian bread or French bread

TO PREPARE
1 Preheat oven to 175° F.
2 Take stale leftover bread and cut into cubes. Spread the stale bread cubes evenly on a sheet pan and put pan into the oven.
3 Let bake for about 45 minutes until very dry and lightly brown. Remove from the oven and let cool completely.
4 Place breadcrumbs in a food processor and grind very fine. Place breadcrumbs in a container with a tight-fitting lid. Store in the pantry.

MAMMA'S BREADCRUMBS
Makes about 7 cups

3 cups Homemade Breadcrumbs
2 cups finely-grated Pecorino Romano cheese
6 green onions, finely chopped
1/2 cup fresh Italian parsley, finely chopped
3 cloves garlic, peeled and minced
1/3 cup finely-chopped fresh basil
1/2 tablespoon kosher salt
1/2 tablespoon freshly-ground black pepper

TO PREPARE
Place all ingredients in a mixing bowl and mix well. Store, refrigerated in an airtight container or re-sealable plastic bag.

USES
Perfect for most recipes calling for use of bread-crumbs.

Basics & Techniques

MUDDICA
Yield 2 cups

1/2 cup extra-virgin olive oil

2 cups Homemade Breadcrumbs (see page 179)

Kosher salt to taste

TO PREPARE

In a nonstick skillet heat the oil over moderate heat until it is hot but not smoking and cook the bread-crumbs, stirring, for 2–3 minutes, or until they are golden. Season to taste with salt. Transfer the bread-crumbs to a small serving bowl.

BRUSCHETTA
Serves 8

8 slices rustic Italian bread, about 3/4-inch thick

Extra-virgin olive oil

4 large garlic cloves, peeled and cut in half

Salt and freshly-ground black pepper

TO PREPARE

1 Place bread slices on a baking sheet and toast under a preheated broiler until the bread is lightly toasted on both sides. In Italy the bread is placed on the charcoal grill to give it a nice smoky flavor.

2 Remove from the oven and rub one side of the bread with the cut side of a garlic clove. Repeat with remaining slices of bread and garlic cloves.

3 Drizzle toast with a liberal amount of olive oil. Season with salt and pepper.

Basics & Techniques

RICOTTA CHEESE
Makes about one pound

1 gallon whole milk
1 quart buttermilk

TO PREPARE

1 Combine the milk and buttermilk in a 8-quart stainless steel pot over low heat. Place a thermometer in the liquid, without allowing it to touch the bottom of the pan, and continue to heat until the liquid reaches 175° F.

2 While the liquid is heating, rinse some cheesecloth and use it to line a strainer or small colander placed in a bowl.

3 When the ricotta forms on the surface of the milk, remove it with a slotted spoon or skimmer and place it in the lined strainer.

4 Let the ricotta drain in the cheesecloth for 1 hour. Then place the lined strainer in a bowl and place in the refrigerator to let drain for a few more hours.

5 Store in an airtight container. Ricotta is best when used in a few days.

RICOTTA SALATA
Makes about one pound

1 batch of Ricotta (see opposite left)
1–2 cups kosher salt
Cheese molds, or plastic containers with holes punched in them for drainage

TO PREPARE

1 Divide the ricotta into two equal parts and place each in plastic containers with holes punched in for drainage. Then add the kosher salt on top. (It should cover with up to 1/4-inch thickness of the salt.)

2 Place containers in the refrigerator with a pan underneath for drainage. Let them stand for 3–4 days, checking every few days to see that there is still salt covering the top of the cheese. Add more salt if needed.

3 After 4 days, take the cheese out of the containers and wash the salt off the top.

4 Invert the cheese and add more salt to the other end of the cheese covering it again with 1/4-inch of salt. Every few days check to see that there is still salt covering the top of the cheese. Add more if needed.

5 You will know that it is done when the ricotta is crumbly, the consistency of Feta cheese. Wash off all the salt and pat dry. You can store this cheese for up to two months in the refrigerator.

Basics & Techniques

VANILLA CREAM FILLING
Yields 2-1/2 cups

2 cups milk
8 tablespoons sugar
6 tablespoons cornstarch
4 egg yolks
1/2 teaspoon vanilla

TO PREPARE

1 Heat milk and 2 tablespoons of the sugar over medium heat until very hot but not boiling.
2 Combine the remainder of the sugar and the cornstarch in a mixing bowl and then add egg yolks. Whisk until thick.
3 Add the hot milk, a little at a time, to the mixing bowl. Return the mixture to the stove over medium heat to thicken. When it achieves a custard consistency, remove from heat.
4 Add vanilla, mix until cool.

USES

Great for various desserts. Use rubber utensils so that the cream will stay yellow.

FIG PRESERVES
Makes 3 1-pint jars

3 pounds figs, stemmed
2 quarts water
1 teaspoon baking soda
2 cups water
4 cups sugar
4 tablespoons of lemon juice or slice up one whole lemon

TO PREPARE

1 Soak figs in the water and the baking soda for 15 minutes.
2 Drain and rinse figs.
3 In a stainless steel pot over medium-high heat bring 2 cups of water and the sugar to a boil and simmer uncovered for 15 minutes.
4 Add figs and boil gently for 20 minutes.
5 Remove from heat and bring to room temperature and then refrigerate, covered, overnight.
6 Return to the pot to medium-high heat and bring the figs back to a boil and boil gently for 30 –40 minutes and add the lemon juice.
7 Place the figs into sterilized preserve jars, leaving 1/2-inch of head space jar. Seal and process in boiling water for 45 minutes.

NOTE

Historians argue about whether the Greeks sent figs to Egypt or whether figs traveled the other way. Regardless of their origin, figs are grown extensively in India, Turkey, Greece, and Sicily. To our taste, Sicilian figs are especially wonderful

Basics & Techniques

PREPARING AN ARTICHOKE

This is the basic method for trimming an artichoke. By using this method the artichoke can then be prepared in many different ways.

1 Taking care not to break the stem, begin bending back and snapping off the outer green part of the leaves, letting only the whitish, tender bottom of each leaf remain, this is the edible portion. Use a lemon half to squeeze juice over the cut portions so they won't discolor.

2 As you get deeper into the artichoke, the leaves will snap off farther and farther from the base. Keep snapping off leaves until you expose a central cone of leaves that are green only at the tips. The paler, whitish base of the leaves should be at least 12 inches high. Slice at least an inch of the top of the artichoke eliminating the green tip, rub with the lemon half so that the leaves won't discolor.

3 You can now see into the center of the artichoke where you will find at the base of the choke some very small leaves with prickly tips curving inward. With a teaspoon or a tomato corer, scrape away the little leaves and the fuzzy choke beneath them, being careful not to cut away any of the heart or other tender parts. Return to the outside of the artichoke and pare away the green parts of the leaves around the base, leaving only the white.

4 All there is left to trim now is the outer part of the stem. Turning the artichoke upside down, you will note from the bottom of the stem that the stem has a whitish core surrounded by a layer of green. Trim away all the green up to the base of the artichoke, keeping only the white part. Be careful not to detach the stem and always rub the cut portions with lemon juice so that they will not discolor.

NOTE

The artichoke is now ready to be used in any recipe that may call for a whole artichoke that is completely edible, such as *Carciofi alla Romana*. If the artichokes are going to be halved, quartered, or sliced then it would be easier to trim away all green areas from the exterior of the artichoke first, including the base, then cut artichoke in half and scoop out the small leaves and fuzzy choke.

Basics & Techniques

PREPARING AN EGGPLANT

1 Slice off and discard ends of eggplant, but do not peel. Cut eggplant into slices or cubes as specific recipe directs.

2 Salt eggplant lightly on both sides and place in a colander.

3 Cover eggplant with plate and weight down, a cast iron skillet lid works well to help squeeze bitter fluids from the eggplant. Allow eggplant to drain for 30 minutes.

4 Rinse away salt, pat dry, and proceed with recipe instructions.

NOTE If you have young, slender eggplant, and are in a hurry, you may skip the salting and draining steps and proceed directly to sauté or grill the eggplant slices.

An alternative to sautéing the eggplant: is to slice or cube the eggplant, place in a Pyrex baking dish, drizzle with a little olive oil, season with salt and freshly-ground pepper, and bake at 450°F. for 20 minutes or until tender. Keeps down the calorie count and saves time for other preparation steps!

BLANCHING AND ROASTING VEGETABLES

Blanching is a process used to remove the skin of vegetables, keep vegetables looking fresh, or speed up the cooking process.

TO BLANCH VEGETABLES

1 Clean and cut the vegetables into the desired shape. Keep cut vegetables similar in size to avoid overcooking or undercooking them.

2 Bring a large pot of water to a boil and add vegetables. For green vegetables, add salt to the boiling water *before* adding the vegetables to help keep them a brighter green. Cook the vegetables *al dente*, 2–4 minutes.

3 To avoid overcooking the vegetables and to stop the cooking process, place blanched, vegetables in a bowl of ice water. The ice water will also keep the vegetables crisp and their color bright.

TO BLANCH TOMATOES

1 Prepare the tomatoes by turning them so the stem is on the cutting board. With a sharp knife, score the skin on the bottom of each one with a small "x", making sure not to cut them too deep.

2 Place the tomatoes in boiling water and cook for 8–12 seconds, depending on the ripeness of the tomatoes.

3 When the skin starts to peel away from the flesh, remove the tomatoes from the boiling water with a slotted spoon and place them in ice water.

4 Once they are cool enough to handle, take them out of the water and remove the skins.

5 To stuff the tomatoes, slice them into halves and scoop out the seeds and the pith.

Basics & Techniques

TO ROAST PEPPERS WITH A GAS STOVE

1 If you have a gas stove, take the peppers and place them directly on the flame, making sure that you don't let them fall down between or into the burners.

2 Char the skins to a blackened state, turning the peppers to evenly brown them.

3 Once they are completely blackened all over, place the peppers in a bowl and cover with plastic wrap for 10–15 minutes. This will let the peppers sweat and make them easier to peel.

4 When the peppers are ready, remove them from the bowl. Rub or scrape off the skin and then julienne or dice, depending on your needs.

NOTE Don't wash roasted peppers—this will take away the flavor you are trying to enhance.

TO ROAST PEPPERS WITH AN ELECTRIC STOVE

1 For electric stoves, you can get the same roasted effect by placing the peppers under the broiler.

2 First, cut your peppers in half and remove the seeds and stems.

3 Turn your broiler on high, place the peppers on a cookie sheet, cut-side-down, and drizzle with olive oil.

4 Place the cookie sheet in the oven about 3–4 inches away from the broiler element of the oven. Broil 15–18 minutes until the peppers are blistered.

5 Remove from the oven and place the peppers in a bowl and cover with plastic wrap for 10–15 minutes. Let them sweat and cool so they will be easier to peel.

6 When the peppers are ready, remove them from the bowl. Rub off the skin and then julienne or dice them, depending on your needs.

NOTE Don't wash roasted peppers—this will take away the flavor you are trying to enhance.

Basics & Techniques

PEELING GARLIC

1 Place the garlic bulb on a steady surface with the tapered end facing up at a slight angle. Hit the garlic bulb with the palm of your hand to separate the cloves.

2 With the flat side of a chef's knife, lightly crush a garlic clove to break the skin. Peel away the skin and cut off the root end. The garlic is now ready to slice, chop, or mince.

3 Always chop garlic as close to the time you are going to use it. Never boil, deep-fry or soak garlic in water in order to peel it—it changes the taste and removes a lot of the essential oil.

ROASTING GARLIC

Garlic can be roasted in different ways, depending on how you want to use it. The whole bulb of garlic can be roasted or the bulb can be separated into individual cloves and be roasted. Shallots should be left whole.

TO ROAST GARLIC OR SHALLOTS

1 Preheat your oven to 300° F.

2 Slice the tip off both ends off the garlic or shallot. Peel away the excess papery covering around the outside of the garlic bulb. For the shallots, make sure not to remove too much of the paper.

3 Keeping the bulb whole, place in a small pan. With the garlic you could break the whole bulb into individual cloves depending on how you want to serve it.

4 Drizzle a little olive oil over the shallot or garlic bulb, or toss the individual cloves of garlic with a little olive oil. Season garlic or shallots with kosher salt and freshly-ground black pepper. Cover the pan with foil or a lid and bake for 30–40 minutes.

5 Remove from the oven and let cool.

6 The garlic and shallot will have the consistency of a paste, that can be squeezed out and placed on bread or crackers, or used in salad dressings. You can also serve the garlic bulb whole as an accompaniment, with chicken, beef, or fish, or with cheese as a first course.

Basics & Techniques

ROASTING NUTS

Nuts may be roasted either on the stove top or in the oven. Some people prefer to roast the nuts in the oven because it requires less attention. Also, you can reserve the oil from the blanched or roasted nuts and use the oil in vinaigrettes or dressing.

TO ROAST NUTS IN THE OVEN

1 Preheat oven to 325° F.

2 Place the nuts in a sauté pan or on a cookie sheet. If you plan to reserve the nut oil, add enough extra-virgin olive oil or a high-grade vegetable oil, to cover the bottom of the pan or cookie sheet.

3 Place the nuts in the oven for approximately 20 minutes.

4 For even roasting make sure to flip the nuts over.

5 If you used oil in your pan, carefully strain the nuts and reserve the oil in an airtight container for later use.

TO ROAST NUTS ON THE STOVE TOP

1 Place the nuts in a sauté pan on medium-low heat. If you want to reserve the nut oil for later use, add enough extra-virgin olive oil or a high-grade vegetable oil, to cover the bottom of the pan.

2 If you do not want to reserve any oil, place the nuts in a dry pan.

3 Toast on medium-low heat, turning the nuts with a spatula so they are evenly browned. You will need to watch them carefully using this method because the nuts tend to burn quickly.

4 The nuts should cook about 10–15 minutes, depending on the size.

5 If you added oil to the pan, carefully strain the nuts, and reserve the oil in an airtight container for later use.

Acknowledgements

West 175 Productions, Inc.
Executive Producers: Elizabeth Brock, Jamie Hammond
Director: Cassy Soden
Culinary Director: Chris Fitzgibbon
Culinary Team: Tom Bennett, Melissa Nyffeler, Brian Quinn, Eugene Stoddard
Associate Producers: Marla Poland, Garland Hooker
Editor: Alex Carrillo

With great thanks to all who contributed and helped with the food
preparation, props, platters, and photography:
Pepa Brower; June Jackson; Diana Neely; Carol Cates; and Ardon Judd;
Kitchen 'N Things, Kathy Casey Food Studios, and Larry's Markets of Seattle,
Washington; Kitchen Works and Brookshire's Grocery of Albany, Texas;
Central Markets and HEB Groceries of Texas.

Photo Credits

Images by Christine and Torry Bruno:
Pgs; 1, 4 (top right), 14, 44, 92, and 124

Images from Mandola Family:
Pgs; 5 (bottom left), 6, 7, 8, 11, 12, 13, 30, 135 (center and bottom), 147, and 192

Images from PhotoDisc:
Pgs; 19, 29, 50, 55, 64, 69, 91, 98, 101, 111 (top and bottom), 135 (top),
137, 141, 157, 160, 162 (top and center), 165, 166 (bottom), 170, 172 and 177

All other Photography ©Watt Matthews Casey Jr.

"No more pictures! Let us get back to dessert!"

Left to right: Aunt Angelina LaMonte, Aunt Annette 'Sanina' Romano, Grandma Margherita Mandola, and Grandma Rosa Testa, relatives of Damian and Johnny

CD-ROM Contents

Exercise 1: Name Stories
Exercise 1 Handout

Mini-Exercise A: Read a Little More for Fun
Top Baby Names by Decade
100 Most Common Surnames in America

Exercise 2: A Special Home
Exercise 2 Handout
Floor Plan Grid

Exercise 3: Make a Choice
Exercise 3 Handout

Exercise 4: Holiday Traditions
Exercise 4 Handout
Blank Mind Map: Fill in the Bubbles

Mini-Exercise D: Adding Art
Draw a Cake Template
Wrap a Package Template
Draw a Path Illustration

Exercise 5: Family Leisure Time and the 1950s
Exercise 5 Handout

Mini-Exercise E: Adding Music to the Mix
Popular Broadway Musicals from the 1950s
Popular Hollywood Musicals from the 1950s

About the Author

Kathy Laurenhue, M.A., is CEO of Wiser Now, Inc., a company focused on training and product and curriculum development related to older adults, with an emphasis on brain aerobics and other positive mind stimulation, life stories, dementia, and caregiving. For the past 15 years, Kathy has given training seminars throughout the United States and Australia, and has developed multimedia training materials for national companies in both countries.

In the 1990s, Kathy was president of Better Directions, Inc., a multimedia training company that emphasized a practical, but light-hearted approach to Alzheimer's care. She was also the editor of *Wiser Now,* an international award-winning monthly newsletter for Alzheimer's caregivers.

Her interest in life stories began in the early 1970s as she began interviewing relatives to try to make sense of her father's complicated genealogy. This was followed by a home business of writing the life stories of others, teaching life stories through the local community college, leading programming sessions in long-term care, and ultimately writing ***Getting to Know the Life Stories of Older Adults***.

Kathy has a master's degree in instructional technology and an undergraduate degree in English and journalism. She began putting these skills to work in the field of dementia while serving as the primary caregiver for her ever-cheerful mother, who died of Alzheimer's disease in 1996.

Kathy is the author of two additional books, *Alzheimer's Basic Caregiving—An ABC Guide* and *Activities of Daily Living—An ADL Guide for Alzheimer's Care*. Additional information can be found on her Web site, http://www.wiser-now.com.

Introduction

"God made man because he loves stories."
—Yiddish proverb

I have written this book with three goals in mind. The first is to build positive relationships and foster understanding as we discover how our life stories are unique and what we have in common. I believe much of the fear and discord in the world today could be overcome if we simply took the time to get to know one another.

Thornton Wilder wrote a play many years ago called *Our Town,* which started me on the road to teaching life story sharing. One of the main characters in the play is the Stage Manager whose role is partly to set the stage for what the audience is about to see. At one point he notes, "This is the way we were; in our growing up and in our marrying and in our living and in our dying." (p. 33) It is a *universal* story; the action takes place in the early 1900s, but could have easily been a hundred years earlier or later.

Yet it is also a unique story. Wilder wanted us to appreciate the individual precious moments that make up our lives. In Act III, Emily, one of the main characters, has died in childbirth and she asks the Stage Manager to be allowed to relive one day in her life—her 12th birthday. As she goes back, she sees everything with new eyes—how wonderfully ordinary and happy the day was, and how oblivious they all were to it. It is too painful, and before breakfast is even eaten, she begs the Stage Manager to let her return to her grave. She says one last tearful good-by: "Good-by, world, Good-by, Grover's Corners, . . . Mama and Papa . . . Good-by to clocks ticking . . . and Mama's sunflowers. And food and coffee. And new ironed dresses and hot baths . . . and sleeping and waking up. Oh, earth, you're too wonderful for anybody to realize you." She turns to the Stage Manager and asks, "Do any human beings ever realize life while they live it?—every, every minute?" The Stage Manager answers, "No," but after a pause adds: "The saints and poets, maybe—they do some." (p. 108)

There are elements of our life stories that we have in common and there are elements that are uniquely ours. It is in sharing *both* that we build bonds with one another. And it is in realizing the wonder in *every* moment that we learn to treasure life rather than compromise it.

My second goal for this book is to foster self-awareness. It is one thing to lead these exercises, but another to do them yourself. You will be surprised by what you learn about a subject you thought you knew well—who you are. I also hope those who do the exercises with you will have the same awakening. That leads to the third goal.

I hope you and those who do these exercises with you will have revitalized self-esteem. Most of us are oblivious to all we've lived through, the character we've shown, the fun we've had, the talents we've exhibited. These exercises can provide reminders.

Lastly, my underlying goal is to build your brain power. There is a tendency to dismiss reminiscence as useless chatter about boring bygone days, but these exercises are designed to help you to look at your life experiences in new ways. Every time you make new connections—even to old memories—you are building brain power.

WHO SHOULD BUY THIS BOOK

This book is intended to give groups of people fun, interesting, and energizing ways to get to know one another with a minimum amount of preparation and props. Although my experience has been primarily working with older adults, I hope it will be used any place that people might benefit from greater understanding of one another, including:

- School and after-school settings/youth groups
- Organizations and churches
- Adult day centers and senior centers
- Residential care settings for older adults
- Training sessions as ice-breakers or team builders (exercises like "Make a Choice" are especially good in this regard)
- Among families, including those who are caring for someone who is disabled and need ideas for visits or daily activities

In some places the references are to experiences only older adults are likely to have had—such as the focus on the 1950s—but it would be easy to update the references if your group consists only of young people, and if it is a mixed group, sharing viewpoints will benefit both young and old.

I have tried to offer specific ideas for adapting these exercises for people with dementia (see Appendix A). Most people with dementia are likely to be older adults, but you may find useful ideas in those directions for working with people who have developmental disabilities, too. Other ideas work with everyone, in part because the focus is genuine interest in each others' lives.

A WORD ABOUT TERMINOLOGY

Dementia and Alzheimer's Disease: I tend to use these words somewhat interchangeably in this book, even though in reality dementia is a symptom of dozens of diseases and Alzheimer's disease is the most common of those diseases. Often I will refer to specific skill losses common in people with Alzheimer's disease, and more general memory loss in people with dementia. There is tremendous variation among the capabilities of people with mild cognitive impairment, those in the end stages of Alzheimer's disease, and individuals in any stage. Most of my advice is aimed at a middle level.

Families: I refer often to families, and although I generally mean either the family in which we grew up or the family of which we were a part after marriage,

I am open to a diversity of meanings. Not everyone married and had children; not everyone grew up in or raised a traditional family. Not everyone who once was, still is part of a traditional family. Many people live a large part of their lives alone or with a same-sex roommate or partner. Many of us are as close to certain friends as we ever were to certain family members. Many of us consider coworkers, fellow volunteers or club members, or fellow residents in our care setting part of our family. When you read the word "family" in any of the following exercises, interpret it any way you want.

Participants: Because I hope this book will be used by a wide variety of people, young and old, male and female, healthy in mind and body or not, living at home or in a residential care setting, I have tried to use the word "participants" as a generic, all-inclusive term. It may seem a little odd if you are a family caregiver doing these exercises with a parent or spouse, but it is the best I can do with the English language.

WHAT THIS BOOK IS NOT

There are hundreds of books about how to write your life story. This book is not one of them. Most people will never get around to putting their stories in print, and, I'm sorry to say, even if they do, their readers will likely be few. This book is not about *writing* your life story, but about *sharing* it and learning from others. The goal is not literary, but love—mutual understanding. And fun. Definitely fun.

For the Reader

WHY I EMPHASIZE THE POSITIVE

Throughout this book, with only slight exceptions, I have emphasized drawing on positive memories. Here is my reasoning:

1. The fastest way to build a bond with another person is to smile, and the second fastest is to find that you laugh at the same things. If we emphasize positive memories, chances are good there will be lots of opportunities to laugh together.
2. There is enough depression in the world already, and certainly justification for depression if we focus on the world's problems. If we focus on what's good and right, we can build from there—and we'll have a stronger basis for friendships and facing problems together when we need to.
3. For many years it was thought that people had to relive trauma to heal from it. Now more and more studies are suggesting that attitude toward life plays a huge role in overcoming hardships. People who admit the tragedies in their lives and move on tend to live longer and happier lives than those who dwell on their troubles. Research is still coming in, but I see no harm in looking for silver linings. Every tragedy in my life came with wonderful gifts and many kindnesses wrapped in the barbed wire.

If There Are Tears Anyway

That said, there will still be tears sometimes. Often tears well up with tender memories—play a certain song, and you are young and in love again. It may hurt, but your life would be poorer without the memory, so you don't really mind. Often tears are cathartic; after a good cry, the body releases endorphins that can be as relaxing as laughter. And sometimes an exercise evokes genuine sorrow. If we talk about family vacations and you never took one with your family and have a terrible sense of deprivation from that, it's probably something I won't know in advance, and will therefore be surprised by your tears (and you may be, too). But maybe I can use that new knowledge to draw out other good memories—perhaps you made up for it by taking vacations with your own children or with adult friends. Or perhaps you would be pleased now to go on a day, weekend, or longer trip, and we can try to arrange it.

Many sorrows in our lives are much deeper and an integral part of who we are. In many cases it can be argued that they had a larger role in shaping us than our joys. If such sorrows are expressed, it is a sign that you and your participants have indeed bonded with one another, that they trust you to treat them gently—to sustain and safeguard them. Perhaps in another book I will talk more about how we can proactively share those deeper feelings, but here I remain determined to start by enjoying one another.

Allen Klein wrote a wonderful book in the late 1990s called *The Courage to Laugh.* Early on he recounts the story of a woman with ovarian cancer who had "worked hard over the oven" to prepare a meal that everyone enjoyed. When she popped into the bathroom before serving dessert, she saw herself in the mirror and gasped. She had apparently gotten *too* close to the oven and the entire front of her wig was "a solid melted glob of plastic fibers." She looked hilarious, and she couldn't believe that all through dinner no one had said a word and all had kept a straight face. When she walked back into the dining room laughing, everyone else began laughing, too. That led to a heart-to-heart conversation about her diagnosis. The shared humor had opened the doors to sharing the pain. "The shields were down and hearts connected." (p. 24) So let's begin by sharing our joys.

HOW THIS BOOK IS ORGANIZED

The exercises in this book are divided into four parts. Within those four parts are:

- Nine main exercises,
- Resources for Digging Deeper, and
- A series of mini-exercises that extend the topic of the main exercise.

At the end of the book are four appendixes:

- Special hints for working with people with dementia,
- Where to find the resources and games referenced in the book,
- Handout samples, and
- Art templates for some of the exercises.

Also at the end of the book is a CD-ROM containing printable versions of the handouts and art templates.

Note: The opening and closing of each exercise is not included in the script but the outline for beginning and ending each session is provided below.

The mini-exercises are not scripted, but I hope provide enough detail for the nonprofessional to have fun with them. Although I have tried to put this series of exercises in a logical order, you may also have success just picking and choosing from among them.

Make Each Exercise Yours

The nine main exercises are almost completely scripted so that *anyone* reading the script can easily lead the exercise. I've tried to include all the "patter" you are likely to need, along with ideas for expanding the discussion or keeping it moving based on my experiences. However, you can add to or condense this based on your time frames, your *own* experiences, and the appropriateness of the material for your group. (You may want to go through the exercise before leading it, and highlight what you consider the key points in your circumstances.) If things aren't going well, or the group goes off on a tangent, or if you have an idea you'd like to try, don't be limited by the script.

Don't be limited by the mini-exercises intended to expand the script either. For example, ideas for adding art are found in Mini-Exercise D, but could certainly be used with any exercise that might benefit from a new form of creative thinking.

The Resources for Digging Deeper in each section list many activity books from Bifolkal, ElderGames, and ElderSong, all of which have produced hundreds of trivia quizzes and other ideas to insert for a change of pace. If possible, always bring one of those resources to class so that you have a new idea to substitute if needed.

> *Quick Tip:*   One way to use trivia quizzes is to divide your group into two teams giving each team half the questions to ask the other team. Assign arbitrary points (1,000 each is always impressive) to the questions. Always have a bonus question ready for breaking ties. Encourage team cheering. Prizes can be stickers to add to name tags, a 2-foot length of ribbon hung around the winners' necks, or, if you have a button-making machine, silly buttons that say "Brain power" or "Trivia whiz."

USING THIS BOOK EFFECTIVELY

Potential Settings and Participants

Most of these exercises can be done in a variety of settings, such as:

- A group exercise led by a formal leader (Some could serve as energizers or ice-breakers, too.)
- A spontaneous exercise while people are waiting (to enter the dining room? For a bus to take them somewhere? *On* the bus taking them somewhere?)
- A small group exercise when you have just two to four people gathered together
- A one-on-one exercise with a person who is sitting alone or who is bedridden
- In a person's home as a family game or in a residential care setting by family visitors
- By staff (aide, housekeeper, maintenance person) in a residential care setting as a conversation starter that creates a diversion when you are dressing or bathing the person or cleaning his or her room or replacing a light fixture, and so forth.

People of almost any age can participate in almost all the exercises. Part 3, which covers "The Historical Perspective" and concentrates on the 1950s, is the only section that might seem like a history lesson to those born later. Nevertheless, it provides multiple opportunities for comparing "then and now."

Ideal Group Size

Almost all of these exercises can be done with as little as a leader and one participant or as much as a leader and 200 participants, but as scripted here they probably work best with a group of 8 to 20 people. If you have a large group, consider dividing participants into smaller groups frequently, such as whenever they have been given a series of questions to discuss. That way many more people can actively participate and share their stories.

In a group of 25 or more, it is possible to call on only a limited number of participants. Ideally, if this is done in a day center or residential care setting, you will have aides, volunteers, or other staff in each small group to listen and learn, so that insights gained can be shared in a debriefing. ("Mrs. Jones absolutely loves the beach and has wonderful memories of family vacations on the Jersey shore," gives us an instant topic for reminiscence or distraction with Mrs. Jones during daily care.)

Know Your Group

Mobility Concerns: The general focus of each exercise is discussion. That provides exercise for the jaw, but little else. As noted below, I encourage leaders to add movement and motion, energy, and enthusiasm to each class, but do so keeping in mind the specific abilities of your participants. If they can stand and move about the room, give them an opportunity every chance you get. On the other hand, if participants are unsteady on their feet or the room is not conducive to moving about, don't take unnecessary risks. Look for other ways (and other body parts, such as arms) to move about.

Hearing Concerns: If you are leading a group of older adults, chances are good that some of them will have hearing deficits which may be further exacerbated by background noises or other activities nearby. You can at least partly alleviate these challenges by

- Providing handouts in fairly large type;
- Writing key questions and answers on a flip chart, white board, or overhead transparency;
- Always facing your audience as you speak so that your lips can be clearly seen; and
- Using a microphone, when possible.

Visual Concerns: People with visual impairments may need

- Handouts printed in larger type;
- Seating near the front so that they can see the flip chart, white board, or overhead transparency more clearly;
- Stronger lighting; and
- Assistance with any activity involving movement, such as moving from one side of a room to the other.

Dementia Concerns: Appendix A provides a number of things to keep in mind when doing these exercises with people with dementia. I have also included a few brief notes related to each exercise in the introduction to that exercise, since many will require making certain adaptations. I feel strongly about giving people with dementia every possible opportunity to participate because they are frequently underestimated. They have much they can still contribute, including a wonderful sense of humor.

Some of these adaptations may also work for people who are developmentally disabled. The primary focus of my advice is how to make the activity successful for *anyone* who might be easily confused, frustrated, or fearful of making a mistake.

Opening the Session When You Are Leading a Group

When you lead a formal group activity, it is always reassuring to participants if there is some routine to follow. Here are suggestions for what to do as people enter the room:

- Greet them warmly and ask how they are doing today.
- Give them name tags to wear with their names in large print, or if they are sitting at tables, encourage them to make a tent card (have folded card stock ready) with dark markers. Be sure they write the name they want to be known by in large letters on both sides of the card so that it can be seen by the maximum number of people.
- Introduce or re-introduce each person to the other participants. I also advocate beginning each class with introductions of participants, but when everyone is introduced as he or she comes into the room, it creates a more pleasant atmosphere and also provides multiple occasions to repeat (and remember) the person's name. Never assume that name tags are enough to assure everyone knows everyone.
- If refreshments are served, encourage people to get a cup of coffee or a glass of lemonade or whatever is available.
- Make small talk. Discuss the weather, a popular TV show, or some other "safe" subject that anyone can have an opinion about and that everyone can be drawn into.
- Unless there are special circumstances, such as lunch having been served late, begin the class on time.
- At the beginning of the class, ask participants to say their names, using the name they prefer to be called by. (Some prefer Mrs. Jones, others a first name, and still others an informal nickname. Chances are, we all need reminders.)
- Be sure participants know where the bathrooms are and encourage them to "get up and go" whenever they need to rather than waiting for a formal break.

Closing the Session When You Are Leading a Group

Bringing closure to a class is also important. It does not have to be elaborate, but there should be some activity that signifies the end. I have made simple *preliminary* closing suggestions for each main exercise throughout this book. After that closing activity:

- Thank participants for their interesting input.
- If you have served refreshments, encourage them to have more coffee or cake (or whatever is left over) as they leave.

- Give them a hint of what will be discussed the next time you meet. (You don't have to follow the order listed.)
- Suggest any resources they might want to try out during the intervening time.
- Tell them you hope to see them ____. (Whenever you are meeting again.)
- Collect their name tags or tent cards.

That may all seem obvious, but many meetings that lack those niceties feel awkward.

Approach Is Always Key

In a group setting to which people come specifically for an activity, these exercises can be easily introduced if you simply show respect for and interest in the participants. Most of us are pleased to be asked about our lives, interests, and opinions.

However, if an activity is done spontaneously because you are helping a person in her room or you are waiting together for a meal to be served, asking a question "out of the blue" may confuse the person or make her suspicious, as if you are trying to invade her privacy. Instead, make conversation. Tell her about where you heard of this idea and share your own answer, because *sharing* shows interest and respect. Here is a sample beginning for a spontaneous conversation:

"We did an exercise in a class I took in which we were asked to choose our preferences between opposites. For example, 'Are you more of a morning person or more of a night owl?' I'm a night owl. Which are you?"

The Goal Is Connection

Most of the people who could benefit from using these exercises are not officially activity directors, recreational therapists, or even social chairpersons, but if you *are* one, you know that activities were once seen by many as frivolous— a way of keeping people busy and killing time. People were often envious of you because they thought you had all the fun, but they didn't take you seriously and had no idea how hard you worked.

"Only connect!"—E. M. Forster

In more recent years, we have come to see activities as a way of *connecting*. We encourage people to be involved because we build strong relationships by being **engaged** with one another, by actively participating in something together. That is the primary goal of everything on the pages that follow.

But here is a warning to leaders: Not everyone will be active. You know this is true of yourself when you are less sure of your abilities or less familiar with the group. In those situations, you may prefer to be **passively engaged.** You may want to watch and observe and react to the activity, but you don't want to be performing (such as singing along or dancing) or speaking up (such as answering questions in a game). That's fine, too. We are sharing the experience with others when we are just part of the audience, too.

On the other hand, there are also levels of engagement. If I am *completely independent,* without disabilities of any incapacitating sort, chances are I am the leader of the group activity, or at least capable of being an ultra-active participant. However, if I am too young, too old, too frail, or have a memory impairment, I may be able to do only a part of an activity. As leader, it is your role to look for participants' strengths within their *partial dependency.*

- One person may be able to *repeat one part of an activity* over and over, such as putting each picture, after it has been discussed, into an envelope.
- Another person may be able to *do something only peripherally related,* such as sweep up scraps of paper that have fallen to the floor while we were cutting up pictures for an art collage of our lives.
- At the very least, a person can *offer an opinion.* "Did you enjoy this?"

In each of these exercises look for ways to involve people who might be comfortable being more than passively engaged if they were given a specific role.

And at still other times, you may want to be ***positively disengaged,*** by which I mean no matter what is going on around you, you are happy to be doing something else. For example, in the midst of a music program, one woman may be completely ignoring the performers, but happily watching the birds outside the window at the bird feeder. Our minds wander. When we're waiting in line at the grocery store, we often think our own thoughts—how to prepare the meat we bought or what weekend plans to make. Our participants are often happy in their own thoughts, too. So *sometimes* when they appear to be doing nothing, that's exactly what they want to be doing.

But then there are the people who are ***unhappily disengaged.*** These are the people who are uncomfortable for any of a thousand reasons. Maybe they are:

- Cold, hot, hungry, thirsty, need to use the bathroom, or wearing clothing that is too tight;
- Feeling physically ill or in pain or simply tired;
- Discomforted by an environment that is too noisy or crowded or where there is too little light or too much glare or they feel unsafe; or
- Confused or frustrated by what they perceive is expected of them.

In all cases, do what you can to discover the cause and make the person more comfortable. Sometimes that means the person needs to leave and come back another time.

Share What You Learn

George Eliot once said, "What do we live for if it is not to make life less difficult for each other?" It's a good point, but I also believe we are here to enjoy one another. If we are drawn closer to one another because of what we learn through these exercises, the world will be a better place. If you share what you learn with others who could benefit from knowing the preferences, interests, and strengths of your participants, the world will be even better. In various settings, those others may include family members, friends, caregivers, teachers, administrators, health professionals, or many others. Don't betray confidences. Do promote understanding.

PROPS AND MATERIALS

Virtually all of the nine main exercises in this book can be done spontaneously without props, but all of them would be enhanced by them.

The Essentials

If you are doing any of the exercises in this book in a group, I strongly suggest that you come prepared with:

- **Name tags or tent cards.** See tips and techniques for opening a class below.
- **Handouts.** Samples of the handouts that would enhance each session are presented in Appendix C and on the accompanying CD-ROM.
- **Pens, pencils, or markers.** Always provide writing implements for people who want to take notes. Personally, I also like to provide stickers, highlighters, and post-it "flags" so people can mark up their papers in creative ways. (For instance, I provide star stickers for "bright ideas," and heart stickers for "ideas I love.")
- **Flip chart or white board or overhead transparencies with appropriate markers.** Handouts are helpful, but when you write the question and responses for all to see, it helps people stay focused on the current topic and adds another visual for the hard-of-hearing.

An LCD projector with key points may also be helpful if one is readily available to you, but since at the time of this writing there is still no easy way to write participants' responses on an LCD screen, I still suggest that you have a flip chart or other large writing surface handy.

> *Quick Tip:* Whenever possible, use volunteers—preferably a participant—to write on flip charts, transparencies, or white boards. That builds self-esteem in the volunteers, gives participants another person to look at (which perks up audience interest), and frees you to concentrate on participants and their input.

The Nice-to-Haves

When we talk about something from our past, it helps a great deal to have a tangible reminder from that past. Sometimes that's easy to do. When we talk about toys of the 1950s in Part 3, you may find in your own home many of the toys that were first introduced in the 1950s, such as hula hoops, Silly Putty, Frisbees, Barbie dolls, and Mr. Potato Head. Other things may be harder to find "in the flesh" but pictures are readily available in books or on the Internet.

Whenever you can plan ahead and provide either photos or tangible products related to the topic, do so. Each exercise is followed by a review of Resources for Digging Deeper, and the Reference section at the end of the book includes more than 100 books and websites; you aren't likely to be able to find all of these in your local library or afford all through the vendors listed in Appendix B, but chances are you can obtain some.

The Nearly Essential: Make It Multisensory

Although I have tried to choose activities that can be done spontaneously, or nearly so, any activity is enhanced if it is multisensory. In addition to the Nice-to-Haves listed above, energy and enthusiasm are generated by your positive attitude as a leader, and by

- Movement;
- Color;
- Things to touch, hold, or toss;
- Music (except where it interferes with hearing); and
- Things to taste or smell, when appropriate (including refreshments).

See the notes that follow for adding exercise.

Combine Reminiscence and Exercise

Wherever possible, I advocate adding physical exercise in some form to each of these mental exercises. When you move, you help your brain think more clearly. (Experiments have been done showing that people who squeeze a small rubber ball whenever they start to tire or get tense while taking a test perform better than those without—dare I say it?—balls.)

Movement in general creates energy, excitement, and interest in a room. For that reason, I suggest that whenever possible, you find ways to move people around the room according to their answers to a question. For example, in Exercise 3, Make a Choice, I usually have everyone move to one side of the room if they answer a question one way and to the other side if they answer it the other (e.g., "Stand to my right if you are a morning person; stand to my left if you are a night owl. And if you couldn't be either one without an afternoon nap, stand in the middle.") Of course, if you are working with frail older adults or people with physical or mental disabilities, that may not work. Then try the variations listed below.

The simple act of having people raise their hands if they agree with an answer or want to give a specific answer is movement, and it *is* good exercise. Every time we move our arms above the level of our heart, we are exercising our heart as well as our arm. It's just not very *interesting* exercise.

If an exercise has no built-in movement to it or my suggested movement doesn't work for your group, try:

- Tossing a **soft ball** (Koosh, Nerf, beach) to each person before he or she gives a response; ask that person to toss it back to you or to the next person who wants to speak.
- Making raised hands more visible by putting something in them such as **scarves, ribbons, or colorful plates.** Ribbons and scarves move in graceful ways, but colorful plates make an inexpensive alternative. Personally I prefer the plastic versions found in party stores because they are washable (for infection control), compact, fairly durable, and, unlike paper plates, colored on both sides. I use them in two ways. Sometimes I give them out randomly ("Choose a color you like") and then ask participants to wave them back and forth according to their responses ("How many of you agree? . . . Who disagrees?"). At other times I give everyone a red plate and a green plate, and ask them to all vote at once, raising their green plate if they agree and their red plate if they disagree. You will be surprised how the energy level changes in a room simply by adding bright colors and waving arms. Try this every time you ask an opinion question, and ask opinion questions often in each exercise. (Everyone has a right to an opinion so no answer is ever "wrong," even when we disagree.)
- **Making signs** to wave using small sticks and heavy paper (see directions below) so people can "vote" on any question.
- **Sounding it out** by making ugly buzzer sounds when you disagree and tinkling bell sounds when you agree, both with appropriate hand movements.

Make Them Laugh

Although most people don't realize it, laughter is also a form of exercise. Norman Cousins, a pioneer in humor as therapy, called laughter "internal jogging." In reality, laughter brings oxygen to the brain, so it literally freshens our thinking. It also boosts the immune system, reduces stress, promotes creative thinking, and builds camaraderie among people. In the scripts for each exercise, I have tried to incorporate dialogue that will make people smile.

However, don't be afraid to go a step further and add an element of silliness—and then back off if it isn't working. Some people will have fun tossing bean bags in the shape of whales ("That's a whale of an idea") or pigs (making pigs fly) or raising rubber chickens in the air as a symbol of their readiness to answer a question. (See Appendix B for vendors.) Others will think that is "going too far." They are willing to have a good time, but only within the limits of what they consider proper decorum. Know and respect your participants.

Bottom line: If you have fun, the participants are likely to have fun, too.

Possible Graphics for Signs

As noted above, one way to make participation in these exercises more interesting is to call frequently for votes. "Do you agree or disagree with this statement?" or

"Do you like this idea or not?" At the beginning of each class, participants will have been given a sign for easy voting. For example, they may have a sign with a thumbs up or a thumbs down or a smiling or frowning face (see Appendix D).

AVOID FAVORITES

Most of us have a tendency to make conversation by asking things like:

- What's your favorite color?
- What's your favorite food?
- What's your favorite vacation spot?
- What's your favorite TV program?

If you are on the receiving end of those questions, you may feel like a ping-pong ball being batted about—it's too much too fast. Each is also the wrong question.

If I ask you, "What's your favorite color?" and you answer "blue," that's often the end of the conversation—not very satisfying. For people with dementia or others with decision-making difficulties, it's also a question loaded with pressure. In my mind I may be thinking, "Well, I like blue and green and yellow and purple, but my favorite? I'm not sure. What am I supposed to say? Is there only one right answer? Will I have to live with this choice? Why is she asking me this anyway?"

Instead, ask the question like this: "I see you're wearing a pretty blue blouse today. Do you like the color blue?" Assuming she is flattered, and answers yes, I can then make conversation with her, sharing my own likes and asking her additional questions. Here are some possibilities:

- "I like some shades of blue, too, but not all of them. Do you prefer pale blues or navy blue?" or "Are there any shades of blue you don't like?"
- "I've noticed you wear blue a lot—it brings out the color of your eyes; do people tell you that often?"
- "I have a pair of blue jeans and a grubby old sweatshirt that I love to wear when I am just relaxing. Do you have a blue relaxation outfit?"
- "Have you ever had an unusual item of clothing in blue—like blue suede shoes or a blue hat? Tell me about it."
- "I once had a bedroom decorated all in blue, yellow, and white, with lots of flowers. I thought it looked like a French country house and I just loved it. In your home, did you have a blue bedroom, or were any other rooms painted blue?" (Again, if she says yes, ask her to tell you more.)
- "Blue in nature is wonderful, too, I think. I love seeing a bright, blue cloudless sky; do you?" (And suggest other natural blues—turquoise waters on a tropical beach, the shimmering royal blue necks of peacocks, blue hyacinth flowers)

If I've tried two or three questions like this and the conversation isn't going anywhere, didn't lead to anywhere new (e.g., to talking about nature or home decorating), or you've exhausted it, it's easy to move on to another color, because you are not talking about favorites anymore, but simply colors you like. For example, you might say something like, "Blues and greens are considered cool and soothing colors. Are there any warm colors like red or orange or yellow that you like?" And then you can take off from there with colors for clothes, home decorating, in nature, and so on.

The same is true with foods, vacation spots, TV programs, or any other "favorite" question you may be tempted to ask. By simply asking what a person "likes" rather than which is a "favorite" anything, you have many more opportunities for conversation and you learn much more about the person.

Using What You Learn

The reason for asking about favorites has always been to learn what pleases another person. We want to know what will bring a smile to another's face, especially if that person is having a down day. But most of us are pleased by more than one thing, and if we ask for favorites, the one thing we have mentioned may not be readily available. If I tell you my favorite thing in the whole world to eat is poppyseed kolaches like my grandmother used to make, chances are you aren't going to be able to offer me that snack very often. But if we have a general conversation about treats that leads to a detailed conversation about chocolate, and you learn that I like dark chocolate with nuts, Reese's peanut butter cups, and brownies, you have a range of ways to bring a smile to my face.

A conversation can pleasantly distract a person when you might have to assist with something private such as dressing, bathing, or toileting. It can also make walking, waiting, or dining more enjoyable. We build self-esteem in others when we show genuine interest in them.

But at least equally important is what we learn about that person and can share with others about that person's interests and preferences. The conversation about blue suggested above can potentially tell me the following things about this particular woman:

- What color and style of clothes are among her preferences,
- What sort of décor she is comfortable in,
- How she feels about nature, and
- Special memories related to this color.

Do you get the idea? Start asking and sharing.

> "People are beginning to realize that self-knowledge is not an end in itself.
> It's for the purpose of better relationships, so that we can give to our community."
> —*Jennifer James*

Part 1
Who I Am and Where I Lived

Part 1 consists of two primary exercises and multiple mini-exercises related to identity and shelter.

Most people don't consciously think much about their names—first, last, or middle—but most people are more profoundly shaped by their names than they realize, which is one reason Exercise 1 on names is one of the longest. Our names are an integral part of our identity; we have a tendency to immediately think well of people who remember our names and we berate ourselves for forgetting names. We respond to our names until the day we die—even people with severe Alzheimer's disease tend to recognize their own names until the end, as long as you use the name they were familiar with in childhood. This exercise is likely to bring out many more stories than you might imagine and may take much longer than you intended.

The second exercise, Where I Lived, is a new way of looking at an old idea—a home with warm memories. The simple act of drawing the floor plan tends to draw out many more recollections than a simple discussion would. For those who cannot draw a floor plan (even though we set very low standards for proportion and accuracy), photographs, books on architecture, and, most of all, field trips provide lively alternatives. Many of us are surprised by the reflections stirred up by simple architectural details—roof lines, door knobs, window seats, transoms. These may lead to memories of long forgotten conversations, well-loved books read in a special hiding place, or the feelings generated in the rooms beyond the door knobs.

Although field trips are only mentioned lightly in this section, try to get out and about with your group as often as possible. Remember that fresh air and physical exercise stimulate the brain; participants will not only be primed to remember more, but they will have a richer experience than a stuffy room can provide. (Or when the weather is pleasant, at least conduct your class outside.)

Exercise 1: Name Stories

THE BASIC EXERCISE

This exercise consists primarily of telling stories about our names or about the names of people we know. Names are fascinating, and once one person begins to tell a name story, it prompts reminiscence in others.

What would seem to be just a simple exercise, however, can actually be drawn out into hours of reminiscence in a lively group, so consider dividing this exercise into multiple shorter sessions. For example:

- One on first names,
- Another on surnames and ethnic heritage,
- Another on nicknames or middle names or unusual names, and
- Perhaps another on the evolution of names and their meanings.

Alternatively, consider skipping some of the questions if your time is limited or if there is little interest in a particular question.

KEY ELEMENTS

The stories generated by this exercise are often both hilarious and moving. Most of us have overcome any embarrassment about our names over time (kids will make fun of *any* name) or have had reason to develop pride in our names. Because the United States is an immigrant nation, our last names tend to identify our immigrant heritage, or at least that of our spouses if a woman is married, or of one parent if she is single. Most immigrants were discriminated against when they first arrived and some still are, so in this discussion stay attuned to sensitive issues related to race and ethnicity. At the same time, be open to all the wonderful nuances of names. Names go straight to the core of who we are. As such, life story discussions can have no better beginning than telling one another about our names.

Quick Tip: One way to add immediate energy to any discussion is to burst into song. When you are talking about names, there are dozens of possibilities. Let participants come up with their own that may have special meaning to them, but here are some you might consider coming prepared with to get things off the ground. (Most lyrics can be found on the Internet or in old songbooks):

- Once in Love with **Amy**
- **Bill Bailey,** Won't You Please Come Home
- My **Bonnie** Lies Over the Ocean
- My Darling **Clementine**
- **Daisy, Daisy** (Bicycle Built for Two)

- **Dinah** Won't You Blow Your Horn (I've Been Workin' on the Railroad)
- **Ida,** Sweet as Apple Cider
- **Jimmy** Crack Corn (Blue Tail Fly)
- **John Jacob Jingleheimer Schmidt**
- **K-K-Katie,** Good-bye
- **Maria** (I've just met a girl named Maria)
- Waltzing **Matilda**
- Wait Till the Sun Shines, **Nellie**
- Oh, **Susanna**
- **Tom Dooley**

DEMENTIA CONCERNS

People with mild confusion or whose verbal skills are still intact may handle this exercise easily. Those whose dementia has progressed further are still likely to enjoy listening to the stories told by others and can still offer opinions ("Do you like your name?").

If this exercise is done in a mixed group of people with dementia and their family caregivers, the care receivers might enjoy hearing what the family name or their individual name has meant to their spouses, sons, or daughters. For example, many of us grew up with a nickname or term of endearment that meant our parent was well-pleased with us or enjoying the moment with us; we tend to have great affection for that nickname throughout our lives. On the other hand, many of us also knew that when a parent used our full, formal name, including our middle name, we were usually in big trouble. Talking about times when either the nickname or formal name was used can often stir warm memories. (Even when we were in trouble, it often became a favorite family anecdote over the years.)

THE COMPLETE SCRIPT

 Dialogue: Today we're going to talk about names. Everyone has at least one name story, even if it takes you a while to think of one. Our primal identity comes from our name and most of us have been shaped in some way by our names—first and last and nicknames. Sigmund Freud once wrote, "A human being's name is a principal component in his person, perhaps a piece of his soul." Some of us have had to live up to a name; others of us have had to overcome negatives associated with our names or heritage, but most of us are very attached to our names. Some name stories are funny, others are sad, but each one tells us something about who that person is. So let's start at the beginning:

- Who named you?

- What do you know about how your name was chosen?

Direction: In the dialogue, we ask only one or two questions at a time, but as the discussion gets going, many people may jump ahead or answer a different question altogether. That's fine, since the point is simply to tell stories about names. The order in which they are told doesn't matter. However, if the discussion seems to have moved prematurely ahead to the heritage of names, for example, you might give people an opportunity to go back, asking, "Does anyone else have a story about who named you and how your name was chosen?"

In any group there are always interesting stories related to who chose a person's name—father, mother, brother, sister, aunt, friend, and so forth—and why. It's always interesting to me—and says something powerful about the family dynamics—when someone other than the child's parents chooses the name. There are also often amusing or touching stories about fathers choosing names. One childhood friend was named "Uneeda" ("You need a") after the biscuit available in grocery stores at the time, because her father was at a loss for what else to choose. I also know a sweet story of a father who chose a daughter's name because it meant "Dear to my heart."

If you have a name story of your own you want to share to get the group going, that's fine, but keep it short—our goal is to learn about others, not to tell our own stories. (On the other hand, if you are asking these questions during personal care, you can often break the ice by telling your own story first.)

▶ ***Dialogue:*** Some of us were given a formal name, but a nickname stuck. Many a child with a perfectly acceptable given name was saddled with what he or she later perceived as an embarrassing nickname because her 2-year-old sister couldn't pronounce it correctly (I'm thinking of a "Louise" who became known as "Weezie") or her 6-year-old brother started calling her "Zippy" as she began to crawl.

Other children were given a pet name by a parent that they will always treasure. Some parents used the same name for everyone, such as "darling" or "honey," but as children we still feel a warm association with that parent when we hear the word. And as adults, spouses or lovers often have pet names for each other that may be embarrassing, but that they treasure nevertheless.

- Do you have a nickname? How did you acquire it?

- Do you prefer the use of your real name or nickname? Why? Does it depend on the situation?

- Do you only allow certain people to use the nickname? Who?

Direction: Whether or not we like our nicknames usually relates to two factors: 1) whether we like the person who gave us the nickname and 2) whether or not the incident that gave rise to the nickname was embarrassing. But it can also relate to our overall personality. President Ronald Reagan was nicknamed "Dutch" by his father when he was a baby, because he said he looked like "a fat Dutchman." That hardly sounds flattering, but the origins were eventually forgotten, and the congenial president never seems to have minded being called "Dutch."

This discussion may also lead to the cruelty of children and playground bullies. We all know that the ditty "Sticks and stones may break my bones, but names can never hurt me," is patently false. When I was in elementary school, a mass murderer was arrested in my state whose surname was unfortunately similar to mine, and my classmates were unmerciful in their teasing.

On the other hand, some childhood nicknames conjure up fond memories. Explore that possibility, too. When participants have said all they want about nicknames, go on to the next questions.

▶ *Dialogue:* Many people are named after someone—a grandparent, favorite aunt or uncle, a brother who died in a war, a godparent, or a movie star or other celebrity. Others are given a name to carry on a tradition, which may mean they are named after their father, with "Junior" after the name, or if it's a long-standing tradition, maybe they are the third (III) or fourth (IV). Other people are given their mother's maiden name as a first or middle name or another family name that has meaning.

- Were you named after someone?

- What names recur within your family?

Direction: The stories related to whose name we bear are also endless and interesting. I met a man named "Warren" who was named after the then current U.S. President Warren Harding. I have met Marilyns named after Marilyn Monroe and Shirleys named after Shirley Temple.

Cultures vary. It can be good luck or bad luck to name a child after a relative who is living or one who has died, depending upon your heritage. I had a German great-grandfather who in the 1860s renamed each male child John until one of them lived beyond the age of 1 year, which meant that the John who lived had two brothers before him also named John. This was not just a German custom. The famous painter Salvador Dali was named after a brother who died, and perhaps in part because his parents kept a picture of the first Salvador Dali over their bed, the second spent all of his life looking for attention in his own right.

Encourage participants to talk about who they were named after, about their family customs, and whether they carried on (or plan to carry on) those same customs in naming their own children. If they didn't marry and have children, ask about the stories related to siblings or friends.

This could also be a good time to insert an opinion question: Which statement do you agree with?

- Naming a child after a parent is a good way to carry on a tradition and build pride in one's name.
- A child is better able to develop his own identity if he has a name that is uniquely his.

Then go on to the next questions.

► **Dialogue:**   Some people who are named after a parent, grandparent, or beloved relative take great pride in their heritage; others find their name a burden and are determined not to do the same to their own children, so they simply choose for them names they think are attractive or that are popular. Those children are just as likely to love or hate their names as their parents loved or hated theirs. If you grew up with a name that set you apart because it was unusual, and you try to give your child a common name, she may ask why you had to give her the same name as three other children in her class. If you grew up with a common name and wanted your child to have her own identity, she may complain if you give her a name that no one else shares, because she feels awkward and alone. And others love their names for the very same reasons.

Let's talk about that:

- Do you like your name?

- Why or why not?

- Do you like only part of your name? (First, middle, surname) Which part? Why?

Direction: Watch out for participants who have a tendency to condemn a name altogether rather than just as the right appellation for them. Just because a person says she doesn't like the name Jane, never felt like a "Jane," and thinks it's a name that is too plain, doesn't mean that Jane is a bad name for everyone. It's easy to step on toes here.

At the same time, watch how people show their empathy. If a woman named "Bertha" loathes her name, it's okay to agree it isn't currently fashionable, but try to find something positive to say. It means "glorious, shining one," which is certainly positive. Or perhaps you had a beloved relative or friend named Bertha, so she shouldn't automatically assume that it has negative connotations for others.

Most of us like or dislike a name because of the associations we have with it—people we knew/know, literary heroes or villains, or what does or doesn't sound musical to us. It's highly individualized.

► **Dialogue:**   Many people who don't like their name are simply tired of having to spell it, pronounce it, or repeat it for others. Many people with unusual names, whether first names or surnames, have come up with stories for helping others to remember it. For example, consider the woman named Susan Stubbs who met a young man at a dance a few decades back and hoped he would remember her and ask her out. She pointed to his cigarette and told him he could remember her name by thinking of her when it was finished and he stubbed it out. She was the remainder, the stub. She saw him the next weekend at another dance and he came up to her and introduced her to his friend as Suzie Butts. For her, it wasn't close enough.

- Do you have a way of helping people remember your name or how it is spelled or pronounced? Tell us.

Direction: This question needs no further explanation, but you might also ask another opinion question at this point.

► *Dialogue:*   Child development expert Lee Salk said that "parents who give their kids weird names are weird themselves." (As quoted in *The Language of Names*, p. 125; see Resources for Digging Deeper.) Do you agree or disagree?

Direction: Note that not all names that are difficult to spell or pronounce are weird, and encourage people to define "weird," while also being sensitive to others' feelings.

Then go on to the next question.

► *Dialogue:*   Choosing a child's name is highly significant in some cultures and is said to influence one's success in terms of wealth, career, and marriage/love relationships. The Chinese have a saying that a bad name "is worse than being born to a bad life." (*The Language of Names*, p. 18; see Resources for Digging Deeper.)

- How would you define what makes a good name?

- How important is a good name? Do you know people with odd names who have been successful?

- How important is *making* your name good (i.e., living an honorable life)?

Direction: These are mostly opinion questions and need no further explanation. Simply listen and go on to the next question.

People who want to dig deeper on this question might turn to the resources at the end of this exercise and consider reading up on the meanings of names and trivia about names.

A question somewhat related that you might also ask is:

► *Dialogue:*   If you could choose any name for yourself, what would you choose and why?

Direction: That may lead us into the next question as well.

► *Dialogue:*   Now let's talk about your heritage. The United States is a nation of immigrants, and in spite of the message on the Statue of Liberty, most immigrants were discriminated against when they first arrived. Some still are. Over the years many groups underwent various transformations. They were proud of their nationality or ethnic heritage. They tried to hide it and assimilate. They found enclaves of people with the same background and grew proud again. A war came along and they tried to hide it again.

A multicultural nation is richer for its diversity, but that is not universally recognized. Let's begin to talk about how your name fits into American culture.

- What does your name say about your (family or ethnic) heritage? Is that a positive or negative for you?

Direction: Although we hope everyone will be sensitive to each other in this discussion, pay attention to body language and facial expressions that might suggest greater tact is needed. When I was growing up, I was called a "Bohunk" because of my Bohemian heritage, but it never seemed derogatory because half the county was made up of Bohemian-Americans. Other ethnic groups have truly suffered discrimination, racial slurs, and obstacles beyond my imagining. If this discussion can help others understand one another better, it will provide a service to humanity.

On the other hand, there are many funny stories related to our names and heritage, often based on misunderstandings. Some of them are related to the next question, but try to draw out all those, too.

▶ **_Dialogue:_**   When immigrants came to the United States, they often changed their names or had their names changed for them by immigration officers or those recording the ship manifests. Immigrants were not required to present visas for admission to the United States until 1924, so most names—either as they were boarding the ship from Europe or other ports, or as they arrived in the United States—were recorded as they were heard. It is not too difficult to imagine then how if the recorder were English-speaking, "Yitzchak" could become "Hitchcock," or "Yankele" could become "John Kelly," or "Ilyan" could become "Williams." Similar changes occurred when census-takers walked from farm to farm or house to house in the late 1800s.

Many other people changed their names in order to "get along or go along." One man tells the story of his great-grandfather who came to the United States from Russia. His original name was 28 letters long, but as people were going through customs (sic), he watched carefully. He noticed that a man about five people ahead of him told the official his name was Miller and he was passed right through. People who didn't speak English or who had complicated names had more trouble. Therefore, when his turn came, he just said, "My name is Miller," and he, too, passed right through. He wrote back to his relatives in Russia, who were thinking of emigrating, to try the same ruse. (A _Celebration of American Family Folklore_, p. 79; see Resources for Digging Deeper.)

But not everyone who changed a name was a commoner. During World War I, the British royal family renounced their German name of "Wettin of Saxe-Coburn-Gotha," which came from Queen Victoria's consort, and chose the name Windsor after William I's 1,000-year-old castle on the Thames.

Other people—most notably movie stars—change their names to something viewed in our society as more glamorous. In the 1920s and the decades that followed, many stars changed their names to hide their Jewish heritage and the discrimination that often accompanied its revelation. Thus Leo Jacoby cleverly became Lee J. Cobb, Issur Danielovitch became Kirk Douglas, and Bernard Schwartz became Tony Curtis. We may think we are more enlightened now, but most celebrities still seem to be people with names that are easy to pronounce and no obvious ethnic heritage.

- Talk a little more about your ethnic heritage. How important is it to your identity?

- Did your surname change when your ancestors arrived in America? Was it hard to adjust or did it make things easier?

- Does your family still speak another language? Cook ethnic foods? Celebrate ethnic holidays? Are these traditions you have carried on or hope to carry on with your own families?

Direction: This is an interesting topic that could easily take an hour on its own, particularly if you have broad ethnic diversity in your group. If you don't have much diversity, you may also find a lively discussion ensues as people talk about their common experiences growing up within a particular ethnic group—Italians, Chinese, Russians, and so forth.

If the discussion seems to be getting out of hand, you might consider a follow-up session at which you have a party with participants bringing a food representing his or her ethnic heritage, or wearing native clothing, or bringing a souvenir/antique that may have been passed down through the generations. On the other hand, many people who are no longer interested in preparing elaborate recipes still love to *talk* about the foods that represent their heritage, or their holiday customs or favorite expressions.

Some people, especially those who are the first native-born Americans in their families or who came to the United States at a very young age, have been anxious to give up their heritage and fit in as Americans. This often causes great intergenerational tension, so be aware that this could be a sensitive topic for some participants.

People who want to learn a little more about their heritage or their surnames might consider perusing one of the books recommended at the end of this exercise. (See also the mini-exercises that follow this one.)

▶ ***Dialogue:*** The most common way in which names are changed is when people marry. This is based on long tradition. In the 1700s William Blackstone wrote in his *Commentaries on the Laws of England* "that when a man and woman exchange marriage vows, they become one person, and 'the husband is that person.'" (*The Language of Names*, p. 136; see Resources for Digging Deeper.) It is no longer a law (in the United States at least) that a woman must change her name when she marries, and the etiquette of names has also eased up a bit. However, it remains a controversial subject and although some women retain their birth names and some couples combine their last names, the vast majority of women still take their husband's name.

So let's talk about changing names when one marries.

- Do you think women should take their husband's name as their surname when they marry? Why or why not?

Direction: Remember to use opinion questions like this as opportunities to "vote" by waving signs, scarves, or paper plates. This tends to be a lively discussion starter, especially if a diversity of *ages* is represented. Even though answers are purely a matter of opinion, you may be surprised how strong the feelings are.

- Some women were very proud to take their husband's name and never thought twice about it.

- Some women were proud at the time, but now think it's unfair.
- Some women think it may be unfair, but it's less confusing for their children.
- Some women think, why should I marry and keep my father's name? Why not my mother's name (which is done in a few cultures)?
- Some women think it is best to meld both the husband's and wife's last names (often hyphenating them).
- Some women see social status in being "Mrs. John Smith." Others see total loss of personal identity.

And what do the men think? They, too, may have wide-ranging opinions, but because most have never considered giving up their names (and were never asked to do so), most don't see what the big deal is. Therefore, this, too, is a discussion that calls for tact on the part of the leader!

A follow-up question, now that divorce is common, is:

- What name does or should a woman take after divorce? What factors contribute to one's choice?

Then give people one last chance to tell a name story.

▶ ***Dialogue:*** Are there any other stories associated with names in your family that we haven't covered yet?

Direction With Closing: Discuss whatever comes up, then end the session by letting each person tell something he or she learned about another person in the group that he or she hadn't known before. Learning each other's names—and in this case, the stories behind them—is the first step in building bonds with others.

Resources for Digging Deeper—Exercise 1

As purely a discussion topic, the questions in Exercise 1 should reveal many wonderful stories among participants. However, others will have their curiosity aroused by this topic and will want to learn more and perhaps discuss more.

If you are working with people with Alzheimer's disease or some other form of dementia, their ability to answer many of the discussion questions may be compromised by a loss of verbal skills. However, they usually can still read (if the print is large enough) and tend to enjoy interesting, concise information, especially if some humor is involved.

For both of these needs, the following list includes a few books that are available through on-line bookstores and useful for delving further into the topic of names:

FIRST NAMES

- ***Beyond Jennifer & Jason, Madison and Montana: What to Name Your Baby Now*** by Linda Rosenkranz and Pamela Redmond Satran, © 2000,

ISBN 0312974620. This book is more than anything a compilation of lists, offering lots of categories of names: popular names, old-fashioned names, comfy names, creative names, and so on. It also has essays on a history of American naming traditions, the psychological impact of names, and a variety of tips for choosing names. It's interesting and fun, but it says nothing about the historical meaning of all these names, which may still be important to some people.

- ***The Secret Universe of Names*** by Roy Feinson, © 2004, ISBN 0739453335. This is a fascinating book, but probably shouldn't be taken too seriously. The preface asks a series of questions such as why people whose names begin with J are 250% more likely to become millionaires than people whose names begin with the letter N or why the name Emma evokes stronger romantic feelings than the name Kate. The majority of the book focuses on significant letter combinations in first names such as A-N-T in Anita, Annette, and Anthony and then ascribes a variety of characteristics to people with these names from personality traits, to charisma, career success, and their likelihood of triumphing in love and friendship. How much you believe this probably has a lot to do with how favorable the descriptions are for the letter combinations in your name. Is it really significant that the name Jesus has less charisma than the name Jeremy? In my opinion, no, but it can be fun to read and discuss.

- ***Name Your Baby*** by La Reina Rule, © 1986, ISBN 0553271458. When I was pregnant with my first child, I used this simple little paperback (in an edition that predates the latest version named here by many years) as my chief means for choosing my daughter's name. The book is divided into girls' names and boys' names and provides a name, an origin, a brief meaning, and variations for each, with most listings being less than 25 words. This was perfectly adequate for my needs, and remains fascinating to me.

- ***What's in a Name?*** by Susan Osborn, © 1999, ISBN 0671025554. Note that this is one of three books on this list with the same title, all quite different in content. This one is only about first names, but it covers more about each of 3,000 names than you may care to know or choose to believe: origin; meaning; evolution and popularity throughout history; its numerical significance; astrological association; and its relationship with particular herbs, colors, metals, and stones. It's fun and fascinating, but since it groups together what it considers similar names (for example, Diane, Dick, Dion, Dirk, Dolly, Domenica, and 20 others), it's not easy to find a specific name you might be looking for.

SURNAMES

- ***What's in a Name? Surnames of America*** by La Reina Rule and William K. Hammond, © 1973, ISBN 0515044601. Although quite old, this book is still available on-line in "used" condition. It has a brief, but interesting introduction on how surnames came about (from occupations, locations, physical characteristics, and personality traits, for example) and then consists almost entirely of brief descriptions of thousands of surnames from "Aaron" (Hebrew, "lofty, exalted one") to "Zyto" (Czech, "Raiser of rye for flour").

- *American Surnames* by Elsdon Coles Smith, © 1997 (third printing), ISBN 0806311509. If you want to find a name in this book, you must search the index, where some names have multiple page listings. However, this isn't really a hardship, and if you are mostly curious about names in general, this book provides far more detail than *What's in a Name?* It's clearly arranged under six chapter headings which include a general classification of names; names that come from places, fathers, occupations, actions, or nicknames; and a last miscellaneous chapter that is perhaps the most fascinating of all.

GENERAL BOOKS ABOUT NAMES

- *The Ethnic Almanac* by Stephanie Bernardo was published in 1981, but is amazingly still available (ISBN 0385141440). This 500-page volume has been a favorite of mine since it first came out because it has something good to say about everybody, and forces us to question history as it is commonly taught. (For example, Bernardo points out that when the white settlers won a battle against the Indians, it was called winning a "war." When the Indians won, it was called "a massacre.") The book provides a brief history of more than 30 ethnic groups as they arrived in the New World and summaries of what these men and women contributed to the wider world. It also covers food, celebrations, genetics, music, and many other topics. This isn't really a book about names, but it's an excellent beginning resource on ethnicity.
- *The Language of Names* by Justin Kaplan and Anne Bernays, © 1997, ISBN 0684807416. This is a broad-ranging and well-researched book, but my favorite chapters are those on immigration ("Names in the Melting Pot"), "Maiden Names," and "Literary Names."
- *A Celebration of American Family Folklore* by editors Steven Zeitlin, Amy Kotkin, and Holly Cutting Baker, © 1992, ISBN 0938756362. This is a book of family stories, only some of which are about names, but many of which are delightful. It is a source I quote often in this book.

WEB SITES USED

http://www.ssa.gov/OACT/babynames/
http://www.mybirthcare.com/favorites/babynames.asp
http://www.babycenter.com/babyname/popnames.html (also names for
   each decade)
http://www.last-names.net/
http://www.genealogyforum.com/gfaol/surnames/Top100.htm
http://surnames.behindthename.com/top/lists/100usss1990.php
http://www.jimwegryn.com/Names/CommonSurnames.htm

Mini-Exercise A: Read a Little More for Fun

> *Quick Tip—Read Aloud:* One way to change the energy level in a group is to give participants someone new to focus on. It also builds self-esteem when participants become adjunct leaders. An easy way to accomplish both of these goals is to ask participants to read aloud questions on the handout or interesting information such as can be found in Exercises 2–4 below and in the resources named in the previous section on digging deeper. If you are using book excerpts, it also helps if you can print out the passages ahead of time, and enlarge them on your copier for easier reading. Then simply hand the passages to anyone who expresses a willingness to read aloud at the appropriate spot.

The books related to names described in Resources for Digging Deeper as well as web sites on related topics are rich resources for taking this topic on interesting tangents. Here are a few suggestions:

1. **How does the meaning of your name compare to the person you are?** You can look up your given name in the books above or on the Internet by searching for "Meaning of Names." Many people are surprised by the meanings (e.g., John means "God is gracious" and comes from the old Hebrew) and how well or badly it suits them or others they know with that name. For example, is every Charles you know really "strong and manly"? Is every Ann you know graceful as the name implies?

2. **How does your name compare to fashionable names through the last century?** According to the Social Security Administration, the top 10 names for babies born in 2005 (the most recent year available at the time of this writing) were:

Rank	Male name	Female name
1	**Jacob**	**Emily**
2	Michael	**Emma**
3	**Joshua**	**Madison**
4	**Matthew**	Abigail
5	**Ethan**	**Olivia**
6	**Andrew**	**Isabella**
7	Daniel	**Hannah**
8	Anthony	Samantha
9	Christopher	**Ava**
10	Joseph	Ashley

According to the BabyCenter (*www.babycenter.com*), which represents the largest *private* list available in the United States, the top 10 names for babies born in 2005 were:

Rank	Male name	Female name
1	Aiden	**Emma**
2	**Jacob**	**Emily**
3	**Ethan**	**Madison**
4	Nicholas	Kaitlyn
5	**Matthew**	Sophia
6	Ryan	**Isabella**
7	Tyler	**Olivia**
8	Jack	**Hannah**
9	**Joshua**	Makayla
10	**Andrew**	**Ava**

I have highlighted the names that are common to both lists. They don't agree because the Social Security Administration's list is larger. Nevertheless, they show an interesting trend when compared with names from other years. (See the decade lists that follow.)

BOYS' NAMES

Until about 10 years ago, boys' names in the top 10 changed little. For example:

- The names James, John, Robert, Joseph, and William were popular throughout the 20th century, and almost always in the top 10. According to the Social Security Administration, Joseph is still in the top 10.
- The names Charles, David, and Michael were in the top 10 for at least 50 years; Richard and Thomas for at least 40; Christopher and George for at least 30; Frank, Matthew, Joshua, and Edward for at least 20 each.
- Of the names popular in 1900, only Frank, George, Henry, and Harry are rare among today's newborn boys.
- Names like Gary, Steven, and Mark were among those popular in the mid-20th century but seem to have fallen out of favor again.
- Names like Nicholas, Anthony, and Andrew were around throughout the 20th century, but have only recently made it to the top 10.
- Biblical names like Zachary, Jacob, and Joshua have seen a resurgence lately.
- Recently there has also been some "trendiness" in boys' names, less stability than before as shown by the fact that Jason and Justin went in and out of the top 10 fairly quickly and names like Ethan, Ryan, Tyler, and Aiden are just showing up.

GIRLS' NAMES

- Girls' names are definitely more trendy. Among the girls' names, Elizabeth is the only one that has been consistently popular since at least 1880. (It dropped to #11 in 1990, but was back up to #10 in 2000.)
- Mary and Margaret were popular throughout the first half of the 20th century, but dropped out of the top 10 in 1950.
- Names like Helen, Ruth, and Dorothy were popular for about 30 years after the turn of the century, but names like Rose, Florence, Bertha, Mildred, Alice, and Ethel had a shorter run at popularity and none of those names are common anymore among newborns.
- Names like Betty, Barbara, and Patricia tend to mark you as someone born between 1930 and 1950+, although the latter two names were still seen for another decade or two.
- Names like Carol, Kathy, Karen, Judy, Linda, Susan, Sandy, Nancy, Donna, and Debbie are very mid-20th century.
- There was a shift over the next couple of decades, so that names like Jennifer, Lisa, Kim, Michelle, Melissa, Angie, and Amy were popular in the 1970s, and by 1980, names like Jessica, Heather, Amanda, and Sarah were added.
- In 1990, the 1970s names were definitely gone and had been replaced by names like Ashley, Brittany, Stephanie, Samantha, Megan, and Lauren.
- By the year 2000, all of the popular 1990 names except Ashley, Sarah, and Samantha had disappeared, and now the top names were Hannah, Emily, Madison, Brianna, Kaylee, Kaitlyn, Hailey, and Alexis—and once again Elizabeth.
- Until the year 2003, Emma last appeared in the top 10 names for girls in 1890, but most of the other new names on the 2005 list had *never* been in the top 10 before the 21st century (Sophia, Isabella, Olivia, Makayla, Abigail, and Ava).

Here are the lists of top 10 baby names for the last 11 decades according to *www.babycenter.com:*

1900

Rank	Male name	Female name
1	John	Mary
2	William	Helen
3	James	Anna
4	George	Margaret
5	Charles	Ruth
6	Joseph	Elizabeth
7	Frank	Marie
8	Henry	Rose
9	Robert	Florence
10	Harry	Bertha

1910

Rank	Male name	Female name
1	John	Mary
2	William	Helen
3	James	Margaret
4	Robert	Dorothy
5	Joseph	Ruth
6	Charles	Anna
7	George	Mildred
8	Edward	Elizabeth
9	Frank	Alice
10	Henry	Ethel

1920

Rank	Male name	Female name
1	John	Mary
2	William	Dorothy
3	James	Helen
4	Robert	Margaret
5	Joseph	Ruth
6	Charles	Virginia
7	George	Elizabeth
8	Edward	Anna
9	Thomas	Mildred
10	Frank	Betty

1930

Rank	Male name	Female name
1	Robert	Mary
2	James	Betty
3	John	Dorothy
4	William	Helen
5	Richard	Barbara
6	Charles	Margaret
7	Donald	Maria
8	George	Patricia
9	Joseph	Doris
10	Edward	Ruth

1940

Rank	Male name	Female name
1	James	Mary
2	Robert	Barbara
3	John	Patricia
4	William	Carol
5	Richard	Judith
6	Charles	Betty
7	David	Nancy
8	Thomas	Maria
9	Donald	Margaret
10	Ronald	Linda

1950

Rank	Male name	Female name
1	John	Linda
2	James	Mary
3	Robert	Patricia
4	William	Barbara
5	Michael	Susan
6	David	Maria
7	Richard	Sandra
8	Thomas	Deborah
9	Charles	Kathleen
10	Gary	Carol

1960

Rank	Male name	Female name
1	David	Mary
2	Michael	Susan
3	John	Karen
4	James	Maria
5	Robert	Lisa
6	Mark	Linda
7	William	Donna
8	Richard	Patricia
9	Thomas	Debra
10	Steven	Deborah

1970

Rank	Male name	Female name
1	Michael	Jennifer
2	David	Lisa
3	John	Kimberly
4	James	Michelle
5	Robert	Angela
6	Christopher	Maria
7	William	Amy
8	Mark	Melissa
9	Richard	Mary
10	Brian	Tracy

1980		
Rank	Male name	Female name
1	Michael	Jennifer
2	Jason	Jessica
3	Christopher	Amanda
4	David	Melissa
5	James	Sarah
6	Matthew	Nicole
7	John	Heather
8	Joshua	Amy
9	Robert	Michelle
10	Daniel	Elizabeth

1990		
Rank	Male name	Female name
1	Michael	Jessica
2	Christopher	Ashley
3	Joshua	Brittany
4	Matthew	Amanda
5	David	Stephanie
6	Daniel	Jennifer
7	Andrew	Samantha
8	Joseph	Sarah
9	Justin	Megan
10	James	Lauren

2000		
Rank	Male name	Female name
1	Michael	Hannah
2	Jacob	Emily
3	Matthew	Sarah
4	Nicholas	Madison
5	Christopher	Brianna
6	Joseph	Kaylee
7	Zachary	Kaitlyn
8	Joshua	Hailey
9	Andrew	Alexis
10	William	Elizabeth

Now think about yourself, your parents, siblings, friends, and children.

- Does your name "date" you?
- Do you or any of your friends or relatives share the names of those in the top 10 of these decades?
- Do you particularly like or dislike any of these top 10 names in any decade?
- Are you surprised by what is or was popular at any given time?

3.   How does your name compare with common surnames in the United States? Partly because we are a nation of immigrants, the United States is unusually rich in its variety of surnames, which even 20 years ago numbered 1.7 million within 350 million records, according to *The Language of Names,* p. 51. (See Resources for Digging Deeper.) The following list contains the 100 most common surnames in the United States according to the 1990 census (which is the most recent available on-line) as shown at *www.jimwegryn.com.* Is your name here?

1. Smith (2.5 million)	35. Green	69. Gray
2. Johnson (2 million)	36. Adams	70. Ramirez
3. Williams (1.7 million)	37. Baker	71. James
4. Jones (1.5 million)	38. Gonzalez	72. Watson
5. Brown (1.5 million)	39. Nelson	73. Brooks
6. Davis	40. Carter	74. Kelly
7. Miller	41. Mitchell	75. Sanders
8. Wilson	42. Perez	76. Price
9. Moore	43. Roberts	77. Bennett
10. Taylor	44. Turner	78. Wood
11. Anderson	45. Phillips	79. Barnes
12. Thomas	46. Campbell	80. Ross
13. Jackson	47. Parker	81. Henderson
14. White	48. Evans	82. Coleman
15. Harris	49. Edwards	83. Jenkins
16. Martin	50. Collins	84. Perry
17. Thompson	51. Stewart	85. Powell
18. Garcia	52. Sanchez	86. Long
19. Martinez	53. Morris	87. Patterson
20. Robinson	54. Rogers	88. Hughes
21. Clark	55. Reed	89. Flores
22. Rodriguez	56. Cook	90. Washington
23. Lewis	57. Morgan	91. Butler
24. Lee	58. Bell	92. Simmons
25. Walker	59. Murphy	93. Foster
26. Hall	60. Bailey	94. Gonzales
27. Allen	61. Rivera	95. Bryant
28. Young	62. Cooper	96. Alexander
29. Hernandez	63. Richardson	97. Russell
30. King	64. Cox	98. Griffin
31. Wright	65. Howard	99. Diaz
32. Lopez	66. Ward	100. Hayes
33. Hill	67. Torres	
34. Scott	68. Peterson	

If not, you might want to look up your name in the U.S. census and discover just where it fits (*www.census.gov/genealogy/www/namesearch.html*).

4. **What is the derivation of your name?** *Note:* All of the following information was gleaned from *What's in a Name? Surnames of America* by La Reina Rule and William K. Hammond (See Resources for Digging Deeper) and focuses primarily on the 100 most common names in the United States as listed in item #3 above. The authors of *American Surnames* (also noted in Resources) provides greater detail and sometimes offers other explanations for names, but this is a good starting point.

Most surnames didn't come into being until sometime between 1100 and 1500 and most express physical characteristics, personality traits, patron saints, geographical locations, structures, and ancestors or relationships. Some are obvious; others are not.

Flanagan (Ireland), **Roux** (French), **Rossi** (Italy), **Roth** (Germany), and **Reed** and **Russell** (English) all denote an ancestor with red hair, which is obvious if you know the word for "red" in that language. (**Ross,** on the other hand, which might seem to refer to red hair, is the Gaelic word for peninsula.)

Names that are colors most often refer to physical characteristics (**Gray** for a gray-haired man, **Brown** for a dark complexion), but **Green** is one exception, as it generally refers to the town square. **Long** or **Lang** indicates a tall ancestor, which is not particularly surprising, but other names referring to physical characteristics are hidden. **Campbell** seems like a simple, strong Scottish name, but its origin—crooked mouth—has probably been forgotten by most. **Griffin** refers to a ruddy complexion and **Morris** to a dark complexion. **Young** might seem to refer to a young-looking person, but actually refers to the descendants of a younger son. (If you were a gold-digger in those days, you would only marry the oldest son who inherited his father's estate.)

The origins of personality traits are also almost always hidden. Who would know today that:

- **Hernandez** is "the son of the peaceful and bold one";
- **Hughes** refers to "the intelligent one";
- **Phillips** derives from "lover of horses";
- **Powell** is the "son of the young alert one";
- **Ramirez** is "son of the mighty counselor"; and
- **Sanchez** is "son of the pure one"?

Quite a few names have to do with prowess in war or having a warlike personality such as **Allen** (fierce one); **Price** ("son of the fiery one"); **Garcia** and **Rogers** (spearman); **Kelly, Lewis, Martin, Martinez,** and **Watson** (warlike, or son of a warrior). **Gonzalez** means son of the *young* warrior. **Cole** or **Coleman** has to do with men in a victorious army.

Other names are associated with power: **Reynolds** means "mighty ruler," **Richardson** is the son of a *powerful* ruler, **Rodriguez** of a *famous* ruler, and **Roberts** and **Robinson** both mean "shining with fame." **McDonald** is the son of the "ruler of the world."

Patron saints may or may not be more obvious—**Sinclair** (St. Clair), **St. John,** and **Sample** (St. Paul). **Simmons** refers to the Biblical Simon— "One who hears." Some ancient names seem more like prayers. **Jackson, Jenkins, Johnson,** and **Jones** all mean "God is gracious." **Ellis** means "Jehovah is my God."

Most location names (**Brooks, Forest, Hill, Woods**) and structures (**Barnes, Hall**) are obvious, but there are exceptions. Does anyone still know that

- **Foster** refers to a home in the forest,
- **Hayes** are hedges,
- **Hamilton** is a weather enclosure,
- **Lee** is a pasture or meadow,
- **Murray** is a seaside settlement,
- **Rivera** is a property on a stream, or
- **Torres** refers to a tower?

(If you speak Spanish, the answer to the latter two is probably, "yes.")

Some names refer to where people came from: **West** is from the west; **Scott** is from Scotland; **Wallace** is a Welshman settled in Scotland.

Many names based on occupations are obvious (**Miller, Baker, Cook, Taylor, Steward/Stuart**). However, many occupations no longer exist or are called by different names. We no longer use the word "**Wright**" to describe a maker of carts or a carpenter; nor do we associate those named **Carter** with someone who once hauled goods with a cart or **Coopers** with barrel-makers. We don't think of people named **Meyer** or **Myers** as stewards of a nobleman's estate or those named **Parker** as the custodian of a hunting forest. Yet those are the origins. **Butler** may seem obvious, but butlers were originally keepers of the wine cellar. **Clark** may seem to have a strong relationship to clerk, but the origin is "scholar and reader." Can you tell that **Flores** derives from the descendants of flower-growers or that **Turners** were once specialized carpenters, skilled at using a lathe?

Many names indicate "son of" including names beginning with "O" and "Mac" or "Bar" and "Ben" and names ending with

- son, sohn, or sen;
- kin;
- poulos;
- ez or es;
- ski and sky;
- ich; and
- ian.

Have you learned anything about your own ancestry from this little essay? If not, you might want to delve deeper into one of the resource books on surnames listed in Resources for Digging Deeper or look up "Meaning of surnames" on the Internet.

Exercise 2: **A Special Home**

THE BASIC EXERCISE

Draw the floor plan of a home or apartment that brings back warm memories. Some people will choose a home in which they were raised; others will choose the home in which they raised their own family. Alternatively, draw a map of a neighborhood that was important to you.

KEY ELEMENTS

There are some people who don't want to mess up their paper, and therefore hesitate to get started. That's why it's important to have extra grid sheets so that participants essentially have "permission" to mess up, or to take a sheet home for later. Other people plunge right in and are amazed at the forgotten memories it stirs up. Be sure no one feels there is a "right" way to do this exercise. Some people end up putting all their energies into one room of the house—their bedroom or the kitchen; others expand and position their home in relation to their friends' homes, their school, and so forth.

DEMENTIA CONCERNS

One symptom of Alzheimer's disease in many people as their disease progresses is a loss of visual-spatial skills. They can no longer load a dishwasher or understand where to put the plates to set the table. That means this exercise is not likely to work well in this form with people with dementia. They will not only be unable to draw a floor plan, but probably would find one you drew for them meaningless. However, you are still likely to generate fond memories through pictures. Details for doing this effectively are provided in Mini-Exercise B, which follows this exercise.

THE COMPLETE SCRIPT

Direction: Put a sample floor plan up on an overhead screen or draw one on a flip chart. (See sample on page 39.) Ask a volunteer to help you pass out grid paper and pencils (as needed) while you say the following:

▶ *Dialogue:* Today we're going to try an exercise that is good for the brain as well as, we hope, for your spirits. One of the principles of exercising the brain is to give it a chance to make new connections, so we're going to ask you to pull up old memories in a new way. You're getting some grid paper and a pencil if you need one, and I'd like you to draw the floor plan of a house or apartment that is associated with pleasant memories for you. If you moved a lot, draw a place associated with some of your best memories. You might choose to draw a home where you lived as a child or a home where you raised children of your own. It doesn't matter; the idea is simply to conjure up pleasant memories. Here is a sample to give you the idea.

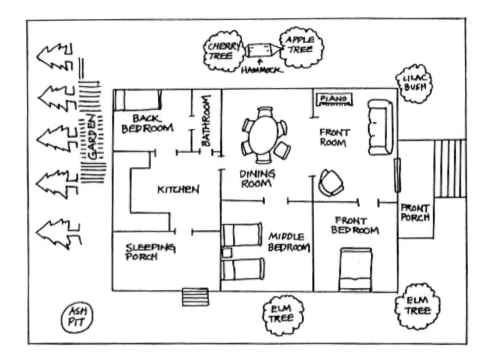

Direction: If possible, put the sample page on a transparency and show it on an overhead projector. You might also consider drawing it out on a flip chart. A smaller version is also included on the handout, which provides an abbreviated version of the following questions and directions. The sample floor plan is likely to serve as a visual reminder of most of the directions and questions, but the handout is a helpful backup—or you could also write these directions on flip chart sheets hung at the front of the room. Participants are not likely to remember all these instructions and questions on their own.

▶ ***Dialogue:*** As you draw your floor plan:

- Don't worry about proportion. We don't really care if you draw your kitchen three times larger than the living room.

- And don't worry about making "mistakes." They don't matter. And we have extra grid sheets if you really want to start over.

- If you lived in a two-story house or if you had a playroom in the basement, draw the floor plan on multiple pieces of paper or draw the plan smaller so each story fits on the sheet.

- Try to remember and draw details. Are there certain colors or certain architectural or furniture styles you associated with this home? Did it have any striking features—nooks and crannies, round windows, pocket doors, old plumbing? What about a mail slot, laundry chute, or a milk box for deliveries that was accessible inside and out?

- Do you remember any distinctive wallpaper, curtains, flooring, or carpeting? What about paintings or prints? Did you hang pictures of movie stars in your room?

- Put in as many details as you can. Think about furniture or beloved objects that were special to you or to another family member. Did your father have a chair in the living room where no one else was allowed to sit? Was your bed near a window where you could see the stars at night? Did you have enough closet space? If closets were jammed, what were they jammed with?

- Draw details outside, too. Was there a porch with a rocker? Was there a hammock tied to trees? Did you have a vegetable or flower garden? A special climbing tree or a treehouse? Was there a detached garage that connected to an alley behind the house? What about lilac bushes, fruit trees or other foliage that pleased the nose or eye?

- Some people grew up on a farm or have fond memories of a grandparent's farm home. If you're one, draw the area around the farm, too—barns, chicken coop, pasture, and so on.

- Some people would rather draw their neighborhood than their home. If you're one, include your house (or apartment), your friends' houses, favorite hangouts or secret hiding places, your school, and any other places that influenced you (e.g., candy store, music store, museum, church or temple, park).

- If you lived in an apartment building, chances are you lived in an urban environment and city life was important, so you may want to suggest other influences.

There aren't any rules with this exercise, except to try to draw a place where you were happy or about which you have fond memories. Do you have any questions? Okay, let's get started.

Direction: Give participants about 10 minutes to draw. Answer any questions as they come up. Most people become quite absorbed in this activity as they look for more details to add. People who have done reminiscence exercises may have often been asked to think about their childhood or being a young mother, but there is something about the physical act of drawing out the floor plan where their memories took place that unleashes long-forgotten elements.

When people seem to have had enough time and are looking for the next step, ask for volunteers to tell about what they have drawn. Usually one person is especially eager to share something he or she is surprised to have remembered. However, if no one volunteers immediately, don't be afraid to wait in silence for a while. Someone who is initially shy almost always speaks up when given time and encouragement.

▶ *Dialogue:* Who is willing to share his or her plan and tell us a little about it?

Who I Am and Where I Lived

Direction: Depending upon the size of your group, you may want to give people only a minute or two to hit the highlights of their plan. If the group is small and you have enough time, you may want to encourage lengthier sharing and even combine this with the mini-exercise that follows or Exercise 3.

After a few people have spoken, ask the group if anything someone else mentioned conjured up similar memories for them.

- For example, perhaps someone remembered push-button light switches, where the top button was white for turning an overhead light on, and the lower button was black for turning the light off. Did you have them in your house, too? (These were common for a while in the 1900s but tended to disappear in homes built at least since the 1950s.)
- Perhaps someone else remembers when pesticides were not a big concern and we ate carrots right out of the ground—or at most, gave them a cursory rinse with the hose. Or did the rabbits get yours?
- Or perhaps their memories were more general:
  - The pain and pleasure of sharing a room with a sibling, or
  - The warmest places in the house in winter and coolest places in summer.

All of these are possibilities for discussion if the group doesn't offer plenty of their own, but in my experience, one memory leads to another and this is an exercise that ultimately simply has to be cut off.

Depending upon the amount of time you have, here are some other questions you might want to ask about the multisensory memories and feelings this floor plan generates:

- How was your bedroom decorated? Was it distinctive in any way? Did it reflect the "real" you? Did you share it with anyone?
- Are there certain colors or certain architectural or furniture styles you associated with this house? Did your family have any prized possessions?
- Did the house have squeaks or groans that were either frightening or comforting? Do you remember giggling, singing, or bickering in these rooms?
- What memories are associated with the kitchen? What happened at the kitchen table? Is that where you did your homework? Learned to bake? Chatted with neighbors?
- Where did your family relax? How did they relax? Did you have a favorite place to curl up and read or listen to the radio or watch TV?
- What were your chores? Did you do them willingly?
- Did you have a yard? What was in the yard—flower garden, vegetable garden, trees, sandbox, basketball hoop, hammock, glider, chicken coop, dog house, driveway where you played hopscotch?
- Who were your neighbors and friends? Where did they live in relation to you? Describe the neighborhood on a summer evening.
- How far away was school? Were there any favorite spots along the way— a park, a candy store, construction site?

▶ ***Dialogue:*** Before we close, does anyone have anything else they want to add?

Direction for Closing: Give participants a chance for a final comment or two. Then close with one or both of the following questions:

▶ ***Dialogue:*** How many of you were surprised by the long-forgotten memories this exercise conjured up?

Direction: Encourage a show of hands or a voice vote. Unless earlier discussion already mentioned many of the surprising memories, ask participants to name something that surprised them.

▶ ***Dialogue:*** Can you give me some examples?

Direction: If they have already given examples or after a few more are mentioned, ask their opinion of the exercise.

▶ ***Dialogue:*** Did you enjoy this?

Direction: Encourage a show of hands or a voice vote. If there is enthusiasm, you may want to mention some of the suggestions in the mini-exercise or share some of the Resources for Digging Deeper.

Resources for Digging Deeper—Exercise 2

I had been teaching autobiographical writing for many years when I first encountered this exercise in Mary Borg's book, ***Writing Your Life*** (see References) which was originally published in 1989. Since I have always been fascinated by the floor plans of homes, I quickly added it to the exercises I recommended. Many of the other exercises in her book were ones that I had long been using, and many appear in other texts, but if you are looking for a single, user-friendly book for people interested in writing their life story, this would be my top choice. As is obvious from this exercise, many of the suggested activities can also be the basis for life story *sharing,* not just writing. I have mentioned specific exercises in her book elsewhere in mine, but could have suggested more.

Dover Publications is known for publishing copyright-free or long out-of-print books inexpensively. They have a number of publications on building plans and architectural features from houses built in the first half of the 20th century. For example, you might order ***Sears, Roebuck Homebuilder's Catalog, the Complete Illustrated 1910 Edition***. This book includes a sampling of the floor plans and housing kits that were once available from Sears—portable cottages, ready-made garages, and dozens of pages on doors, stained glass windows, door knobs, lighting fixtures, bathroom fixtures, fireplaces, and more. If you ever lived in an old house or if you visited a grandparent in an old house, some of these details are bound to look familiar. They also have many books of floor plans from the early 1900s through the 1930s as well as books on art deco and art nouveau styles. Go to *www.doverpublications.com* and click on architecture or antiques. The one thing to be aware of is that Dover often seems to be republishing the original from photocopies which lower the quality of the photographs and text, and sometimes make the volumes hard to read. Small, closely spaced print doesn't help. Two (of actually many) exceptions that are likely to bring back the sense of familiar neighborhoods to many older adults are:

1. The Brown Blodgett Company's *100 Small Houses of the Thirties;* and
2. Harris, McHenry, and Baker Company's *101 Classic Homes of the Twenties.*

Another source for interesting books that talk about daily life is **Time-Life.** In the early 1970s they produced a series of eight volumes called *This Fabulous Century.* The first volume covered 1870–1900, and each of the next seven books covered one decade of the 20th century. This was a marvelous series that may still be found in some libraries, but otherwise must be ordered from out-of-print book sources and is quite expensive. This was followed by an updated version of 20+ books called *Our American Century* that not only had a theme for each decade, but also had separate volumes for topics like *A Century of Flight, Events That Shaped the Century, A Century of Sports, 100 Years of Hollywood,* and *People Who Shaped the Century.* I love these books because they are filled with photographs and useful commentary on each decade's take on topics ranging from art, entertainment, and advertising to politics, war, and social issues, from sports and cars to fads and fashion. Most of these books are no longer available from Time-Life Books directly (http://www.time.com/time/bookstore/) but can be ordered from www.Amazon.com or may be available through your local bookstore. Try editor Richard Stolley's *The American Dream: The 50s,* for example. Or if you want more on music, look up *The Rock and Roll Generation: Teen Life in the 50s.* (These books are also useful for the exercises in Part 3.)

For a completely light-hearted look at life in the middle decades of the 1900s, consider the two Time-Life Books that have been compiled from the humorous photographs in *Life Magazine.* Both *Life Laughs Last* and *Life Smiles Back,* edited by Philip Kunhardt, Jr., which were published in 1989 and 1988 as Fireside Books from Simon & Schuster, are still available as of this writing. They are bound to produce laughter as well as fond memories.

There are many books that consist of lists of questions for helping you to write or tell your life story or that have those lists as part of the text. My favorite, however, has long been *To Our Children's Children: Preserving Family Histories for Generations to Come* by Bob Greene and his sister D. G. Fulford. What I like about this more than others is that while it covers the obvious, such as your family ancestry, your childhood, high school, college, military, career, parenthood, and so forth it also covers the less obvious, such as habits, appearances, moods, attitudes, philosophies, and 20/20 hindsight. It also, conveniently for this topic, has chapters entitled "The House of Your Growing Up," "The House You Raised Your Family In," and "Your House Now."

Note that Greene followed this book in 1998 with the similarly titled *To Our Children's Children: Journal of Family Memories* which consists of one question for each day of the year and space for families to write their own answers. I prefer the earlier book, so be careful you are getting the title you want if you order it or check it out of your local library.

Mini-Exercise B: **Photographs and Field Trips**

Many people who cannot draw a floor plan, and many of those who can, will also enjoy seeing photos of this special home or seeing similar architecture in books or taking a field trip to their own or a similar neighborhood.

1.   Generate fond memories through pictures. Start with an exterior view of the home—one in which the person grew up or raised a family. Then move to interior pictures of that same home that may have architectural features or furnishings in them that could be memory-stirrers, such as:

- A porch, perhaps with a rocker or glider
- A garden—flowers or vegetables
- A quiet or busy street in front or an alley behind—What games were played there?
- A hose or sprinkler—Who was in charge of watering the lawn? How was the hose used on hot summer days?
- A cozy alcove or window seat
- A staircase with a banister that has sliding possibilities
- Artwork or photos hanging on a wall that had some significance
- A dining room table—Who sat where and why?
- Antiques and heirlooms—What were their origins?
- Toys—a rocking horse, doll house, fire truck?
- Your father's chair in the living room—Did he read there, watch TV, listen to the radio, smoke?

The possibilities are limitless. The key to success is: **Use large pictures.** Many people have old photo albums filled with tiny pictures in which each human head is no larger than a quarter of an inch. Put them on a photocopy machine and blow them up to at least an 8 × 10 size. Then give the person plenty of time to peruse the picture.

If the person has dementia, recognize that if you ask six questions about one picture before any are answered, it will only cause more confusion. It is also likely to take time for the person to "tune in" to the picture and pull out the memories associated with it. Since time is a difficult concept for people with dementia, memories may easily slip back and forth between multiple homes, such as the one in which they grew up and the one in which they raised a family. The idea is to conjure up pleasant memories for that person; they don't necessarily need to make sense to *you*. Moreover, many people with dementia may not be able or willing to tell all the memories associated with a picture, but may enjoy silently contemplating it.

You can also still use family pictures with someone whose vision is severely impaired or even blind. In that case, it will be up to you to describe the visual details of the picture, and then ask the person for the memories associated with it. For example, I remember an old photograph of my great-grandparents seated on a couch next to what looked like a very short adult. In reality, it was a replica of Edgar Bergen's ventriloquist dummy, Charlie McCarthy—a very popular character from the mid-1930s until the mid-1950s. Talking about the wise-cracking Charlie McCarthy led to a discussion of other popular entertainment during that time.

Many photographs are likely to have been perused many times over the years, so if you simply say, "Here's a young boy in a rowboat," or "Here's a group of people sitting around a table in what looks like a grape arbor," the visually impaired person is likely to recognize it instantly by description, or at least have memories of a similar occasion to the one shown.

2. **Use photos to study architecture from the period.** Consider stimulating memories by spending time with a book on architecture or architectural features that represent the time period when your house was built. See Resources for Digging Deeper or look on-line.

3. **Take a field trip.** Try an architectural walking tour. If possible, walk through the town associated with the person's floor plan. If that's not possible, try for a neighborhood that is similar in age and architectural style to the person's experiences. You may get help from your local historical society; at the very least, they are likely to have wonderful memory-producing pictures. If they don't offer a walking tour, try making up one of your own by looking for a place with the architectural details that brought back memories for the person or the group. Or go to an antique store that sells architectural features and look for lighting fixtures, mantels, ceiling tiles, and other elements that bring back memories.

Part 2

Preferences, Routines, Customs, and Celebrations

The two main exercises in this section are intended to be lively means for drawing out memories of little events that have shaped us, and the mini-exercises that follow them are also creative memory-stirrers. Exercise 3: Make a Choice is essentially a simple game for learning about participants' preferences and routines. What do they find satisfying or meaningful? Maya Angelou once said that you can tell a lot about a person by how they handle a rainy day, lost luggage, and tangled Christmas tree lights. We tend to think it's life's big events that shape us, but it's more often little events that make a day pleasurable or upsetting, simply because the little events happen daily; weddings and funerals (thank goodness) are rarer. Even the celebrations discussed in Exercise 4: Holiday Traditions tend to occur only once every month or two; the idea behind Part 2 is finding what you can cheer about each day.

Participants will learn to use games, mind mapping, and art for conjuring up recollections in this section. All three are techniques that can be adapted for nearly any exercise and tend to not only liven up discussions, but awaken dormant memories. Most people are delighted with what they discover about themselves in this section and what they learn about others. These exercises are great connectors.

Exercise 3: Make a Choice

THE BASIC EXERCISE

Ask participants to make a choice between two essentially opposing ideas and stand on opposite sides of the room, according to their decision. Participants who can't decide, or aren't sure what the question means, can always stand in the middle.

KEY ELEMENTS

The fun in this exercise is generated both by the discussion of the questions and the movement of people from side to side of the room. If physically moving people isn't practical, see "Props and Materials" on page 11.

DEMENTIA CONCERNS

This is an exercise that generally works well with people who have dementia because (1) it's an opinion exercise, so there's no wrong answer; and (2) they only have to choose from two things, each of which is only one word or a short phrase, so they can usually pick an answer readily, and *look* like they are succeeding, even if they are not precisely sure what they are doing.

The trickier part is the metaphors. As the disease progresses, they may not be able to ascribe characteristics to a rose or a clothesline, but don't underestimate them. They can still make choices based on their likes and dislikes and some may think more complexly than you expect. Nevertheless, if the metaphors aren't working with a particular person or a particular group, return to concrete questions. "Do you like dressing up or do you prefer casual clothes?"

THE COMPLETE SCRIPT

▶ *Dialogue:*   Today we're going to do an exercise called "Make a Choice," in which we will ask you to decide between two opposite, or at least different, ideas. If your answer is one thing, I'm going to ask you to stand on the side of the room to my left, and if your answer is the opposite, I'm going to ask you to stand on the side of the room to my right. If you can't decide, or aren't sure what the question means, you can always stand in the middle. If you're feeling a little confused, I think you'll get the idea pretty quickly.

Okay, let's get started. The first question is, Are you an early riser or a night owl? Do you wake up early with lots of energy for the day and fade toward evening, or do you start your day slowly but start to come alive at night and love to stay up late? If you are an early riser, I'd like you to go to this side of the room (point), and if you are a night owl, I'd like you to go to this side of the room (point in the opposite direction). If you are a person who is only awake in the middle of the day, stand in the middle.

Direction: If your group is not fully mobile and you have decided to use signs or wave scarves or use some other alternative for "voting" on each question, modify the dialogue to reflect those changes. It's important to take each question a little bit further before going on to the next one. You will see why as the discussion unfolds.

▶ *Dialogue:*   Now those of you who like to get up early, give me examples of what you like to do then.

Direction: Get a few examples from the early risers and then ask the same of the night owls. What you are likely to find is that some people get up early to *work*—they have bills to pay or lunches to make for school-age kids or they just start work early either because their job demands it or because they are most alert and creative then. Others get up early so they can start their day slowly. They like to have quiet alone time to have a cup of coffee, read the newspaper, meditate, do some yoga, or whatever. The point is they like to *ease* into the day.

The night owls are often very much the same. Some people do like to party all night, but many night owls really are most alert or creative then and do their best *work* then. Others use that late night time when their kids are in bed or the house is quiet to pay bills, read the newspaper, do some yoga, and wind down from the day—very much like their morning counterparts. Their internal clocks are opposite, but their interests are much the same. Therefore, as you can see, answers that seem different can have similarities if you probe deeper.

▶ *Dialogue:*   Let's go on to another question. Are you a city person—someone who likes to be part of the hustle and bustle and culture and shopping of a city, where there are lots of people and activities day and night—or a country person, who likes a more quiet life out in nature—which may include the beach or the mountains as much as the country? If you are a city person, stand on this side of the room (point). If you are a country person, stand over here. (Point to the opposite side of the room.) If you need both, stand in the middle.

Direction: Some people are clearly one thing or another, but many people express a need for balance in their lives—time in nature, time with people. This may be a good time to pause and talk about balance in *all* of our lives.

It's also important to ask about what people like to *do* in each place, because this tells us a lot about the person, too. Many people tend to think of city people as extroverted and nature lovers as introverted, but the opposite can be true.

▶ *Dialogue:*   What do you like to do in the city or the country? What does it symbolize for you?

Direction: Give people a chance to respond and then use any of the following dialogue that seems appropriate.

▶ *Dialogue:*   Some people feel most *alive* out in nature—taking a hike, surfing the waves—while others feel most alive when they are in the city which bubbles with energy.

Others like to be *passively engaged*. They like the city because it's easy to remain anonymously in the background, while they watch people and observe everything going on around them. They can be as much or as little a part of things as they choose to be. They can be unaccountable for a while and ignore all of their other responsibilities.

But there are people who love being in nature for those same reasons. They don't go to hike, but to sit on a rock and listen to the birds or watch the sunset—they just want to *be*.

▶ ***Dialogue:*** Let's try another: Are you more physical or mental? Do you prefer to be actively doing something that requires physical energy or mental energy? If you are more physical, stand over here. (Point.) If you are more mental, stand here. (Point to the opposite side of the room.) If you need both kinds of activities, stand in the middle.

Direction: Again, some people are clearly one thing or another, but many people express a need for balance of both physical and mental activities in their lives. Reinforce the likelihood that everyone needs that balance.

It's also important to have participants specify what physical and mental activities they like to do. For some, it's about leisure activities—going for a bike ride rather than doing a crossword puzzle—but for others, it may involve household chores or physical work. Would you rather wash dishes or pay bills? Would you rather mow the lawn or look through a seed catalog? So ask the following questions.

▶ ***Dialogue:*** Those of you who like physical activities, what do you enjoy doing? Those of you who like mental activities, what do *you* like to do? Those of you in the middle, what's a good balance for you?

Direction: When you feel comfortable with what you've discussed go on to the next question.

▶ ***Dialogue:*** Here is another question. Are you more like a tortoise or the hare? Think of the old folk tale. Are you more like the tortoise—someone who moves along slowly and steadily—or the hare—someone who races through life? Some of you are hares because you actually move faster than others, but others of you are hares because you'd rather leap right into a project and correct your mistakes as you go along. Tortoises prefer to analyze things and plan them out before they begin. So, tortoises, stand over here. (Point.) Hares, stand here. (Point to the opposite side of the room.)

Direction: Allow discussion, if anyone has something they want to say, and then move on to the next question.

▶ ***Dialogue:*** Next question. Are you more of a saver or a spender? Spenders stand over here. (Point.) Savers stand over here. (Point to the opposite side of the room.)

Direction: This time you are likely to gain insight into people by *what* they save, so ask. Many people just like to save money, which may mean they like having a savings account and other assets or simply that they like to find a bargain. Other people are packrats and save everything: paper bags, string, gift wrap, or what one man described as "future usables." If the savers are older adults, this may stem from surviving the Great Depression in the 1930s or from another time when their financial security was weak. Spenders usually spend money, but you can get insights into what they value by *how* they spend it—on clothes, travel, their children, charities, and so forth.

I usually end the discussion on this topic by noting that the spenders should make note of the savers so they know where to borrow money, but the savers may not be willing to lend it.

▶ *Dialogue:* Now things are going to get a little trickier. The next question is, "Are you more like a rose or a daisy?" If you are more like a daisy, stand over there. (Point.) If you are more like a rose, stand over there. (Point to the opposite side of the room.) If you have no idea what we are talking about, stand in the middle.

Direction: Let people move about. Usually at least one person understands enough to make a choice and once you ask him why he is what he is, the others will catch on. If possible, though, it's best to first ask the daisies why they are daisies.

▶ *Dialogue:* Daisies, why are you daisies?

Direction: This question begins to get into people's value systems and sense of self. Daisies almost always say things like this: I'm a daisy because . . .

- I'm simple and down to earth; what you see is what you get.
- I am flexible; I can thrive almost anywhere.
- I am cheerful and bring a smile to people's faces.
- I'm a little "wild."

If your daisies don't bring these characteristics up, note them yourself.

The reason it's important to ask daisies to define themselves first, is that they often don't like roses. They think of roses as aloof and sophisticated. They think that roses think they are better than others and that they look down on daisies.

But here is where the discussion can turn to the labels we give people, and the way we judge them without asking what they really think. It's time to ask roses why they are roses.

▶ *Dialogue:* Roses, why are you roses?

Direction: Roses most often say things like this:

- They simply like roses—they feel pampered and well treated when someone gives them roses; they like the beauty and smell of roses.

- They know and like someone *named* Rose.
- Roses are complex—they have many layers, many facets, and they come in many varieties; they are not easily understood.
- They require nurturing and gentle care. (Others describe them as "high maintenance.")
- They are beautiful, but they have thorns—goes with their complexity and the idea that "Much about me is good and wonderful, but cross me and you will get hurt!"
- When they seem to be withering, you can just peel off a few layers of petals and the buds look fresh and new—they have more life in them than people sometimes think!

Give people a chance to give their own reasons, and just bring up any of the above that aren't mentioned. The funniest comment I have heard related to this seemed at first to go along with the nurturing that roses require, but the way she phrased it is, "I'm a rose because I take a lot of manure in my life." It's a good line that many of us can relate to.

Assuming that they did, also note that all of the roses defined themselves completely by how they viewed roses—not because they thought daisies were beneath them.

The next question is also a metaphor.

▶ *Dialogue:* Are you more like a kite string or a clothesline? Kite strings, stand over here (point) and clotheslines stand over here (point in opposite direction).

Direction: Again some people may be confused by this question, but most people find it easier than defining themselves as a flower. Start with the kite strings and ask the following question.

▶ *Dialogue:* Kite strings, why are you kite strings?

Direction: Allow for some discussion. Like the previous question, this one says a lot about how people see themselves and either want to be (usually kite strings) or know other people see them as (usually clotheslines).

Kite strings almost always see an element of freedom and soaring and believing in one's dreams in being a kite string. Others note that they still are attached to the ground and are indeed "grounded" by family, friends, life work, and other good elements.

The funniest response I have had so far to "Why are you a kite string?" was "Because I get jerked around a lot."

▶ *Dialogue:* Clotheslines, why are you clotheslines?

Direction: Again, allow for some discussion. Clotheslines almost always see themselves as practical and reliable. They are the people to whom others always come to get the job done. People hang things on them all the time. But that's okay, because clotheslines usually enjoy being useful and dependable. They are literally well grounded and they know it.

Some of the discussion depends upon how people picture a clothesline. If you see two upside-down "U" shaped poles with parallel lines of rope strung between them for attaching the clothes to, "well grounded" is especially appropriate. But some people think of a single pole with strings emanating out in a sort of diamond pattern. Those people may say they "are spun around a lot."

The funniest response we have had to "Why are you a clothesline?" was "Because I am always strung out."

Then move on to the remaining questions. Consider skipping some if time is limited. Directions for these are shorter, assuming you have the idea by now.

▶ *Dialogue:*   Let's move on to the next question. Which do you find more comforting, spring or fall?

Direction: As always, ask people to choose one side or the other and then ask "Why?"

The premise behind this question is that some people find greater pleasure in spring—in the idea of rebirth and renewal—and others see comfort in the earth, after one last blaze of color, settling down into a quiet, dormant time. The answers you get, of course, may be completely different. Seasons do influence moods, however, so this can be a good thing to know about others.

> *Quick Tip: Ask "Why?" at Every Opportunity:* Asking "Why?" not only gives us more information about people, but often expands our view of the question. As we found with "Are you more like a rose or a daisy?" my reasoning for preferring a daisy may be different from the reason you prefer them, and the way I see roses may be very different from the way those who prefer them see them. Listening to others opens up new possibilities. In addition, sometimes we find that we are closer in our thinking than our opposite responses would indicate.

▶ *Dialogue:*   Here's the next question. Are you a person who is more intuitive—going with gut feelings—or more rational, always weighing both sides?

Direction: Give people a chance to move to one side of the room or the other and give them a chance to answer "Why?"

Ask them to consider different applications, such as making a decision about buying a new refrigerator or listening to political debates. Do they handle ethical decisions differently from business decisions?

▶ *Dialogue:*   Next question: Are you more like a business suit or a t-shirt and jeans? (or, for women, high heels or sneakers?) In other words, do you feel more comfortable and confident dressing up or dressing informally?

Direction: Give people a chance to move to one side of the room or the other and give them a chance to answer "Why?"

Adding "comfortable and confident" can make this a loaded question. Some people feel more "real" in informal clothes, and definitely more physically comfortable, but they feel more confident around others (that is, more emotionally comfortable) when they are more formally dressed. In a residential care setting, this can be helpful to know.

▶ ***Dialogue:*** Are you more comfortable on a mountaintop or in a valley?

Direction: Give people a chance to move to one side of the room or the other and give them a chance to answer "Why?"

The responses to this tend to fall into two categories: those related to control and those related to the comfort of communities. In my experience, the people who like the mountaintops like to have oversight, to have a view of the big picture, and to feel in control of their lives. They are exposed to more light than people in the valleys in a literal and figurative sense. The people who prefer the valleys often see mountaintops as lonely places. The cities are in the valleys; that means that's where the action is, where their friends are. Also, the roads that connect them to other places are in the valleys. People who prefer valleys tend to feel a greater sense of control *there* because that's where their physical and emotional support systems and connections are.

▶ ***Dialogue:*** Are you more like a screened porch or a picture window?

Direction: Give people a chance to move to one side of the room or the other and give them a chance to answer "Why?"

This is one of those questions where people giving opposite answers often have the same reasoning for their preferences. Some people think they are more "real" and visible in a picture window—what you see is what you get—than when they are on a screened porch which can actually keep them somewhat hidden from view, depending on the light. Others will say, "No, I am more 'out there'—more visible and part of the community—when I am out on my screened porch as the world walks by than when I am 'hidden' and protected behind glass."

▶ ***Dialogue:*** Are you more *Carpe diem* (Seize the day) or *Que sera sera* (What will be, will be)?

Direction: Give people a chance to move to one side of the room or the other and give them a chance to answer "Why?"

This question tends to highlight the difference between people who believe they can take charge of their destiny and those who are at ease going with the flow. Talk about it in different circumstances: Do you like a thoroughly planned vacation or one that lets you decide what to do with each day as it comes? Do you actively pursue a goal or do you head yourself in the right direction and then let life unfold?

▶ *Dialogue:* Are you more a hot weather or cold weather person?

Direction: Give people a chance to move to one side of the room or the other and give them a chance to answer "Why?"

This seems like an ordinary, completely innocuous question, but it's one that tends to garner strong feelings.

▶ *Dialogue:* Are you more like a violin or a bongo drum? (Or some other musical instrument altogether?) Why?

Direction: Some people can easily answer this. People who see themselves as violins often appreciate their versatility and complexity—music played on violins ranges from the intensely sorrowful to the utterly toe-tapping happy. Those who see themselves as drums often do so because they have always marched to their own beat. Drawing out additional responses is bound to be interesting.

People who see themselves as other instruments usually have widely varying reasons—they resemble the shape of a cello; they prefer the sound of a flute; they played a trumpet in a high school band. This is a good question to ask people you want to know better because it tends to give you clues about their musical tastes, their personal history, and their view of themselves.

Directions for Closing the Session: If you have gotten through all the questions and time has still not run out, ask if any of the participants have an idea for a Make a Choice question. The possibilities are limitless. If there is time, try out some they suggest.

Because each question in this exercise asks for a vote in which everyone is encouraged to participate by moving about or waving scarves or signs, this exercise tends to be lively and laughter generating. As you end the session, ask participants whether they enjoyed this exercise.

▶ *Closing Dialogue:* Did you enjoy this exercise? Would you like to do more exercises that are similar?

Direction: Give participants a chance to respond. If they did enjoy this, consider trying out some of the games in Mini-Exercise C that follows.

PUTTING THE ANSWERS TO WORK

The exercises in Part 2 can be particularly useful in residential care settings if we apply the answers of participants to their daily care. For example, learning who among our residents is a morning person and who is a night owl, and how they like to start and end their days, helps us to:

- Know how to help them have a good start and end to each day by following these preferred routines.
- Know how to schedule more complex tasks for the times they are most alert (bathing, appointments, physical and mental exercises).

- Know when they may need extra help. For instance, a person sitting in the common area in the evening—when we know she is a morning person—may need assistance finding her way back to her room. Once there, she may need help with bedtime preparations. She may be perfectly capable of getting herself together in the morning, but by evening her brain has just given out.

In more general terms, here are examples of things we can learn based on the responses to other questions in Exercise 3:

- From the question of whether they prefer physical or mental activities, we can learn which activities they might be most interested in.
- From whether they are more like a tortoise or a hare, we can understand how they like things presented—carefully laid out and explained ahead of time or explained as we go along.
- For whether they are a rose or a daisy, we can learn something about how they like to be seen and treated.
- From whether they are a clothesline or a kite string, we might learn whether it was more important to them to be free and independent or to be useful.
- From whether they prefer warm weather or cold, we learn something about whether they like to sit in the sunshine and how much bundling they might need.
- From whether they are more like high heels or sneakers, we learn which way they feel most comfortable (or perhaps safer) and therefore what to help them wear.

Keep potential applications to care in mind as you do other exercises in this book.

Resources for Digging Deeper—Exercise 3

Many of the questions for this exercise came from the book *Values Clarification,* by Sidney B. Simon, Leland W. Howe, and Howard Kirschenbaum, which they wrote as a "handbook of practical strategies for teachers and students" in 1978 and which I began using with older adults a few years later. This exercise was updated in the 1995 version of their book (published by Warner Books) and appears on pages 69–71 with a number of new questions. Dr. Simon, who is professor emeritus at the University of Massachusetts, Amherst and who has made a lifelong career of helping people to identify and live their values, also wrote *In Search of Values* (Warner Books) in 1993 (as well as a number of other books). Although I prefer *Values Clarification,* both of these books have lots of ideas for identifying what's important to individuals through engaging, intriguing, and fun exercises. See Mini-Exercise C.

A small warning: Some of the exercises involve sharing information on a deeper level than participants may be willing to do. Avoid those exercises unless there is a high level of trust in confidentiality and a high level of intimacy among group members. Always allow people to "pass" if they don't want to share.

If the people in your group enjoyed the metaphors ("Are you more like a kite string or a clothesline?") in the Make a Choice exercise, they may also enjoy the game *Imaginiff.* See details in Mini-Exercise C-1.

There are also many other games that encourage people to talk about themselves and learn more about others in the group. There are two versions, for example, of **Penny Ante.** In that game, after being given a set number of pennies to start, players take turns drawing a card from the pile and following the directions, such as "Give a penny to everyone wearing glasses" (which in an older crowd can quickly use up a supply of pennies) or "Take a penny if you've been to the Grand Canyon." Trying to build up or maintain your supply of pennies adds a level of competition that many find fun, but the real intent of the game is to stimulate discussion about travel, experiences, family, and other topics. Another good game for reminiscing about daily life is called **Shake out the Truth.** This is described in greater detail in Mini-Exercise C-2. The makers of *Shake out the Truth* have also created similar reminiscence games—**Shake up the Relatives** and **Shake Loose a Memory** are two—based on rolling a die and answering questions that are easy discussion starters.

LifeStories produced a board game of that name in the early 1990s and followed it with a series of card games called **Conversation Pieces** shortly thereafter. The board game has four categories of cards, most of which are related in some way to reminiscing. ("What was a happy time in your life?" or "Describe something you like about one of your relatives.") It was designed as an intergenerational game to get family members talking to one another and was originally offered by Talicor, Inc., the same company that produced **The Ungame,** another relationship-building product.

For those who need ideas for discussion questions more than they need board games, *Conversation Pieces* is simplicity personified. There are four versions. My favorite—because it's the most versatile—is *Ice-Breakers.* Participants simply draw one of 100+ cards and respond to the statement or question on the card. For example:

- What do you think is the perfect age? Why?
- Describe the best surprise you ever received.
- What do you hope someone will invent? What does it do?

One of my pet peeves about the manufacturers of many of today's interesting games is that they use very tiny type, sometimes in blue and often against a busy background. All of the games listed here are exceptions. All use black type and most have a background of white or cream. In all of these games the words are large and clear so most older adults can probably read them fairly easily. *Imaginiff* has a yellow background on the bottom and reverse print against a dark burgundy/brown background on top. However, the six choices on each card are easy to read and that is probably the most important part.

All of these products can be found in bookstores, toy stores, on-line, or from one of the vendors listed in Appendix B.

Mini-Exercise C: **Play a Game**

Many of the exercises in this book focus on simple discussions. If your group is talkative, they may produce lots of energy and laughter through their stories, but for a change of pace or for another way of drawing out participants, games can be a great boon. With practice, just as you learn to get people to "vote" their agreement or disagreement by waving signs or scarves or moving around the room, you will learn to spontaneously add games to discussions. In the meantime, here are some ready-made solutions.

All of the following can be played as games the way they were designed or you can simply use the hundreds of cards which are part of each to come up with new questions worthy of discussion.

1.　**More metaphors.** As noted in Resources for Digging Deeper, people who enjoyed the Make a Choice exercise may also like **Imaginiff**. In this board game, players are asked to imagine others as an object or in a specific situation. For example, "*Imaginiff* _____ (your spouse, son, best friend):
- Were a color. Which color would he/she be?
- Were a soup. Which would he/she be?
- Bought a newspaper. Which would he/she read first?
- Needed a laugh. Who would be the most likely to provide it?
- Could invite a famous historical figure home for dinner. Whom would he/she invite?

The question is followed by six choices, and if you choose the most popular answer you get to move your marker forward. Part of what I like about this game is the adaptations that are possible. For example:
- If you play it straight, you simply fill in the name of one of your fellow players in the blank on the card, and say, for example, "*Imaginiff* Jill were a piece of jewelry. Which would she be?" Your choices are diamond ring, anklet, stud in nostril, Rolex, brooch, or earring. Of course, it's sharing the justification for your choice that makes the game especially interesting. When you play it this way, the game changes every time the players change.
- A second version is to play in teams and the person you are imagining as a piece of jewelry is one person in a group of perhaps six famous people. (For example: Albert Einstein, Sean Connery, Jane Austin, Bill Gates, Barbara Walters, and Mother Teresa. The possibilities are limitless.) The winner of each point is the team that comes up with the most creative answer. (Or you can play it like *Family Feud.* Have 50 people submit their votes before this game and see which team can guess which were most popular with the "audience.")
- You can also simply take the nearly 200 questions and ask participants to say which of the six answers is most like them, and why.

2.　**Shake out the Truth.** In this game, each player is given a laminated card which has "No" printed on one side and "Yes" on the other. In addition, there are 100+ cards with one to six dots on the back corresponding to the dot patterns on a die. Players take turns rolling one die (I use an oversized foam die) and drawing a card from the pile that matches their number. Each card has a statement like:

- I am the baby of the family.
- I have been on a cruise.
- I have worked a night job.
- I have been thrown from a horse.

The player reads the statement on the card and the other players guess whether or not it is true of that person—voting with their "Yes" and "No" cards. When all have voted, the player reveals the truth. Like *Penny Ante,* there is additional fun in sharing the stories the statement engenders, but I have found that the element of "Did she or didn't she?" is also intriguing to players. Let us say the card I draw says, "I have played hooky from school." If the others think I am full of mischief and was probably never concerned about a perfect attendance record, they will turn up "Yes." If they think I live by the rules, they will probably turn up "No." When everyone has voted—and only then—I tell them the truth.

That is, the truth as I remember it, and we are bound to accept what the person says, which makes this an easy game for people with dementia, because whatever they *say* is the truth, is accepted as the truth. In my case, I remember being a "Goody Two-shoes" in school, always trying to please, always trying to do the right thing, so I don't ever remember skipping school. That, too, could be a topic for discussion. If I had it to do over again, I would be less earnest about school. What would you do differently?

Shake out the Truth comes with 10 "Yes/No" cards, and I have played it in even larger groups in order to demonstrate it, but I would recommend playing it in groups of 6 to 8 so that people do not have to wait a long time between turns.

3.   Try another reminiscence game. As noted in Resources for Digging Deeper, there are also a number of other games with a similar purpose: fostering reminiscence discussions. Most of these have been around for a decade or two and have proven successful as designed. *Conversation Pieces* is the most spontaneous of these, but if you throw out the rules and simply ask one of the questions from one of the games whenever a small group is gathered together, you can have reminiscence discussions anywhere anytime.

Here's another idea. In a residential care setting or adult day center or anywhere there are multiple participants and staff, assign the staff a question a day from one of the games. For example, on Monday the staff assignment is to learn about the pets of their care receivers, and to come back at the end of the day and report to the rest of the staff what they learned.

Exercise 4: Holiday Traditions

THE BASIC EXERCISE

When we talk about holiday traditions, the first thing that comes to mind for the majority of Americans is Christmas, but we are a diverse society and in this exercise we are going to be talking about many celebrations.

PROPS AND MATERIALS

One can talk about celebrations without props, but this is one exercise that could be greatly enhanced with symbols of multiple holidays, both religious and secular. If you have decorations, hats, trinkets, balloons, banners, or any other representations of holidays, drag them out. Fill up the walls and tables. Make the room as festive as possible. With some planning, you might be able to serve a variety of foods representing one or more holidays, or make the cooking or baking part of the exercise. At the very least, put decorative symbols on your flip chart sheets, overhead transparencies, or Power Point slides.

KEY ELEMENTS

Celebrations are natural uppers. Put a helium balloon in a room, and suddenly it's a more welcome place, so generating enthusiasm for this exercise shouldn't be difficult. On the other hand, many people are depressed by traditional holidays. Perhaps December has never quite lived up to the person's expectations; perhaps Valentine's Day is only a reminder of a lost love; perhaps the person never had a birthday party in his or her honor. Be sensitive to these issues, and remedy them where you can. Someone never had a birthday party? Then throw one! Someone's spouse has died so Valentine's Day is a sad reminder? Start a new tradition of secret Valentines; send cards, candy kisses, and smiley hearts, for the first 13 days of February and on the 14th day, let people reveal themselves to their secret Valentines and give real hugs. Listen for the celebrations that were meaningful to the people in your group and then find ways to carry on those traditions.

DEMENTIA CONCERNS

As with several other exercises, this generally works well with people who have dementia because we are asking them to think about pleasant events from their past. Be aware, however, that they may be able to think about something that they can't necessarily articulate; that doesn't mean they don't enjoy thinking about it.

Also remember that it takes people with dementia time to tune in to the topic of discussion. If you are covering a dozen holidays in one class, they may well still be thinking of Valentine's Day when you have moved 9 months forward to Thanksgiving. You may need to slow down or cover fewer holidays in one class. The goal as always is to stir up pleasant memories, not add to their confusion. Therefore, if they do talk about Valentines when you are covering Thanksgiving sweet potatoes, go with the flow and give them positive reinforcement for whatever memory they bring forth.

THE COMPLETE SCRIPT

▶ *Dialogue:*   Today we're going to talk about celebrating holidays—many kinds of holidays. We're going to jump right in and begin by asking you to tell us:

- What is a holiday you especially enjoy? Why? What makes it special?

Direction: Give participants a chance to express themselves, but don't let anyone dominate the conversation from the beginning. At the start of this exercise, we just want a general sense of the holidays that are meaningful to participants. When someone mentions one, ask for a show of hands—or a waving of signs or streamers—from everyone who agrees that that's a pleasant holiday. We don't want to get into the negatives here or put people on the spot, so don't ask who disagrees. (In some cases, it may simply be a holiday of little significance in other people's lives or outside their faith.) After the request for agreement, simply ask for input on another holiday.

▶ *Dialogue:*   Who else can give me the name of a holiday you enjoy celebrating and tell me why it's important to you?

Direction: Do this four or five times so that you get an idea of what people like to celebrate in your group and use that as the basis for the questions you ask from here on. This opening exercise also enables you to eliminate certain holidays from discussion. For example, if your group is primarily Jewish, Christmas is not likely to be a holiday with which the participants have particularly pleasant associations.

   If no one has mentioned birthdays or anniversaries, let them know that we'll also be talking about those.

▶ *Dialogue:*   Okay, since we can't talk about every holiday, we'll concentrate mostly on those which seem to be among the favorites of this group. Now I'm going to ask you more detailed questions.

Direction: One way to make this exercise more engaging is to draw "mind maps" for each holiday. (See samples in Appendix D and on the following pages.) The example we have is for a birthday, and we've only included general categories in each bubble. You can draw your own mind maps on a flip chart or overhead transparency using as many bubbles as you need and changing the categories to suit you. Encourage those who are interested to create their own mind maps, perhaps related to a holiday that was especially memorable.

Sample Mind Map: Birthday Ideas

Whether or not you use the mind-map format, go through each of the four or five holidays mentioned at the beginning and ask participants the following questions about them. Try to give a variety of people a chance to respond and try to draw out both comments that participants have in common—"Oooh, I like that, too"—and ones that are perhaps unique to a specific family or culture. There are great differences, for example, in how people of different cultures celebrate Christmas. Here are the questions to repeat for each holiday you want to discuss in depth:

- How do you celebrate it? What are the traditions associated with this holiday that you work hard to preserve?
- With whom do you celebrate it?
- Where do you celebrate it? Do you go anywhere specific?
- What foods do you associate with this holiday? Do you prepare them yourself or help in the preparation?
- Is there specific music associated with this holiday? What is it? Can you sing something related to it?
- Are gifts a part of this holiday? What kinds of things are given? Did you ever give or receive something special?

Sample Mind Map: Fill in the Bubbles

Event

- Are there costumes or special clothing associated with this holiday? Talk about that.
- Are there funny stories that are told year after year at this celebration? Tell one.
- Was this also a special holiday to you when you were a child? Why or why not? What has changed?

When you feel people have said most of what they want to say about a particular holiday, go on to the next holiday you initially chose as special and begin the questions again.

Remember that we're looking for stories, not just lists. Here's an example paraphrased from *A Celebration of American Family Folklore* (by Zeitlin et al., 1992) on a gag Christmas gift:

My cousin Keith brought back a can of seal meat from Newfoundland. Everyone in the family was horrified, so for a joke, he wrapped it up and put it under the Christmas tree for his sister; she gave it back to him and he wrapped it up again the next Christmas. This time she recognized it and relabeled it as a present for me. I gave it to Keith's wife as a wedding present; she gave it back to me the next Christmas, and I gave it to Keith's sister for her wedding last summer. I expect it will be back under the tree next Christmas. (p. 169)

▶ *Dialogue:* Sometimes there are holiday traditions that are deeply rooted in your family's experiences. One person talked about how her family came to the rolling prairies of Kansas in a covered wagon. Her grandfather planted and lovingly cared for a grove of maple trees. Trees were rare and therefore sacred within her family. No one ever dreamed of cutting a Christmas tree; instead presents were put at each person's place at the dining room table, and generations later they still are. (*A Celebration of American Family Folklore*, pp. 163–164)

- Are there any traditions in your family that have come from life experiences?

Direction: Give participants a chance to respond.

▶ *Dialogue:* Sometimes the holiday and the traditions are less important than the social aspects. Nonreligious families may celebrate a religious holiday because of the excuse to fix good foods and share them with family and friends.

One family described their aunts and uncles and parents as elderly, sober people, "pillars of the church," but when they got together there was always laughter and rowdiness. One said, "They are people who enjoy themselves and they have a spirit of fun about them and a spirit of nonsense" that only surfaced when they all got together." (*A Celebration of American Family Folklore*, p. 180)

- Do you have or did you ever have family members who surprised you by their unaccustomed silliness? Do any of your own celebrations center more on food and good times than whatever the holiday was supposed to be about?

Direction: Give participants a chance to respond.

▶ *Dialogue:* Now let's talk about birthdays and anniversaries.

- Did your family make a big deal of birthdays when you were growing up?

- Did you do the same in the family you raised or do you do it in the family you are part of now?

Direction: Get a general consensus of how people felt or feel about birthdays. Was it special once, but not so special anymore? We would love to have people be excited for every birthday, so try to generate again the excitement that they once felt. Ask a few people to respond to the following questions.

▶ *Dialogue:*

- How did your family celebrate birthdays when you were a child?

- Describe a special birthday or birthday party or gift. What made it special?

- How did you celebrate birthdays with your children? (Did your own childhood experience influence what you did?) Was any child's birthday particularly memorable?

- Is there a party game you especially like? One that you don't like?

- Do you have any birthday traditions in your family that are unusual? Describe them.

Direction: People will have their own answers for each of these questions, but if you need a story or two to get you started, here is one from my childhood and one from *A Celebration of American Family Folklore:*

On birthday games—

When I was about 7 or 8 my mother arranged a treasure hunt game that I absolutely loved. She made us all go into my room to play for about 20 minutes behind a closed door. When we opened my bedroom door, on the outside were strings tied to the door knob, each with a name attached. We took the string with our name and followed it all through the house—down the stairs, over and under furniture, straight out to the backyard. At the end of each string was a small present—my mother was not only tolerant about furniture being climbed on, she also believed in giving people who came to birthday parties as many gifts as they gave! I tried this treasure hunt many years later at my own daughter's party, but one child wound the string around her wrist and cut off her circulation. We suddenly noticed her hand was blue and had to snip through the layers quickly.

On traditions—

In another family it's traditional to wake up the person whose birthday it is by putting butter on her nose. One sister thought it was to give the person a shiny day, but another said it was to elicit comments from fellow students, coworkers, or people passing by. When they ask, "Why do you have butter on your nose?" you can say, "Because it's my birthday!" and presumably they will wish you a happy birthday. (*A Celebration of American Family Folklore*, p. 178) But would you really go through the day without wiping it off your nose?

► *Dialogue:* Some people, particularly in Roman Catholic households, grew up celebrating their saint's day, as well as their birthday. Did you? Did you get presents then, too?

Direction: Give people a chance to respond.

► *Dialogue:* Some people only have or had grand celebrations for milestone birthdays—turning 21, 30, 65 or each decade. Did you ever have a special milestone birthday celebration? What did you do?

Direction: Give people a chance to respond.

► *Dialogue:* Some people still love to celebrate their birthdays with a big bash and others don't like to think about getting older, so they prefer to let them pass unnoticed—or so they say.

- How do you feel about celebrating your birthday now?
- What would be the ideal birthday celebration for your next birthday?

Direction: Give participants a chance to respond.

> ***Quick Tip: Insert a Change of Pace:*** Here are the months, the character associated with them, birthstones, and flowers of the month. This sheet is repeated in the handout section. Ask participants if they were aware of these and whether the characteristic, stone, and flower suit them.

Month	Character trait	Birthstone	Flower
January	Constancy	Garnet	Carnation
February	Sincerity	Amethyst	Violet
March	Courage	Aquamarine	Jonquil
April	Innocence	Diamond	Sweet Pea
May	Success in love	Emerald	Lily of the Valley
June	Health and longevity	Pearl	Rose
July	Contentment	Ruby	Larkspur
August	Married happiness or friendship	Peridot	Gladiolus
September	Clear thinking	Sapphire	Aster
October	Hope	Opal	Calendula
November	Fidelity	Topaz	Chrysanthemum
December	Prosperity	Turquoise	Narcissus

Reprinted with permission from Bifolkal's *Remembering Birthdays* (see Resources for Digging Deeper).

► *Dialogue:* What about anniversaries? The stereotype is that women always remember wedding anniversaries and men never do. Is that or was that true in your household?

Direction: Give participants a chance to respond.

▶ ***Dialogue:*** Did you celebrate anniversaries and were they important to you? What did you do? Go out to dinner? Exchange gifts? Take a trip?

Direction: Give participants a chance to respond.

▶ ***Dialogue:*** What about other kinds of anniversaries, like the anniversary of quitting smoking or getting an important job? Do you celebrate anything like that?

Direction: Give participants a chance to respond.

▶ ***Dialogue:*** Has anyone ever thrown a surprise party for you in honor of a birthday, anniversary, or other occasion? Tell us about it. Were you truly surprised? Were you pleased?

Direction: Give participants a chance to respond.

▶ ***Dialogue:*** Are there any nontraditional holidays celebrated in your family? For example, is there a historical figure or a celebrity who is much admired in your household so you bake a cake each year, say on Albert Einstein's birthday?

Direction: Give participants a chance to respond.

▶ ***Dialogue:*** Are there any other occasions in your family when you are likely to send flowers or give gifts? What are they?

Direction: Give participants a chance to respond.

▶ ***Dialogue:*** Finally, let's talk about starting new traditions. Elizabeth Berg in the Reader's Digest book *Family Traditions* says celebrations not only give us something to look forward to, but they make "a formal statement that life is full of things to be grateful for." She defines traditions much like habits: "something you do once and it feels right; and so you do it again and again." Some "traditions" are little things—like sleeping with a particular pillow that has been your key to feeling ready for slumber for 25 years or more, or always having a big breakfast on Sunday or pizza on Friday nights. These small things, Berg says, "identify us like a fingerprint. They anchor us." (p. 9)

However, in a world that is constantly changing, especially if we have moved away from family and old friends, or they have moved away from us, we may need to create new traditions. We may have an idea for something and be eager to try it out but meet with resistance or apathy from others. Berg says we shouldn't let others rain on our parade. Forge ahead. Try it. Then try it again. "Give it a few times before you decide whether it's working or not." It may take a few times before your family or friends get used to the idea, or maybe the idea needs some tweaking, but over time you may find you have another way of celebrating. Or you may say, "Well, we found out something that *didn't* work."

What kinds of things are we talking about? Well, it's up to you to decide, but think about something that you have done for a long time that isn't working anymore, or perhaps that you no longer want to do, such as being the chief Thanksgiving cook. Or think of something that you haven't done or aren't doing that you would like to do. Here are a few examples to get you started:

- December has become a time of heavy consumerism for people of almost any faith. If you have thought it would be good to help people less fortunate instead of buying another fondue pot for Aunt Alice, think about what that might be. What would you like to do instead? What and who would need to change?

- Do you no longer celebrate Valentine's Day since your spouse died, and want to make it a happy holiday again? Think about ways to do it.

- Are the people with whom you used to celebrate Thanksgiving out of reach? With whom could you celebrate instead?

- If you consistently have a particular meal on a particular day and are getting bored, how about starting a Tuesday "tantalize your taste buds" lunch in which you try out at least one food that represents another culture or ethnicity or that simply offers a new spice such as anise or tarragon?

- Do you miss intellectually stimulating conversation? Start a group that meets weekly to discuss a predetermined topic.

- Do you like classical music? Could you start a noontime listening group and call it Bach's Lunch?

Think about a celebration you would like to have or like to change. Let's talk about it.

Direction: That's a lot of dialog and a lot of questions. Break it up pausing here and there to give participants a chance to respond.

▶ ***Dialogue Before Closing:*** As you leave today, think about a celebration you will treasure more or change because of today's discussion.

Resources for Digging Deeper—Exercise 4

Elizabeth Berg's book ***Family Traditions*** (see References) quoted in this exercise has hundreds of ideas for celebrating in new and familiar ways. It is particularly oriented toward families with young children, but many ideas are multigenerational or usable by people of any age. It's worth checking out.

I have also quoted again from ***A Celebration of American Family Folklore*** by editors Steven Zeitlin, Amy Kotkin, and Holly Cutting Baker, © 1992, ISBN 0938756362.

If you are simply looking for holiday trivia or activities related to birthdays and holidays, look up:

- Activity Connection: *www.activityconnection.com*
- BiFolkal: *www.bifolkal.org* or 800-568-5357

- ElderGames: *www.ncoa.org* under "publications"
- ElderSong: *www.eldersong.com* or 800-397-0533

All of these represent uncommonly rich resources. **Activity Connection** is a subscription-based web site (to which I am a content contributor) that produces hundreds of pages of new material each month, including activity ideas related to holidays for that month. **ElderGames** and **ElderSong** both have holiday trivia booklets with terrific quizzes for inserting a change of pace.

Bifolkal has an entire kit devoted to *Remembering Birthdays,* which includes song sheets ("My get up and go has got up and went," "The More We Get Together"), a slide show and videotape, poetry, skits, discussion ideas, intergenerational activities, resources and background information (such as the Chinese astrological years, birthstones, flowers that represent each month, and so on.) If you can't afford the whole kit, the 120-page manual can be purchased separately and will prove a rich resource for years.

There are loads of books that teach the concept of mind mapping. The process I have suggested for this exercise is very basic and self-explanatory. My inspiration comes from two books, both of which I have used for about 15 years. Joyce Wycoff's *Mindmapping, Your Personal Guide to Exploring Creativity and Problem-Solving,* is obviously completely devoted to the topic of mind mapping, and I still find it useful. *Writing Your Life* by Mary Borg, the book that inspired the exercise on drawing the floor plan of our home, also has an exercise she calls "rippling" (p. 48) based on the same idea as mind mapping. Just as dropping a stone into a pond has a ripple effect, one topic ripples out into many ideas. In her example, she uses the word "Mom" which leads to bubbles on her children, her family tree, her qualities, the things she loves, and so on. Those, of course, lead to other ideas.

The primary activity medium for the mini-exercises listed on the following pages is art. Just as drawing the floor plan of a home with pleasant associations tends to bring out long-forgotten memories, art allows us to tell our stories in new ways. In the sample mini-exercise that follows, we have suggested a few art projects. Some of the ideas came from the out-of-print ElderGames publication called *Drawing on the Past,* which gives people an idea for drawings to complete. Others have come from my imagination and past art experiences.

Art can be an especially good way to give people with dementia a new voice. The best book I know for providing guidance is *I'm Still Here* by La Doris ("Sam") Heinly, which can be purchased from Sam directly. (Go to *www.alzheimersartspeaks.com* or call 949-673-8231.) *I'm Still Here* provides dozens of amazing full-color examples of the art of people in various stages of Alzheimer's disease and provides wonderful advice about conducting art classes for people with dementia. In the 1990s, Sam began working with the late Selly Jenny whose "Memories in the Making" program for the Orange County (CA) Chapter of the Alzheimer's Association won acclaim nationwide. Now Sam has expanded where Selly left off, and while continuing to work directly with people with dementia, also trains art class leaders. Sam is amazing in her respect for and sensitivity toward people with Alzheimer's disease, which makes her book (which now also comes with a CD) indispensable. Each illustration is enhanced with comments made by the person who drew it and the added insight of Sam as she and others worked with the person. We have no cure yet for Alzheimer's disease, but this book proves that people with dementia can remain uniquely articulate and express a full range of emotions through their art.

Mini-Exercise D: Adding Art

Many people find great satisfaction in crafts and have made holiday decorations and gifts for many years. Others are likely to claim they have no artistic talent whatsoever, but if gently handled, can be persuaded to try a project or two and often surprise themselves. The key is to give the widest possible range for "success." If the standard for a craft project is Martha Stewart quality, I am likely to forego even attempting the activity, but if I have the chance to make it "mine," expressing my individuality, I am much more likely to have fun with it, and perhaps discover something new or long-forgotten about myself. Here are a few examples of how to add art to reminiscence:

1. **Draw a cake.** For this exercise, you will need paper and colored pencils, markers, or water colors. This is adapted from the out-of-print publication *Drawing on the Past* from ElderGames (see Resources for Digging Deeper). You can either give participants a chance to draw a cake from scratch or provide an outline to decorate. (See sample on p. 193 in Appendix D.) If you try the former, start with these directions:

On a blank piece of paper, draw the shape of a cake that represents a happy memory for you.
- What shape is it—round, square, jelly roll–shaped?
- How many layers is it?
- Is there a piece missing from it? If so, who ate it?

If you start participants out with an outline, or once those with blank papers have drawn the shape of their cakes, give them further instructions. *Now decorate your cake.*
- Is it frosted? Is the frosting fancy, perhaps with flowers?
- Is the frosting flavored or colored? What flavor or what colors?
- Is anything written on the cake? What?
- What flavor is the cake? What else is being served?
- What are you celebrating? (A holiday, a wedding, a birthday, an anniversary, the return of someone?)
- Is there a "guest or guests of honor"? Who?
- Who is at the celebration?
- Where is this taking place?

- Is the room decorated? How?
- Are presents being given? Is anything especially fun or interesting in the packages?
- Are games being played? Describe them. Are there prizes for winners?
- Talk about a favorite celebration from your past.
- Talk about a celebration you would like to have.

2. Wrap a package. Just as you can decorate a cake representing a special memory, you can wrap a gift that represents something special to you. For this exercise, you will again need paper and colored pencils, markers, or watercolors. This, too, is adapted from the out-of-print publication *Drawing on the Past* from ElderGames (see Resources for Digging Deeper).

You can either give participants a chance to draw a package from scratch or provide an outline. (See sample on p. 194 in Appendix D.) If you try the former, start with these directions:

On a blank piece of paper, draw a box that represents either a gift you are giving to someone or one you are receiving that evokes a happy memory for you.

The advantage of a blank piece of paper is that they can choose the kind of box—perhaps it is a gift box, or a package that comes in the mail, or a mailbox representing a special greeting, or even a treasure chest. It could even be a cigarette box and represent a pleasure forsaken.

Once they have drawn their boxes, ask:
- Describe the box. Is it a gift box, a mailed package, or some other sort of box?
- How big is the box? How heavy is it? Does it rattle?
- Can you tell anything about what's inside from the shape or the size or the wrapping?
- Is it for you or from you? If it's from you, who is it to? If it's for you, who is it from?
- Or is it to and from someone else? Who?
- Does this box represent a special occasion? What is it?
- Now talk about what's inside the box. Is it something you really received or gave or something you would have liked to have given or gotten? Is there a story connected with it?
- Perhaps the gift is something intangible. Perhaps you received a treasured trait from a beloved relative or a special kindness that is as precious as a gemstone. If so, talk about it.
- If this is a gift you received, did you give anything in return? What was it?
- Is there anything else you want to say about the gift?

3. Draw a path. Again you can give the participants a blank piece of paper or outline an example.

- Imagine the path leads to the past. Talk about it.
- Imagine the path leads to the future. What do you foresee?
- Imagine the path leads to someone you would like to be with. Who?
- Imagine the path leads home. Which home? What or who is waiting there?

4. Imagine yourself on a magazine cover. Draw yourself, the title of the magazine, the headline, and the date. Then talk about what you chose.

5. Imagine yourself as a tree. Like the questions in the Make a Choice exercise of whether you are a rose or a daisy, drawing yourself as a tree forces you to think of yourself as a metaphor. Try to draw without thinking about what you are doing. You may be surprised by what shows up on paper.

- What kind of tree are you? Why? What are that tree's characteristics?
- What time of year is it? (For example: Are you blooming or are your leaves falling or are you an evergreen?)
- Where are you—in a forest, on a city street, in a backyard, on a mountaintop?
- What sort of life is around you—more trees like or unlike you, people, animals, flowers? Do you support a swing, birds' nests, squirrels?

Thinking in metaphor has endless possibilities. You may find participants would prefer to express themselves as a flower, an animal, or a piece of clothing—a hat or shoes or a dress. Perhaps they want to express themselves by drawing the ideal place they would like to be at the moment. This is an exercise that can be done multiple times in multiple ways.

6. Create a life story collage. People have many facets. Perhaps I can draw myself as a lilac bush and imbue it with many characteristics that illustrate me, but that is still just one part of me. Giving people a chance to create themselves as a collage provides opportunities to bring in those other facets. Give people a poster board or a shoe box and tell them to cut out pictures from magazines—or add drawings of their own—that express things they have done or things that are important to them. For example, a person might cut out pictures of:

- An office cubicle or a classroom to represent a career or one's education,
- Children to represent family,
- A cat to represent a beloved pet,
- A house to represent home,

- Mountains or beaches to represent a favorite place to be,
- The Grand Canyon or the Eiffel Tower to represent a special vacation,
- Flowers to represent a garden, or
- Tomatoes to represent a love of cooking.

The possibilities, of course, are endless. Some people cut out important words: "love," "family," "poetry," "laughter." Adding small souvenirs such as ticket stubs, a theatre bill, or a postcard or greeting card is another possibility. People whose dexterity or mental capacity is compromised may need some assistance in clipping pictures or pasting them.

This project may take several sessions to complete, but when it is finished, the participants then tell the meaning of their collages, and you may find they have captured the essence of themselves in amazing ways.

Part 3
The Historical Perspective

This was by far the most difficult section of this book to write, because the resources available for this topic are enormous and almost overwhelming. Ultimately, I decided to try to make a tiny dent by limiting the majority of the focus to the 1950s. This helped only a little. It would have been easy to make this section many times longer, but finally I decided to provide a sampling rather than attempt to make it comprehensive.

I chose to concentrate on the 1950s because it was a watershed decade in which there were both widespread prosperity and hope and widespread unease and fear. There are an equally wide array of fine resources for the decade that preceded the 1950s and the one that followed, but this seemed a decade that most people alive today can relate to in some way—children are playing with some of the same toys introduced in the 1950s; the Baby Boomers, who are the next wave of older adults, were mostly born in the 1950s; current older adults were raising families of their own.

You will also note that I chose to concentrate on social history rather than political history. There were numerous important political events that happened in the 1950s: from Senator Joseph McCarthy's witch hunts for Communists to the Civil Rights Movement; from the American "space race" and Cold War with the Soviet Union to Castro's rise to power. In their own way those events affected all of us, although certainly some more than others. If they made a difference in your life, you will have another chance to talk about them when we talk about "Turning Points" in Part 4, but I have continued to look mostly for the fun in the 1950s. It was the first decade in which, through the medium of television, people across the nation had simultaneous common experiences. It had happened to some degree through the radio, but television literally made the experiences vivid. In Exercise 5, we begin to talk about this.

Note that I have organized the historical perspective into three distinct exercises with specific mini-exercises. In reality, discussions are unlikely to be so neatly divided. Go with the flow.

Exercise 5: Family Leisure Time and the 1950s

THE BASIC EXERCISE

What we do for relaxation and entertainment and who we choose to do it with says a lot about our values and expendable time, such as:

- The value of work versus play,
- The value of family togetherness or time spent with other relatives and friends,
- What we consider pleasurable pastimes, and
- What we can afford to do in terms of time and money.

This exercise focuses primarily on that aspect of our lives related to what was popular in the 1950s, with allowance for people to talk about other times. This choice is based on limited time and space. As noted in the introduction to this section, what is covered here could be adapted for any decade. Suggestions for doing so are covered in Resources for Digging Deeper.

KEY ELEMENTS

If you ask people to name 10 things they love to do, most will start to falter after about five. We don't spend much time actively thinking about how our leisure time has shaped us. Most participants take great pleasure in remembering relaxation and entertainment they haven't thought about in years. Give participants time to think; even if they don't want to volunteer their answers, chances are they are remembering events with warm feelings.

DEMENTIA CONCERNS

This is an exercise that generally works well with people who have dementia, precisely because we are asking them to think about pleasant events from 50+ years ago—which may be where their minds are naturally dwelling anyway. There is one adaptation that you will probably need to make. I have grouped a series of questions together related to each topic. People with dementia are likely to be confused by multiple questions. Ask them one at a time.

Many of the games associated with this exercise and those suggested in the mini-exercise that follows are focused on a single right answer. People with dementia often retain an amazing capacity to fill-in-the-blank, so that when you give them the first words in a title to a song, they can easily finish it. However, if you find that someone is stymied by a question, turn it into a multiple-choice question with only two choices. For example, was Rochester a character on the "Burns and Allen Show" or the "Jack Benny Show"? Chances are good that if they hear the name "Jack Benny" they will remember that's the correct answer.

Again remember that people with dementia may be able to think about something that they can't necessarily articulate; that doesn't mean they don't enjoy thinking about it. As we've also mentioned before, because time is a tricky concept, they may also flip-flop in their minds about entertainment in various decades. That's fine. The goal is a pleasant experience, not accuracy, so don't worry about things which may not make sense to you.

THE COMPLETE SCRIPT

▶ *Dialogue:*   Today we're going to talk about the role of relaxation and entertainment in our lives and a lot of our time will be focused on the 1950s, partly because that was a time when mass entertainment—television, radio, and the movies—gave us common experiences, and partly because we have limited time. But I would like to start by talking a little about the role of relaxation in your life, both as you were growing up and as an adult, perhaps raising a family of your own, and if you are retired, what you do now.

In all our discussions, we have not talked much about work. We will get to it eventually, but in this exercise it only enters in as a sidebar, according to how much it may have interfered with our opportunities for relaxation and vacations.

What we do for relaxation and entertainment and with whom we choose to do it says a lot about our values and expendable time, so this discussion isn't as frivolous as it might seem, but let's start at the beginning. Which of these proverbs do you agree with:

- All work and no play makes Jack a dull boy, or

- Idle hands are the devil's playground?

Direction: Give people a chance to respond. Most people realize that we need to refresh both body and mind with play on a regular basis.

▶ *Dialogue:*   Did your parents have the same view you do? How was leisure time spent in the family you grew up in? Did you even have much leisure time?

Direction: If this is an older crowd, chances are they grew up in the Depression (1929–1940) and may have been struggling to survive—perhaps they had to quit school or had an after-school job. Perhaps they had lots of chores to do or lived in the country where entertainment opportunities were limited. Perhaps they made their own fun. If so, what did they do? Then ask about what they did as a family versus what they did with friends.

▶ *Dialogue:*   In some families children were to be seen and not heard, so children went off to do their own thing, playing with friends while their parents had hobbies of their own—reading, stamp collecting, gardening. Other families enjoyed interacting with their children and may have played Scrabble or Monopoly with them or taught them to play Bridge or other card games or practiced pitching baseballs with them. What was your family's routine?

Direction: Again, give participants a chance to share some of their experiences.

▶ *Dialogue:*   Now let's talk a little about weekends. Did you live in a city where weekends might give you the chance to go to parks, baseball games, museums, movies, live theater, or some other form of entertainment? Did you and the family in which you grew up take advantage of what your city or town had to offer?

Direction: Again, give participants a chance to share some of their experiences.

▶ *Dialogue:*   What about special entertainment that came your way—county fairs, circuses, Chautauqua-style lecturers, vaudeville acts? Did you go to those? Did you enter anything in the county fair?

Direction: Again, give participants a chance to share some of their experiences.

▶ *Dialogue:*   In the 1950s, people loved their cars and gas was $.25 a gallon. Roads were not very good at that time because it was not until 1956 that the interstate highway system was authorized. The first Holiday Inn was built in 1952, but it was years before motel chains replaced the mostly grungy cabins and basic campsites that were the only choices for most travelers. Still, many men loved the open road and took their families with them. Some lucky travelers even went to Disneyland after it opened in 1955. So let's talk about family vacations. Did you take them with your family? What did you do? Where did you go? Can you recall an especially good or especially disastrous experience?

Direction: Again, give participants a chance to share some of their experiences. Try to draw out stories that express feelings—Did they enjoy these family times? Did they fight with siblings? Did they feel enriched by their experiences? Some families had neither money nor inclination for family vacations or outings. Some people will express that as a loss—something they missed out on.

▶ *Dialogue:*   Some people spent part of their summer vacations at a scout, church, or other camp—giving parents and children a break from each other. Did you go to summer camp or send your children? What were your experiences? Good or bad? Do you still remember any camp songs or camp pranks?

Direction: Give participants a chance to respond. Going to camp represents the first time many children spent time away from their parents—the first taste of independence. Some learned new skills such as canoeing or rock-climbing. Others merely learned how to short-sheet another person's bed. If anyone remembers a camp song ("The ants go marching one-by-one" or "I've got six pence, jolly, jolly six pence," for example) encourage your group to sing with gusto.

▶ *Dialogue:* I'm asking all these questions for a purpose beyond reminiscing. I'd like you to think about the ways leisure pursuits in your family shaped your values. For example:

- The value placed on work versus play;

- The value put on family togetherness;

- The value of money spent on food for the table (bread) and food for the soul (beauty, leisure, enriching experiences);

- The value placed on reading, listening to music, watching TV;

- The value placed on exercise and sports (as participant and/or spectator);

- The value placed on creative arts and live performances (museums, theater, dance); and

- The value of hobbies and the ones worth pursuing.

What *did* your family value and how did they do in instilling the same values in you?

Direction: Give participants a chance to respond.

▶ *Dialogue:* In the late 1970s, Morris Massey wrote a book called *The People Puzzle* in which he suggested that we are more influenced as we grow up by what we did without than by what we had. Therefore, if you grew up poor during the Great Depression, financial security is likely to have been a lifelong value for you as an adult. But if you grew up poor and feel you missed out on family vacations or popular entertainment, those are things you are likely to *choose* to spend your money on as an adult. If you grew up in a family that was close knit and spent a lot of time doing things together, you are likely to take a close-knit family for granted and simply *expect* that you will stay close to family members and raise a close-knit family of your own that will do many enjoyable things together.

- Do you agree with Massey's view that what we did without as children remains important to us and what we had we tend to take for granted?

- Can you give me an example to support your viewpoint?

Direction: Give participants a chance to respond.

▶ *Dialogue:* Let's talk specifically about those ideas.

- How did the family in which you grew up influence you as an adult in the ways that you now prefer to relax?

- How did the places that your parents felt were important for their children to see or the experiences they felt were important for them to have influence how you spent time with your spouse or raised a family of your own?

Direction: Give participants a chance to respond.

▶ ***Dialogue:***   All this is very interesting, but now I would like to switch direction and talk about entertainment in the 1950s. The biggest medium of the 1950s was television. In 1948, less than 1% of homes in the United States had televisions sets, but by 1950, that figure had risen to 9% (about 1.5 million sets). By the end of 1951, about a quarter of households had a TV and by 1960, more than 87% of households in the United States had at least one. Can you remember the first time you watched TV? Were you a child or already an adult with children of your own?

Direction: Give participants a chance to respond.

▶ ***Dialogue:***   Let's talk about what you remember about television from the 1950s. Let me start with a little quiz about famous lines from television programs. Can you tell me who was known for saying the following?

Direction: Give each line of dialogue below one at a time and wait for participants to answer before going on to the next one. The answers are given in parentheses.

▶ ***Dialogue:***

- "Tonight we have a really big show"—or as he said it, "a really big shoe." (Ed Sullivan)

- "Well, I'll be a dirty bird." (George Gobel)

- "How sweet it is." (Jackie Gleason)

- "This is another fine mess you've gotten me into." (Oliver Hardy to Stan Laurel)

- "Say kids, what time is it?" (Buffalo Bob Smith; what time was it? Howdy Doody Time!)

- "Oh, Rochester!" (Jack Benny)

- "What a revolting development this is!" (William Bendix in "The Life of Riley")

- "Everybody wants to get into de act." (Jimmy Durante)

- "Say the secret word and take home a hundred dollars." (Groucho Marx on "You Bet Your Life")

- "Say goodnight, Gracie." (George Burns—whose wife would then say, "Goodnight, Gracie.")

- "I kid you not." (Jack Paar)

- "And that's the way it is." (Walter Cronkite)

- "Now cut that out!" (Jack Benny)

- "Goodnight, Mrs. Calabash, wherever you are." (Jimmy Durante)

Direction: Once participants have given their answers, ask them if they have any special memories related to watching those shows. Give participants a chance to respond.

▶ *Dialogue:*   On your handout there are some matching games of TV stars of the 1950s and the programs on which they performed. I'm going to give you a few minutes to see if you can match the stars to their shows. I encourage you to work with a partner on this. See how well you can do and then let's talk about the ones that had meaning for you.

Direction: Below are the categories of programs on the participants' handout (westerns, crime and mystery shows, comedies, and quiz shows) divided by dialogue for leading the group discussion. Encourage everyone to work in groups of two or three. They are likely to come up with more answers in a group and stir up more memories. The goal is not to test their knowledge but to stimulate their memories of early TV. After participants have had a chance to work on their answers, come back together for sharing.

▶ *Dialogue:*   Okay, let's see what memories you were able to dredge up from your past. Westerns were popular in the 1950s—some were continuations of radio programs from the 1940s and others were new. How did you do in matching the star to his TV show?

Direction: Read the name of the TV show, and let participants fill in the answers. Use the following list only to confirm or correct the right answers.

1. Bat Masterson (B: Gene Barry)
2. Bonanza (H: Lorne Greene)
3. Cisko Kid (K: Duncan Renaldo)
4. Gunsmoke (A: Jim Arness)
5. Have Gun will Travel (C: Richard Boone)
6. Hopalong Cassidy (D: William Boyd)
7. Lone Ranger (I: Clayton Moore)
8. Maverick (G: James Garner)
9. Rawhide (F: Clint Eastwood)
10. The Rifleman (E: Chuck Connors)
11. Wyatt Earp (J: Hugh O'Brien)
12. Zorro (L: Guy Williams)

Another bit of trivia: "Gunsmoke," which debuted in 1955, ran for 20 years and during at least part of that period, it was the most watched show on TV. In addition to Jim Arness playing Marshall Matt Dillon, the other main original cast members were Dennis Weaver as Chester Goode, Milburn Stone as "Doc" Adams, and Amanda Blake as Kitty Russell.

The next little section is not part of the handout. Give participants bonus points if they can correctly identify the characters in the following dialogue.

▶ *Dialogue:*   In some cases, the sidekick of the cowboy was as famous as he was. Do you remember them? Can you name them?

- The Cisco Kid was played by Duncan Renaldo. Do you remember his sidekick's name and who played him? (Pancho, played by Leo Corillo) Do you remember their horses' names? (Diablo and Loco)

- The Lone Ranger was played by Clayton Moore. Who was his sidekick and who played him? (Tonto, played by Jay Silverheels)

- Wild Bill Hickok was another cowboy we haven't mentioned yet. Do you know who played him? (Guy Madison) Like the Cisco Kid, Wild Bill Hickok had a somewhat comical sidekick. Do you remember the sidekick's name and who played him? (Jingles B. Jones, played by Andy Devine)

Direction: You may find these are all Baby Boomer questions because many of these shows were on television at a time parents were less likely to be watching, but the Boomers will enjoy the remembrance, so we're going to keep going for a few more.

▶ ***Dialogue:*** You notice that all the heroes we've mentioned so far were men, but there was one western starring a woman. Do you remember who starred in it and who she played? (Gail Davis as Annie Oakley). Do you remember that show?

So far we have not mentioned two of the most popular westerns because the stars played themselves—Gene Autry and Roy Rogers. Both of these western heroes started out with radio programs. Gene Autry was known as "the singing cowboy." Do you remember his theme song? ("Back in the Saddle Again")

Roy Rogers was extremely popular. At least as early as 1949, the Sears catalog offered Roy Rogers' pajamas, shirts, boots, and toy guns with holsters. Did you or your children ever wear any of those things?

Direction: Give participants a chance to wax nostalgic for a minute about any Roy Rogers memories they have; then see if you can trip them up with the following.

▶ ***Dialogue:*** Let's see just how much you remember about the Roy Rogers show. Can you name:

- Roy Roger's wife? (Dale Evans)

- Roy Roger's sidekick? (Pat Brady)

- Roy's horse? (Trigger)

- Dale's horse? (Buttermilk)

- Pat's jeep? (Nelly belle)

- Roy's dog? (Bullet)

At the end of each show, Roy Rogers and Dale Evans sang a song. Do you remember what it was and can you sing it?

Direction: The song was "Happy Trails." Encourage anyone who remembers the song and the tune to sing it. Then move on to discussing the crime and suspense shows of the 1950s.

▶ *Dialogue:* Now let's talk about the second quiz on your handout. Almost all of the cowboy shows were supposed to take place at least a half-century earlier. Some people wanted more contemporary action and suspense. There were a number of crime and mystery shows in the 1950s. "Alfred Hitchcock Presents" had a different cast each week. Others had recurring characters. How did you do in matching those stars to their shows?

Direction: Read the name of the TV show, and let participants fill in the answers. Use the following list only to confirm or correct the right answers.

1. 77 Sunset Strip (E: Efrem Zimbalist, Jr., Roger Smith, and Edd Byrnes)
2. Dragnet (D: Jack Webb and Harry Morgan)
3. M Squad (C: Lee Marvin)
4. Perry Mason (A: Raymond Burr, Barbara Hale, and William Hopper)
5. The Thin Man (B: Peter Lawford and Phyllis Kirk)

Then ask the following question.

▶ *Dialogue:* Do any of these shows bring back fond memories for you?

Direction: Give participants a chance to talk about any they especially liked or remember. Then introduce the next quiz.

▶ *Dialogue:* In the 1950s there were many situation comedies starring men who were either completely inept or always right. How did you do on that quiz, matching the man to his program?

Direction: Read the name of the TV show, and let participants fill in the answers. Use the following list only to confirm or correct the right answers.

1. The Adventures of Ozzie and Harriet (F: Ozzie Nelson—this one's a freebie)
2. The Donna Reed Show (C: Carl Betz)
3. Father Knows Best (I: Robert Young)
4. Leave It to Beaver (A: Hugh Beaumont)
5. The Life of Riley (B: William Bendix)
6. Love That Bob (E: Bob Cummings)
7. Make Room for Daddy (H: Danny Thomas)
8. Mr. Peepers (D: Wally Cox)
9. Sgt. Bilko (G: Phil Silvers)

▶ *Dialogue:*

- Do any of you have fond memories of any of these shows?

- Did they actually reflect the life you were living in any way?

- How are men portrayed on TV programs today? Has anything changed?

84   The Historical Perspective

Direction: Give people a little time to remember these programs. Did father actually know best in their families?

Here's an extra bit of trivia you might want to throw in: Wally Cox, who played Mr. Peepers, was stereotyped as a meek and rather bumbling character. In reality, his best friend and one-time roommate was a famous movie heartthrob from the 1950s. Can anyone name the man? (Marlon Brando)

Then move on to talking about shows featuring women as the primary stars.

▶ *Dialogue:* At a time when women were portrayed in most television programs as stay-at-home mothers, a surprising number of women had their own shows and strong followings. Do you remember the shows with these women as hosts?

- June Allyson
- Dinah Shore
- Ann Sothern
- Loretta Young

Direction: Allow a brief time for responses.

▶ *Dialogue:* Other stars had their own situation comedies. "I Love Lucy" was certainly the most famous of these, but do you also remember:

- "December Bride" starring Spring Byington,
- "Our Miss Brooks" starring Eve Arden, and
- "My Little Margie" and "Oh! Susanna," both starring Gale Storm?

Direction: Allow a brief time for responses. Some people may have only vague memories of the other shows but want to discuss their favorite episodes of "I Love Lucy." You may want to put the following list on a flip chart or white board, since it isn't in their handout.

▶ *Dialogue:* If you liked comedy in the 1950s, you had plenty of shows from which to choose. Here are some of the famous comedians of the time who had their own shows:

- Abbott and Costello
- Steve Allen—the original host of "The Tonight Show"
- Jack Benny
- Milton Berle
- George Burns and Gracie Allen
- Red Buttons
- Sid Caesar ("Your Show of Shows" which also featured Imogene Coca and Carl Reiner)

- Jimmy Durante
- Allen Funt had the original reality show: "Candid Camera"
- Bob Hope
- Jackie Gleason (and sidekick Art Carney)
- George Gobel
- Martha Raye
- Red Skelton

Do any of you have any special memories of those?

Direction: Allow a brief time for responses. You may also want to put the next group of programs on a flip chart or white board.

▶ **Dialogue:** Most of the shows featuring comedians were variety shows with short sketches and guest stars. If these weren't enough for you, there were plenty more that featured amateur and professional talent. Did you ever watch these?

- American Bandstand
- The Nat "King" Cole Show
- The Perry Como Show
- Arthur Godfrey's Talent Scouts
- Grand Old Opry
- Liberace
- Ted Mack's Original Amateur Hour
- The Arthur Murray Dance Party
- Ed Sullivan
- The Lawrence Welk Show
- Your Hit Parade

Were any of these favorites of anyone?

Direction: Allow a brief time for responses.

▶ **Dialogue:** Speaking of new talent, Bert Parks began hosting another sort of talent show in 1955. Does anyone know what that was? (The Miss America Pageant)
One of the quite surprising things about this new medium was the number of original plays that were produced during the 1950s for television—some of which had also been produced on Broadway. One of the most prolific writers was Rod Serling who wrote for Kraft Television Theatre and Playhouse 90 before starting a science fiction show called "The Twilight Zone" in 1959. He wrote 92 of the 156 episodes over the next 5 years. Do you remember any of them?

Direction: Again allow a brief time for responses.

▶ *Dialogue:* Another television format that became popular in the 1950s was quiz shows. Let's look at your handout again. How did you do in matching the host or host and chief panelists for these shows from the 1950s on your handout?

Direction: Read the name of the TV show, and let participants fill in the answers. Use the following list only to confirm or correct the right answers.

1. $64,000 Question (F: Hal March)
2. I've Got a Secret (H: Garry Moore with alternating panelists Kitty Carlisle, Bill Cullen, Jayne Meadows, Henry Morgan, and Betsy Palmer)
3. Name That Tune (C: George DeWitt)
4. The Price is Right (B: Bill Cullen)
5. To Tell the Truth (A: Bud Collyer with alternating panelists Don Ameche, Orson Bean, Polly Bergen, Kitty Carlisle, Peggy Cass, and Tom Posten)
6. Truth or Consequences (E: Ralph Edwards—who also hosted "This Is Your Life" but that wasn't a quiz show—and later in the decade, Bob Barker)
7. What's My Line? (D: John Daly with panelists Bennett Cerf, Arlene Francis, and Dorothy Kilgallen)
8. You Bet Your Life (G: Groucho Marx)

Give participants a chance to comment on any of these programs that they especially enjoyed or remember.

Some participants may bring up the fact that certain types of quiz shows, such as the "$64,000 Question" fell out of favor when it was discovered that the contestants whom the producers wanted to succeed were coached to give the right answers. It caused a tremendous scandal at the time.

▶ *Dialogue:* One show that was popular during the daytime in the 1950s was not a quiz show, but it was a contest. It was hosted by Jack Bailey and the goal was to be seen as the woman who had the saddest life and most needed to be lifted out of her doldrums to become "Queen for a Day." Like contemporary wish-fulfilling programs of the current TV era, it was a real tear-jerker.

Other popular daytime programs were a multitude of "soap operas," also known as daytime serial dramas. They became popular as radio programming in the 1930s and because most aired in the afternoon when the most likely listeners were women, soap and laundry products were common sponsors. By the end of the 1930s there were more than 60 soap operas on radio. When television came along, it took awhile for soap operas to find their new niche. The first three to be successful were "Search for Tomorrow," "Love of Life," and "The Guiding Light." Only "The Guiding Light" was a radio program that made the transition to television. At first these programs were only 15 minutes long. In 1956 the 30-minute soap opera was introduced with "As the World Turns."

Did you ever "get hooked on" soap operas? What were your favorite shows?

Direction: Give participants a chance to make a few comments. Then go on to the next TV genre.

► *Dialogue:*   For decades, most people learned the news from reading newspapers, but in the 1950s television news programs became popular. Perhaps you enjoyed listening to news programs. Can you name the men first associated with these programs?

1.   The Camel News Caravan (sponsored by Camel cigarettes)

2.   Meet the Press

3.   See It Now

4.   TODAY

Direction: Read the name of the TV show, and let participants fill in the answers. Use the following list only to confirm or correct the right answers:

1.   John Cameron Swayze
2.   Lawrence Spivak
3.   Edward R. Morrow (who also hosted "Person to Person")
4.   Dave Garroway

Here is another bit of TV Trivia you might consider adding: Perhaps the most famous of the newscasters in the 1950s were Chet Huntley and David Brinkley who nightly gave us "The Huntley Brinkley Report." Walter Cronkite, who certainly grew more famous over time, was around in the 1950s but as host of what was called a CBS historical recreation series: "You Are There"—not as a newscaster. He later narrated the documentary series "Twentieth Century."

► *Dialogue:*   One of the most famously enduring men on daytime TV in the 1950s was Jack LaLanne. His fitness program aired for 34 years, which means he was over 70 when it ended. Did you ever exercise with him? Have exercise programs changed over the years? In what ways?

Direction: Another bit of trivia: As of this writing Jack LaLanne is in his 90s and says, "I can't die; it would ruin my image."

► *Dialogue:*   Children in the 1950s watched TV anytime their parents let them and most of the programs had little sex or violence likely to do them harm. There were at least some programs, however, specifically aimed at children. Do you remember any of these?

•   "Kukla, Fran, and Ollie"

•   "Howdy Doody Time" with Buffalo Bob Smith

•   "Captain Kangaroo"

•   What about "The Mickey Mouse Club"? Did you or your children long to be a Mouseketeer?

How do you think these programs compare to what children watch today? Has programming gotten better or worse?

Direction: Here's a little more trivia: Bob Keeshan who played the walrus-mustached "Captain Kangaroo" for 36 years, started out as Clarabell the Clown on "Howdy Doody Time." "Captain Kangaroo" featured the puppets Bunny Rabbit and Mr. Moose (who loved knock-knock jokes), plus Dancing Bear and Mr. Green Jeans (Hugh Brannum). Although he was only 27 when the show began, Keeshan said, "I was impressed with the potential positive relationship between grandparents and grandchildren, so I chose an elderly character," and over 36 years he grew into the character.

Give participants a chance to talk about their memories of early children's television programming.

► *Dialogue:*   One other daytime TV program from the 1950s that wasn't aimed at children, but featured them was Art Linkletter's "People Are Funny." He interviewed children on each show and later became famous for the book *Kids Say the Darndest Things.* Did you ever see the program or read the book?

Direction: Art Linkletter also had a program called "House Party." Give participants a chance to respond and then wind things up.

► *Dialogue Before Closing:*   Well, in spite of all that we've talked about today, there's much more we could have covered. We will talk about television more, I'm sure, the next time we meet, but does anyone have anything else that must be said about television in the 1950s?

Direction: Give participants a chance to respond.

Resources for Digging Deeper—Exercise 5

Resources for exploring America's social and political history are abundant and wonderful. My all-time favorite book for doing this is James Trager's ***The People's Chronology, A Year-by-Year Record of Human Events from Prehistory to the Present*** (1992). This book provides brief accounts of 30 categories of information for each year of human life (although the early years around the time of the invention of the wheel are missing some categories), including political events, human rights, science, nutrition, music, sports, theater and film, everyday life, and much more. Nearly every other resource listed here cites this book as one of its references. In 1995, Trager also came out with ***The Woman's Chronology*** which uses the same categories and is an excellent addition, since women tend to get short shrift in most histories.

My second favorite book for a combined political and social history is ***Our American Century: The American Dream: The 50s*** from Time-Life Books which we mentioned earlier. This particular volume is essentially an expanded version of the information for the 1950s in Trager's book, but this time with wonderful black and white and color photos. If you could bring in one book for show-and-tell, this is the one I would recommend. A close second, however, is the other Time-Life book in this series related to the 1950s, ***The Rock and Roll***

Generation: Teen Life in the 50s, which covers not only music but many of the fads and fashions.

Then there are the books that are specifically designed for leading activities related to the 1950s. The most comprehensive of these are Lynne Martin Erickson's *Remembering the Fifties Program Manual* from BiFolkal Productions and Beckie Karras's *Journey Through the 20th Century: Activities for Reminiscing and Discussion* from ElderSong. Erickson's manual is part of a much larger activity kit that includes slides, video, song booklets, a song tape, and multisensory pieces. All the components can be purchased separately, which is handy for those with limited budgets. If you can purchase only one item, the program manual would certainly be enough to provide dozens of creative activities over many hours and weeks.

While Erickson's 100+-page manual is completely devoted to the 1950s (although it has many intergenerational suggestions that draw on more recent times), Karras' *Journey Through the 20th Century* covers multiple decades with about 20 pages per decade. It is conveniently organized with many activity suggestions for approximately the first 10 pages devoted to each decade and then offers a one-page summary of the songs, music and cultural events, fads, fashions, trends, and news events for each year of that decade. The title is slightly misleading because only five decades (the 1920s through the 1960s) are comprehensively covered, but these are likely to be the ones most desired by any group of older adults.

Two other well-known publishers of activities for older adults offer booklets on the 1950s. ElderGames has a 25-page booklet called *The 50s, The 20th Century: Remembering the Decades* and Gary Grimm & Associates offers *The 1950s, Remembering and Reminiscing* (45 pages). Both companies have produced similar booklets for other decades of the 20th century. Gary Grimm's book has more information and more actual activities (fill-in-the-blanks, discussion questions, a word search), but both were also helpful in my research for this part of *Getting to Know the Life Stories of Older Adults*.

One other book by Beckie Karras, *Down Memory Lane, 2nd edition* should also be mentioned at this juncture. The memories are not limited to the 1950s, but it's another book with lots of ideas for creative ways to talk about social history—and to incorporate music into programs.

Since Mini-Exercise E is devoted to adding music to life story sharing, this is also a good time to mention the **ElderSong catalog,** which has dozens of musical resources—books, CDs, videos—from Bing Crosby to Mitch Miller, and much, much more. (See Appendix B for more information.)

ElderGames offers two products that are also useful for the musical discussions suggested in Mini-Exercise E. Two of the packets in their "Flashback" series would work especially well for suggestion #1. They are *Flashback to Hollywood's Golden Age, Music and Comedy Stars* and *Flashback to Stage and Screen Musicals.* Not all of the movies and Broadway shows featured are from the 1950s and the information is not entirely current (Gene Kelly died in 1996 but is still listed as living), because it was produced more than a decade ago. Nevertheless, here are glamour shots of stars like Kelly, Bing Crosby, and Maurice Chevalier (all featured in the mini-exercise) along with brief bios and lists of their classic films. The stage and screen musical packet includes an 8 × 10-inch photo of a scene from the play or movie and loads of trivia on the backside about that production. Among the 10 musicals from the 1950s that are featured are *Singin' in the Rain, My Fair Lady, Guys and Dolls, The King and I,* and *The Music Man.* Both packets come in a plastic bag with loose photos that are easy to pass around in a group.

For people who work specifically with people with dementia, one wonderful book for leading activities and incorporating music is **The Lost Chord** by Melanie Chavin. (See References.) Although published in 1991, the advice is still solid, and there are lots of topical activity themes that are appropriate for life story sharing, all with song suggestions to enhance the activity. Because the part of the brain that sings is different from the part that speaks, many people with diminished verbal skills can still burst into song and enjoy doing so.

I perused dozens of web sites in writing these exercises on the 1950s. Type in any TV show, any Broadway or film musical, or any musical star of the 1950s and you will find many options. One of the general web sites I used for the 1950s was *www.babyboomers.com,* but be forewarned that it has a few errors.

Because I was a child of the 1950s myself, some information comes from my own fond memories. If you are interested in reading more about Morris Massey's book, **The People Puzzle,** it can be found on-line as a used book (Reston Publishing Company, Inc., © 1979, ISBN 0835954773).

Mini-Exercise E: Adding Music to the Mix

People often think of the 1950s as the time Rock and Roll came to prominence and they are right. However, that decade was also when:

- Broadway and Hollywood musicals were perhaps at their prime;
- Big Bands were fading, but pop music still vied for top 10 placement on the music charts;
- Folk music from groups like the Weavers ("Goodnight, Irene"; "Kisses Sweeter Than Wine") and the Kingston Trio ("Tom Dooley") started to rise (soon to be followed by The Limeliters, The Brothers Four, The Chad Mitchell Trio, and The Smothers Brothers, among others);
- Latin dances like the Mambo, Cha Cha, and Merengue were hot;
- Calypso music sung by the likes of Harry Belafonte ("Jamaica Farewell") was all the rage;
- Jazz was "cool" (The first Newport Jazz Festival was held in 1954; Charlie Parker was in his heyday);
- Country music was welcoming new stars as Johnny Cash began to "Walk the Line" and Hank Williams was singing about your "Cold, Cold Heart"; and
- Mitch Miller began to convince us to sing along ("Yellow Rose of Texas").

Adding music and dance to *any* discussion enlivens it. In order to limit the length of this book, we have provided only some suggestions for using Broadway and

Hollywood musicals from the 1950s, but don't let our single example limit your imagination.

MUSICALS FROM BROADWAY AND HOLLYWOOD

Below are some of the most popular musicals of the decade, along with the songs they made popular. Here are some of the things you can do with the lists.

- Try giving the name of the musical and see if people can name some of the songs from it. The lists here are not complete, so some people may remember other hits.
- Let them sing these songs. Do you have a karaoke machine?
- Try looking for CDs (library or music store) of original cast albums. Bring in a sampling.
- Most of the musicals made into movies are available on VHS or DVD. Let your group choose one, rent it, and have a musical movie night.
- Talk about any of the musicals that were particularly moving or inspiring for your participants. Did anyone see the musical on Broadway? How many have seen the movies? (Many of the popular Broadway musicals of the 1950s were made into Hollywood musicals in the 1960s.) Did anyone play a musical role in amateur theater?

Popular Broadway Musicals of the 1950s include:

- *Guys and Dolls* (1950)—"Luck Be A Lady"; "If I Were a Bell"; "A Bushel and a Peck"; "Sit Down You're Rocking the Boat"
- *The King and I* (1951)—"I Whistle a Happy Tune"; "Getting to Know You"; "Hello Young Lovers"; "Shall We Dance"; "We Kiss in a Shadow"
- *Paint Your Wagon* (1951)—"They Call the Wind Mariah"; "I Talk to the Trees"; "I'm on My Way"
- *Carousel* (1952)—"You'll Never Walk Alone"; "June Is Bustin' Out All Over"; "If I Loved You"
- *Kismet* (1953)—"Baubles, Bangles and Beads"; "Stranger in Paradise"
- *The Pajama Game* (1954)—"Hernando's Hideaway"
- *Damn Yankees* (1955)—"Whatever Lola Wants"; "You've Got to Have Heart"
- *Bells Are Ringing* (1956)—"The Party's Over"; "Just in Time"
- *My Fair Lady* (1956)—"The Rain in Spain"; "I Could Have Danced All Night"; "On the Street Where You Live"; "Get Me to the Church on Time"; "Isn't It Loverly"; "With a Little Bit of Luck"
- *West Side Story* (1957)—"Maria"; "Tonight"; "I Feel Pretty"; "Somewhere"; "Something's Coming"
- *The Music Man* (1957)—"Seventy-Six Trombones"; "Marian, the Librarian"; "You Got Trouble"; "Goodnight My Someone"; "Till There Was You"; "Wells Fargo Wagon"; "Gary, Indiana"
- *Flower Drum Song* (1958)—"A Hundred Million Miracles"; "I Enjoy Being a Girl"; "Grant Avenue"; "Don't Marry Me"; "Sunday"

- *Gypsy* (1959)—"Let Me Entertain You"; "Everything's Coming Up Roses"; "Together Wherever We Go"
- *Once Upon a Mattress* (1959)—This one didn't produce popular songs, but did give us a new comedian: Carol Burnett
- *Sound of Music* (1959)—"The Sound of Music"; "Do-Re-Mi"; "Edelweiss"; "My Favorite Things"; "So Long, Farewell"; "Climb Every Mountain"

Hollywood took a cue from that success and produced these movie musicals in the 1950s, some of which had been Broadway plays in the 1940s:

- *An American in Paris* (1951)—"I Got Rhythm"
- *Singin' in the Rain* (1952)—"Singin' in the Rain"; "You Were Meant for Me"; "Make 'Em Laugh"; "All I Do Is Dream of You"
- *Seven Brides for Seven Brothers* (1954)—"Wonderful Day"; "When You're in Love"; "Goin' Courtin'"
- *Oklahoma* (1955)—"Oh, What a Beautiful Morning"; "Oklahoma!"; "The Surrey with the Fringe on Top"; "People Will Say We're in Love"; "I Cain't Say No"
- *Gigi* (1958)—"Thank Heaven for Little Girls"; "The Night They Invented Champagne"; "Gigi"
- *South Pacific* (1958)—"Some Enchanted Evening"; "Bali Ha'i"; "Happy Talk"; "Nothing Like a Dame"; "I'm Gonna Wash That Many Right Outa My Hair"; "Younger Than Springtime"; "This Nearly Was Mine"; "You've Got to Be Carefully Taught"

Some nonmusical movies also produced hit songs, such as *High Noon's* "Do Not Forsake Me," and the theme songs to *Love Is a Many Splendored Thing* (recorded by Nat King Cole), *Tammy* (recorded by Debbie Reynolds), and *Bridge Over the River Kwai*.

Ask: Does anyone remember these? Can you sing them (or in the case of *Bridge Over the River Kwai*, whistle them)?

Exercise 6: How Things Have Changed

THE BASIC EXERCISE

In this exercise we continue to focus on life in the 1950s, but we are especially looking at how things have changed—particularly inventions, objects in daily use, language, food, fads, and fashion. Those may seem frivolous, but in many cases they have had a greater impact on our lives than political events. These are all part of our social history—history made fun.

The mini-exercises at the end give us an opportunity to put our social history, our political history, and our personal history into a timeline.

PROPS AND MATERIALS

If you can, bring in samples or photographs of the items talked about in the following script to enrich the experience for participants. The Resources for Digging Deeper in Exercise 5 are mostly the same in this exercise, so if you have any of them, bring them in again.

KEY ELEMENTS

Most people do not see themselves as part of social history, so this may be a new experience for them. That's good; it means this exercise is a brain builder—making new connections. You may also get into some lively discussion in this exercise over what was and wasn't a positive influence. Have fun with it. As always, give participants time to think; even if they don't want to volunteer their answers, chances are they are remembering meaningful events.

DEMENTIA CONCERNS

The dementia-specific notes that applied to Exercise 5 apply here as well. If you try to do any of the timeline-related mini-exercises with participants, they will probably need assistance because of diminished visual-spatial skills and the fact that it requires sorting through a lot of information. However, using the information provided in the handouts, they may be able to tell you things that were meaningful to them in some way. If you can fill those in on the chart with the year they happened and then figure out how old the person was at the time, all that will be left is for the person to tell you why the event was meaningful or about the feelings related to it. If you know the person's age at the time of the event, it's easy to ask questions that will draw out responses. For example, "You were just a child during the Great Depression. Did you have any sense of being poor as you grew up?" (Many people who *were* poor were surrounded with love and didn't notice.)

Try to keep the questions fairly simple and refer to long ago events rather than more recent ones. (Most people with dementia have only sketchy memories of any political events of the last 20 years or so, unless they had a strong emotional impact on that person.) For those whose verbal skills are compromised, ask questions that can be answered with "yes" or "no" or a simple phrase. As always, be aware that they may be able to think about something that they can't necessarily articulate. When they do speak, they may provide an answer that doesn't seem to correlate to the time you asked about; enjoy the interaction without worrying about pressing for accuracy.

THE COMPLETE SCRIPT

▶ ***Dialogue:*** Today we're going to talk about how things have changed in our lifetimes, and we will be concentrating again on the 1950s, but I want to begin by giving you a sense of how much things changed in the half-century *before* then. Most of this information comes from a book called *The Big Change* by Frederick Lewis Allen.

In 1900:

- Wealthy people usually had running water, bathtubs, and toilets, but if you lived outside of cities, beyond the reach of water and sewer lines, even wealth couldn't buy you a working bathroom. Poor people—factory workers, farmers, servants, indeed, most people—used an outhouse as a toilet, and a pitcher and bowl for washing, if they washed at all.

- People were very fond of tobacco, but they chewed it, put it in a pipe, or smoked cigars. About 4 billion cigarettes were manufactured in the United States in 1900; by 1949 that number would rise to 384 billion or enough for every man, woman, and child in the United States to smoke more than 2,500 cigarettes per year, or about 7 a day.

- Telephones were clumsy and relatively scarce, used primarily by businesses and the status-seeking wealthy.

- Mass communication barely existed. There was no television, no radio, and only the crudest of motion pictures, although that would change in a few years. There were lots of local newspapers for those who could afford them, but the only giants of widespread mass media were the *Ladies Home Journal* with nearly a million subscribers, and those willing to purchase a Sears Catalog for 25 cents. That meant that in 1900 there were sharp limits on the ideas and information that Americans held in common.

- Most people did not have easy access to libraries. That would change in the next 20+ years as endowments from Dale Carnegie would fund nearly 1,700 libraries across the nation.

- Fewer than 10% of children graduated from high school in 1900 and those who did rarely had opportunities for physical education or exposure to sports like tennis, golf, or basketball. There were no Boy Scouts, no 4-H clubs, and rarely bands, orchestras, or glee clubs.

- People still traveled mostly on foot or by horse and carriage on unpaved roads. Henry Ford had not yet started mass production of the automobile, and the Wright brothers hadn't mastered flight.

- There was tremendous disparity between rich and poor. The average annual wage of *all* Americans in 1900 was between $400 and $500. Andrew Carnegie made 20,000 times that, which is something like the difference between most of us and Bill Gates. Many more people than now had servants in 1900, but that was partly because the weekly wage of a cook was $5 and $3.50 for a laundress.

Are you surprised by any of that?

Direction: Give participants a chance to make a few comments and a comparison to their own experiences.

► ***Dialogue:*** Now let's begin to talk about how things have changed in our lifetimes. Remember that I said in 1900 few people had the opportunity to share experiences through mass communication. Television played a huge role in changing that. When Lucy gave birth to Little Ricky on the January 19, 1953 episode of "I Love Lucy," it is estimated that 44 million viewers tuned in. That's close to 30% of the entire U.S. population at the time. The next day, the first presidential inauguration was shown on TV and 15 million fewer viewers tuned in, but that was still amazing. For the first time, millions of people could *simultaneously* witness the same event. Today we don't even think about it, but it made a huge difference in how we experienced life. We had much more common ground than we had ever had before.

Does anyone want to comment on that?

Direction: Give people a chance to say something, if they would like; then move on.

► ***Dialogue:*** When we talk about watching the same television program, we're talking about our social history. Social history is influenced by lots of things—literature, language, fashion, family life, food, health—and much more. We can't talk about all of it, but we're going to talk about some of those things today, at least briefly.

One of the elements of social history that you might not have thought about shaping you is geography. Talk about the geography of the place where you grew up. Did you live in the city or country, on a hill or in a valley, on a flat plain, near mountains, near water? What were you used to seeing as you stepped out of your home each day? And do you still live in or value a similar place?

Direction: Give participants a chance to talk about this. It's a subject most of us don't consider, but there is a reason that immigrants to the United States tended to choose landscapes like those they left behind when they went to the Midwest to farm, for example. People who grew up around mountains or near the ocean or in "Big Sky Country" tend to value those landscapes all their lives.

Conversely, those who grew up in the city are often most comfortable there. We talked a little about this in "Make a Choice," but here is a chance for them to examine how their life experiences influenced that.

Others will have had a life-changing event such as serving in a foreign country or taking a fabulous vacation that changed their views of what is appealing. Others will simply have lived lots of places because of career changes or military postings or educational opportunities, and those, too, are likely to have been influential. Draw out their stories.

▶ *Dialogue:*   Now let's talk about the size of your family. In 1900, fewer than 1% of people lived alone and fully half the population lived in households of at least six people. In 1940, large families were still common, with 1 in every 19 births being an eighth or later child. At the end of the 20th century, however, only 1 in 219 births was an eighth or later child and 10% of people lived alone. Part of this had to do with the fact that the birth control pill for women did not become commercially available until 1960 and some religious faiths oppose birth control. Some of it had to do with economics, and some people think it had to do with the fact that people starting watching TV instead of having sex!

- How many people and how many generations lived together when you were growing up?

- How did this influence your own choices when you were an adult?

Direction: Most people who grew up in a large family seem to have enjoyed it and have wonderful stories to tell, so encourage those. Whether people were part of large or small families, try to find out how close they were to parents and siblings and how that influenced their family relations as an adult.

In the 1960s, many people were concerned about something called ZPG or Zero Population Growth. The idea was that the world population was growing too rapidly to long sustain itself, so it was our civic duty to have no more than two children—enough to keep population steady, but not increase it. If no one brings it up, you may ask whether anyone in your group heard of that movement or was influenced by it.

▶ *Dialogue:*   Another influence on social history is health. Penicillin did not come into common usage until the 1940s, which made a significant difference in life expectancy. In 1900 life expectancy was about 47 years, and the most common causes of death were pneumonia, influenza, tuberculosis, and diarrhea-related illnesses. By 1950, the average life expectancy had increased more than 20 years to 68.2 and the leading causes of death had changed to heart disease, cancer, and stroke. Together they accounted for over 60% of all deaths.

If you were growing up or raising a family in the 1950s the only epidemic likely to have worried you was the outbreak of polio, which struck 50,000 Americans in 1952, but which was largely halted with a massive inoculation effort in 1954, thanks to a vaccine developed by Dr. Jonas Salk. Do any of you have memories related to the polio epidemic of the 1950s?

Direction: Give participants a chance to respond. Then talk about more common health issues.

▶ *Dialogue:*   In the 1950s there weren't vaccinations for most of the childhood diseases, so measles, chicken pox, and mumps were still common, but not usually a serious worry. Schools were often involved in yearly mass inoculations for smallpox and other diseases. You may also remember your school as a drug dispenser: elementary school children in some places in the 1950s were given weekly doses of chewable chocolate goiter pills with their graham crackers and milk.

Mothers had mostly stopped doling out cod liver oil to their children each morning, and their children were glad to do without it. Lots of people had their tonsils or appendix removed and spread colds and ear infections among their family members and classmates, but health worries as children were growing up were the exception rather than the rule.

Talk about how health in your family or among your peers influenced you as you were growing up.

Direction: Some people will have vivid memories of all the cues in those previous paragraphs from cod liver oil to school vaccines to tonsillectomies. Give them a chance to talk about how their health growing up influenced their habits today. Then move on to talking about inventions; stop after each one and see what memories they trigger.

▶ *Dialogue:*   Science brought us great advances in health during the 20th century and many of those were already in evidence in the 1950s. Let's talk about some of the other inventions from that decade.

Lots of inventions were just in their infancy in the 1950s and wouldn't become an everyday part of our lives for another decade or more. We already talked about the birth control pill being developed in the 1950s, but not becoming commercially available until the 1960s. Here are some of the other things that were "not quite ready for prime time" in the 1950s:

- UNIVAC by Remington Rand—the first commercial computer. It was huge and expensive and not yet terribly reliable.

- Computer chip—It would eventually replace magnetic tape, but not yet.

- DNA—Scientists Watson and Crick discovered the structure, but it wasn't ready to be used for solving crimes at that point.

- Xerographic copier—It would eventually take away the pleasures of smelling the purple mimeograph ink and eliminate the need for carbon paper, but in the 1950s the copiers were too rare and expensive to consider frivolously copying your hand or other body parts.

- Microwave ovens—The first ones were as big as a refrigerator and cost $1,200!

- Solar battery—Will we ever "go green" and turn to solar energy for more of our needs?

Direction: Discuss any of the "not ready for prime time" inventions that participants have comments about, but then move on to discussing inventions that *did* have an impact on our everyday lives. Stop after each invention mentioned below and ask if anyone has a comment to make.

▶ ***Dialogue:*** There were lots of inventions that date to the 1950s that you probably don't realize had their beginnings then. For example:

- Automatic elevator doors—Do you remember when every elevator came with a human operator?

- The transistor radio—For the first time people could take their music with them wherever they went. Do you think that was a good thing?

- Motorized lawnmowers—The ride-on models were still a few years away, but this was the noisy beginning. Do you remember when lawn mowers made a soothing clicking or whirring sound?

- Automatic pinsetter—Until the 1950s, bowling alleys had human pinsetters.

- Jet airliners for commercial travel—But in the 1950s many people still took family vacations traveling by train. Did you?

- Bic ballpoint pens—Lots of people experimented with and even patented ballpoint pens earlier, but it wasn't until 1952 that the Frenchman Marcel Bich finally made an inexpensive, practical product. Did you ever get blue ink stains on your fingers from using a fountain pen? Did anyone ever stick your pigtails in the inkwell that once sat on every student's desk?

- The electric typewriter—The first one was built by Thomas Edison in 1872, but the widespread use of them, along with a portable version, arrived in the 1950s.

- WD-40™—Do you know what it stands for? The answer is: "Water Displacement, 40th Attempt." It was named by the chemist who developed it in 1953, Norm Larsen. He was trying to concoct a formula to prevent corrosion, a task done by displacing water. Its first use was in the aerospace industry, but it became commercially available in 1958.

- Raid™ Bug Spray—Before this product became available, wire screens and smoke screens were our best defense.

- Aerosol spray—Of course both WD-40 and Raid owe their popularity in part to Robert Abplanalp's invention, patented in 1953, of a "crimp-on valve" that enabled liquids to be sprayed from a can under the pressure of an inert gas. His invention made spray cans cheap and practical—so cheap and practical that his Precision Valve Company was soon manufacturing one billion cans a year. That's a lot of hair spray!

- The Diners Club Credit Card—This was the beginning of the end of American frugality.

Direction: After participants have had their say about these inventions, ask if they remember any others they would like to mention. Then move on.

▶ *Dialogue:*   If we asked you "What was one of the greatest inventions of your lifetime?" what would you say?

Direction: Give participants a chance to comment. Like most of the questions in this exercise, this is an opinion question so there are no wrong answers.

▶ *Dialogue:*   Some things weren't new inventions, but they became much more popular in the 1950s. Think about telephones. In the 1950s it was still common to have only one telephone, and in the early 1950s you may even have had a party line—a number shared with others that enabled you to listen in on their conversations, if you were indiscreet. Your phone number may have had a word prefix such as:

- Murray-5555 instead of 687-5555 or

- Butterfield-5555 instead of 288-5555.

The telephone was often located in the center of the house where siblings and parents could easily hear what we were saying. That was important because the phone was not supposed to be used for frivolous conversation, and a long-distance call signified either a special occasion or a tragedy.
    Do you remember any of those things? How has that changed?

Direction: Give a few people a chance to respond and perhaps ask for them to vote on the following.

▶ *Dialogue:*

- How many of you are grateful to be able to be so easily in touch with the people you love by phone?

- How many of you feel more secure taking a road trip knowing you have a cell phone handy for emergencies?

- How many feel children and teenagers are less vulnerable because they can call from their cell phones whenever they need to?

- How many think cell phones should be banned in all public places and teenagers should be muzzled?

Direction: Give participants a chance to comment.

▶ *Dialogue:*   There were lots of genuinely new things available in the 1950s, but they may not all qualify as inventions. For example, frozen foods gained tremendous popularity in the 1950s, particularly something called the frozen TV dinner which was served on a TV tray. The TV tray enabled people to eat dinner and watch TV at the same time, because in those days, most televisions were very large and bulky consoles—not something you could put on the kitchen counter while you sat on a bar stool and watched.

Did anyone eat TV dinners in the 1950s? Were they any good?

Direction: Give people a chance to talk about how family dinner times changed over the years and how much influence television had on that change.

▶ ***Dialogue:*** The foods we ate changed a lot in the 1950s, in part because we had many more options and lots of them weren't good for us. For example, until the 1950s, breakfast cereal was reasonably healthy—Wheaties, Shredded Wheat, Cheerios, Rice Krispies, and Puffed Rice. Then manufacturers discovered sugar.

- In 1950, Sugar Pops were introduced.

- In 1952, Kellogg's Sugar Frosted Flakes (29% sugar) entered the market.

- 1953 brought Kellogg's Sugar Smacks (56% sugar).

- 1954 brought Trix (46.6% sugar).

- 1958 brought Cocoa Puffs (43% sugar) and Cocoa Krispies (45.9% sugar).

And we haven't even begun to talk about Blackjack gum, frozen desserts like creamsicles and popsicles, and our love affair with Coca Cola and other sodas.

Besides sugar, we added lots of salt and fat to our diets. In 1953, the United States had 15,000 pizzerias and 100,000 stores that offered frozen pizzas. In 1958, Pizza Hut opened in Kansas City and would soon become the largest pizza chain in the United States. In 1954, Ray Kroc would begin his McDonald's franchise. Folks, the road to our national weight problem began in the 1950s.

- Do any of you have fond memories of its beginnings anyway?

- How have your eating habits changed over the years?

Direction: Give participants a chance to comment on our diets in the 1950s and since.

▶ ***Dialogue:*** The other bad habit that seemed to be at a fever pitch in the 1950s was smoking. Cigarette packages carried no warning labels and they were heavily advertised in every medium, especially on TV. Although the hazards of smoking were strongly suspected, they were mostly unproven until the mid-1950s. Nevertheless, smokers jokingly referred to cigarettes as coffin nails and identified their throat problems as smoker's cough, which would seem to suggest they knew they were not exactly like eating apples in terms of keeping the doctor away. Cigarettes were further glamorized by movie and television stars who smoked frequently and sometimes constantly on air. Think Edward R. Morrow.

- Did cigarette advertising influence you in the 1950s?

- Do you remember candy cigarettes? Did you "smoke" those?

- Were you ever a real cigarette smoker? Are you still?

- Were you exposed to second-hand smoke in your household?

- How has smoking and your attitude toward smoking and smokers changed in recent years or decades?

Direction: Give participants a chance to comment on these changes.

► ***Dialogue:*** If television helped increase the sale of cigarettes, it also proved effective in selling products to children. Here are some of the popular toys introduced in the 1950s:

- Play-doh

- Mr. Potato Head

- Hula hoops

- Pop-it beads

- Tiny Tears doll

- Barbie dolls

- Silly putty

- Frisbee

- Davy Crockett coonskin caps (plus Davy Crockett lunch pails, pajamas, and much more, including 4 million records of "Davy, Davy Crockett, King of the Wild Frontier")

Which of these products hold fond memories for you—either because you had them yourself or bought them for your children?

- How many of you have grandchildren who still play with these toys?

- What other toys did you play with as a child?

- Do you think today's electronic gadgets have changed the way children play? Is that good or bad?

Direction: Give participants an opportunity to comment and then go on to the next topic.

► ***Dialogue:*** One of the articles that circulates regularly on the Internet is called an Age-O-Meter. If you remember these other fads, you were certainly alive in the 1950s, so talk about your memories related to these. Let's start with clothes:

- Poodle skirts (and circle skirts)

- Saddle shoes and penny loafers

- Blouses with "Peter Pan" collars

- Crinolines

- Bermuda shorts
- P.F. Flyers or Keds
- Leather jackets

Did you or your children ever wear any of those?

Direction: Give participants a chance to comment.

▶ ***Dialogue:*** How about primping and accessorizing. Did you have these?

- Charm bracelets
- Cat's eye glasses
- Mum deodorant
- Butch hair wax
- Anything pink (the "in" color, even for men in 1955)

Direction: Give participants a chance to comment.

▶ ***Dialogue:*** Do you remember:

- 45 RPM records
- Milk bottles with cardboard stoppers delivered to your doorstep or left in the milk chute
- Newsreels before the movie in theaters (plus cartoons)
- Metal ice trays with levers
- Roller skate keys
- Blue flashbulbs on your camera
- Vending machines that dispensed glass bottles
- Little wax bottles filled with colored sugar water
- S&H Green Stamps
- Droodles (simple drawings with a humorous title—the one on the right is "Abraham Lincoln in the shower")

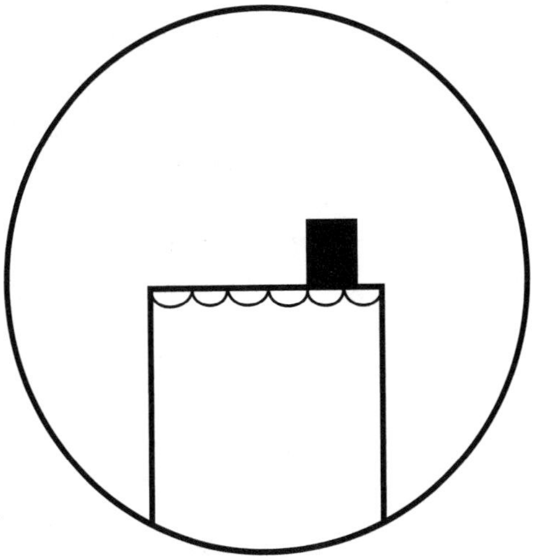

What memories do you have about those?

Direction: Give participants a chance to comment. If you have men in the group, you must mention cars of the 1950s; women may be less excited by the specific brands.

▶ *Dialogue:*   How about cars? Do these things make you feel nostalgic?

- Studebaker

- Nash Rambler

- Ford Thunderbird

- Cadillac convertible

- Chevrolet Bel Air and Impala

- Chevy Corvette

- Kaiser Manhattan

- Hudson Hornet

- Plymouth Fury

- Edsel

- Volkswagen

- Tail fins

- Bright and varied colors

- Gleaming grilles

Direction: Give participants a chance to comment.

▶ *Dialogue:*   How about entertainment? Do you remember these?

- Drive-in movies (and restaurants)

- Tupperware parties

- Stuffing as many people as possible into phone booths or Volkswagens?

Direction: Give participants a chance to comment.

▶ *Dialogue:*

- Do you miss any of these things?

- Are there any other memories you have of things that will "never be the same"?

- Are there any "old ways" you would like to go back to?

Direction: Give participants a chance to respond. Then go onto changes in language. See if participants know the meanings and supply them only when you need to.

▶ *Dialogue:*   Here's one last category of changes: language. Do you remember these expressions from the 1950s? Which ones sound dated or have taken on new meanings?

- BMOC—Big man on campus

- Bombing around—driving around

- Bread—money

- Catch some rays—Sun bathe

- Church key—(Beer) bottle opener

- D.A.—a hairstyle that refers to a duck's tail

- Going ape—wildly enthusiastic

- Greaser—someone who uses lots of hair oil, acts tough, probably wears a D.A. and a leather jacket

- Hanging loose—relaxing

- Having a blast—having a great time

- Out to lunch—person who isn't smart or tuned in

- Pad—house or apartment; where you live

- Parking—going someplace secluded in a car for the purpose of "making-out" (hugging and kissing—not necessarily more!)

- Really hairy—Something difficult or scary; hair raising

- Scuzzy—dirty, shabby, disreputable

- What a riot—something very funny

(Excerpted and adapted with permission from BiFolkal's *Remembering the Fifties Manual.*)

Resources for Digging Deeper—Exercise 6

Frederick Lewis Allen wrote ***The Big Change, America Transforms Itself: 1900–1950*** in 1952. He died about a year after it was published, so he never got to see the tremendous changes of the decades that followed. Undoubtedly, had he lived, he would have written eloquently about them as well. Allen had a unique talent for taking facts related to many aspects of life and meshing them into an engaging story of what Americans once were and how their lives changed over 50 years. I highly recommend this book.

Dover Publications has produced multiple volumes on fashions. For this exercise I used ***Everyday Fashions of the Fifties as Pictured in Sears Catalogs*** by JoAnne Olian. There are also volumes on other decades and all are fun to peruse for astonishment at prices and sometimes bewilderment at the styles we chose to wear. The other books used for this exercise include all those mentioned in Exercise 7.

Mini-Exercise F is devoted to time line variations. Although time lines are found in virtually every book on autobiographical writing, once again Mary

Borg's *Writing Your Life* has easy directions and samples for life's highs and lows or what I call life as a stock market chart (p. 98) and a more typical time line tied to world events (p. 60). I have also adapted the time line as a pie chart idea from Ruth Kanin's book, *Write the Story of Your Life.* My copy dates from 1981, but a reprint edition was published in 1998 and is still available (Genealogical Publishing Company, ISBN 0806311479).

Mini-Exercise F: Time Lines

At the end of this mini-exercise are a basic time line form and brief lists of events from social and political history which can be used to provide "food for thought" in filling out your preferred time line. If you do this exercise with a group, use the time line format on page 195 (available on the CD-ROM). The information in Mini-Exercises E and G provide more ideas on music, movies, and literature. The information in the handouts for *all* the exercises in Part 3 provide additional social history background.

1. Time line in table format. The most common form and easiest time line format is provided in Appendix D with a sample below. Pick an event from political, social, or your personal history and write it under "event." Then fill in the year it happened, how old you were at the time, and the impact it had on you. With this format, it's easy to add events and comments as you think of them without having to worry whether they are in chronological order. (If chronological order is important to you, you can always rearrange the events on a second form after you've finished the first.) To get started, try using the "Brief Historical Time Line" on pages 110–111 or list any of the foods, fashion, fads, TV programs, or inventions that had an impact on you, and write your comments in the last column.

Note: Some people like to fill out multiple forms, such as one for personal growth, one for career, one for travel or other leisure pursuits, one for family life, and so on. There is no "wrong" way to do this exercise.

Time Line of Life of: _____

Event	Year	My age	Impact on me

2.   Time line as stock market chart. Some people prefer to summarize their lives as if they were tracking the stock market. Create a baseline at birth and then place all the experiences you want to measure above or below the baseline depending upon whether they had a positive or negative effect on you. Your choices are purely subjective. For example, if you were a soldier in World War II, the war may have been a negative event, but the character it built in you, the friends you made, and the new skills you developed because of it may all have been positive, making it ultimately a peak experience. Marriage and births of children are usually very positive experiences, while family deaths and job losses are negative, but even those may have mitigating factors. For example, when someone dies after a long illness, the death may be seen as a relief from watching that person suffer.

3.   Time line as pie chart. I first encountered the method of dividing your life into a pie chart when reading Ruth Kanin's book ***Write the Story of Your Life*** (pp. 9–13) in the early 1980s. The general idea is to divide your life into six or eight segments, always saving one segment for the future. Create a narrow band near the outside rim of the circle and in each segment place the time period and your ages during that segment. Then list some of the major events or influences on you during that time period and the general feelings generated by that time period.

For example, you might divide your life into the following six segments:

- Birth and early childhood
- High school and college/military/trade school
- Early career, marriage, and family
- Later career, growing or grown family
- Retirement
- Future

Under birth and early childhood you might fill in such highlights as

- Raised by single mom as Dad was in WWII
- Tonsils out at 4—have hated hospitals since
- Learned to read—loved it!
- Great fifth-grade teacher; spurred interest in science

The main advantage of this format is that it provides limited space, so you are forced to pick highlights. It also enables you to see patterns and to make connections from one segment to another—and ultimately to "come full circle" seeing your life as complete, whole.

An example I created many years ago is shown on page 108.

4.   Time line as map. Some people—generally those with an artistic or imaginative bent—like to draw their lives as a journey and literally draw the map they have followed. They may put in all the pleasant stops along the way

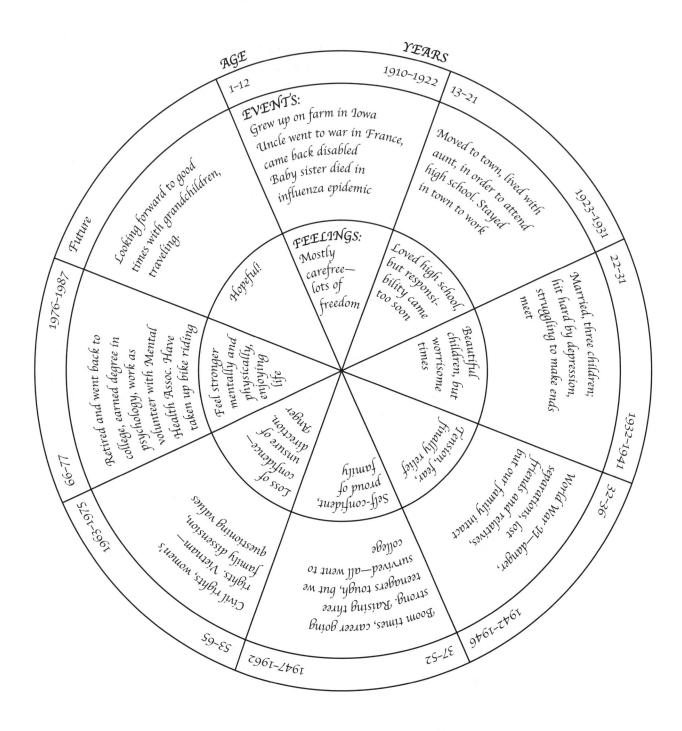

AGE

YEARS

1910–1922

1–12

13–21

EVENTS:
Grew up on farm in Iowa
Uncle went to war in France, came back disabled
Baby sister died in influenza epidemic

Moved to town, lived with aunt, in order to attend high school. Stayed in town to work

1923–1931

Future

Looking forward to good times with grandchildren, traveling.

FEELINGS:
Mostly carefree—lots of freedom

Loved high school, but responsibility came too soon

22–31

1976–1987

Hopeful.

Beautiful children, but worrisome times

Married, three children; hit hard by depression, struggling to make ends meet

1932–1941

Feel stronger mentally and physically, enjoying life

Retired and went back to college, earned degree in psychology, work as Mental Health Assoc. Have taken up bike riding

Loss of confidence—unsure of direction. Anger.

Tension, fear, finally relief

Self-confident, proud of family

World War II—danger, friends and relatives lost, but our family intact

32–36

66–77

1963–1975

Boom times, career going strong. Raising three teenagers tough, but we survived—all went to college

1942–1946

Civil rights, women's rights, Vietnam— family dissension, questioning values.

1947–1962

53–65

37–52

108   The Historical Perspective

(smooth sailing across the pond of early childhood) as well as the obstacles (uphill battles, valley of despair) and the detours (started an unsuccessful rock band, became a flower child for one summer). They may include peak experiences as actual peaks or may draw the geography of the actual location (a chance to study volcanoes in Hawaii or take a trip to Antarctica). These maps can be spontaneous or carefully considered. They can be reconsidered over time and adjusted or new maps can be drawn for new decades of the journey.

5.   Time line as real map. If you and your family have lived many places in your lifetime and if your family is geographically scattered now, using a real map as a time line may make sense for you. If you have lived many places, write the years you lived each place directly on the map. If your family is scattered, write who is where now (or where else they have lived) on the map. Include favorite aunts, uncles, cousins, siblings, children, grandchildren, nieces and nephews, and close friends. You might be amazed at where life has brought everyone.

1945	Roosevelt dies on April 12; World War II ends—estimated 54.8 million have died, mostly civilians; Hitler commits suicide; atomic bomb is dropped.
1946	UN General Assembly opens; Nuremberg trials sentence 12 leading Nazis to death; Churchill speaks of "Iron Curtain"; birth rate soars; Juan Peron elected president of Argentina.
1947	The Marshall Plan that will help Europe recover from World War II is formulated; India is partitioned into India and Pakistan as it becomes independent from Great Britain; the Dead Sea scrolls are discovered.
1948	State of Israel proclaimed; phrase "Cold War" is coined; Gandhi assassinated; a "Universal Declaration of Human Rights" is adopted by the UN; Truman wins election over Dewey.
1949	East and West Germany established; NATO is formed; Chiang Kai-shek moves to Taiwan; Communists Mao Tse-tung and Chou En-lai come to power; apartheid established in South Africa.
1950	Korean war begins; Senator Joe McCarthy begins a 4-year "witch hunt" for communists in the United States; U.S. census reaches 150 million.
1951	Atomic bomb exploded over Nevada; General Douglas MacArthur is relieved of his command; local phone call rates double from 5 cents to 10 cents; food prices also climb steeply.
1952	Eisenhower elected president; Queen Elizabeth II ascends throne; polio epidemic begins—50,000 stricken; hydrogen bomb is tested.
1953	Stalin dies; Korean War ends leaving 4 million dead or wounded; Edmund Hillary and Tensing Norgay reach summit of Mount Everest; Dag Hammarskjold becomes Secretary-General of UN.
1954	Racial segregation in public schools is ruled unconstitutional; Joseph McCarthy is finally discredited; Eisenhower refuses to send troops to Vietnam.
1955	U.S. occupation of Japan ends; "In God We Trust" is added to U.S. currency; Rosa Parks refuses to give up her seat on a Montgomery, AL bus, galvanizing the Civil Rights Movement.
1956	President Eisenhower signs the law creating the interstate highway system; people's revolt in Hungary is crushed by Soviet troops; Grace Kelly marries Prince Rainier of Monaco.
1957	Sputnik is launched; school integration begins in Little Rock, AR with the help of federal troops; pharmaceutical companies are accused of "charging all the traffic will bear" for drugs by Sen. Kefauver.
1958	Gen. de Gaulle becomes French premier; peace symbol is introduced; whalers kill nearly 7,000 blue whales; recession begins in the United States; transatlantic jet service begins.
1959	Fidel Castro becomes premier of Cuba; Alaska and Hawaii are admitted to the Union; Dalai Lama escapes to Tibet; St. Lawrence Seaway opens.
1960	John Kennedy wins presidential election; France explodes her first atomic bomb; lunch counter sit-ins begin as a Civil Rights strategy; Brasilia becomes new capital of Brazil; aluminum cans begin use.

1961	Bay of Pigs invasion in Cuba; Berlin Wall erected; Peace Corps is created; The United States and the Soviet Union both launch first manned space-ships for their countries.
1962	Cuban missile crisis; John Glenn orbits the earth; Cesar Chavez forms National Farm Workers Association; first Wal-Mart opens.
1963	President Kennedy assassinated. Congress passes law guaranteeing women equal pay for equal work; Martin Luther King, Jr. declares, "I have a dream . . . ."
1964	President Johnson wins re-election; Civil Rights Bill becomes law; the Tonkin Gulf Resolution is passed beginning heavy commitment of U.S. Troops to Vietnam.
1965	United States has 125,000 troops in Vietnam by July; Black Muslim leader Malcolm X is assassinated; President Johnson outlines plan for "Great Society" to eliminate poverty.

Sources: James Trager's *The People's Chronology* and Beckie Karras' *Journey Through the 20th Century.*

Exercise 7: Life as Social History

THE BASIC EXERCISE

This exercise continues to explore the effect of social history on our lives, but this time the emphasis is on how *we* have changed. Most of this is done through a discussion of advertising, simply because beginning in the 1950s we were bombarded with advertising at every turn and it affected us in more ways than we realize.

The mini-exercise that follows this main exercise provides ideas for using movies and literature for reminiscence because many of us were deeply moved by these forms of entertainment, and many of us simply set our standards for what is fun by them.

PROPS AND MATERIALS

Again, if you have used any of the resources in Exercise 5 and 6, bring them out again for this one. In several places in this exercise, we ask for volunteer readers. Plan ahead and print those passages out on separate sheets of paper, preferably in large type.

KEY ELEMENTS

The fun in this exercise is generated mostly by the ads themselves and by the essay on "How to Be a Good Wife."

DEMENTIA CONCERNS

People with dementia, as noted elsewhere, are often good at filling in blanks, so many of these advertisements and their slogans will work well with them if you phrase them in a fill-in-the-blanks way. They are also likely to enjoy the humor of the Burma-Shave signs and other aspects of this exercise.

THE COMPLETE SCRIPT

▶ **Dialogue:** Today we're going to talk about how we have changed—and not changed—in our lifetimes. We're going to start by talking about advertising, in part because advertising shapes us in many ways that we don't even realize. The 20th century was the beginning of consumerism fueled in part by clever advertising and in part by many more choices. Before the 20th century, most people used things up or wore them out before they purchased anything new.

According to the author Harvey Green, this all started to change about 1915. He wrote a book called *The Uncertainty of Everyday Life, 1915–1945* and in it he argues that advertisers about that time began to exploit our self-doubts. He says advertisers invented new social diseases like "halitosis," "dandruff," and "body odor." These were all especially frightening, because you might not know you had them. But, the advertisers promised, if you bought the right products you wouldn't need to worry about offending others. According to Green, "Feelings of inferiority . . . were a valuable thing in advertising" (p. 22). In the past, advertisers focused on the product. Now the focus was on the consumer.

Let me give you an example.

Direction: Ask for a volunteer to read the indented passage below. (You may want to print it from the CD-ROM on a separate piece of paper before your meeting begins.) Then introduce the passage by first reading the following dialogue.

▶ ***Dialogue:*** An ad for Listerine, reprinted in the Time-Life series, *Our American Century, The Jazz Age, the 20s* (p. 86) features a painting of a wistful elderly woman over the headline, "Are you sure about yourself?" The woman has an open photograph album on her lap, a wadded hankie in her hand, and she is staring off into space. If this isn't obvious enough, the ad copy provides lengthy and graphic details that read like a romance novel: Long ago she was the object of affection of "a dark-eyed Nashville boy" and she would always know that she had once "been loved passionately, devotedly." But suddenly there was a broken engagement with no explanation and a half-century later, continuously alone, it's all still a mystery to her.

Direction: Ask your volunteer to read the following copy promoting Listerine:

> How often some trivial gesture, habit or fault alters the course of human affairs. On every side you hear of engagements broken for trifling causes. Of marriages that ride into the divorce court on the strange complaint "incompatibility."
>
> If you have ever come face to face with a real case of halitosis (unpleasant breath) you can understand how it might well be an obstacle to pleasant business, professional and social relations.
>
> The insidious thing about halitosis is that you never know you have it. It does not announce itself to the victim. Important to remember also, is the fact that few people escape it entirely.

Then thank the volunteer as he or she sits down again.

▶ ***Dialogue:*** The ad continues for another three paragraphs, but you get the idea. Advertisers became fear-mongers and self-esteem blasters. Not only is bad breath likely to ruin your life, but you won't even know it was the cause because no one will tell you, and you can't escape having it! Horrors!

- What do you think of this as an advertising tactic? Does it work to play on our self-doubts?

- What products use this tactic today?

Direction: Give people a chance to comment. Most will probably be surprised that such blatant attempts to attack our self-esteem were in use 80+ years ago, and many may find the language quaint. But others will see the same trends continuing today. The biggest difference in today's breath freshener ads is that advertisers know they have to get our attention quickly, so ads tell the story on TV in 30 seconds or less. The actual message behind the words hasn't changed much.

▶ ***Dialogue:***   According to author Green, the uncertainty of everyday life was reinforced by the popular books of the day. Emily Post's book of etiquette first appeared in 1915 and would go through five editions in the next 20 years. Her book stressed the importance of manners and pleasing others, of appearances over character. Anyone could learn to behave "properly" in society. Then in 1936 Dale Carnegie's book *How to Win Friends and Influence People* was published and quickly became a best-seller. Carnegie's primary message was that for the best chance of success in life, one had to learn to "fit in" with others' expectation of behavior.

All of this gave advertisers good reason to make appeals that centered on "guilt, status and celebrity." For nearly 20 years, Henry Ford made essentially the same Model T car in the same color—black. But by the mid-1920s, advertising was stressing the *look* of things, not their function. Advertisements for Ford cars began to show them parked in front of mansions to give them a look that symbolized success. Suddenly consumers had style and color choices in almost everything, and advertisers encouraged them to buy in quantity. A woman needed a car as much as her husband in order to avoid isolation. Households needed two or three radios, not just one.

All this was fueled by radios themselves, since shows began to be sponsored by and advertised specific products, and celebrity endorsements became common. The popular crooner Rudy Vallee pitched Fleischmann's yeast, for example. People also learned what was fashionable through motion pictures and magazines.

- Does this advertising tactic of trying to convey status through products work?

- What products use it today?

- What about celebrities? Are you influenced by their endorsements?

- What *does* influence you?

Direction: Give participants a chance to comment. Most of us would prefer to think we resist that kind of advertising, but we don't always.

▶ ***Dialogue:***   You may be thinking, "Why does any of this matter?" Green says, ". . . the material base of society—houses, artifacts, the visual world—is a key signifier of a culture's ideas, identity, and intentions" (p. 14).

Let's illustrate the point. Does anyone remember seeing the little red series of signs with white writing along country roads that advertised Burma-Shave? Do any of you remember any of the slogans?

Direction: Give participants a chance to respond. Most people who traveled at all when the signs were popular have fond memories of them. Here's the background:

Burma-Shave was a brushless shaving cream produced by a company owned by Clinton Odell. In 1925 his son Allan suggested the idea of using small wooden roadside signs to advertise the product. Mr. Odell was not enthused, but ultimately gave Allan $200 to give it a try. Sales soared quickly, so Allan and his brother put up more. At their height of popularity there were 7,000 signs all over America, with each series containing four to six signs. The last sign always said "Burma-Shave," but the verses leading up to the ad were often quite clever—usually some variation of why women like men who use Burma-Shave, although in later years the brothers included signs advocating safe driving and the prevention of forest fires, too. The signs were a staple of driving along country roads for more than three decades, but by the early 1960s, they disappeared. Interstate highways had begun to replace country roads as primary routes and the little signs were overtaken by giant billboards. (This information and the following sampling of the slogans has come from: http://www.fiftiesweb.com/burma1.htm, Burma-Shave Slogans of the '50s.)

If anyone remembers a slogan, give him or her a chance to recite it. Otherwise, print out the following samples and give them to participants to read aloud.

His cheek
Was rough
His chick vamoosed
And now she won't
Come home to roost
Burma-Shave

On curves ahead
Remember, sonny
That rabbit's foot
Didn't save
The bunny
Burma-Shave

The whale
Put Jonah
Down the hatch
But coughed him up
Because he scratched
Burma-Shave

My job is
Keeping faces clean
And nobody knows
De stubble
I've seen
Burma-Shave

No use
Knowing
How to pick 'em
If your half-shaved
Whiskers stick 'em
Burma-Shave

Substitutes
Can let you down
Quicker
Than a
Strapless gown
Burma-Shave

The draftee
Tried a tube
And purred
Well whaddya know
I've been defurred
Burma-Shave

Said farmer Brown
Who's bald
On top
Wish I could
Rotate the crop
Burma-Shave

Dinah doesn't
Treat him right
But if he'd shave
Dinah-might!
Burma-Shave

Ben met Anna
Made a hit
Neglected beard
Ben-Anna split.
Burma-Shave

Don't take
A curve at
Sixty per
We hate to lose
A customer
Burma-Shave

If you don't know
Whose signs these are
You haven't driven
Very far!
Burma-Shave

When you have enjoyed these verses, if you have any men in the room, use the following dialogue.

▶ *Dialogue:*   How many of you men ever used Burma-Shave? Did you like it? Was it a good product? Did it draw women to you like they said it would?

Direction: Give them a chance to answer. Then ask the women the following question.

▶ *Dialogue:*   Now ladies, how many of you ever bought Burma-Shave for your husbands or sons? Did you like the results?

Direction: We also were inundated in the 1950s by shows named after the sponsors—much like sports stadiums are named today. Talk a little about that by giving people a chance to react to the following list.

▶ *Dialogue:*   One of the reasons most of us have fond memories of Burma-Shave signs is that they showed a sense of humor. We felt good about liking the ads. Celebrities can do the same for a product, which is why in the 1950s, TV sponsors often "owned" a show, meaning their name was in the show's title and they were the sole advertiser. If the show was popular, it made the sponsor look good.

In some cases, commercials were worked right into the script. Do you remember how Gracie Allen would manage to talk about Carnation Milk with her neighbor Blanche Morton (Bea Benaderet)? This was a carry-over from the radio shows of the 1940s (when the Burns and Allen show was sponsored by Maxwell House Coffee) and came before TV commercials were too expensive for a single sponsor. Here are some of the sponsored shows. Which of these do you remember?

- Buick Circus Hour

- Camel News Caravan (Camel Cigarettes)

- The Chevy Show (This featured Bob Hope, not Dinah Shore, who promoted the same sponsor on her show)

- Colgate Comedy Hour

- Disneyland—to promote its theme park

- The Ford Show (starring Tennessee Ernie Ford, but sponsored by Ford Motor Company)

- General Electric Theatre (hosted by Ronald Reagan in his prepolitical days)

- Gillette Cavalcade of Stars

- Goodyear TV Playhouse

- Hallmark Hall of Fame

- Kraft Television Theatre

- Lux Video Theatre

- Philco TV Playhouse

- Texaco Star Theatre

- The U.S. Steel Hour

Did any of these shows influence your buying habits?

Direction: Whether or not the people in your group bought any of these products, chances are good that they have bought other products that they have seen or heard advertised.

Tell them you're going to give them a little quiz of advertising slogans. See if they can name them without you giving the answer in parentheses.

▶ **Dialogue:** Most of the time advertising is so pervasive that we don't even know we're absorbing it. Here are slogans from the 1950s for a variety of products. Can you name what is being advertised?

1. A little dab'll do ya. (Brylcreem)

2. Don't squeeze the _____. (Charmin)

3. I'd walk a mile for a _____. (Camel cigarette)

4. When it rains, it pours. (Morton salt)

5. Plop plop fizz fizz, oh what a relief it is. (Alka Seltzer)

6. Good to the last drop. (Maxwell House coffee)

7. The breakfast of champions. (Wheaties cereal)

8. From contented cows. (Carnation milk)

9. Mmmmmm Mmmmmmm good. (Campbell's soups)

10. You'll wonder where the yellow went. (Pepsodent)

11. A day without _____ is like a day without sunshine. (Florida orange juice—not a name brand but a state brand)

12. Double the pleasure, double the fun. (Wrigley's Doublemint gum)

13. You can be sure if it's _____. (Westinghouse)

14. The pause that refreshes. (Coca-Cola)

15. Nothing says lovin' like something from the oven and ___ says it best. (Pillsbury)

Direction: We will assume most of the people in your group did pretty well with that, especially if they are at least 50 years old. Now help them to realize that even if they don't know slogans, they know brand names. Ask them to tell you what product is sold under the following brand names. Answers are again in parentheses.

▶ ***Dialogue:*** Can you tell me what each of these brand names sell?

- Timex (watches)

- Gold Medal (flour)

- Bayer (aspirin)

- Comet (household cleanser)

- Crest (toothpaste)

- Kraft (cheese)

- Lipton (tea)

- Hershey's (chocolate)

- Hellman's (mayonnaise)

- Nabisco (crackers and cookies)

- Arm & Hammer (baking soda)

- Parkay (margarine)

Direction: Since all of these brand names have been around for a very long time now, most people of any age are likely to be able to answer these. The point we're trying to make is just how ingrained those brand names are. So ask a few more questions.

▶ ***Dialogue:*** It's easy to see from these exercises that brand names are deeply ingrained in us. But the question is, "Does that make a difference?" In other words:

- When you go shopping for anything, what influences you most—name recognition, price, quality, attractiveness?

- How tied are you to brand names? Are there certain products that you and your family are very loyal to? What are they? What would make you try something different?

- Has anything else changed your buying habits over the years—things like dietary concerns, for example?

Direction: Give participants a chance to discuss their preferences and how they were formed. Note how they choose a product. Many will find it is sheer habit that creates loyalty. They find something they like and stick with it. That doesn't mean they wouldn't try something else that came along if they had an incentive to do so. Then change direction slightly.

▶ ***Dialogue:*** Some people say we have too many choices. As early as 1929, a man named Joseph Wood Krutch argued in *The Modern Temper* that having multiple choices was not liberating but paralyzing (p. 12 of Green's book). Barry Schwartz makes the same argument in his 2004 book *The Paradox of Choice*.

Schwartz says that he went to his local supermarket and counted 85 brands and varieties of crackers and 285 varieties of cookies, including 21 options for chocolate chip cookies. He also found 275 varieties of cereal and 22 types of frozen waffles—and that's just the beginning of his list.

Schwartz says that studies have shown that because we want to make the "right" choice every time we buy something, if we have too many choices, we often won't buy anything at all, out of fear of making the "wrong" choice.

Do you find there are too many choices these days? Are you ever afraid of making the wrong choice?

Direction: Give participants a chance to comment on this idea. If anyone has any doubt that this is true, ask how many people have seen a man in a grocery store on a cell phone trying to get clearer information from his wife on what to buy. My guess is everyone has witnessed this.

Here's a little background on the study that Schwartz cited: It was called "When Choice Is Demotivating." What the study showed was that when consumers were given a choice of six jams in a taste sample, and then a coupon for buying any of 24 varieties, they were 10 times more likely to buy a jar of jam than people who were given a choice of taste testing all 24 varieties.

We're going to change direction now. Ask the following questions one at a time and give people a chance to respond before you go to the next one.

▶ ***Dialogue:*** Our confusion about what to buy is one sign of uncertainty that is still with us in the 21st century. Let me ask you another question in a totally different direction: How confident are you that this is a world worthy of your trust? For example:

- Do you trust your neighbor?

- Do you lock your house and car doors whenever you go out? Did you always? How has your sense of security changed over the years?

- Do you feel safe walking the streets in your city or neighborhood?

- Do you think most people are trustworthy?

- Do you trust big business or the government to look out for your best interests?

- Do you think the world is a safer or less safe place than it was in the midst of the Cold War in the 1950s?

Direction: Give participants a chance to talk about these things and to argue why they feel one way or the other. Then change tactics again. Ask again for a volunteer to read the passage indented below. If possible, print it from the CD-ROM ahead of time on a separate paper.

Introduce this passage by saying the following dialogue.

▶ ***Dialogue:*** I'm going to illustrate another way we have changed in the last generation or two. The passage I have asked _____ (volunteer's name) to read is from a home economics textbook printed in 1950. It was reprinted in the BiFolkal *Remembering the Fifties Program Manual.*

Direction: Then have the volunteer read the following:

How To Be a Good Wife

Have dinner ready. Plan ahead, even the night before, to have a delicious meal—on time. This is a way of letting him know that you have been thinking about him and are concerned about his needs. Most men are hungry when they come home and the prospect of a good meal is part of the warm welcome needed.

Prepare yourself. Take 15 minutes to rest so that you'll be refreshed when he arrives. Touch up your makeup, put a ribbon in your hair, and be fresh looking. He has just been with a lot of work weary people. Be a little gay and a little more interesting. His boring day might need a lift.

Clear away the clutter. Make one last trip through the main part of the house just before your husband arrives, gathering up school books, toys, paper, etc. Then run a dust cloth over the tables. Your husband will feel he has reached a haven of rest and order, and it will give you a lift, too. Prepare the children. Take a few minutes to wash the children's hands and faces (if they are small), comb their hair, and if necessary, change their clothes. They are little treasures and he would like to see them playing the part.

Minimize all noise. At the time of his arrival, eliminate all noise of the washer, dryer, or vacuum. Try to encourage the children to be quiet. Be happy to see him. Greet him with a warm smile.

Some don'ts. Don't greet him with problems or complaints. Don't complain if he's late for dinner. Count this minor compared to what he might have gone through that day.

Make him comfortable. Have him sit down on a comfortable chair or suggest that he lie down in the bedroom. Have a cool or warm drink ready for him. Arrange his pillow and offer to take off his shoes. Speak in a low, soft, soothing and pleasant voice. Allow him to relax and unwind.

Listen to him. You have a dozen things to tell him, but the moment of his arrival is not the time. Let him talk first.

Make the evening his. Never complain if he does not take you out to dinner or other places of entertainment. Instead, try to understand his world of strain and pressure, his need to be home and relax.

The goal: Try to make your home a place of peace and order so that your husband will stay and not stray.

(Reprinted with permission.)

▶ *Dialogue:* How many of the women here follow this advice today?

Direction: Give a few people a chance to respond, or ask for a show of hands and then give participants a chance to comment. Most people will find the passage hilariously outdated.

▶ *Dialogue:* How many men here are treated like this by their wives? How many would want to be?

Direction: Give a few people a chance to respond, or ask for a show of hands and then give participants a chance to comment.

▶ *Dialogue:* How many of you would say that women as a whole have gained confidence and a stronger sense of identity in the last 50 years?

Direction: Give a few people a chance to respond and perhaps ask for a show of hands. Also encourage people to comment. Some are likely to say we have a long way to go yet. Perhaps a few men would like to go back to the old ways. Perhaps some women never changed.

▶ *Dialogue to Precede Closing:* What we have been trying to explore here is both how things have changed over the years, and how some have stayed the same. The fact that advertisers are still trying to chip away at our self-esteem, or tie our sense of success to the car we drive or the makeup we wear speaks to some things unchanging. The fact that most women's roles have evolved shows that changes do occur. But some things haven't changed and shouldn't change. The last thing I'd like us to talk about today is:

- What things in life can you count on staying the same?

Direction: See what ideas participants come up with. Give them time to think. Some of their ideas are likely to be fun or funny, others quite serious. Here are a few ideas, but these are by no means complete:

- The sun and the moon and stars
- Beauty

- The search for truth
- Love matters
- Always finding comfort in chocolate
- People needing people
- My thighs will never be thin and that's okay, darn it.

Resources for Digging Deeper—Exercise 7

Again, I have primarily used resources mentioned in Exercise 5. One is new here, however. *The Uncertainty of Everyday Life, 1915–1945* by Harvey Green provided the opening background for this exercise as well as a resource for doing further research. The title of his book would seem to give it limited appeal, but it is a quite fascinating take on the early decades of the 20th century. Since it was written in 1992, it also provides perspective.

If anyone is interested in pursuing *The Paradox of Choice* by Barry Schwartz, it is still readily available (HarperCollins, © 2004. ISBN 0060005688).

Mini-Exercise G: **Movies and Literature**

Not everyone grew up loving literature or seeing movies as anything but pure entertainment, but many of us *were* influenced by, even changed by, what we saw on the screen (TV or movie) or what we saw in our minds as we read the classics, the best-sellers of the day or even comic books. The following mini-exercises suggest ways to use movies and literature from the 1950s to continue our discussion of social history.

1.   Children's literature. If you were a child growing up in the 1950s, or if you were a parent reading to your children or buying books for them, the following list may bring back fond memories for you.
- Which of these are you familiar with?
- Which did you personally enjoy as a child or as a parent reading to a child?
- Did any of them have life lessons for you? (If not these, did others? Which?)
- Did any of these inspire in you a love of reading or at least of hearing stories? (If not these, did others? Which?)

Popular children's literature of the 1950s includes:
- *Henry Huggins* by Beverly Cleary—1950
- *Yertle the Turtle* (Dr. Seuss begins his rise)—1950
- *Dennis the Menace* begins to appear in newspapers—1950
- *Charlotte's Web* by E. B. White—1952
- *The Borrowers* by Mary Norton—1953
- *Eloise* by Kay Thompson—1955

- *Old Yeller* by Fred Gipson—1956
- *The Cat in the Hat* by Dr. Seuss—1957

Comic books were also very popular in the 1950s. In 1954 the monthly sales had reached 24 million. Among the favorites of those who liked pure amusement were:

- Little Lulu
- Nancy
- Casper the Friendly Ghost
- Spooky
- Felix the Cat
- Donald Duck

However, that was also the heyday for:

- Super heroes: Batman, Superman, Wonder Woman, Captain Marvel, and others.
- Archie comics were aimed at teens, but popular with a younger crowd, too.
- Then there were other comic book genres: Mystery and detective, romance, science fiction, westerns, horror, jungle-based, war stories, and those based on movies and TV programs.

Were you a comic book reader? Which ones did you enjoy?

Mad magazine began publication in 1952 and children who read it tended to feel subversive for doing so. Were you one of them?

2. Adult literature—fiction. Many of the books we now consider classics made their debut in the 1950s. Many are now taught in literature classes. Many were made into movies. Which of the following have you read, and which influenced you in some way? How?

- *Catcher in the Rye*—J. D. Salinger, 1951
- *From Here to Eternity*—James Jones, 1951
- *The Caine Mutiny*—Herman Wouk, 1951
- *East of Eden*—John Steinbeck, 1952
- *Giant*—Edna Ferber, 1952
- *The Old Man and the Sea*—Ernest Hemingway, 1952
- *Casino Royale*—Ian Fleming, 1953
- *Invisible Man*—Ralph Waldo Ellison, 1953
- *Fahrenheit 451*—Ray Bradbury, 1953
- *Lord of the Flies*—William Golding, 1954
- *The Lord of the Rings*—J. R. R. Tolkien, 1955
- *Lolita*—Vladimir Nabokov, 1955
- *Auntie Mame*—Patrick Dennis, 1955
- *Andersonville*—MacKinlay Kantor, 1955
- *Howl* (poetry)—Allen Ginsberg, 1955
- *Peyton Place*—Grace Metalious, 1956
- *Atlas Shrugged*—Ayn Rand, 1957
- *By Love Possessed*—James Gould Cozzens, 1957

- *Rally Round the Flag, Boys!*—Max Shulman, 1957
- *On the Road*—Jack Kerouac, 1957
- *Dr. Zhivago*—Boris Pasternak, 1957
- *The Ugly American*—Eugene Burdick and William Lederer, 1958
- *A Raisin in the Sun*—Lorraine Hansberry, 1958
- *Breakfast at Tiffany's*—Truman Capote, 1958
- *Goodbye, Columbus*—Philip Roth, 1959
- *The Miracle Worker*—William Gibson, 1959
- *Hawaii*—James Michener, 1959

3.   Adult literature—nonfiction. Nonfiction best-sellers reflect the hot topics of our times—and almost always include a cookbook or two. Did any of these have special meaning for you? Which did you read or use? Did you keep any of them?

- *Betty Crocker's Picture Cook Book*—1950
- *Kon-Tiki* (Thor Heyerdahl)—1950
- *Better Homes and Gardens Garden Book*—1951
- *Better Homes and Gardens Handyman's Book*—1951
- *Anne Frank: The Diary of a Young Girl*—1952
- *The Power of Positive Thinking*—Norman Vincent Peale, 1952
- Revised Standard Version of the *Bible*—1952
- *Tallulah*—Tallulah Bankhead, 1952
- *Sexual Behavior in the Human Female*—Alfred Kinsey, 1953
- *Betty Crocker's Good and Easy Cookbook*—1954
- *The Guinness Book of World Records*—1955
- *Why Johnny Can't Read*—Rudolf Flesch, 1955
- *Gift from the Sea*—Anne Morrow Lindbergh, 1955
- *The Secret of Happiness*—Billy Graham, 1955
- *Better Homes and Gardens Barbecue Book*—1956
- *The Nun's Story*—Kathryn Hume, 1956
- *Profiles in Courage*—John F. Kennedy, 1956
- *The Organization Man*—W. H. Whyte, 1956
- *Kids Say the Darndest Things!*—Art Linkletter, 1957
- *'Twixt Twelve and Twenty*—Pat Boone, 1958
- *Dear Abby*—Abigail Van Buren, 1958
- *The Status Seekers*—Vance Packard, 1959
- *The Elements of Style*—William Strunk, Jr. and E. B. White, 1959

4.   At the movies in the 1950s Following is a sampling of the movies that were popular in the 1950s. Were any of these movies meaningful or especially memorable for you? Who were your favorite movie stars in the 1950s? What movies and stars from this decade aren't mentioned below? (There are many!)

1950
- *All About Eve* (Bette Davis, Anne Baxter, Celeste Holm)
- *The Father of the Bride* (Spencer Tracy, Elizabeth Taylor, Joan Bennett)
- *Born Yesterday* (Judy Holliday, William Holden, Broderick Crawford)

- *Harvey* (James Stewart)
- Walt Disney's animated *Cinderella*

1951
- *African Queen* (Katherine Hepburn, Humphrey Bogart)
- *A Streetcar Named Desire* (Marlon Brando, Vivien Leigh)
- *Death of a Salesman* (Frederic March, Mildred Dunnock)
- *An American in Paris* (Gene Kelly)

1952
- *High Noon* (Gary Cooper, Grace Kelly)
- *Singin' in the Rain* (Gene Kelly, Debbie Reynolds, Donald O'Connor)

1953
- *Roman Holiday* (Audrey Hepburn, Gregory Peck)
- *From Here to Eternity* (Burt Lancaster, Montgomery Clift, Deborah Kerr, Frank Sinatra)
- *The Robe* (Richard Burton, Jean Simmons, Victor Mature)

1954
- *On the Waterfront* (Marlon Brando, Eva Marie Saint)
- *Rear Window* (James Stewart, Grace Kelly)
- *20,000 Leagues Under the Sea* (Kirk Douglas, James Mason)

1955
- *Picnic* (William Holden, Kim Novak, Rosalind Russell)
- *Rebel Without a Cause* (Natalie Wood, James Dean)
- *Blackboard Jungle* (Glenn Ford, Anne Francis)

1956
- *Lust for Life* (Kirk Douglas, Anthony Quinn)
- *The Man in the Grey Flannel Suit* (Gregory Peck, Jennifer Jones, Frederic March)
- *Bus Stop* (Marilyn Monroe)

1957
- *The Bridge on the River Kwai* (William Holden, Alec Guinness, Jack Hawkins)
- *Twelve Angry Men* (Henry Fonda, Lee J. Cobb)
- *Peyton Place* (Lana Turner, Hope Lange)

1958
- *Gigi* (Leslie Caron, Louis Jourdan, Maurice Chevalier)
- *Cat on a Hot Tin Roof* (Elizabeth Taylor, Paul Newman, Burl Ives)
- *Vertigo* (James Stewart, Kim Novak)

1959
- *Pillow Talk* (Doris Day, Rock Hudson, Tony Randall)
- *Some Like It Hot* (Jack Lemmon, Tony Curtis, Marilyn Monroe)
- *The Diary of Anne Frank* (Millie Perkins, Shelley Winters)

Part 4
Life From a Personal Perspective

The last two exercises in this book focus on the big picture of who we are. Exercise 8 is about turning points in our lives—milestone events that changed us—and Exercise 9 is about looking at our best qualities—how we define ourselves overall.

Not all turning points in our lives are happy—though many are—so Exercise 8 may produce strong emotions in some people. That's all right. As always, we are using these exercises to build relationships, sharing both joys and sorrows, and to build self-esteem in each participant. The people in your class have no doubt survived formidable hardships. Make sure they feel proud for doing so. Even people who swear their lives are perfectly ordinary have done extraordinary things.

Exercise 9 gives participants a chance to brag. Most of us don't often receive praise from others or spend much time praising ourselves. Most of us are much more practiced at being self-critical. The last exercise is intended to end this first volume of life-story-sharing exercises on an upbeat note, recognizing our strengths. One of the delightful results I have found in doing this exercise with people who may be involved in some rocky relationships is its ability to change both attitudes and realities. No one wants to be known as a crabby old woman or a stubborn old man. When a woman who has been known by others as "difficult" describes herself as "fun-loving," two things happen. One is that she begins to live up to that (perhaps long forgotten) image of herself. She liked the fun-loving person she once was and decides to draw that person out again. She looks for opportunities to have fun—to liven things up. The second thing that happens is that caregivers or family members who hear her describe herself as fun-loving begin to look for that characteristic in her and draw it out, too. The relationship begins to change.

The last mini-exercise in this volume is about heroes and role models. We are living in an age when it is much easier to disparage people than admire them, and yet the world is filled with amazing human beings who nurture us and inspire us. The last exercise encourages us to build on the goodness of others and pass it on.

Exercise 8: Turning Points

THE BASIC EXERCISE

So far we have talked about moments in our lives, but we haven't really looked at the big picture. One way to do that is to consider the turning points in our lives. There are many ways to look at turning points. This script focuses on discussion, but this is another time when mind mapping works well, especially as a means of showing that tragedies often have a positive element, as is discussed in the script. The end of this exercise provides a sample mind map for a job loss, but any turning point can be mind mapped. Use this technique wherever it seems appropriate to help participants see an event as a growth experience.

KEY ELEMENTS

Most of us haven't given much thought to turning points. We realize they exist in our lives, especially the big things like marriage, children, job opportunities, but we don't connect them to the ways in which they shaped our lives—so this is another exercise in making new associations.

DEMENTIA CONCERNS

As their dementia progresses, people with Alzheimer's disease tend to have increasing difficulty carrying on a conversation, but they still feel the full range of human emotions, so turning points is an important topic. You may find that the mind map process works well because it condenses ideas into short phrases ("lost job," "no future in this field," "back to school") and creates a visual to help participants stay focused. They probably cannot draw their own mind maps, but they can talk about the thoughts that a turning point triggers so that either you as the leader or a volunteer working with them can draw a mind map of their thoughts for them. As always, be aware that they may be able to think about something that they can't necessarily articulate. Watch body language and facial expressions for clues.

One turning point that people with Alzheimer's disease (or any other debilitating disease) have faced is the diagnosis. They are likely to go through the classic signs of mourning: disbelief, anger, bargaining, sadness, and, finally, acceptance. They may not go through all those stages or in that order, but as the disease progresses, most people—if they are well supported by people who love and accept them—come to live each day quite cheerfully. If your group consists of all people with dementia, you may want to make that a specific topic of discussion. If it's an important turning point for only a few people, you might want to put them together for a small discussion group.

THE COMPLETE SCRIPT (Before you begin, please read)

Of all the exercises in this book, this one is most likely to provoke tears, but if you have been doing these in order, your group will have shared a lot by this point and be likely to be supportive of one another. If they do not automatically do so, it is very important that you show your leadership in that regard. If you provide a hug, hold a hand, or give an encouraging word, the rest of the group will do so, too. The goal of this exercise is both to develop a broader understanding of one another and to bolster each other's self-esteem as we recognize what we have triumphed over—or at least learned to live with. Lead with compassion.

► ***Dialogue:*** Today we're going to talk about turning points in our lives. So far we've been talking about "moments" and "incidents," but we haven't looked at the big picture of our lives. We're going to do that today, but I want to start out by asking a simple question.

- Do you think you've had a good life?

Direction: Give participants a chance to answer. If a few people want to elaborate, that's fine. Get a sense of how they define "good." It will quickly become clear that a good life is not one free of tragedy.

A 2005 op-ed piece by Daniel Gilbert in the *New York Times* noted that human beings as a whole are good at seeing the bright side. I've quoted excerpts of it below. Assuming your group has tended to agree that they have had a good life, note that they are not alone.

► ***Dialogue:*** In 2005, Daniel Gilbert wrote an editorial for the *New York Times* that said: "Research suggests that human beings have a remarkable ability to manufacture happiness. For example, when people in experiments are randomly awarded one of two equally valuable prizes, they quickly come to believe that the prize they won was more valuable than the prize they lost." Gilbert noted that even if you offered these people extra cash to swap prizes, they refused, still believing that what they already had was the best. He said this was important, because it illustrated our natural tendency to believe that things turn out for the best. It doesn't mean that bad things don't happen to us, but that we tend to remember the good that came from it. He said that we may dread divorce or financial hardships or a natural disaster, but when they happen, "we recognize them as opportunities to reinvent ourselves, to bond with our neighbors," and to transcend the tragedy. We look for silver linings, and because we are looking, we almost always find them.

We're going to talk about turning points today. Some we chose for ourselves, but many we would not have wished for ourselves or anyone else, and still we found joy in the kindness of others or the new opportunities we wouldn't have otherwise known. Helen Keller said, "The world is full of suffering; it is also full of the overcoming of it."

Direction: Obviously, some people do not see silver linings. Some people are defeated by tragedy and that compounds the tragedy. Others, Gilbert noted, like

Abraham Lincoln are spurred to action by their melancholy and do great things in spite of their despair. They never know how far their influence has reached over the years, and that in itself is a kind of miracle—that someone who saw his life as far short of his goals, has inspired many others to carry on. If your group does not mention those who do not overcome their despair, you may choose not to bring it up at this point.

Begin this discussion by making some lists of possible turning points. You can talk about them in greater detail a little bit later.

▶ **Dialogue:**   I'd like us to begin to talk about turning points by making some lists of where to look for the turning points in our lives. Let's start by talking about "firsts." Can you name some of the firsts in your life that might have been turning points?

Direction: If people don't come up with their own, you can suggest a few:

- First day of school, or first day you discovered you could read
- First close friend or first pet
- First job (babysitting, paper route, or something bigger)
- First kiss or first time you fell in love (discovering the power of attraction!)
- First day of college or first day in the military
- Birth of first child
- First time you recognized injustice

Write participants' ideas on a flip chart or white board. Then give them time to talk a little about which of these firsts really were turning points for them, and what they meant.

The dialogue lists a number of things that are potential positive events. You may want to ask about each individually rather than as one massive group.

▶ **Dialogue:**   We've touched on some of the firsts that are life events. Are there other positive life events that were turning points you want to talk about? For example:

- Sometimes we are influenced by a particular teacher or a subject that we hadn't known we were interested in.

- Sometimes it isn't a first job that matters, but a career choice or a career change.

- Sometimes new adventures begin because we move to a new city or country.

- Sometimes we discover new things about ourselves when we take a vacation or serve as a volunteer.

- Sometimes we discover we have a talent or an affinity for doing something that causes us to start in a new direction.

- Sometimes hard-won success is a turning point.

- Sometimes we are just in the right place at the right time.

Talk about the turning points that happened in your life because of personal choices or good fortune or mentors.

Direction: This could be a long discussion all by itself and may lead in other directions, but when participants have had their say, change direction slightly and talk about the "little things" that made a difference in your life.

▶ ***Dialogue:*** Sometimes it's not anything dramatic that marks a turning point in our lives; sometimes it's just a "little epiphany." Here's what one 86-year-old woman said in Wendy Lustbader's book *What's Worth Knowing* as she sat at her kitchen table just day-dreaming while the sunlight faded in and out from the clouds:

> All of a sudden, a sunbeam crossed my kitchen table and lit up my crystal saltshaker. There were all kinds of colors and sparkles. It was one of the most beautiful sights I'd ever seen. But you know, that very same saltshaker had been on that kitchen table for over 50 years. Surely there must have been other mornings when the sun crossed the table like that, but I was just too busy getting things done. I wondered what else I'd missed. I realized this was it, this was grace. (p. 76)

Have you ever had a little moment like that when life changed for you?

Direction: Give participants a chance to respond. Although we are trying to present this discussion in a logical progression that begins with the discussion of only positive events, it may not turn out that way. If your discussion doesn't flow the way we have outlined it here, don't worry. Try to cover all the ground within this topic—that is, both positive and negative events—but if conversation is flowing well, don't stop it prematurely. The script is only a guideline. It is possible that the above topic could take all of your remaining time, or lead naturally into the other aspects of turning points outlined below without any further intervention from you.

This is the shortest of the exercises in terms of scripted pages, but because turning points are usually something we feel strongly about, discussion is likely to quickly fill in for unscripted dialogue.

If conversation does wind down naturally, move on to discussing how big things, such as world events, may have influenced your participants' lives.

▶ ***Dialogue:*** Let's move on to talking about how your lives may have been influenced by world events. For example, if you lived through the Great Depression, World War II, the Korean or Vietnam conflicts, or the struggle for equal rights, chances are they affected you in some way. Perhaps you fought in a war, struggled to find a job, or became active in a political movement. Most people have vivid memories of seminal events they lived through, such as the bombing of Pearl Harbor, the death of Franklin Roosevelt, President Kennedy's assassination, and the assassination of Martin Luther King, Jr. Talk about an event in world or national history—which may be either positive or negative—and how it changed you or changed the direction of your life.

Direction: This, too, is a huge topic. Not all life-changing events were the result of national tragedies. For example, some people have *happy* memories of becoming involved in the movements for equal rights of African Americans and women. If you are working with people now in their 50s or 60s, they may have fond memories of being flower children, hippies, or active in the Peace Movement. People who served in the military often leave the service with lifelong friends and a sense of having been part of something important, in spite of whatever hardships they endured.

Give people a chance to talk about how national and world events may have been influential in shaping them. Then—if this hasn't come up earlier—discuss with your group the personal tragedies they have endured. If you haven't used the mind map technique earlier in this session, this is an especially good time to do it, because our goal in this last section is to talk not just about tragedy, but about who and what helped us endure those difficult times.

Sample Mind Map:
One Thought Leads to Another

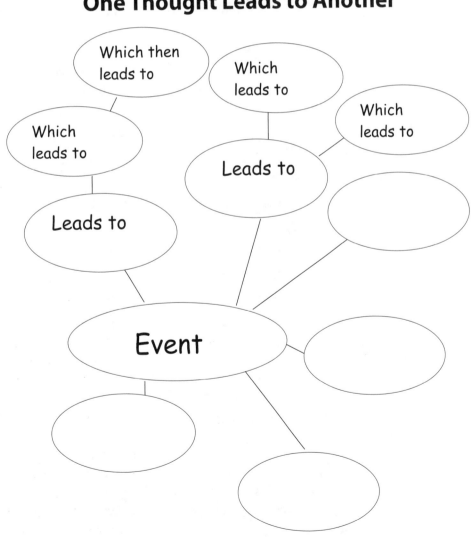

Dialogue: Now I'd like us to talk about the personal tragedies that we've endured—the turning points that you wouldn't have chosen, such as the loss of a job or a divorce or a health issue or the death of someone close to you.

- How did such events affect you and how did you get through them? Did they ultimately turn out all right?

Is anyone willing to share a personal experience?

Direction: Give participants a moment to respond, as some may not want to jump right into this. When someone does respond, give the person a chance to tell the story, and then ask if the person minds if you mind map the event. A blank mind map is found on page 197 (and on the CD). The example below illustrates a lost job. Fill in the central event and the negative effects in the out-lying bubbles, but then connect those negative bubbles with more bubbles that explain how the person began to move on again. The human spirit is quite amazing in its ability to regenerate itself through the love of family and friends, through faith and by sheer force of will.

Sample Mind Map: Lost Job

Once you have done this with one event for one individual, ask for others to tell their stories. Try to mind map their stories, too. In all these life-story-sharing classes we are emphasizing talking over writing, but many people will find that if you put their story on a piece of flip chart paper, even in this simple form—here's the tragic event; here's what happened next; and here's how I moved on—they have a concrete sense of accomplishment.

But for many people, moving on did not come easily. Talk about that, too.

▶ *Dialogue:* Most of us have endured a lot of things in our lives. Sometimes when something bad happens we can bounce back quickly and other times it is much more difficult. What makes the difference?

Direction: Give participants a chance to share their ideas. Pay attention to their answers, because the people or things that can bring us back from despair are vital to who we are as human beings. If you want to have a strong relationship with someone, knowing what that person needs in times of sorrow is key. Plus, the stories they tell are marvelous.

▶ *Dialogue:* Sometimes we're proud of a turning point because it means we've accomplished a goal or given up a bad habit or gained new confidence. Talk about a turning point that makes you proud. Does anyone want to volunteer?

Direction: Give participants a chance to respond.

▶ *Dialogue:* The last thing I would like to talk about are missed opportunities, especially those that are legends within your family. In *A Celebration of American Family Folklore,* there are a series of stories that illustrate what I mean. For example, a teenage girl in Massachusetts tells this family story:

> My great-grandfather was a great traveler. He'd go off for years at a time, and my great-grandmother would never see him. She'd just be suffering along trying to make do until one day he'd walk in and say, "I'm home!" "Yes, I see that," she'd say. But he went out west with two other men and they bought a small claim. And they didn't have enough money to try it out. So they had to sell it for fifty dollars. The man who bought it tried it out and it became very famous. It was known as the Comstock Lode. And now it's a great symbol of remorse in our family. (p. 89)

Direction: It should be noted that the Comstock Lode (discovered in the late 1850s) was considered the richest silver deposit in American history, but various web sites give conflicting stories on how it was discovered. My guess is that this young girl's story is more legend than fact, but it makes a great story, and is symbolic of many family stories of missed opportunities.

▶ *Dialogue:* Are there any stories in your family about real estate investments passed by, jewels lost, or other missed opportunities? Talk about them.

Direction: Give participants a chance to vent a bit on this one. Most people at least *think* they have missed a chance to get rich at some point in their lives, and some of the stories are quite funny.

▶ *Dialogue:* Now let's talk again for a few minutes about opportunities that you might have turned around. You thought you were going to miss out in some way, but managed to turn things right. Let me give you another example paraphrased from the *Celebration* book:

> On the day of the opening of the Golden Gate Bridge, my dad was about 17. He and a friend thought they could be the first people to cross it, but when they went down early in the morning to the bridge, there were already about 5,000 people there, some in track suits. They realized they didn't have a chance to be the first to cross it, so they went into San Francisco and bought a checkerboard. When the bridge opened, they went to the middle and sat down and played checkers. So now they can say they were the first people to play checkers on the Golden Gate Bridge. (p. 44)

Are there any stories like that in your family—of substituting one goal for another when the first thing didn't work?

Direction: Give participants a chance to tell their stories. Close this session by thanking participants for sharing their turning points, and perhaps by applauding each other's strengths.

Resources for Digging Deeper—Exercise 8

The idea of writing about turning points appears in virtually every book on writing autobiographies, because these tend to be the dramatic moments that make a good story, but the book that was my inspiration for this exercise was *Family Tales, Family Wisdom* by Robert U. Akeret et al. Although the book is now quite old and out of print (available used on-line), I still think it provides great ideas for helping older adults tell their stories. Akeret actually stretches out the topic of turning points into four chapters from which I have adapted some of his ideas in Exercise 8 and Mini-Exercise H.

As noted in greater detail under Exercise 4, my resource for mind mapping was Joyce Wycoff's *Mindmapping, Your Personal Guide to Exploring Creativity and Problem-Solving.* Once again, I have used *A Celebration of American Family Folklore* by Steven J. Zeitlin et al. as a wonderful source of stories to prime the pump for your participants telling their own.

Mini-Exercise H: Telegrams and Letting Go

1.   Telegrams. Thinking of turning points tends to put us in mind of the people who have been influential in our lives—in both good and bad ways. If we quit a job because we had a terrible boss, we learned something about the person we didn't want to be—neither someone like that boss nor someone who would work for such a boss. If we had an outstanding teacher who influenced our career or a grandparent who was a childhood comfort, we learned something about the person we *did* want to become.

Robert Akeret, one of the authors of *Family Tales, Family Wisdom* (See Resources for Digging Deeper) suggests we write telegrams to the people who influenced us. Telegrams are short and to the point. "Thank you for being a terrific teacher. You made a wonderful difference in my life." If the teacher is no longer living, write the telegram anyway and send it with your thoughts out into the universe. It is like a prayer of gratitude and who knows what happens to such prayers?

If you have harbored ill will toward the bad boss, recognize what you learned because of him, and send him a telegram, too. If you can forgive him, that's terrific, but if not, write down your angry thoughts and burn the telegram, sending it out into the universe through smoke.

If the person who helped you through a hard time is still living, send a thank-you note. It doesn't need to be longer than the telegram; just send a line saying you were thinking of him and wanted to express your gratitude. Most of us never know what our acts of goodwill toward another mean to that person, and once we have done a favor or a kindness, we usually forget about it. To be reminded that it still resonates is like getting a precious gift.

2.   **Letting go.** One of the best uses I have found for mind maps is as a means of letting go. When we talk about turning points, some people dredge up old anxieties. Most of us have at least something in our past we wish we would have done differently. And if our lives are stressed, many of us are anxious about something every day. Mind map those anxieties out of your life. Put the phrase "I give up" in the center bubble. Then draw bubbles around it that list all of the things you want to give up, such as:

- Guilt,
- Trying to do too much,
- Trying to please everyone, and
- Always putting responsibility before pleasure.

Then draw more bubbles extending from each of those bubbles that tell what you intend to do instead or that give you affirmation:

- I am doing the best I can, and that's pretty darn good most of the time.
- I can leave some things undone; I can ask for help from others.
- Some people are not worth pleasing.
- I am going to do *something* for my own pleasure each day.

We all have different things we need to give up—anger, bitterness, feeling hurt, regret, or obsessing over something insignificant in the larger scheme of things. Whatever it is, mind map an alternative plan, post it where you see it daily, and practice it.

Exercise 9: **Best Qualities**

THE BASIC EXERCISE

Many of us grew up with the admonition to avoid being proud—or simply being told that we had no reason to be so because we didn't pick up our clothes, take out the garbage, or get an A in algebra. Consequently, the primary purpose of this exercise is to build self-esteem by giving participants credit for all their best qualities. We also hope that you and others who interact with the participants in other venues will gain some insight into how they see themselves and how they want to be seen by others. The second half of the exercise—which you may not choose to do—is intended to help participants better understand someone they are close to or would like to be closer to.

This is one of the simplest exercises in this book and one of the most effective as well. However, many of its strengths are subtle, so I have provided long explanations of things to look for. Read them before you conduct the class, but don't let them interfere with the spontaneous fun of this exercise.

PROPS AND MATERIALS

Since this is an exercise that requires people to circle items on a chart, it's a good idea to provide writing utensils. Simple pencils will do, but I encourage you to consider colored pencils, markers, even stickers (stars, smiley faces) so that people have a sense of celebration as they note their good qualities.

Some people may want to take extra copies of the Best Qualities handout (see Appendix C) to share with others, so be sure to make more than enough copies.

ONE-ON-ONE

If you want to have a good visit with someone, you can ask the person to fill out the form, and then add your own comments on positive traits you think the person has missed.

This is also a good way to find out how a person would *like* to be seen. If a woman describes herself as considerate and you happen to see her as rude, ask for more input in a diplomatic way. For example, you might say, "I imagine that as you raised your family you often had to sacrifice your own desires to be considerate of their needs. Can you give me examples of things you did?" If you then start looking for ways in which that person *is* considerate—or trying to be—and you notice and appreciate that trait, you might also find that your relationship improves. Most of us go through each day trying to be good, and most of the time it isn't noticed by anyone, but any crabby comment we make is.

Also if you are assisting someone with care, you might say something like: "I took a class in which we had to name our best qualities—things like being fun-loving or compassionate. If I asked you what you think are your best qualities, what would you say?" Then add your own assessment of any good qualities the person failed to mention.

KEY ELEMENTS

The fun in this exercise is generated in praising yourself—something we are seldom given permission to do—and in getting praise from others. It's a feel-good session, through and through.

DEMENTIA CONCERNS

People with dementia may need assistance in naming their qualities. Rather than giving them the whole sheet at once, it may be best to name two or three characteristics at a time. "Do you think of yourself as adventurous, someone who likes to try new things?" If they agree they are, follow up with a related question: "Do you think you are a risk taker, or just high-spirited? Or are you both?" If they don't see themselves as adventurous, go for characteristics in another direction: "Do you think you are a kind and considerate person?" If they say yes, you might ask, "Are you generous, too?" There are many characteristics on this list that could be easily paired such as:

- Diplomatic and peacemaker
- Cheerful and optimistic
- Supportive and empathetic
- Courageous and bold
- Fun-loving and young at heart
- Intelligent and quick-witted (people with dementia lose some of their brain connections, but not their intelligence)
- Patient and forgiving

When you get a yes answer, encourage people to tell you more if they can, without putting them on the spot. Always look for stories. Do they see themselves as adventurous because they climbed a mountain or because they like to keep learning new things? Those are different definitions of adventurous, but both are valid.

Also read the directions under the one-on-one section above in which we noted the importance of understanding how people see themselves. Many people we might label as "constantly critical" may see themselves as having "high standards and expectations"—of themselves and others.

On the other hand, feel free to point out characteristics on the list for which they may not have given themselves credit. Most people do not think of themselves as courageous, for example, but anyone with Alzheimer's disease or any serious illness has probably shown courage just by getting up and facing each day. Use this list to give the person with dementia compliments that you might not have otherwise thought to do. If a person is a constant walker, praise the energy; if a person is known to always look for sweet treats, praise the decisiveness or the determination. Remember that we all like to be thought of as attractive, so find something to praise—a smile, pale blue eyes, soft hands. If a person protests and says, "Oh, I'm not that," you can always follow up by saying, "And you're modest, too."

THE COMPLETE SCRIPT

▶ *Dialogue:*   Today we're going to spend some time looking at our best characteristics and qualities. This is a simple exercise, but it's an important one. How many of you grew up in a household where you were taught that pride was a character flaw or praise was hard to come by?

Direction: Give people a little time to answer that. Up until perhaps 30 years ago, many, maybe most, children were criticized on a regular basis in order to teach them to keep reaching for higher goals. Girls in particular were taught that modesty and self-sacrifice for the men in their lives were virtues. In more recent years some parents are being criticized for going to the opposite extreme, giving praise so easily that children's expectations of themselves may actually be lowered. That's not a debate we are encouraging you to have with your participants, but the fact is that most of us have spent our lifetimes trying to be good people and we're overdue to take time to look at what's best about us. *Note:* Print out two copies of the handout for Exercise 9 (page 187) for each participant.

▶ *Dialogue:*   You have a handout with two identical forms. Each has a list of 75 positive qualities. I want you to begin with the first one and mark it up for yourself. Be generous to yourself. Circle every quality that you think applies to you and then try to think of things not on the list and add them to the bottom of the list.

I'm going to give you about 5 minutes to do this before we stop to discuss your answers, but take more time if you need it. If you haven't given yourself the praise you deserve in a year or more, 5 minutes is hardly enough, but it is a beginning.

Direction: If you have provided colored pencils and stickers, encourage people to decorate their sheets as they highlight their best qualities.

Answer any questions participants may have, but then give them some quiet time to concentrate. I used to ask people to circle a limited number of characteristics—15 or 20—but then I stopped for four reasons:

1. I found people were spending their time debating "Am I more A or more B?" instead of basking in the glory of having potentially 75 wonderful characteristics.
2. Lots of people emphasize in their own way the things they feel most strongly about by adding thicker circles or stars around those items. When you ask them in the next step to pick a sampling of what they circled, they automatically tend to pick those.
3. Participants also tend to naturally do some self-evaluation as they go through the list if there are no restrictions on it. They may say to them-

selves, "Well, I used to be zany and fun-loving, and I want to draw that person out more. I'm going to circle those." Alternatively, they decide to forego circling them at this time, but decide they will become that zany, fun-loving person in the months ahead.

4. If you give them a limited number of characteristics, they won't add any others to the bottom of the list and what they perceive as missing from the list can be the most revealing of all.

When you think participants have had enough time to go through the list, ask for a few volunteers to tell you their qualities. I have never had a group where there weren't people who were eager to speak up. Most people haven't been asked in many years what they think their strengths are, and this exercise is freeing.

▶ *Dialogue:* Who would like to share some best qualities? Is there a volunteer who will give us a sampling?

Direction: If you have a small group, give everyone a chance to share. Here is where you can limit the number of qualities they name by asking for 10 or 15 that they are especially pleased to mention. Don't be a stickler about it since lists can be read quickly. If someone says she is proud to say she circled 70 of the 75, tell her that's terrific, but resist the temptation to ask what she *didn't* circle because it's what she wants others to know about her that is important—what she *is,* not what she thinks she is *not.*

If it is a group of people who know each other—or through meeting for the exercises in this book have gotten to know each other—ask for affirmation from the group: "Who would agree that these are some of Mary's wonderful characteristics?" (Most people will do so willingly, in part because they hope the group will agree when they read their own lists.) Then ask, "Does anyone think Mary missed one of her most outstanding qualities in this sampling? Do you have anything else to add?" If no one in the group adds anything, be ready to add something yourself. For example, "Well, I would add 'mysterious' to Mary's list because in these meetings I have gotten to know all kinds of things about Mary that I would have never guessed about her life." Or "I would add 'bold' since Mary bravely started the discussion."

In a small group you may also have time to ask follow-up questions, such as "Why do you see yourself as a risk taker? Can you tell us about a time you took a risk?" As always, it's the stories behind the lists that are most revealing in helping us to build a relationship with that person.

That's also the reason that if you have a large group—more than 20 people—it's best to divide them into smaller groups of 4–6 people and give them perhaps 10 minutes for sharing among the people in the smaller group. That way everyone is heard by at least some of the other people in the room. Give the small group instructions to: 1) affirm those qualities in each person that they have witnessed; 2) add to them if they know the person and feel the person has left out something important; and 3) ask for the stories behind the quality.

If you do divide into smaller groups, be sure to give a spokesperson from each group a chance to summarize or present highlights to the whole group about what they learned. That doesn't mean repeating each person's list of qualities, but perhaps telling stories that formed the qualities. For example, "Jane said she learned patience and flexibility from raising seven children, and Mary said she learned determination from growing up in a family of eight children and fighting for her share of the meal." That tells us something interesting and helps us understand them better.

Once everyone who wants to speak has been given the opportunity, be sure to ask about what they added to the bottom line.

▶ *Dialogue:*   Did anyone add any qualities that weren't on the list?

Direction: If anyone did, encourage those people to share what they added, and, if there is time, to say why each addition is an attribute that helps define them.

Sometimes people have a hard time seeing what is missing from the list, so you might suggest a few qualities: persevering, easy-going, sweet, affectionate, organized, versatile, observant, and so on. (Looking through a thesaurus helps.)

One thing that comes up fairly often is "sexy." On the list "sensuous" and "vivacious" are as close as we come to mentioning sexy, and sensuous can also mean being attuned to things which stimulate the senses—fragrances, textures, beauty, savory food. Vivacious may simply mean bubbly and enthusiastic. The main reason we left "sexy" off is to avoid controversy if this exercise is done intergenerationally with children. In addition, while sex remains a great delight to many older people, it can also be a source of sorrow for those who have lost a spouse or produce feelings of inadequacy in those whose body image isn't strong. Since our emphasis is on making people feel good, we didn't want to include any obvious words that might trigger self-doubt. When participants bring "sexy" up themselves, I think it's great. For those who have—or can find—a partner, an active sex life tends to be good for both physical and mental health throughout one's life span.

Now move on to savoring the list participants have created.

▶ *Dialogue:*   Now that you've created and shared this list that describes how wonderful you are, I'd like you to save and savor it. Most of us accept praise badly. Someone tells us, "What a lovely outfit you're wearing!" and we tend to say, "Oh, this old thing; I've had it for years." That is rejecting a gift. We think we are simply being modest, but we are actually being ungracious. If I give you a compliment, I do it to make you feel good, but I also do it to make myself feel good for saying something nice. If you refuse the compliment, you don't feel good for the praise I gave you, and I don't feel good because you didn't accept that praise. How much better we would both feel if you said, "Thank you. That's kind of you to say. I like this outfit, too."

So why am I telling you this? Because we've just spent some time talking about all our good qualities, praising ourselves, and if we now just put it aside and refuse to truly accept the compliment we've given ourselves, this exercise won't be much good. Here's my request:

Fold this paper and put it somewhere safe—in your purse, your wallet, in your sock drawer—somewhere that you are likely to see it often or at least be able to take it out if you want to. Then every time you are having a day when you are feeling a little blue and inadequate, I want you to pull it out and slowly read every quality on the list. Say "I am this and this and this," naming each quality. Maybe you made a mistake or lost your temper, but that doesn't change the essential you. Read the qualities and believe them. Bask in them. Will you do that for me?

Direction: Even though this is a compliment participants have given themselves, I have found that people do treasure the list and return to it for a personal boost. They may not feel patient on a particular day, but by looking at the list, they realize that they are more often than not; patience is one of their qualities, and to see it in print and circled, somehow gives it greater validity. This is positive self-talk in black and white.

If people in your group know each other well, you might think it's a good idea to put each person's name at the top of one form and pass them around in the group asking the other members to put checkmarks next to the qualities of the person whose name is on top of the form. In fact, it can have a negative effect, because our minds too often work in perverse ways. Instead of being pleased that five out of six people labeled you "loving" you will wonder why the sixth person didn't. If you think being cheerful is one of your best qualities and no one checked it, you will wonder why. This particular exercise is designed for us to compliment ourselves and works best in that way.

1.   **You may choose to close the session here** and simply encourage participants to share the second form with someone they care for to be filled out by that person.
2.   Alternatively, you may choose to continue this exercise in the manner described below.

▶ ***Dialogue:*** You will note that we have given you two copies of this list. The second list is for you to fill out for someone you care for. This can be a friend, a spouse, a child, or parent—anyone you are close to. Many parents find it useful to fill this out for a teenage child and teenagers find it useful to fill it out on a parent. Many family caregivers find it useful to fill out about their care receiver. If you are a professional caregiver and take care of lots of people, then consider filling it out for a care receiver with whom you would like to have a better relationship.

When we are close to someone, we are usually aware of that person's faults as well as their good qualities, and perhaps there are a few things that drive you crazy about this person. Remember that for this exercise we are only going to circle positive qualities or add to the bottom of the list qualities not shown here. If, for example, your teenager is driving you crazy because he is always looking for a way to circumvent the rules you have laid down, describe him as "enterprising." If he is a "risk taker" but one who lacks judgment about the consequences of those risks, still try to see the positive side of his willingness to try new things.

But also recognize that while I am pushing you to look for strengths, not flaws in this person's character, I want you to fill it out without having any intention of showing it to that person. The purpose of this exercise is solely for you to gain a new perspective.

Direction: I have often found that once people have paused to be gentle with themselves, they are more willing to look for the good in others, so filling out the form on a person for whom they have mixed feelings is a step toward transforming the relationship. Although I have done this exercise most often with family and professional caregivers who then fill out a form on their care receiver, it also works well among:

- Older adults or residents in long-term care settings considering spouses, adult children, or other relatives (especially if they have felt neglected by that person);
- Parents of teenagers, as noted above (and teenagers considering their parents); and
- Supervisors considering staff and vice versa.

The reason I emphasize not sharing the list with the person directly is the same reason I gave above for not letting someone else fill out a form about you. If I show you this list of 75 qualities and fail to circle even one, you may be upset that I don't regard you as that. On the other hand, if I circle "zany" and you don't view that trait in the same positive light that I do, you may say, "Zany? Why do you think I'm zany?" and completely miss my good intentions. And if in filling out the form, I am censoring my own true feelings in order to please the person to whom I am going to show it, I have defeated the purpose of the exercise.

The goal of this part of the exercise is simply to step back and remember that person's strengths. If I am my husband's caregiver and I have been overwhelmed by the responsibilities I now have, it helps to stop and think about the man I fell in love with who was friendly and kind, a mentor to others, a problem solver—and to see what remains of those fine characteristics. It may also help me to be more patient, understanding his own frustrations with what he can no longer be or do.

Similarly, if I am a professional caregiver and I have begun to dread having to care for Mrs. Smith, if I can stop and look again for her good qualities—try to see her life through her eyes—chances are my change in attitude will be felt by her and we will have an improved relationship.

That can also work in other situations and other relationships.

Give participants a chance to share what they have learned in filling out the form a second time.

▶ ***Dialogue:*** Who would like to share the characteristics of the person they were thinking of in this second part of the exercise?

Direction: Again, there is usually someone who has had an awakening in doing this and is eager to share. Another thing I have found in doing this with professional caregivers is that once one person describes Mrs. Jones as sensitive and kind, others tend to chime in with other good qualities and examples. Suddenly the person who was only seen as someone with *dis*abilities—needing help with bathing, eating, and so on—is seen with wonderful abilities remaining.

And while I still don't recommend that you show that care receiver the form, it would be lovely to have you tell her of all the good qualities you see in her.

▶ *Dialogue:* Now that you've thought about the good qualities of the people on your second form, I hope you will compliment them the next time you see them. And keep those qualities in mind the next time you are frustrated with that person!

Potential Closing: If this is your last meeting and you are not going to do the mini-exercises, you may want to have some ceremony of closure. Think about how much you've learned about each other through all these exercises. Express your gratitude. Eat cake!

▶ *Dialogue:* Thank you all very much for your participation. I've enjoyed getting to know you. I hope you've enjoyed getting to know each other.

Resources for Digging Deeper—Exercise 9

Exercise 9 is an adaptation of an activity I have done with groups for more than 20 years, so there is no particular book I can recommend directly related to it. There are probably thousands of books on building self-esteem, and choosing one that is right for you is a matter of going to a bookstore or library and looking for one that you find appealing. It really is a matter of personal preference.

As for digging deeper as you look for personal heroes (the topic of the mini-exercise that follows), one way I have found my heroes is by reading books of quotes. When I read a quote I like, it often makes me want to know more about that person, so I read more. Books of quotes are a quick way to expose myself to a wide variety of thinkers. Here are just a few short books of quotes that are among my favorites (See References for more details):

- *Funny Ladies* by Bill Adler
- *Pearls of Wisdom* by Jerome Agel and Walter Glanze
- *"Age doesn't matter unless you're a cheese"* by Katherine and Ross Petras
- *Brilliance* compiled by Dan Zadra

Although not a book of quotes, Wendy Lustbader's compilation of *What's Worth Knowing* based on her interviews of dozens of older adults definitely has many quotable passages. (See References.)

The only activity book I know on the subject of heroes is by Jean Vetter and is simply called *Heroes* (ElderSong © 2002). It offers brief biographies (less than a page each) of about 35 people, mostly Americans from Patrick Henry to Christopher Reeve, and including the sled dog Balto and comic book superstars. The bios are followed by four ways to take the topic further:

- Point/counterpoint (discussion questions)
- Taking credit where it's due (simple ways you may have done something similar in your own life)
- Group fun (which ranges from debates to sing-alongs and word games)
- Furthermore (other things that happened in a critical year related to this person, including news, books, songs, movies, and sports)

The list is broad enough to cover people I would not have considered (i.e., supports multiple political viewpoints) while offering tantalizing facts on people whom some participants may want to study further.

Mini-Exercise I: Heroes and Role Models

1. Tell us about the people who influenced you. When we think of our best qualities, we usually owe them to someone we admire or admired. Who were your heroes and role models when you were growing up?

- Some of us had a parent, grandparent, sibling, aunt or uncle, or other relative whom we respected.
- Others were influenced by a teacher or a religious leader.
- Others were determined to become Nancy Drew or Superman, taking our heroes from fiction or even comic books or TV.
- Many young boys and girls took their heroes from sports.
- Others were influenced by national and international celebrities such as Gandhi, Martin Luther King, Jr., Albert Schweitzer, Einstein, or Gregory Peck or Katherine Hepburn—the possibilities are endless.
- Some of us were influenced by a role model in a career that we wanted to pursue—art, medicine, business, science.

Give participants a chance to think about their answers and talk about what they gained from these people.

2. Tell us about your present heroes. Most of us learned over time that the people we admired had flaws. In some cases that was a bitter disappointment; in other cases it simply meant it was okay to be human. Think about who your heroes are now.

- Have your heroes changed over time? Have you dropped some, added others?
- Have the characteristics you admire in others changed? In what ways?
- Do you think we live in an era when heroes are harder to find because the popular media exposes their flaws? Or are they harder to find because the media tells us too much about the wrong people—celebrities vs. the people who are working hard to make real differences in the world?
- What do you think makes a person a hero or a role model in today's world?

3. Heroes as dinner partners. In the 1970s Steve Allen produced a series of television programs called "Meeting of Minds" in which he imagined the dinner conversation among a disparate group of famous historical figures. For example, shows #5 and #6 featured Charles Darwin, Emily Dickinson, Galileo Galilei, and Attila the Hun. If you could have dinner with anyone you wanted from the present day or history, who would you choose and why?

If you have trouble thinking of people, I've put together some combinations below to consider. They are meant to stimulate your ideas, not limit them.

If your interests lie outside the areas shown below, make your own lists. I do not expect you to want to have dinner with everyone in any group or even anyone in a group. If there is an accomplished person you admire, choose that person, regardless of whether the name is on the list below. Then tell us why.

Accomplished Women
- Helen Keller
- Margaret Mead
- Maria Montessori
- Eleanor Roosevelt
- Gloria Steinem

American Politicians
- George Bush (Senior or Junior)
- Jimmy Carter
- Bill or Hillary Clinton
- John McCain
- Your governor or senator

Artists
- Leonardo Da Vinci
- Frida Kahlo
- Grandma Moses
- Pablo Picasso
- Andy Warhol

Authors
- Jane Austen
- Agatha Christie
- Ernest Hemingway
- Jack Kerouac
- William Shakespeare

Businessmen
- Andrew Carnegie
- Walt Disney
- Henry Ford
- Bill Gates

Explorers/Adventurers
- Neil Armstrong
- Edmund Hillary
- Lewis and Clark
- Magellan

Historical Figures
- Aristotle
- Winston Churchill
- Benjamin Franklin
- Sigmund Freud
- Abraham Lincoln

Inventors
- Marie Curie
- Thomas Edison
- Buckminster Fuller
- Isaac Newton

Musicians
- Ludwig van Beethoven
- Duke Ellington
- John Lennon
- Itzhak Perlman

Religious Leaders
- Confucius
- Martin Luther King, Jr.
- Dalai Lama
- Moses
- Mother Teresa

Royalty
- King Arthur
- Princess Diana
- Elizabeth I
- Queen Victoria

Wits
- Woody Allen
- Dorothy Parker
- Will Rogers
- Mark Twain

World Leaders
- Tony Blair
- Mahatma Gandhi
- Mikhail Gorbachev
- Nelson Mandela

Appendixes

Appendix A:
When Participants Have Dementia

One of the things we tend to forget is that the brain craves novelty. Human beings are naturally curious. That doesn't disappear with dementia, which means that people with memory impairments are as likely to enjoy reminiscing and sharing their stories as anyone else. Nevertheless, it is wise to be aware of some of the challenges they may face in doing so. Dementia, by definition, is progressive, so early in their disease process, people may communicate quite easily and well. Over time, they may need greater accommodation.

First, a little perspective: There are many forms of dementia, but the most common is still Alzheimer's disease (AD), so that is what we will concentrate on here. Many people think people with Parkinson's disease or those who have had a massive stroke have dementia because their words may be slurred or mumbled or they are slow to respond. ***Never* underestimate the people with whom you are trying to share stories.** Whatever difficulties they have, chances are great that they understand much more than they can express.

If I could give only three rules for communicating effectively with a person with dementia or speech difficulties, they would be the following:

1. **Be patient.** Many times it takes an enormous effort for people to "tune in" to the topic and process the information. Trying to rush them to express their thoughts flusters them. Trying to move on too quickly to another topic when you don't get an immediate response confuses them.

2. **Keep your sense of humor.** One of the blessings within Alzheimer's disease is that people do not lose the ability to smile until they are very close to death. People with dementia are drawn to laughter just as we all are, and they are often surprisingly witty themselves. Enjoy them.

3. **Relax.** Anyone who has worked with people with dementia for any length of time will tell you that they have an uncanny ability to pick up on body language and demeanor. If you are nervous around them, they are likely to be nervous, too. If you relax and accept them as they are, they will relax, too. So you make a mistake? So they will forgive you, just as you would forgive them.

COMMON CHANGES TO KEEP IN MIND

When a person has Alzheimer's disease, it means that certain parts of his or her brain have been damaged. Exactly which parts and how that person is affected varies among individuals. Many people with AD have either expressive aphasia (difficulty speaking coherently) or receptive aphasia (difficulty understanding what is being said). Often the challenges this represents can be overcome if we simply follow the three rules above: relax, keep our sense of humor, and remain patient. Additionally, here are some specific things to consider:

- **People often have trouble remembering names.** (Don't we all?) Make it easier by always introducing yourself, even if you're the daughter. ("Hi, Mom; it's me, Susie. I'm here for our regular Tuesday lunch.") If you're a professional caregiver, introduce yourself even if you're wearing a name badge—often the print is too small for older adults to see. Many people (especially spouses and daughters) tend to be hurt by the inability of a person to call them by name. My colleague Mary Lucero tells the story of a tearful daughter who confronted her mother with dementia saying, "Mom, I'm not going to stay if you can't tell me what my name is." The mother, doing the best she could, said to her daughter, "Well, Honey, if you don't know who you are, how should I know?"

- **People mix up relationships.** It is quite common for a woman in an adult day center to ask, "When is my mother coming to pick me up?" She means "daughter," but the word "mother" comes out, either because of language deficits and "mother" is the only word she can think of to express a close relationship, or because she is living in a past reality now and imagines herself in her twenties, so that 50-something woman who comes to get her each day must be her mother.

- Be aware that **as short-term memory diminishes, people may think they are living in a past reality**—when they were young parents or even when they were children themselves. But also be aware that they may slip in and out of that time period. A person talking about playing with her young children one minute may suddenly be talking about playing with her siblings the next. A woman who remembers she is a widow one minute may think of herself as a young bride a few minutes later. Sequencing of events can be equally difficult because of this time travel. Try to go with the flow. It may be disconcerting for you, but it is often surprisingly easy for the person with dementia.

- **People may have great confusion over numbers.** When you are reminiscing with someone with dementia, it is natural for most of us to say things like: "When did that happen?" or "How long ago was that?" or "How many years were you married?"—all of which can be impossible for people with dementia to answer. I once inadvertently embarrassed a woman by asking how many children she had, something she was sure she was supposed to know but didn't. She vacillated between 4 and 8 and finally settled on 6, but I have no idea whether that was the actual number. (Nor could she reliably remember their names or how many were boys or girls—perhaps partly because she kept confusing them with her siblings.)

  - The rule with number questions related to time is: Try not to ask them. We may feel an urgency to ground ourselves in a certain time frame, but chances are the person with dementia is unconcerned, and any answer you get may vary by the reality the person is living in at the moment.

- The rule with number questions related to amounts is: Don't ask those either. If quantity is really important, try to get a range: "Do you come from a large family?" or "Did you have several different jobs in your career or did you stick to one?"

- **Generalities tend to substitute for specifics.** People with dementia have a tremendous need to feel safe and secure. This shows up in their language, too. If you say, "Tell me about the house in which you grew up," and I'm not able to articulate all the things I may be picturing in my mind, I am likely to play it safe, and say, "It was nice." You will learn more if you ask specific questions, particularly if they allow me to provide short responses, or make a choice between two things: "Was the house one story or two?" or "Did you have your own room?"

- **Repetition may be comforting.** Just as people use generalities to "play it safe," they often use repetition. First, we all have favorite stories to tell, and second, because of their short-term memory loss, people with dementia don't realize they've already told you the story. There is an Australian videotape that demonstrates a woman telling a brief anecdote about her husband over and over within a 5-minute time frame. She always laughs when she tells it—it's clearly a fond memory—and the first few times at least, the staff members who hear it laugh, too. The woman who repeats it sees it not only as a fond memory but as a "safe story," one that helps her fit in. I see in her repetition nervousness—a need to have her hand held, to be reassured that she is valued, and to be redirected to another topic. But if none of those distractions work, keep laughing with her.

- **Holding an object can be reassuring.** People are often comforted by things, not because they are materialistic, but because they're tied to their identity. A man jingling coins in his pocket or a woman clinging to her purse is essentially saying, "This is part of who I am; this gives me confidence." The same is true of the man carrying a newspaper under his arm or wearing a cowboy hat or the woman who carries around silverware ever-ready to set the table. In a life-story-sharing class, that means that people may be more grounded and focused if they have a photograph or fabric or some other tangible form of memorabilia to hang onto. But as the disease progresses, it also means it may get harder to get someone to pass that object to the next person unless you give her another object to replace it.

- **Emotion may increase coherency.** Some of us splutter incoherently when we are angry, but surprisingly, many people with dementia who feel a strong emotional attachment to a subject become more articulate. A woman whom I once interviewed used the phrase "very nice" four times in four basic sentences when I asked her about a house in which she had lived. But when I asked her about her reaction when a son decided to break family tradition and forego an appointment to West Point, she said, "I let him go where he wanted to go. I think afterwards he was a little bit sorry he hadn't gone, but he's doing very well, so there's no reason to worry about it." You may also find this phenomenon at work when a person describes peak experiences.

As their disease progresses, coherency usually decreases in people with AD:

- People who learned English as a second language may revert back to their native language.

- A person who cannot think of the right word may substitute another or make one up. (We all do that when we say "thingamajig" for "hammer." They may say "branch" or "bratch" for "brush.") If English is the person's second language, he is likely to do this in his native language, too, which can be confusing to translators.

- Behavior and tone of voice substitute for language. You can read a great deal about the comfort of a person with dementia by his tone of voice, body language, and actions. A person who walks out of your class may just have to go to the bathroom, but he is definitely saying, "I am uncomfortable." Pay attention to potential unspoken needs and to whether a topic of discussion—or others' specific comments—are causing that person discomfort.

Remember these two absolutes:

1. **A person with dementia always makes sense to himself.**

2. **A person will always stay where he feels he belongs**—where he is welcomed and valued.

TIPS FOR COMMUNICATING WELL

I have included some ideas above for improving your chances of success in reminiscing with people with dementia, particularly as the person's verbal skills diminish, but here are a few more:

- **Call the person by name.** The first part of "tuning in" is to realize we're the one being addressed. Call me by name and I will understand that you mean me and not my neighbor. Plus, knowing you know me feels good.

- **Use concrete terms.** Not, "Did you like that?" but "Did you like your high school?" On the other hand, as dementia progresses, avoid asking questions that require concrete answers, especially if short-term memory is involved. If you ask a woman what she had for lunch, she knows she ought to know. Since she can't remember, it is logical to think she hasn't eaten, and that's what she is likely to say. If you ask, "Did you have the grilled cheese or the tuna sandwich?," she at least has a clue as to what is an acceptable answer.

- **Use short sentences and give directions one step at a time.** Some of the questions in this manual are complex and may need simplifying for people with dementia.

- **Repeat questions using the same words.** If you feel the need to repeat a question and change your wording when you do so, a person who is still trying to tune in and process the first question is likely to think you have asked a new question and now has to try processing that.

- **Avoid open-ended questions.** A person who is newly diagnosed with Alzheimer's disease may be able to respond easily if you say, "Tell me about your high school." As verbal skills become more compromised over time, however, you will find that questions with short answers, ones that can be answered "yes" or "no," or ones that offer a choice between two answers work more easily.

- **Avoid asking questions that begin, "Do you remember . . . ?"** Try to substitute, "Did you ever . . ." or "Did you like . . . ?" For example:
  Did you ever:
  - skate on a frozen river?
  - meet a movie star?
  - ride an elephant?
  - sleep in a tent?
  - eat frog legs?

  Did you like:
  - your first day of school (or just school)?
  - your first kiss?
  - shoveling snow?
  - swimming in a fresh water lake?

- **Use multisensory clues.** When we are reminiscing about hula hoops, it's great to bring in a hula hoop to demonstrate, and to pass it around for everyone to hold. Pictures—provided they are large enough to see clearly (always at least 8 × 10 inches)—are also helpful. People with dementia tend to have a severely compromised sense of smell, but that doesn't mean they won't enjoy talking about and remembering favorite smells—or tasting the brownies you were just discussing. Remember to use those multisensory cues and clues in all possible situations. If a newcomer arrives, you might say, "Welcome, Mary; sit beside me in this chair," and then give it a little pat and maybe pull it out for her. If she still looks confused, get up and assist her to the spot. (Many people with dementia have a compromised visual-spatial sense that makes it difficult for them to maneuver through a crowded room.)

- **Don't pepper people with questions.** If you ask multiple questions in a row, you may make the person feel as if you are prying. For example, "Did you grow up in a small town? Did you walk to school? Was it far away? Did you like your teachers?" represent easy-to-answer questions, but if you don't slow the pace and volunteer information about your own life, it feels more like an interrogation than a conversation.

- **Don't give pop quizzes.** My father had a hard time accepting my mother's dementia, and he consistently (and persistently) asked her questions like, "What day is it?" My mother had no idea, and since they were both retired, it rarely mattered anyway. Putting her on the spot only frustrated both of them.

- **Tap into rote memory.** Rote memory represents the things we have learned so thoroughly that we don't even have to think of them. Saying, "please," "thank you," and "How are you?" are a few examples. People often find comfort in religion because of the unchanging prayers, responses, and hymns. Many people memorized Bible verses and passages from the Torah in childhood and never forgot them. Many people also learned various works of famous poets. Thus, people with dementia are often quite good at finishing proverbs, familiar quotations, and song titles and lyrics. They can easily give you the second item in pairs ("salt and . . . pepper," "cream and . . . sugar," "Laurel and . . . Hardy"). For some, the memorization also applies to numbers. They may no longer be able to add up a golf score, but if you ask them, "What's 7 times 8?" they will answer "56" without missing a beat.

- **Practice conversation helpers.** If I ask most grandmothers about their grandchildren, they will have no trouble bragging. However, a person with dementia may need help. For example:
  - Your granddaughter sure is full of energy. I bet she's fun to be around.
  - Is she bright? Does she do well in school?
  - I think she's cute as can be, but I would guess all that energy can be exhausting. Do you take a nap when she leaves?

- **Substitute statements for questions.** Sometimes we put people on the spot inadvertently. The question, "What did you do today?" seems innocent enough, but can completely stymie a person with dementia. A better comment would be, "You look like you had a good day at the senior center"—to which a person can then respond in any way that she's able.

- **Ask for opinions and advice.** Everyone has a right to his opinion, so opinions represent instant success. You don't have to take the person's advice, but you may be surprised by how good it is. In any case, asking for opinions and advice shows respect.

- **If you don't understand, it's okay to say so.** When a person's coherency diminishes, but he is clearly trying to communicate something important, tap into the emotion he is demonstrating through his tone of voice or behavior. For example: "I'm not sure what you're saying, but you look sad" (or happy). Perhaps the person will then indicate in some way that you are on target. Provide reassurance or affirmation: "I'm sorry you had to go through that, but you certainly turned out to be a good person to have around," or "That sounds like it was a wonderful experience for you. I'm so happy for you."

- **Take the blame for miscommunication.** When I inadvertently embarrassed the woman in asking about her children, it was easy to say, "Oh, I'm sorry to confuse you. Some days I have trouble keeping track of such things myself. You lived for a long time in Baltimore, didn't you? Did you like it there?" Substituting an opinion question for a number question is likely to meet with much greater success, while giving the person a chance to save face.

- **Don't let silence discourage you.** Many people will listen to a conversation and feel little need to respond. They will chime in if they want to, but that may be rarely. Let them be content to think their own thoughts. If you are enjoying being with them, they will enjoy being with you, and that is a stronger measure of success than the range of conversation.

- **Provide reassurance.** People with dementia are often painfully aware of their limitations and of others' impatience. They need—as much as the rest of us—to be reassured that they are doing well enough, that they are loved and valued. They want to be liked for who they are now, not just the person they once were.

WHEN YOU ARE ASSISTING WITH CARE

These tips may also work when you are trying to make conversation while assisting someone with dressing or changing a light bulb in her room. Be aware, however, that some people are distracted from the task at hand when you talk to them. For some people that is a welcome diversion. For others, it interferes with their concentration and slows the process of eating or dressing or whatever else they are trying to do.

Sometimes it's not the question you ask that's the problem, but the *way* it is asked. When people seem unsure of you or are easily threatened by questions, it sometimes works to ask indirectly. For example, if I were trying to carry on a conversation with a woman while I was assisting her with dressing, I might say, "Mrs. Jones, in a class I took, we were asked to choose our preferences between opposites, such as, 'Are you more of a morning person or more of a night owl?' I'm a night owl. *If I asked you, how would you answer?*"

That indirect phrasing feels less like a test. She might say, "I wouldn't answer at all," or "I'm not sure I could decide," or "I'm a night owl, too," and all of those would be perfectly fine. None of those answers are "wrong."

If she answers in one of those first two ways, the next step is to decide:

- Is she shutting me out? Does she need to focus all her concentration on getting dressed? Would it be better to work in silence with her? Or

- Is she just unsure of where I'm going with this conversation? Do I need to ask simpler questions or just provide more encouragement?

To find out, try asking a follow-up question: "Do you like to watch late night TV?" If she says, "Yes," I can ask another follow-up question. "Do you like the late night comedy shows?" If she says "Yes" again, I have a pretty good idea that my first question was gentle enough, but probably too complex.

If she says, "No," to liking late night TV, I still need a follow-up question: "Does that mean you prefer to go to bed early?" If she says, "Yes" this time, I know she is tuned in and probably answering honestly. If she says "No" again, it may be an indication that she is not comfortable with this conversation and I need to give it a rest. Refusing to answer can also be an indication of depression that bears watching. Perhaps I can make a final innocuous comment, followed by silence: "Personally, I think the world would be a better place if we all went to bed at night laughing."

She will know that I have tried to be friendly and open, and that I like being with her, whether she participates or not. Next time I can try having a conversation when we are not trying to complete a task. Over time the relationship will build simply because I am consistently friendly.

A smile is still the shortest distance between two people.

Take that route at every opportunity.

ADDITIONAL RESOURCES

The best book I know on how to reminisce with people with dementia is *Reminiscing with People with Dementia: A Handbook for Carers* by Errolyn Bruce, Sarah Hodgson, and Pam Schweitzer. However, it was published in London by the Age Exchange for the European Reminiscence Network (ISBN 0947860258) so it may be hard to find in the United States. Try looking it up on the internet (*www.age-exchange.org.uk*) or send an e-mail to *age-exchange@lewisham.gov.uk.*

Many of the materials produced by or offered by Bi-folkal, ElderGames, and ElderSong also work well, and I have tried to suggest specific resources from them throughout this book. One not mentioned earlier is *Remembering Our Town* by Dace Rollis Teegardin which is available from ElderSong and was designed specifically for working with people with Alzheimer's disease. Most of the book consists of suggestions for filling in blanks and making lists—activities that tend to work well with people with AD. Although the title suggests a somewhat limited theme, this book is wide-ranging—family, home, work, school, faith, weekend pursuits, and a day in the country in addition to neighborhood, Main street, and government.

Another book that I like that was specifically designed for people with Alzheimer's disease to read themselves is *When We Were Young* from Alzheimer's Readers, Ltd. and written by Maxine McQueen. It's a book of 21 black and white photographs, one to a page, and 21 sentences in large print, all intended to stir up memories. For example, one page shows two little girls intently rearranging the items in their dollhouse. The sentence under it is "My sister and I played with our dollhouse every day." For male readers, another page notes that "A new jeep was a terrific toy!" The uncluttered pages and sweet, clear pictures are bound to bring back memories of fishing, playing baseball, playing with toys, and so forth. In addition, it is easy to talk about what else you see. (Did you ever have a bike like that? Did you ever dress like that?) This is one in a set of books available from NASCO (see Appendix B). You can also contact Alzheimer's Readers directly (phone 800-252-1955 or e-mail *Maxine@AlzheimersReaders.com.*)

Reading is an "overlearned" skill, meaning it comes so naturally to most people that they don't even think about it. Most people with Alzheimer's disease can read until quite late in the progression of their disease, but most people don't realize this since they are seldom given anything in large enough print for their deteriorating vision. They will not always read with comprehension, but most enjoy reading because it is a retained and "adult" skill. There are not many reminiscence-related books in large print designed for people with AD. *When We Were Young,* as noted in the previous paragraph, is an exception. Another is **Gene Kelly** from the Myers Research Institute. It's one of a growing series (currently six titles) from the institute's Reading Roundtable. The roundtable books are a result of years of research related to finding stimulating activities for people with AD. Participants in the weekly clubs, which are usually led by someone with mild cognitive impairment or early-stage dementia for people with moderate dementia, take turns reading the large print book (such as a biography of Gene Kelly) and discuss the questions. For more information, visit their web site (*www.myersresearch.org*) or call 1-888-693-7774.

Of course, if you simply want a book on general activities and Alzheimer's disease, there are many. One of my favorites is **The Best Friends Book of Alzheimer's Activities** by Virginia Bell et al. (see References) which is available from several of the vendors mentioned in Appendix B. Only some of the activities are tied to reminiscence, but all are about building stronger relationships.

Appendix B: Finding Resources

ACTIVITY BOOKS

All of the books I have referenced, except those currently out of print, are available from a variety of sources. The activity books are available from one or more of the following catalog and on-line vendors, most of which specialize in materials for older adults:

BiFolkal Productions, Inc.
800-568-5357
www.bifolkal.org

Dover Publications, Inc.
31 East 2nd St.
Mineola, NY 11501-3582
www.doverpublications.com
http://store.doverpublications.com

ElderSong Publications, Inc.
800-397-0533
www.eldersong.com

ElderGames
800-637-2604
www.ncoa.org (look under publications)

NASCO
800-558-9595
http://www.nascofa.com/senioractivities/

S&S Primelife
800-243-9232
www.ssww.com

Most of the nonactivity books listed are not readily available in bookstores but may be able to be special ordered. Virtually all can be found on-line at *www.amazon.com* or *www.barnesandnoble.com* in new or used condition.

GAMES

These are the games we suggested using in this volume:

- *Conversation Pieces*
- *Imaginiff*
- *LifeStories*
- *Penny Ante*
- *Shake out the Truth*
- *Shake up the Relatives*
- *Shake Loose a Memory*
- *The Ungame*

Many of these are available from the vendors listed above. Some, like *Imaginiff*, may also be found in toy stores, or you can contact the manufacturer (Buffalo Games (*www.buffalogames.com*). Conversation Pieces is sometimes found in bookstores like Barnes & Noble or Borders.

Appendix C: Handouts

Handout—Exercise 1: **Name Stories**

Many of us have been shaped by our names—first and last and nicknames. Some of us have had to live up to a name; others of us have had to overcome negatives associated with our names or heritage. Think about what your name means to you—or if you would rather begin by thinking of someone else because you have a name story in mind, that's fine, too, but come back then to yourself.

- Who named you?

- What do you know about how your name was chosen?

- Do you have a nickname? How did you acquire it?

- Do you prefer the use of your real name or nickname? Why? Does it depend on the situation?

- Do you only allow certain people to use the nickname? Who?

- Were you named after someone?

- What names recur within your family?

- Do you like your name? Why or why not?

- Do you like only part of your name? Which part? Why?

- Do you have a way of helping people remember your name or how it is spelled or pronounced? What is it?

- How would you define what makes a good name?

- How important is a good name? Do you know people with odd names who have been successful?

- How important is *making* your name good (i.e., living an honorable life)?

- If you could choose any name for yourself, what would you choose and why?

- What does your name say about your (family or ethnic) heritage? Is that a positive or negative for you?

- Talk a little about your ethnic heritage. How important is it to your identity?

- Does your family still speak another language? Cook ethnic foods? Celebrate ethnic holidays? Are these traditions you have carried on or hope to carry on with your own families?

Getting to Know the Life Stories of Older Adults: Activities for Building Relationships by Kathy Laurenhue © 2007 Health Professions Press, Inc. All rights reserved.

- If your name has changed since you or your ancestors came to America, talk about what that has meant in your life. Was it hard to adjust or did it make things easier?

- Do you think women should take their husband's name when they marry? Why or why not?

- Are there any other stories associated with names in your family that you would like to share?

Handout—Exercise 2: A Special Home

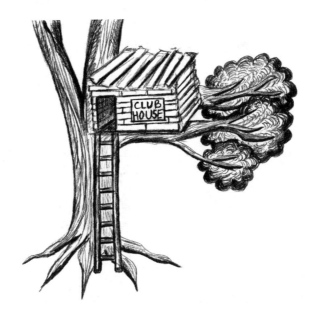

When drawing the floor plan of a place that brings back pleasant memories:

- Don't worry about proportion.

- If you lived in a two-story house or if you had a playroom in the basement, use multiple pieces of paper or draw each story smaller so it fits on one sheet.

- Think about the colors and architectural or furniture styles you associate with this house. Did it have any striking features or peculiarities such as nooks and crannies? What about a mail slot, laundry chute, or milk box for deliveries that was accessible inside and out?

- Think about the wallpaper, curtains, flooring or carpeting, paintings, or prints in each room. Put in as many details as you can.

- Think about furniture and where it was placed.

- Draw details outside, too. What was on the porch or in the yard? Did you have a vegetable or flower garden? A special climbing tree or a treehouse? Was there a detached garage that connected to an alley behind the house? What about lilac bushes, fruit trees, or other foliage that pleased the nose or eye?

- Some people grew up on a farm or have fond memories of a grandparent's farm home. If you're one, draw the area around the farm, too—barns, chicken coop, pasture, and so forth.

- If you would rather draw your neighborhood than your home, include your friends' houses, favorite hangouts or secret hiding places, your school, and any other places that influenced you (e.g., candy store, music store, museum, church or temple, park).

- If you lived in an urban environment and city life was important, include other influences.

Draw the floor plan of a home or apartment with pleasant memories (use grid on next page).

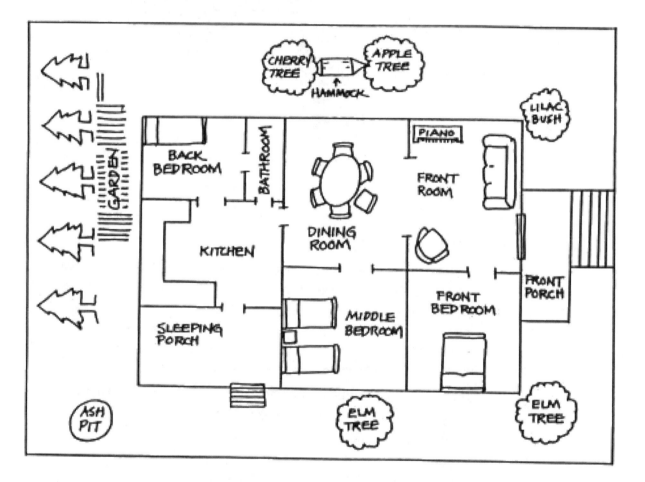

Sample floor plan from *Writing Your Life,* by Mary Borg, 1998. Reprinted with permission from Cottonwood Press, Inc., Fort Collins, CO.

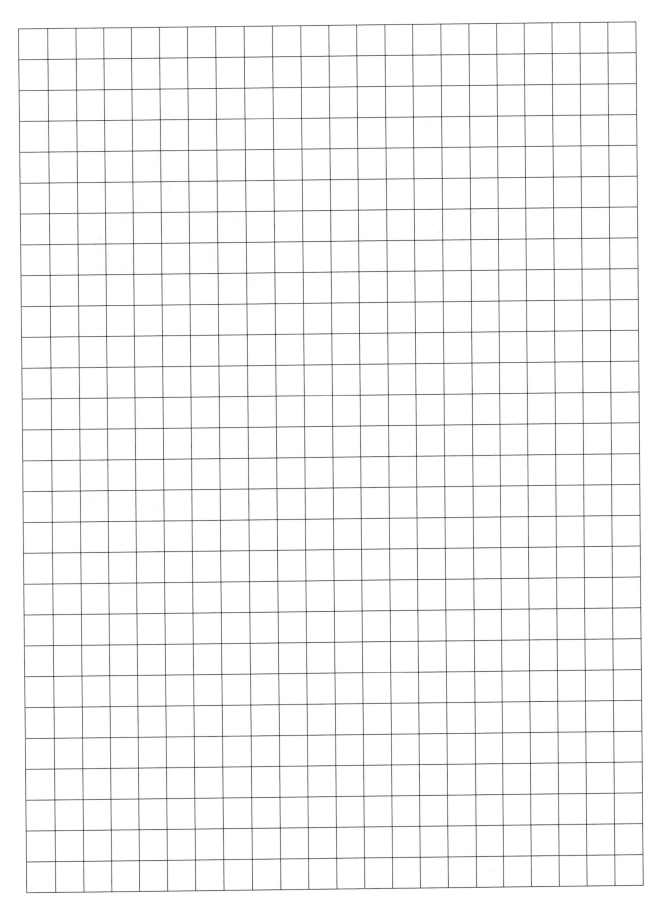

Handout—Exercise 3: **Make a Choice**

Are you:

1. More of an early riser or a night owl?

2. More like the city or the country?

3. More physical or mental?

4. More like the tortoise (slow and steady) or the hare (racing along through life)?

5. More of a saver or a spender? Savers, what do you save? (Many save more than money.)

6. More like a rose or a daisy? Why?

7. More like a kite string or a clothesline? (Why?)

8. More like spring or fall? (That is, which do you find more comforting, spring or fall?)

9. More intuitive (go with your gut feelings) or more rational?

10. More like a business suit or a t-shirt and jeans? (or, for women, high heels or sneakers?)

11. More comfortable on a mountaintop or in a valley?

12. More like a screened porch or a picture window? Why?

13. More *carpe diem* (Seize the day) or *Que sera sera* (What will be, will be)?

14. More a hot weather or cold weather person?

15. More like a violin or a bongo drum? (Or some other musical instrument altogether?) Why?

Handout—Exercise 4: **Holiday Traditions**

Think about the holidays that are most enjoyable for you and then answer the following questions about each:

- What is a holiday you especially enjoy? Why? What makes it special?

- How do you celebrate it? What are the traditions associated with this holiday that you work hard to preserve?

- With whom do you celebrate it?

- Where do you celebrate it? Do you go anywhere specific?

- What foods do you associate with this holiday? Do you prepare them yourself or help in the preparation?

- Is there specific music associated with this holiday? What is it? Can you sing something related to it?

- Are gifts a part of this holiday? What kinds of things are given? Did you ever give or receive something special?

- Are there costumes or special clothing associated with this holiday? Talk about that.

- Are there funny stories that are told year after year at this celebration? Tell one.

- Was this also a special holiday to you when you were a child? Why or why not? What has changed?

Next, think about holiday traditions that define your family.

- Are there any traditions in your family that have come from your ancestors or your life experiences?

- Do you have or did you ever have family members who surprised you by their unaccustomed silliness or celebrations that centered more on food and good times than whatever the holiday was supposed to be about?

Then think about birthdays.

- How did your family celebrate birthdays when you were a child?
- Describe a special birthday or birthday party or gift. What made it special?
- How did you celebrate birthdays with your children? (Did your own childhood experience influence what you did?) Was any child's birthday particularly memorable?
- Is there a party game you especially like? One that you don't like?
- Do you have any birthday traditions in your family that are unusual? Describe them.
- Some people, particularly in Roman Catholic households, grew up celebrating their saint's day, as well as their birthday. Did you? Did you get presents then, too?
- Did you ever have a special milestone birthday celebration? What did you do?
- How do you feel about celebrating your birthday now?
- What would be the ideal birthday celebration for your next birthday?

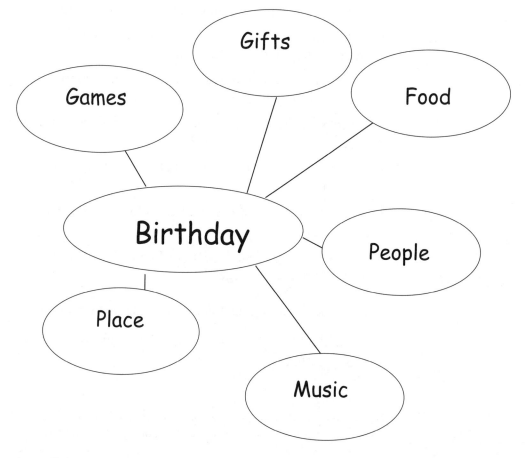

Think about anniversaries.

- Do you (or did you) celebrate anniversaries and are they important to you? What have you done to celebrate? Go out to dinner? Exchange gifts? Take a trip?

- What about other kinds of anniversaries, like the anniversary of quitting smoking or getting an important job? Do you celebrate anything like that?

Do you have any unusual celebrations?

- Has anyone ever thrown a surprise party for you in honor of a birthday, anniversary, or other occasion? Tell us about it. Were you truly surprised? Were you pleased?

- Are there any nontraditional holidays celebrated in your family? For example, is there a historical figure or a celebrity who is much admired in your household so you bake a cake each year, such as on Albert Einstein's birthday?

- Are there any other occasions in your family when you are likely to send flowers or give gifts? What are they?

Over the years many things change and we may not always be able to carry on old traditions—or we may not choose to. Perhaps giving up your role as chief cook is not a hardship.

- Think about a new celebration you would like to have or an old one you would like to change. Talk about it.

What month were you born? Do the character trait, birthstone, and flower suit you?

Month	Character trait	Birthstone	Flower
January	Constancy	Garnet	Carnation
February	Sincerity	Amethyst	Violet
March	Courage	Aquamarine	Jonquil
April	Innocence	Diamond	Sweet Pea
May	Success in love	Emerald	Lily of the Valley
June	Health and longevity	Pearl	Rose
July	Contentment	Ruby	Larkspur
August	Married happiness or friendship	Peridot	Gladiolus
September	Clear thinking	Sapphire	Aster
October	Hope	Opal	Calendula
November	Fidelity	Topaz	Chrysanthemum
December	Prosperity	Turquoise	Narcissus

Reprinted with permission from Bifolkal's *Remembering Birthdays.*

Handout—Exercise 5: **Family Leisure Time and the 1950s**

Let's talk about leisure.

- How was leisure time spent in the family in which you grew up?

- Did you do things together with your family? If so, what kinds of things?

- What did you do with your friends? Did you make your own fun?

- Did you live in a city where weekends might give you the chance to go to parks, baseball games, museums, movies, live theater, or some other form of entertainment? Did you and the family in which you grew up take advantage of what your city or town had to offer?

- If you lived in a more rural area, what leisure activities did it offer?

- What about special entertainment that came your way—county fairs, circuses, Chautauqua-style lecturers, vaudeville acts? Did you go to those? Did you enter anything in the county fair?

- What about family vacations? Did you take them with the family in which you grew up? What did you do? Where did you go? Can you recall an especially good or especially disastrous experience?

- Did you ever go to summer camp? Talk about that experience.

How did leisure pursuits in the family in which you grew up shape your values? For example:

- The value placed on work vs. play

- The value put on family togetherness

- The value of money spent on food for the table (bread) and food for the soul (beauty, leisure, enriching experiences)

- The value placed on reading, listening to music, watching TV

- The value placed on exercise and sports (as participant and/or spectator)

- The value placed on creative arts and live performances (museums, theater, dance)

- The value of hobbies and the ones worth pursuing

What *did* your family value and how did they do in instilling the same values in you?

In Morris Massey's book *The People Puzzle,* he suggested that we are more influenced as we grow up by what we did *without* than by what we had, and the things we had we tend to take for granted.

- Do you agree?

- Can you give me an example to support your viewpoint?

- How did the family in which you grew up influence you as an adult in the ways that you now prefer to relax?

- How did the places that your parents felt were important for their children to see or the experiences that they felt were important for them to share influence how you spent time with your spouse or raised a family of your own?

TV IN THE 1950S

Can you match the star to the TV show?

Westerns

1. Bat Masterson	A. Jim Arness
2. Bonanza	B. Gene Barry
3. Cisko Kid	C. Richard Boone
4. Gunsmoke	D. William Boyd
5. Have Gun will Travel	E. Chuck Connors
6. Hopalong Cassidy	F. Clint Eastwood
7. Lone Ranger	G. James Garner
8. Maverick	H. Lorne Greene
9. Rawhide	I. Clayton Moore
10. The Rifleman	J. Hugh O'Brien
11. Wyatt Earp	K. Duncan Renaldo
12. Zorro	L. Guy Williams

Crime and Mystery Shows

1. 77 Sunset Strip
2. Dragnet
3. M Squad
4. Perry Mason
5. The Thin Man

A. Raymond Burr, Barbara Hale, and William Hopper
B. Peter Lawford and Phyllis Kirk
C. Lee Marvin
D. Jack Webb and Harry Morgan
E. Efrem Zimbalist, Jr., Roger Smith, and Edd Byrnes

Comedies

1. The Adventures of Ozzie and Harriet
2. The Donna Reed Show
3. Father Knows Best
4. Leave It to Beaver
5. The Life of Riley
6. Love That Bob
7. Make Room for Daddy
8. Mr. Peepers
9. Sgt. Bilko

A. Hugh Beaumont
B. William Bendix
C. Carl Betz
D. Wally Cox
E. Bob Cummings
F. Ozzie Nelson (this one's a freebie)
G. Phil Silvers
H. Danny Thomas
I. Robert Young

Quiz Shows

1. $64,000 Question
2. I've Got a Secret
3. Name That Tune
4. The Price is Right
5. To Tell the Truth
6. Truth or Consequences
7. What's My Line?
8. You Bet Your Life

A. Bud Collyer with alternating panelists Don Ameche, Orson Bean, Polly Bergen, Kitty Carlisle, Peggy Cass, and Tom Posten
B. Bill Cullen
C. George DeWitt
D. John Daly with panelists Bennett Cerf, Arlene Francis, and Dorothy Kilgallen
E. Ralph Edwards (who also hosted "This Is Your Life" but that wasn't a quiz show) and later in the decade, Bob Barker
F. Hal March
G. Groucho Marx
H. Garry Moore with alternating panelists Kitty Carlisle, Bill Cullen, Jayne Meadows, Henry Morgan, and Betsy Palmer

Handout—Exercise 6: How Things Have Changed

In this exercise we're going to concentrate on how everyday things in our lives have changed and what ordinary things influenced us.

Talk about the geography of the place where you grew up and the geography that is most appealing to you now.

Talk about the size of your family. How many people and how many generations lived together when you were growing up? How did this influence your own choices when you were an adult?

Talk about health, particularly in the 1950s, but during other times, too, if they had an influence on you. Do you have any memories related to the polio epidemic of the 1950s? What about childhood diseases or tonsillectomies? Did your school provide inoculations to all children? What health prevention measures were taken in your household?

Talk about inventions of the 1950s: Do you remember these?

- Automatic elevator doors
- The transistor radio
- Motorized lawnmowers
- Automatic pinsetter in bowling alleys
- Jet airliners for commercial travel
- Bic ballpoint pens
- The electric typewriter
- WD-40
- Raid Bug Spray

- Aerosol spray
- The Diners Club credit card

What was one of the greatest inventions of your lifetime?

Think about phones.

- Did you ever have a party line?
- Did you ever have a letter exchange instead of numbers? (Murray, Butterfield, Plaza)
- Did you have only one phone? Where was it located? How often was it used?
- How has the use of phones changed?

Think about food in the 1950s.

- Did you eat TV dinners in the 1950s? Were they any good? Did you eat them on TV trays?
- Did you eat sugared cereal in the 1950s? What about other sugar-heavy products?
- Did you like pizza and hamburgers? How important was going to the drive-in for food in your life during the 1950s?
- How have your eating habits changed over the years?

Talk about smoking.

- Did cigarette advertising influence you in the 1950s?
- Do you remember candy cigarettes? Did you "smoke" those?
- Were you ever a real cigarette smoker? Are you still?
- Were you exposed to second-hand smoke in your household?
- How has smoking and your attitude toward smoking and smokers changed in recent years or decades?

Think about popular toys from the 1950s. Do you have any memories related to these?

- Play-doh
- Mr. Potato Head
- Hula hoops
- Pop-it beads
- Tiny Tears doll
- Barbie dolls
- Silly putty
- Frisbee
- Davy Crockett coonskin caps (plus Davy Crockett lunch pails, pajamas and much more, including 4 million records of "Davy, Davy Crockett, King of the Wild Frontier")

Do you have children or grandchildren who still play with these toys? What other toys did you play with as a child? Do you think today's electronic gadgets have changed the way children play? Is that good or bad?

Talk about the fashion fads you remember from the 1950s.

- Poodle skirts (and circle skirts)
- Saddle shoes and penny loafers
- Blouses with "Peter Pan" collars
- Crinolines
- Bermuda shorts
- P. F. Flyers or Keds
- Leather jackets

Did you or your children ever wear any of those? Do you remember any other clothing styles?

Consider primping and accessorizing. Did you have these?

- Charm bracelets
- Cat's eye glasses
- Mum deodorant
- Butch hair wax
- Anything pink (The "in" color, even for men in 1955)

Do you remember?

- 45 RPM records
- Milk bottles with cardboard stoppers delivered to your doorstep or left in the milk chute
- Newsreels before the movie in theatres (plus cartoons)
- Metal ice trays with levers
- Roller skate keys
- Blue flashbulbs on your camera
- Vending machines that dispensed glass bottles
- Little wax bottles filled with colored sugar water
- S&H Green Stamps
- Droodles (Simple drawings with a humorous title—The one on the right is "Abraham Lincoln in the shower")

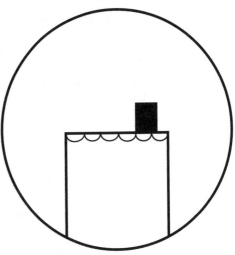

What memories do you have about all these things?

How about cars? Do these bring back memories?

- Studebaker
- Nash Rambler
- Ford Thunderbird
- Cadillac convertible

- Chevrolet Bel Air and Impala
- Chevy Corvette
- Kaiser Manhattan
- Hudson Hornet
- Plymouth Fury
- Edsel
- Volkswagen
- Tail Fins
- Bright and varied colors
- Gleaming grilles

How about entertainment? Do you remember these?

- Drive-in movies (and restaurants)
- Tupperware parties
- Stuffing as many people as possible into phone booths or Volkswagens?

How do you feel about these changes?

- Do you miss any of these things?
- Are there any other memories you have of things that will "never be the same"?
- Are there any "old ways" you would like to go back to?

Here's one last category of changes: language. Do you remember these expressions from the 1950s? Do you know what they mean? Which ones sound dated or have taken on new meanings?

- BMOC
- Bombing around
- Bread
- Catch some rays
- Church key
- D.A.
- Going ape
- Greaser
- Hanging loose
- Having a blast
- Out to lunch
- Pad
- Parking
- Really hairy
- Scuzzy
- What a riot

Handout—Exercise 7: **Life as Social History**

Today we're going to talk about how we have changed—and not changed—in our lifetimes. We're going to start by talking about advertising, in part because advertising shapes us in many ways that we don't even realize.

Long, long ago advertisers who had a product to sell told us why it was a good product and hoped that would be enough to make us want to buy it. But early in the 20th century, advertisers changed tactics. They created social diseases like halitosis and began to play on our self-doubts. One writer said that our natural tendency toward feelings of inferiority were good for advertisers. Now instead of telling us why this breath freshener was a good product, they focused on us as consumers—we need this product in order to be sure we don't offend others, because everyone has bad breath sometimes.

- What do you think of this as an advertising tactic? Does it work to play on our self-doubts?
- What products use this tactic today?

In addition to playing on our self-doubts, many advertisers focused on our desire to have status or to be like the celebrity who used the product. Ford Motor Company at first tried to make cars that anyone could afford, but over time, they began to show their cars in ads in front of mansions—conveying status.

- Does this advertising tactic work?
- What products use it today?
- What about celebrities? Are you influenced by their endorsements?

Some products have used the idea that men will "get the girl" if they use this product or buy this car, but have done it in a way that was fun.

- Do you remember Burma-Shave road signs? Did they influence you to buy the product?

In the 1950s, before commercials became too expensive, whole shows often had the same sponsor. Do you remember these?

- Buick Circus Hour
- Camel News Caravan (Camel Cigarettes)
- The Chevy Show (This featured Bob Hope, not Dinah Shore, who promoted the same sponsor on her show)
- Colgate Comedy Hour
- Disneyland—to promote its theme park
- The Ford Show (starring Tennessee Ernie Ford, but sponsored by Ford Motor Company)
- General Electric Theatre (hosted by Ronald Reagan in his prepolitical days)
- Gillette Cavalcade of Stars
- Goodyear TV Playhouse
- Hallmark Hall of Fame
- Kraft Television Theatre
- Lux Video Theatre
- Philco TV Playhouse
- Texaco Star Theatre
- The U.S. Steel Hour

Did any of these shows influence your buying habits?

Most of the time advertising is so pervasive that we don't even know we're absorbing it. Here are slogans from the 1950s for a variety of products. Can you name what is being advertised?

1. A little dab'll do ya.
2. Don't squeeze the ____
3. I'd walk a mile for a ____
4. When it rains, it pours.
5. Plop plop fizz fizz, oh what a relief it is.
6. Good to the last drop.
7. The breakfast of champions.
8. From contented cows
9. Mmmmmm Mmmmmmm good
10. You'll wonder where the yellow went with ____.
11. A day without ____ is like a day without sunshine.
12. Double the pleasure, double the fun.
13. You can be sure if it's ____.
14. The pause that refreshes.
15. Nothing says lovin' like something from the oven and ___ says it best.

Even if you don't always know the slogan, chances are you know brand names. What product is sold under the following brand names?

- Timex
- Gold Medal

- Bayer
- Comet
- Crest
- Kraft
- Lipton
- Hershey's
- Hellman's
- Nabisco
- Arm & Hammer
- Parkay

These have all been around a long time and are deeply ingrained. You could probably name many more. But the question is, does knowing brand names help the advertiser?

- When you go shopping for anything, what influences you most: name recognition, price, quality, attractiveness?

- How tied are you to brand names? Are there certain products that you and your family are very loyal to? What are they? What would make you try something different?

- Has anything else changed your buying habits over the years—things like dietary concerns, for example?

Some people say we have too many choices. Barry Schwartz in his 2004 book *The Paradox of Choice* says having too many choices paralyzes us. We want to make the "right" choice and having lots of choices increases our chances of making the "wrong" choice so we don't buy anything at all.

- Do you agree that there are too many choices these days? Are you ever afraid of making the wrong choice? Give an example, if you can.

We have talked about how products can sometimes make us unsure of ourselves. Now let's go another direction. How confident are you that this is a world worthy of your trust? For example:

- Do you trust your neighbor?

- Do you lock your house and car doors whenever you go out? Did you always? How has your sense of security changed over the years?

- Do you feel safe walking the streets in your city or neighborhood?

- Do you think most people are trustworthy?

- Do you trust big business or the government to look out for your best interests?

- Do you think the world is a safer or less safe place than it was in the midst of the Cold War in the 1950s?

During this class we have been mostly using advertising to show how in some ways our behavior has changed over the years and in some ways it has stayed the same. Let's end this session by talking about what hasn't changed and shouldn't change.

- What things in life can you count on staying the same?

Handout—Exercise 8: **Turning Points**

This exercise is about the turning points in your life. Sometimes the first time we do something represents a turning point. Can you think of any "firsts" that were a turning point for you?

- First day of school
- First job
- First time you fell in love

What positive life events were turning points for you?

- Sometimes we are influenced by a particular teacher or a subject that we hadn't known we were interested in.
- Sometimes it isn't a first job that matters, but a career choice or a career change.
- Sometimes new adventures begin because we move to a new city or country.
- Sometimes we discover new things about ourselves when we take a vacation or serve as a volunteer.
- Sometimes we are just in the right place at the right time.

Talk about the turning points that happened in your life because of personal choices or good fortune or mentors.

- Were any world events turning points for you? If so, which ones and how did they change you?
- What personal tragedies were turning points for you?
- How did such events affect you and how did you get through them? Did they ultimately turn out all right?

Most of us have endured a lot of things in our lives. Sometimes when something bad happens we can bounce back quickly and other times it is much more difficult.

- What makes the difference?
- What is a turning point you are proud of?

Sometimes turning points come from missed opportunities or from purposely changing direction.

- Are there any stories in your family about real estate investments passed by, jewels lost, or other missed opportunities? Talk about them.
- Are there any stories in your family of substituting one goal for another when the first thing didn't work?

A Mind Map for Turning Negatives to Positives

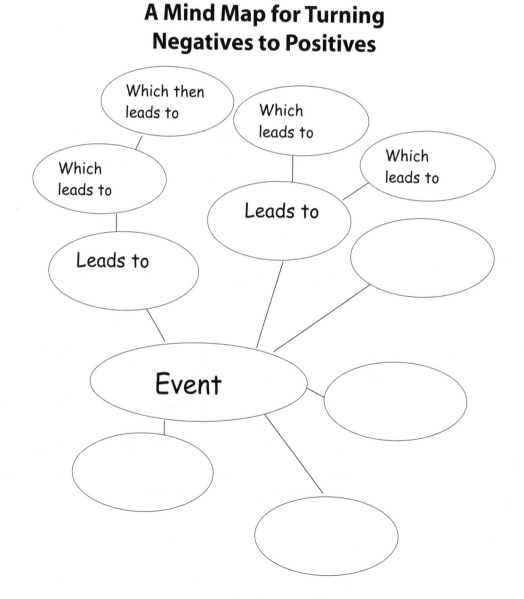

Handout—Exercise 9: **Best Qualities**

Use this handout in one of two ways: (1) Circle everything on this list that you think is one of your best qualities; and (2) do the same for somebody you care for. Add to the bottom any traits you think are missing from the list. Praise yourself!

accepting	achiever	adventurous
attractive	bold	charming
cheerful	companionable	compassionate
competent	confident	considerate
content	courageous	creative
cultured	dauntless/determined	decisive
devout	diplomatic	disciplined
efficient	empathetic	energetic
enterprising	enthusiastic	even-tempered
flexible	forgiving	friendly
fun-loving	generous	gentle
graceful	high-spirited	honest
intelligent	intuitive	kind
leader	loving	loyal
mentor	modest	mysterious
natural	open-minded	optimistic
passionate	patient	peacemaker
personable	plucky	problem-solver
quick-witted	relaxed	respectful
responsible	risk-taker	secure
self-aware	self-reliant	sensitive
sensuous	snazzy	spontaneous
supportive	tenacious	tolerant
trusting	understanding	vivacious
well-balanced	young at heart	zany

Others_____

Appendix D: Art Templates

Note: The artwork in this appendix is available on the CD-ROM.

This appendix includes the following:

- Graphics for signs
- Mind Map: Fill in the Bubbles—Exercise 4
- Draw a Cake for Mini-Exercise D
- Wrap a Package for Mini-Exercise D
- Time Line Chart for Mini-Exercise F
- Mind Map: One Thought Leads to Another—Exercise 8
- Mind Map: Turning Points—Exercise 8
- Pie Chart Time Line—Mini-Exercise F

For the signs on this page and the following pages, using heavy card stock, either:

- Print one double-sided sign for each participant. They can then simply hold up their sheet of paper to cast their votes; or

- Print out two single-sided signs for each participant and glue a popsicle stick or a throat lozenge between them. (These are readily available in craft stores.)

Mind Map: Fill in the Bubbles—Exercise 4

(Fill in the event or idea in the central balloon and then add whatever additional bubbles are needed as one idea leads to another.)

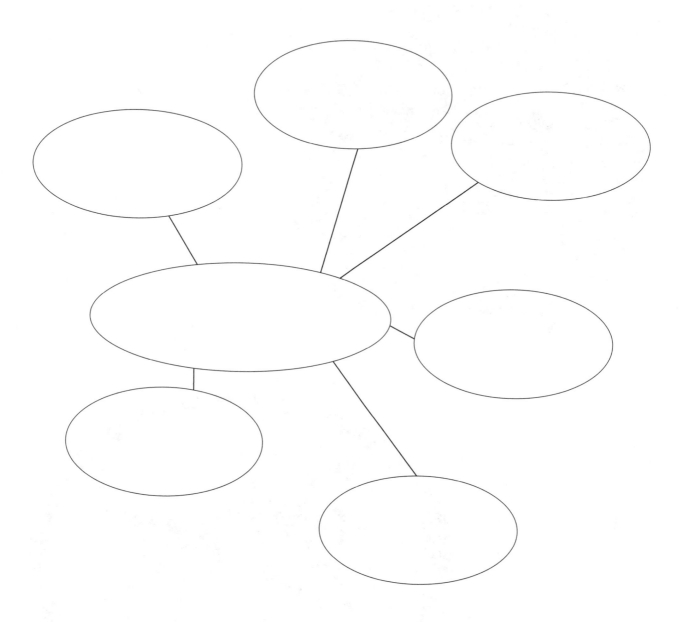

Draw a Cake for Mini-Exercise D: Adding Art

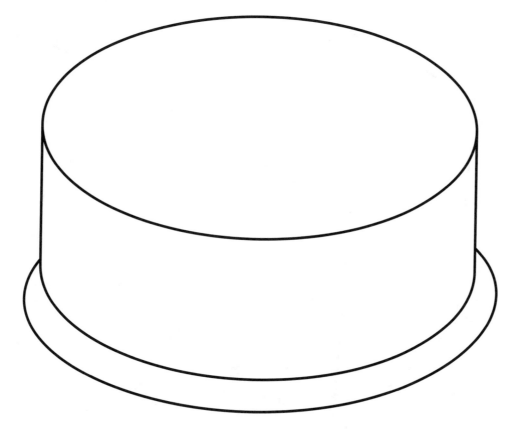

Wrap a Package for Mini-Exercise D: Adding Art

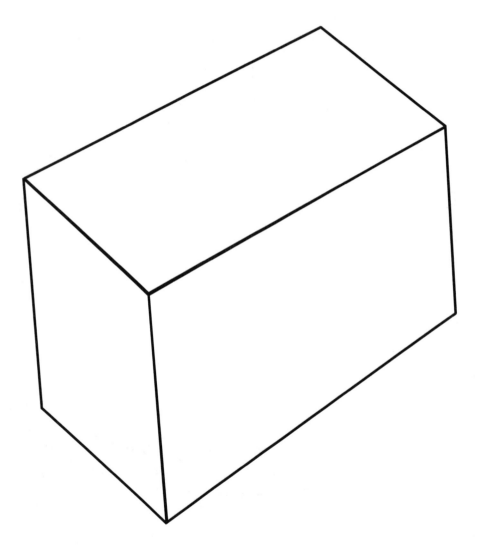

Appendixes

Time Line of Life of: _____

Event	Year	My age	Impact on me

Mind Map: One Thought Leads to Another—Exercise 8

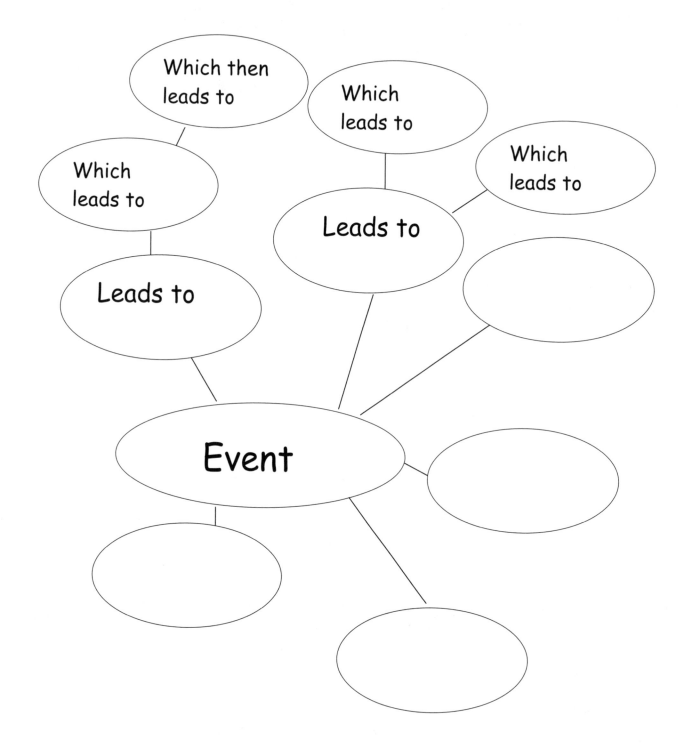

Mind Map: Turning Points—Exercise 8

(Fill in the event or idea in the central balloon and then add whatever additional bubbles are needed as one idea leads to another.)

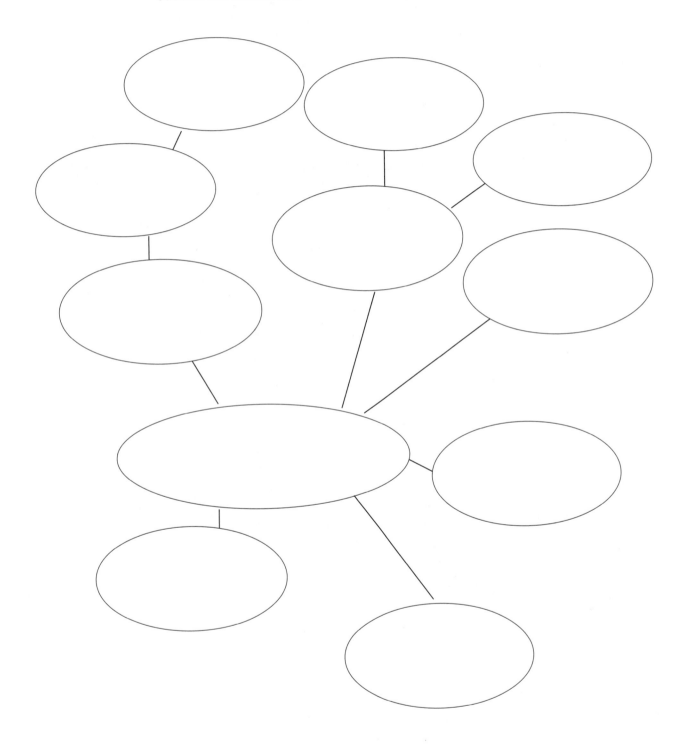

Pie Chart Time Line—Mini-Exercise F

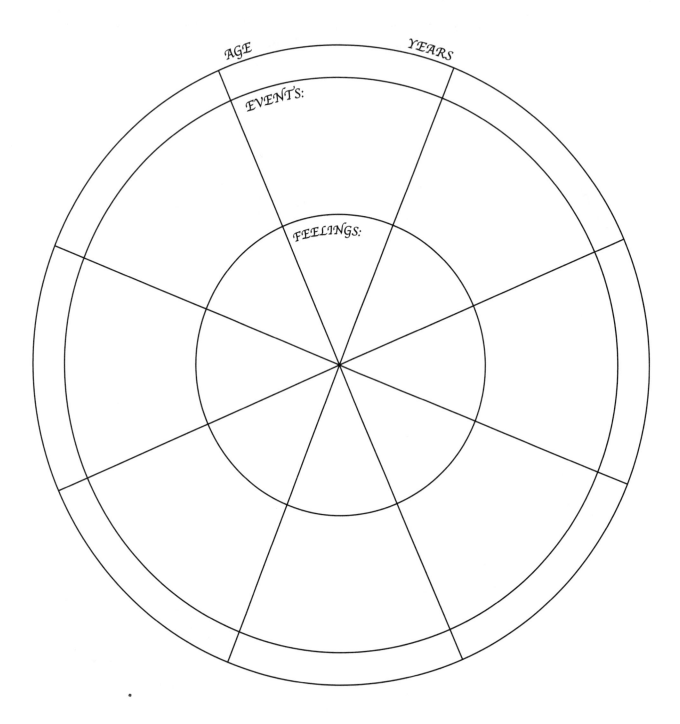

References

BOOKS/BOOKLETS

Adler, B. (2001). *Funny ladies.* Kansas City, MO: Andrews McMeel Publishing.

Agel, J., & Glanze, W. D. (1987). *Pearls of wisdom: A harvest of quotations from all ages.* New York: Harper & Row.

Akeret, R. U., Klein, D., & Klein, D. M. (1991). *Family tales, family wisdom: How to gather the stories of a lifetime and share them with your family.* New York: An Owl Book (Henry Holt and Company).

Allen, F. L. (1993). *The big change: America transforms itself: 1900–1950.* New Brunswick, NJ: Transaction Publishers.

Artman, J., & Grimm, G. (2000). *The 1950s remembering and reminiscing.* Carthage, IL: Gary Grimm & Associates.

Bell, V., Troxel, D., Cox, T., & Hamon, R., (2004). *The Best Friends book of Alzheimer's activities.* Baltimore: Health Professions Press.

Berg, E. (1992). *Family traditions.* Pleasantville, NY: Reader's Digest Association, Inc.

Bernardo, S. (1984). *The ethnic almanac.* Garden City, NY: Doubleday Books.

Borg, M. G. (1998). *Writing your life: An easy-to-follow guide to writing an autobiography.* Fort Collins, CO: Cottonwood Press, Inc.

Brown-Blodgett Company (n.d.). *100 small houses of the thirties.* New York: Dover Publications.

Bruce, E., Hodgson, S., & Schweitzer, P. (1999). *Reminiscing with people with dementia: A handbook for carers.* London: Age Exchange for the European Reminiscence Network.

Chavin, M. (1991). *The lost chord: Reaching the person with dementia through the power of music.* Mt. Airy, MD: ElderSong. [out of print]

ElderGames. (2003). *ElderTrivia, Vol 4.* Washington, DC: NCOA.

ElderGames. (n.d.). *Flashback to stage and screen musicals.* Washington, DC: NCOA.

ElderGames. (n.d.). *Flashback to Hollywood's golden age: music and comedy stars.* Washington, DC: NCOA.

Erickson, L. M. (2002). *Hi-Fi hits.* Madison, WI: BiFolkal Productions, Inc. (Source of "How to be a good wife.")

Erickson, L. M. (2000). *Remembering the fifties program manual.* Madison, WI: BiFolkal Productions, Inc.

Erickson, L. M., & Leide, K. (1996). *Remembering birthdays program manual.* Madison, WI: BiFolkal Productions, Inc.

Feinson, R. (2004). *The secret universe of names.* Woodstock, NY: Overlook Duckworth, Peter Mayer Publishers, Inc.

Green, H. (2000). *The uncertainty of everyday life, 1915–1945.* Fayetteville, AR: The University of Arkansas Press.

Greene, B., & Fulford, D. G. (1993). *To our children's children: Preserving family histories for generations to come.* New York: Doubleday.

Harris, McHenry, & Baker Co. (n.d.). *101 classic homes of the twenties: Floor plans and photographs.* New York: Dover Publications.

Heinly, L. (2005). *I'm still here.* Retrieved from *www.alzheimersartspeaks.com.*

James, J. (1986). *Success is the quality of your journey.* New York: W.W. Norton & Company.

Kanin, R. (1981). *Write the story of your life.* New York: Hawthorne/Dutton.

Kaplan, J., & Bernays, A. (1997). *The language of names.* New York: Simon & Schuster.

Karras, B. (2005). *Down memory lane* (2nd ed.). Mt. Airy, MD: ElderSong Publications.

Karras, B., & Hansen, S. (2005). *Journey through the 20th century: Activities for reminiscing and discussion.* Mt. Airy, MD: ElderSong Publications.

Klein, A. (1998). *The courage to laugh.* New York: Jeremy P. Tarcher.

Kunhardt, P. B. (1988). *Life smiles back.* New York: Fireside Book (Simon & Schuster).

Kunhardt, P. B. (1989). *Life laughs last.* New York: Fireside Book (Simon & Schuster).

Lustbader, W. (2001). *What's worth knowing.* New York: Jeremy P. Tarcher/Putnam.

Massey, M. (1979). *The people puzzle.* Reston, VA: Reston Publishing Co.

McQueen, M. (2001). *When we were young.* Peru, IL: Alzheimer's Readers, Ltd.

Olian, J. (Ed.). (1992). *Everyday fashions of the forties as pictured in Sears catalogs.* New York: Dover Publications.

Olian, J. (Ed.). (2002). *Everyday fashions of the fifties as pictured in Sears catalogs.* New York: Dover Publications.

Osborn, S. (1999). *What's in a name?* New York: Pocket Books.

Petras, K., & Petras, R. (2002). *"Age doesn't matter unless you're a cheese."* New York: Workman Publishing.

Radford Architectural Co. (n.d.). *100 Turn-of-the-century house plans.* New York: Dover Publications.

Reader's Digest. (1996). *Life in these United States: True stories and humorous glimpses from America's most popular magazine.* Pleasantville, NY: Reader's Digest Association, Inc.

Rosenkrantz, L., & Redmond, P. (2000). *Beyond Jennifer & Jason, Madison & Montana: What to name your baby now.* New York: St. Martin's Paperbacks.

Rothschild, M. (2000). *The 50s: the 20th century: Remembering the decades.* Washington, DC: NCOA.

Rule, L. (1986). *Name your baby.* New York: Bantam Books.

Rule, L., & Hammond, W. K. (1977). *What's in a name? Surnames of America.* New York: Jove Publications.

Schwartz, B. (2004). *The paradox of choice.* New York: HarperCollins.

Sears, Roebuck and Co. (1990). *Sears, Roebuck homebuilder's catalog, the complete illustrated 1910 edition.* New York: Dover Publications.

Simon, Sidney. (1993). *In search of values: 31 strategies for finding out what really matters most to you.* New York: Warner Books.

Simon, S. B., Howe, L., & Kirschenbaum, H. (1995). *Values clarification.* New York: Warner Books.

Smith, E. C. (1986). *American surnames.* Baltimore, MD: Genealogical Publishing Company.

Stolley, R. B. (2000). *The American dream: The 50's.* (From the Our American Century Series) Richmond, VA: Time-Life Books.

Teegardin, D. (1999). *Remembering our town.* Mt. Airy, MD: ElderSong Publications.

Time-Life Books. (1998). *The rock and roll generation: teen life in the 50s.* (From the Our American Century Series) Richmond, VA: Time-Life Books.

Trager, J. (1992). *The people's chronology: A year-by-year record of human events from prehistory to the present.* New York: Henry Holt and Company.

Trager, J. (1995). *The women's chronology: A year-by-year record from prehistory to the present.* New York: Henry Holt and Company.

Vetter, J. (2002). *Heroes.* Mt. Airy, MD: ElderSong Publications.

Wenckus, E., & Seemuth, M. (1994). *Drawing on the past.* Washington, DC: ElderGames. [out of print]

Wilder, Thornton. (1938/2003). *Our town.* New York: HarperCollins.

Wycoff, J. (1991). *Mindmapping, your personal guide to exploring creativity and problem-solving.* New York: Berkley Books.

Zadra, D. (Compiler). (1995). *Brilliance.* Edmonds, WA: Compendium Books.

Zeitlin, S., Kotkin, A., & Baker, H. C. (Eds.). (1992). *A celebration of American family folklore: Tales and traditions from the Smithsonian collection.* Summerville, MA: Yellow Moon Press.

ARTICLES

Gilbert, D. (2005, January 20). Four more years of happiness [Op-Ed]. *New York Times.*

WEB SITES

http://www.babyboomers.com

http://www.babycenter.com/babyname/popnames.html (also names for each decade)

http://www.boyscouts.com/history.htm (Boy Scout History, The Earliest Days)

http://www.brainyquotes.com

http://www.census.gov/Press-Release/www.releases/archives/education/ (High School Graduation Rates Reach All-Time High)

http://www.cnn.com/2004/SHOWBIZ/TV/01/23/obit.kangaroo/index.html (Entertainment: TV's "Captain Kangaroo," Bob Keeshan dead)

http://www.crazyabouttv.com/decades/1950s.html (1950s TV Show Pages)

http://www.creativequotations.com/

http://www.extension.iastate.edu/4H/history.html (The History of 4-H)

http://www.fiftiesweb.com/burma1.htm (Burma-Shave Slogans of the '50s)

http://www.fiftiesweb.com/fashion/slang.htm (Slang, A Hepcat's Guide)

http://www.fiftiesweb.com/fashion/fads/htm (It's Only a Fad)

http://www.fiftiesweb.com/pop/1950.htm
(Pop History of the Fifties)

http://www.fiftiesweb.com/quizshow.htm
(Quiz Shows)

http://www.genealogyforum.com/gfaol/surnames/
Top100.htm

http://www.ideafinder.com/history/inventions/
story055.htm (Ballpoint pen)

http://www.ideafinder.com/history/inventions/
story097.htm (Typewriter)

http://www.inventors.about.com/library/inventors/
blwd40.htm (According to the WD-40 Company:
by Mary Bellis)

http://www.inventors.about.com/od/astartinventions/
a/aerosol.htm (The History of Aerosol Spray
Cans from Mary Bellis, Your Guide to Inventors)

http://www.jimwegryn.com/Names/Common
Surnames.htm

http://www.last-names.net/

http://www.lifebio.com (Ethical wills)

http://www.mediafamily.org/facts/facts_histv_print.
shtml (National Institute on Media and the Family
Fact Sheet on the History of Television)

http://www.mybirthcare.com/favorites/
babynames.asp

http://www.myersresearch.org

http://www.museum.tv/archives/etv/l/htmll/
ilovelucy/ilovelucy/htm (U.S. Situation Comedy,
I Love Lucy; U.S. Musical Variety, The Nat
"King" Cole Show; U.S. Talk Show Host, Jack
Paar)

http://www.nces.ed.gov/programs/digest/d04/tables/
dt04_102.asp (*Digest of Education Statistics,
2004*)

http://www.ok-history.mus.ok.us/enc/carnegie.htm
(Carnegie Libraries)

http://www.pbs.org/fmc/book/5living1.htm (The
First Measured Century, living arrangements)

http://www.searsarchives.com/catalogs/history.htm
(History of the Sears Catalog)

http://www.scifi.com/twilightzone/serling (Rod
Serling, The creator of The Twilight Zone)

http://www.ssa.gov/OACT/babynames/

http://www.surnames.behindthename.com/top/lists/
100usss1990.php

http://www.wiser-now.com

Index